HOUGHTON MIFFLIN

math
CENTRAL

 HOUGHTON MIFFLIN

Boston • Atlanta • Dallas • Denver • Geneva, Illinois • Palo Alto • Princeton

Kindergarten

Patsy F. Kanter
Consultant, Teacher, Author
Isidore Newman School
New Orleans, Louisiana

Janet G. Gillespie
Title 1 Specialist, Author
Woodlawn Elementary School
Portland, Oregon

Levels 1–6

Laurie A. Boswell
Profile Jr./Sr. High School
Bethlehem, New Hampshire

Mary Esther Reynosa
Elementary Mathematics Curriculum Specialist
Edgewood School District
San Antonio, Texas

Dr. Juanita Copley
Associate Professor of Education
University of Houston
Houston, Texas

Dr. Jean M. Shaw
Professor of Elementary Education
University of Mississippi
University, Mississippi

Dr. Robert Gyles
Community School District 4
New York, New York

Dr. Lee Stiff
Associate Professor of Mathematics Education
North Carolina State University
Raleigh, North Carolina

Audrey L. Jackson
Assistant Principal
Parkway School District
St. Louis County, Missouri

Dr. Charles Thompson
Professor of Mathematics Education
University of Louisville
Louisville, Kentucky

Edward Manfre
Mathematics Education Consultant
Albuquerque, New Mexico

Consultants and Contributing Authors

Carole Basile
University of Houston
Houston, Texas

Cindy Chapman
Inez Science and Technology
Magnet School
Albuquerque, New Mexico

Dr. Deborah Ann Chessin
University of Mississippi
University, Mississippi

Dr. Richard Evans
Plymouth State College
Plymouth, New Hampshire

Dr. Karen Karp
University of Louisville
Louisville, Kentucky

Casilda Pardo
Armijo Elementary School
Albuquerque, New Mexico

Caitlin Robinson
Mitchell Elementary School
Albuquerque, New Mexico

Acknowledgments   See page 560.

Printed in the U.S.A.

ISBN: 0-395-91737-9

23456789-VH-03 02 01 00 99

Contents

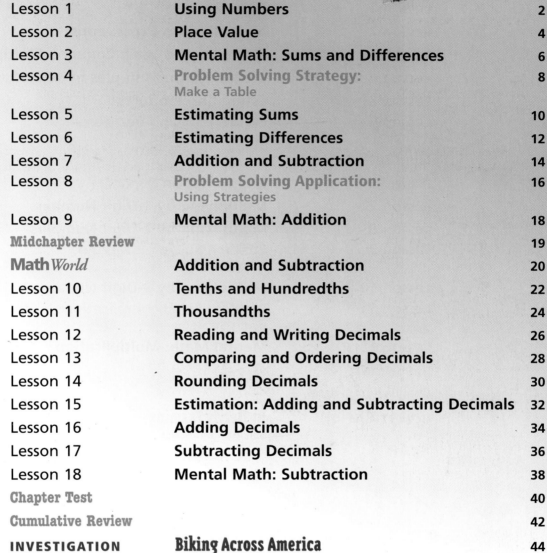

Multiplication of Whole Numbers

page 46

Division of Whole Numbers

page 80

Collecting, Organizing, and Using Data page 122

5 Measurement and Geometry

page 152

CHAPTER 6 Multiplication of Decimals

page 194

CHAPTER 7 Division of Decimals

page 226

8 Geometry

·9· Fractions and Mixed Numbers   page 292

HOUGHTON MIFFLIN
math CENTRAL

CHAPTER 10

Addition and Subtraction of Fractions page 328

Multiplication and Division of Fractions

page 360

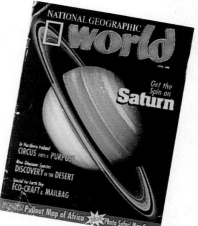

Ratio, Percent, and Probability

page 392

Area and Volume

page 432

Whole Numbers and Decimals

Math Power

Use What You Know

Thousands	Hundreds	Tens	Ones	Tenths	Hundredths
3	7	9	1.4		5

- place value

6982
6437
6982 > 6437

- how to compare numbers

3245 =
three thousand
two hundred
forty-five

2.85 =
two and eighty-
five hundredths

- word forms for numbers

Try This!

Numbers can be written in many ways. Use what you know about numbers to write a 30-second radio commercial.

What You'll Need

pencil, paper

1

In your commercial, describe what your favorite product is, what it does, and its cost.

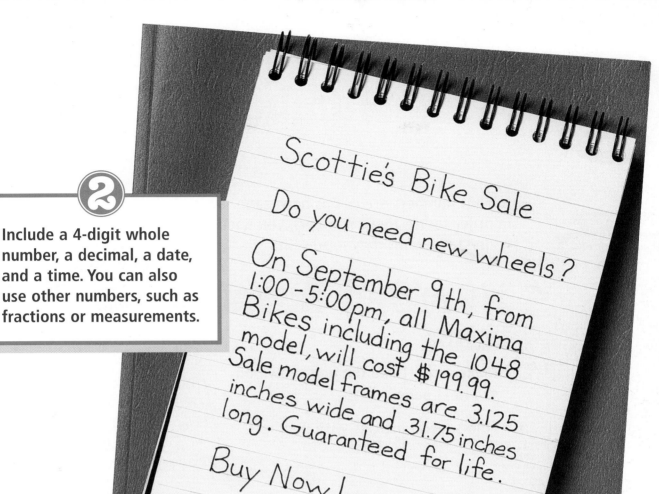

2 Include a 4-digit whole number, a decimal, a date, and a time. You can also use other numbers, such as fractions or measurements.

Scottie's Bike Sale

Do you need new wheels?

On September 9th, from 1:00 - 5:00pm, all Maxima Bikes including the 1048 model, will cost $199.99. Sale model frames are 3.125 inches wide and 31.75 inches long. Guaranteed for life.

Buy Now!

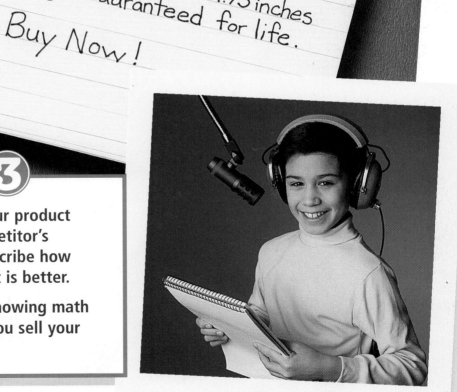

3 Compare your product with a competitor's product. Describe how your product is better.

How does knowing math ideas help you sell your product?

How did you use whole numbers and decimals in your commercial?

Ready to Go!

LESSON 1

Using Numbers

Cooperative Learning Checklist

☑ Work alone.
☑ Work with a partner.
☐ Work with a group.

Getting Started

What You'll Need:
▶ pages from a newspaper

What numbers are in this newspaper article? In order to use these numbers, you need to understand what they represent.

Number Hunt

Activity

• Make a chart like the one shown on the next page.

• Find several articles with numbers.

MONEY BRIEFS
Common Cents

There are believed to be about 132 billion pennies in circulation, and about 89,600,000 disappear from circulation each year. Pennies are 3/4 in. across and are worth $8.82 a pound when new. Pennies are now made of zinc and

Number	Type	Sentence
3/4	Fraction	

1
Use pages from a newspaper. Find at least six different numbers on the pages. Record the numbers in your chart.

2
Classify each number as one of the following:
- whole number
- fraction
- decimal
- other

3
For each number, write a sentence to tell what information the number gave in the article.

Number	Type	Sentence
$\frac{3}{4}$	Fraction	Pennies are $\frac{3}{4}$ in. across.
$8.82	Decimal	When pennies are new, they are worth $8.82 a pound.

Show What You Know!

Discuss each question and explain your answer.

1. Choose five of the numbers you listed. For each type of number, write a sentence that gives the same type of information about you, your school, or your community. Example: Three fourths $\left(\frac{3}{4}\right)$ of the people in my family are females.

2. Tell whether each number is a whole number, a decimal, or a fraction.
   a. 3500   b. 4.9   c. $\frac{3}{5}$ d. $\frac{2}{3}$ e. 0.03

3. **Create Your Own** Write a sentence that uses each number.

   a. 5000   b. 68°F   c. $\frac{1}{2}$ d. 12   e. $10.98

4. **Number Sense** Write a number in the same form, but greater.
   a. 286   b. $\frac{1}{4}$ c. $\frac{3}{5}$ d. 0.5   e. 1.8

②

Place Value

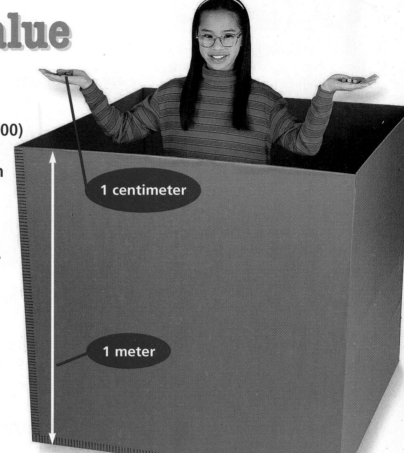

One million (1,000,000) centimeter cubes will fit into the box shown here. It would take about 53,946,592 centimeter cubes to fill a large school bus.

A place-value chart can help you understand this number.

1 centimeter

1 meter

Here's A Way! Write 53,946,592 three different ways.

Billions			Millions			Thousands			Ones		
Hundreds	Tens	Ones	Hundreds	Tens	Ones	Hundreds	Tens	Ones	Hundreds	Tens	Ones
				5	3	9	4	6	5	9	2

1 Short word form: 53 million, 946 thousand, 592

2 Expanded form:
50,000,000 + 3,000,000 + 900,000 + 40,000 + 6000 + 500 + 90 + 2

3 Standard form: 53,946,592

Talk About It! If you add 10,000 to 53,946,592, what digit will change?

22

Show What You Know!

Write the number in the place-value chart in:

Billions			Millions			Thousands			Ones		
Hundreds	Tens	Ones	Hundreds	Tens	Ones	Hundreds	Tens	Ones	Hundreds	Tens	Ones
				7	1	0	0	0	9	2	1

1. short word form
2. expanded form
3. standard form

Write the number in standard form.

4. 900,000 + 60,000 + 8000 + 4   5. 35 million, 206 thousand, 42

6. 100,000 + 9000 + 50   7. 403 thousand, 432   8. 26 thousand

Write the number in short word form.

9. 6,000,000 + 500,000 + 8000 + 40 + 1   10. 811,290,653   11. 12,980,700

12. **Critical Thinking** Write the value of each digit in the number 444,444. Do you see a pattern? Explain.

Work It Out!

Write the number in standard form.

13. 64 thousand   14. 5,000,000,000 + 400,000,000 + 90,000 + 600 + 20 + 5

15. 84 million, 56 thousand   16. 400,000 + 20,000 + 5000 + 3

Write the number in short word form.

17. 427,004   18. 63,866   19. 4,980,300   20. 98,000,000   21. 62,035,020

Write the number from the box that matches each statement.

22. This number is closest to 34,569,200.

23. This number has a 4 in the hundred thousands place.

52,040,212	50,431,260
36,100,439	48,700,184

24. This number has the same digit in the tens place and in the millions place.

Problem Solving

25. A refrigerator can hold about 1,146,242 centimeter cubes. Write the number in short word form.

26. A small school bus for 20 people can hold about 27,431,945 centimeter cubes. Write the number in expanded form.

More Practice Set 1.2, p. 462

Mental Math: Sums and Differences

Peter Menzel is a photographer from Napa, California, who travels the world taking pictures. Suppose he travels from Bamako, Mali, to Cairo, Egypt, a trip of about 3000 mi. He then flies from Cairo to Houston, Texas, a journey of about 7000 mi. Then he flies another 5000 mi to London, England. How many miles does he travel in all?

Peter Menzel, in Cairo, Egypt

Basic addition facts, such as $1 + 9 = 10$ and $2 + 6 = 8$, can help you add greater numbers that are multiples of 10, 100, and 1000.

Here's A Way! Find $7000 + 3000 + 5000$.

1 Think of the addends in short word form.

$$7000 + 3000 + 5000$$

7 thousand + 3 thousand + 5 thousand

2 Look for sums that are multiples of 10.

7 thousand + 3 thousand + 5 thousand

10 thousand

3 Add. Write the standard form.

10 thousand + 5 thousand = 15 thousand or 15,000

So, Menzel traveled 15,000 mi.

Talk About It! Why can using the short word form help you add using mental math?

Other Examples Use the short word form to help you subtract.

$$17,000 - 9000 = 8000$$

17 thousand − 9 thousand = 8 thousand

Use mental math to add or subtract.

1. 500 + 200   2. 9000 − 4000   3. 50 + 40   4. 400 + 900

5. 6000 − 800   6. 4036 + 4000   7. 2600 + 600   8. 40 + 80 + 60

9. **Critical Thinking** Discuss different ways you can think of to add 320 and 70.

Work It Out!

Use mental math to add or subtract.

10. 400 + 300   11. 2000 + 6000   12. 60 + 40   13. 80 − 40

14. 6000 − 2000   15. 120 − 80   16. 500 − 30   17. 400 − 20

18. 5000 − 400   19. 620 + 200   20. 550 − 200   21. 750 + 30

22. Write each pair of numbers in the box whose sum is 100.

23. Write each pair of numbers in the box whose sum is 1000.

30		10		80
	50		40	
20		50		90
	60		70	

	900		600
400		800	
	200		500
100		300	
	500		700

Use mental math to add.

24. 50 + 40 + 50   25. 400 + 200 + 800   26. 30 + 20 + 40

27. 30 + 60 + 70   28. 40 + 30 + 55   29. 200 + 300 + 250

Problem Solving

30. **Create Your Own** Write a word problem that can be solved by doing the following computation: 2000 + 5000 − 1000.

31. When you travel on the gameboard at the right, you collect points. For example, when you travel from A to B, you get 30 points. List three different ways to travel from GO to END so that you collect exactly 150 points.

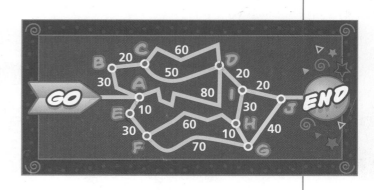

More Practice Set 1.3, p. 462

Problem Solving
Make a Table

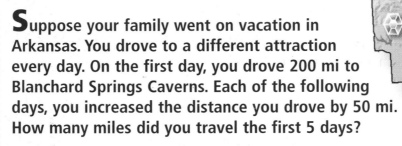

ARKANSAS

Blanchard Springs Caverns

Crater of Diamonds

Suppose your family went on vacation in Arkansas. You drove to a different attraction every day. On the first day, you drove 200 mi to Blanchard Springs Caverns. Each of the following days, you increased the distance you drove by 50 mi. How many miles did you travel the first 5 days?

You can make a table to find the distance.

Here's A Way! Use Make a Table to solve the problem.

1 Understand

- What do you know about the distance you traveled each day?
- How will knowing this information help you to solve the problem?

2 Plan

- How can you make a table to show the distance traveled daily?
- What title will you give each column?
- What numbers will you write in the rows?
- How will you begin to fill in the table?

Day	Distance	Daily Total
1	200	200
2	200 + 50	250
3	?	?
4	?	?
5	?	?

3 Try It

- How will you complete the table?
- What should you do to find the total?

4 Look Back

- You traveled 1500 mi.
- Since you traveled at least 200 miles each day, the total must be greater than 5 × 200 = 1000. So, 1500 miles is a reasonable distance.

Day	Distance	Daily Total
1	200	200
2	200 + 50	250
3	200 + 50 + 50	300
4	200 + 50 + 50 + 50	350
5	200 + 50 + 50 + 50 + 50	400
Total miles traveled in 5 days		?

Make a Table to solve the problem.

1. Your family makes a large batch of brownies to take on your trip. It takes 3 eggs to make 12 brownies. How many eggs does it take to make 60 brownies?

2. **Critical Thinking** How is making a table a useful strategy when increasing recipes?

Rafting on the Arkansas River

Work It Out!

Make a Table or use any strategy to solve the problem.

3. Suppose your family visits Cape Breton in Nova Scotia for one week. You collect sea rocks each day. You collect 3 on the first day, 5 on the second, 7 on the third, and 9 on the fourth. If the pattern continues, how many rocks will you collect by the end of your stay in Cape Breton?

Blanchard Springs Caverns

4. Your family likes to listen to CDs while traveling. The first day, you listen to 4 CDs. The number you listen to increases by 1 every day. How many CDs do you hear by the sixth day?

Day	1	2	3	4	5	6
Number of CDs	4	?	?	?	?	?

5. Your family drives a car that travels 30 mi on a gallon of gas. The gas tank holds 15 gal. How many tanks of gas will your family need to buy on a trip of 1800 mi?

6. One week, 7000 people visit a museum near your house. The next week, 9000 people visit it. How many people visit in all during the two weeks?

7. You go to several stores to check prices on a tape player for your trip. In the first store, the player is $60. At each of the next 5 stores, the price decreases by $3. What is the lowest price you find?

8. The first hour of your vacation, your family drives 48 mi. Each hour you travel, you decrease your distance by 2 mi. How many miles do you travel after 4 hours?

Share Your Thinking

9. Explain the strategy you used to solve problem 8.

10. How does making a table help you to solve problems?

Estimating Sums

Use What You Know

To round numbers, look at the number to the right of the place to which you are rounding. If the digit is less than 5, round down. If it is 5 or greater, round up.

Have you ever been to Paris? Besides being the capital of France, Paris is also the name of some small cities in the United States. Is the total population of Paris, Missouri; Paris, Idaho; and Paris, Arkansas, more than 5000?

ID
Paris
pop. 581

Paris
pop. 1486

MO

AR
Paris
pop. 3674

You can use rounding or front-end estimation to find the answer.

Here's A Way! Estimate 1486 + 581 + 3674.

Rounding

1 Round each number to the nearest thousand.

$$\begin{array}{r} 1486 \\ 581 \\ + \ 3674 \end{array}$$

581 rounded to the nearest thousand is 1000.

2 Add the rounded numbers.

$$\begin{array}{r} 1000 \\ 1000 \\ + \ 4000 \\ \hline \end{array}$$
Rounded estimate: 6000

So, the population of the cities is greater than 5000.

Front-end

1 Add the digits in the greatest place.

$$\begin{array}{r} 1486 \\ 581 \\ + \ 3674 \end{array}$$

Think:
1000 + 3000

Front-end estimate:
4000

2 Adjust your estimate to the next greatest place.

$$\begin{array}{r} 1486 \\ 581 \\ + \ 3674 \end{array}$$

Think:
$$\begin{array}{r} 400 \\ 500 \\ + \ 600 \\ \hline 1500 \end{array}$$

Adjusted estimate:
4000 + 1500 = 5500

3 If necessary, use the remaining digits to adjust your estimate again.

You can see that 5500 is greater than 5000, so you do not need to use the other digits.

So, the population of the three cities is greater than 5000.

Talk About It! In front-end estimation, why would you adjust your estimate to the next greatest place?

Round to the underlined place.

1. 3<u>6</u>7   2. <u>4</u>216   3. <u>7</u>210   4. <u>5</u>5   5. 63,<u>2</u>14

Estimate. Use the method of you choice.

6.	4276	7.	654	8.	488	9.	3298	10.	4540
	539		74		321		1832		1282
	+ 388		+ 325		+ 67		+ 433		+ 526

11. **Critical Thinking** Is the exact sum in exercise 8 greater than or less than 800? How can you tell?

Work It Out!

Round to the underlined place.

12. 5<u>6</u>   13. <u>2</u>2,761   14. <u>7</u>7,771   15. 6,3<u>2</u>1   16. 1<u>1</u>1

Estimate. Use the method of your choice.

17.	436	18.	2016	19.	4325	20.	5412	21.	1047
	58		325		243		679		445
	243		582		+ 4529		+ 2208		29
	+ 61		+ 3254						+ 421

Mental Math Estimate. Write > or <.

22. 4675 + 793 ■ 6000   23. 547 + 88 + 492 ■ 1000

24. 4552 + 332 + 1352 ■ 7000   25. 1694 + 1030 ■ 2500

26. 499 + 152 + 480 ■ 1000   27. 98 + 324 + 25 ■ 500

Problem Solving   Using Estimation

28. About how many people live in the places named Florida?

29. Do more people live in U.S. cities named Paris or Florida?

30. In Pennsylvania, you can live in places named New York (population 1755), Wyoming (3655), or California (5703). Is the total number of people living in Wyoming, PA, and New York, PA, greater or less than the number of people living in California, PA?

Population of Places Named Florida

Place	Population
Florida, New York	2497
Florida, Ohio	304
Florida, Missouri	2
Florida, Puerto Rico	5748

Source: 1990 Census Bureau

More Practice Set 1.5, p. 462

Estimating Differences

Mount Everest is the tallest mountain in the world. The first people to climb to the top were Sir Edmund Hillary and Tenzig Norgay. They pitched their base camp at 5486 m. About how many meters did they have to climb from their base camp to reach the summit of the mountain?

You can use rounding or front-end estimation to help solve this problem.

Tenzig Norgay and
Sir Edmund Hillary, 1953

Summit 8848 m

Base camp 5486 m

Here's A Way!   Estimate 8848 − 5486.

Rounding

1 Round each number to the nearest thousand.

8848
− 5486

2 Subtract the rounded numbers.

9000
− 5000
4000

So, they had to climb about 4000 meters.

Front-end

1 Subtract the digits in the greatest place.

8848
− 5486

Think:
8000 − 5000

Front-end estimate: **3000**

2 Get a closer estimate by using the digits in the hundreds place.

8848
− 5486

Think:
800 − 400

Adjusted estimate:
3000 + 400 = 3400

So, they had to climb about 4000 meters.

Talk About It!   In the example above using front-end estimation, why was 400 added to the estimate?

Estimate. Use the method of your choice.

1. 9647 -2719	2. 475 $-\ 88$	3. 5481 $-\ 327$	4. 6181 $-\ 868$	5. 7365 $-\ 842$

6. **Critical Thinking** Would front-end estimation without adjusting provide a good estimate of the difference between 3496 and 3175? Justify your answer.

Write the letter of the closer estimate.

7. 5847 $-\ 156$	8. $84{,}823$ $-\ 8912$	9. 4588 $-\ 856$	10. 5032 $-\ 542$
a. 5000	a. 76,000	a. 3300	a. 5000
b. 5700	b. 80,000	b. 3800	b. 4500

Which number is a reasonable estimate? Write a or b.

11. $8342 - 321$
   a. 5000
   b. 8000

12. $6932 - 423$
   a. 6000
   b. 2000

13. $9684 - 621$
   a. 9000
   b. 3000

14. $5325 - 338$
   a. 4000
   b. 5000

15. $455 - 38$
   a. 400
   b. 100

16. $862 - 67$
   a. 800
   b. 600

Estimate. Which two numbers in the box to the right have a difference of:

17. about 3500?   18. about 3000?

19. about 3700?   20. about 700?

496		1287
	5217	
1584		4008

21. Mt. Kilimanjaro in Tanzania rises to 5896 m, making it the highest point in Africa. About how much taller is Mt. Everest?

Write the answer.

22. 594 $+\ \ 29$	23. 735 -264	24. 2906 $+6752$	25. 4000 $-\ 738$	26. 886 -579	27. 4867 $+\ 352$

More Practice Set 1.6, p. 463

13

Addition and Subtraction

Valencias and Hamlins are two types of oranges grown in Florida. In 1996, there were 307,878 acres of Valencia oranges in the state. There were 216,157 acres of Hamlin oranges.

You can ask addition and subtraction questions about this data.

Florida oranges

Here's A Way! | Find the sum and difference.

Addition

Find the total number of acres of Valencia and Hamlin oranges.

1 Round to estimate.

$$307,878$$
$$+\ 216,157$$

Think:
300,000 + 200,000

Estimate: 500,000

2 Add.

$$\overset{1\ 1\ \ 1\ 1}{307,878}$$
$$+\ 216,157$$
$$524,035$$

The answer is close to the estimate, so the answer is reasonable.

The total number of acres is 524,035.

Subtraction

Find how many more acres of Valencias than Hamlins there were.

1 Round to estimate.

$$307,878$$
$$-\ 216,157$$

Think:
300,000 − 200,000

Estimate: 100,000

2 Subtract.

$$\overset{2\ 10}{307,878}$$
$$-\ 216,157$$
$$91,721$$

The answer is close to the estimate, so the answer is reasonable.

There were 91,721 more acres of Valencias than Hamlins.

Talk About It! How can you use addition to check subtraction?

Write the answer.

1. 2407
    + 1363

2. 3491
    − 2384

3. $89.03
    − 35.24

4. 75,097
    + 89,302

5. 67,392
    − 28,767

6. In 1984, there were a total of 761,365 acres of citrus fruit grown in Florida. Ten years later, that number increased by 92,377. How many acres of citrus fruit were there in 1994?

7. **Critical Thinking** If you add 342,506 and 217,480 on your calculator and get a 7-digit sum, how will you know if your answer is reasonable?

Work It Out!

Write the answer.

8.   2438
    + 1582

9.   8243
    − 6325

10.   5580
     − 3628

11.   45,089
     − 32,492

12.   4309
     + 3244

13. $2356.89
      421.56
    +   35.07

14.   4365
     − 3828

15.   5823
      4209
    + 1874

16.   730,010
     − 618,455

17.   4 yd 8 in.
     + 5 yd 7 in.

18. 53,809 − 8476

19. $3.20 − $.55

20. 2 h 12 min + 5 h 3 min

21. $50.95 − $12.99

22. 8 ft 3 in. + 17 ft 9 in.

23. 50,000 − 6000

24. 3428 + 2672

25. $4635.99 + $3523.56

26. 4598 − 409

Problem Solving

Use the chart to answer the questions below.

27. How many more acres of grapefruit were grown in 1996 than in 1966?

28. Between 1976 and 1986, was the decrease in acres of oranges greater or less than the decrease in acres of grapefruit?

29. In 1996, what was the total number of acres of oranges and grapefruit?

Acres of Florida Citrus Fruit

Year	Oranges	Grapefruit
1966	673,086	103,224
1976	628,567	137,909
1986	466,252	117,845
1996	656,598	144,416

Source: Florida Agricultural Statistics Service, 1996

More Practice Set 1.7, p. 463

Problem Solving
Using Strategies

You can read more about Galápagos tortoises in the pages of *Zoo Nooz*.

We're Talking Tortoises!

How old are they? How much do they weigh? Zookeepers hear these questions again and again at the San Diego Zoo's Galápagos exhibit. The exhibit has a herd of 39 huge Galápagos tortoises. Nearly 200 million visitors have come to see these creatures since their arrival more than 65 years ago.

Galápagos Islands

Problem Solving Process
- ✓ Understand
- ✓ Plan
- ✓ Try It
- ✓ Look Back

Choose a Strategy You Have Learned
- ✓ Make a Table
- Act It Out
- Guess and Check
- Look for a Pattern
- Work Backward
- Make a List
- Work a Simpler Problem
- Draw a Picture
- Write an Equation

Suppose in 1990 the attendance at the San Diego Zoo was 2,750,000 people. The attendance increased in 1991 by 75,000, and each year after 1991 the attendance increased by 10,000 more than the year before. If the pattern for attendance continued to increase by 10,000 each year, what was the attendance in 1997?

- What is the question you have to answer?
- What was the increase in attendance in 1991? In 1992?
- What was the attendance in 1991? In 1992?
- For how many years do you need to find the attendance?
- Will making a table help you to organize the information?

Work It Out!

Use any strategy to solve each problem. Show your work.

1. One tortoise, hatched in 1994, weighed 2.8 oz at birth. About one year later, the tortoise weighed 8.5 oz. If this tortoise continued to gain the same amount of weight each year, how much would it weigh in the year 2005?

2. The San Diego Zoo received 16 tortoises in 1929. They are still living. If they were at least 25 years old when they arrived, how old are they now?

3. The tortoises are identified by numbers painted on their shells. For example, tortoise 67-5 is the fifth tortoise hatched in 1967. Suppose that there were 6 tortoises hatched in 1963, 7 in 1964, 13 in 1965, 6 in 1966, and 11 in 1967. How many numbers had to be painted to mark these tortoises? (Hint: Three numbers must be painted to mark tortoise 67-5.)

4. The oldest known tortoise lived to be 154 years old. If that tortoise died in 1982, when was it born?

5. Female tortoises are smaller than males. The largest of the zoo's females is 306 lb. The largest male is 660 lb. What is the difference in weight between the largest male and the largest female?

6. The combined weight of 2 tortoises shipped to the zoo was 800 lb. One tortoise was three times the weight of the other. What was the weight of each tortoise?

7. Three tortoises have a combined age of 76 yr. One tortoise is 10 years old. The second tortoise is twice as old as the third tortoise. How old are they?

8. Many baby Galápagos tortoises have hatched successfully at the San Diego Zoo since 1958. Suppose 3 hatched that year and 3 for every year since then. How many baby tortoises have hatched at the zoo from 1958 until now?

Share Your Thinking

9. Explain how the strategy, Make a Table, can work with problem 8.

10. Explain the strategy you used to solve problem 7.

Mental Math: Addition

LESSON 9

You want to buy two African beads. One costs 25¢, and the other costs 26¢. How much do the two beads cost?

You can use mental math to help solve the problem.

One way is to think about coins.

25¢ + 26¢

25¢ + 25¢ + 1¢

50¢ + 1¢ = 51¢

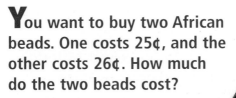

Quarter, Quarter, Penny

Another way is to think about multiples of 10.

25 + 26

25 + 10 + 10 + 6

45 + 6 = 51

The two beads cost 51¢.

Talk About It! What is another way to find 25 + 26 using mental math?

Show What You Know!

Use mental math to find the sum.

1. 46 + 24
2. 59 + 11
3. $32 + $29
4. 54 oz + 28 oz
5. 34 + 26
6. 68 + 12
7. 22¢ + 66¢
8. $46 + $37
9. 41 + 29
10. $64 + $34
11. 25 + 48
12. 46 + 49
13. 35¢ + 36¢
14. 12¢ + 49¢
15. 57 + 38
16. 35¢ + 23¢

17. **Critical Thinking** To add 48 and 32, Ken writes 50 + 30. Will he get the exact answer? Justify your answer.

More Practice Set 1.9, p. 464

Midchapter Review

for Pages 1–18

Solve using Make a Table. Show your work. (pages 8–9, 16–17)

1. When Miss Kitty was found, she weighed 64 ounces. She gained 6 ounces a week for 3 weeks and then gained 4 ounces a week. How many weeks did it take until she weighed 126 ounces?

2. The first week of your exercise program, you walk 1 mile each day. Each week you increase the amount you walk by $\frac{1}{2}$ mile. How many miles a day will you walk the fifth week?

Concepts

Find the answer. (pages 2, 6, 10)

3. Explain how you can use mental math to find $6000 + 8000 + 4000$.

4. Explain how to use front-end estimation to tell which is greater, $458 + 372$ or $399 + 504$.

5. What does 1 above the 3 show?

$$\begin{array}{r} \overset{1}{386} \\ +\ 431 \\ \hline 817 \end{array}$$

6. Classify 0.56 as a whole number, fraction, or decimal.

Skills

Add or subtract. Show your work. (pages 14, 18)

7. $\begin{array}{r} 3654 \\ +\ 1786 \\ \hline \end{array}$

8. $\begin{array}{r} 2791 \\ -\ 1886 \\ \hline \end{array}$

9. $\begin{array}{r} 5412 \\ +\ 8751 \\ \hline \end{array}$

10. $\begin{array}{r} \$54{,}368 \\ -\ 26{,}921 \\ \hline \end{array}$

11. $\begin{array}{r} \$4138.90 \\ 518.66 \\ +\quad 28.40 \\ \hline \end{array}$

12. $23{,}294 - 9651$

13. $3 \text{ h } 16 \text{ min} + 5 \text{ h } 24 \text{ min}$

14. $\$9.45 - \$.96$

15. $20{,}000 - 3000$

16. $11 \text{ ft } 3 \text{ in.} + 9 \text{ ft } 8 \text{ in.}$

17. $5396 - 208$

Estimate the sum or difference to the greatest place. Will the exact answer be greater than, less than, or equal to your estimate? (pages 10, 12)

18. $5123 + 4327$

19. $6000 + 3000$

20. $644 - 395$

21. $6112 - 1911$

Math *World*

Throughout history, people have searched for faster and easier ways of solving math problems.

Ready . . . set . . . add

Although many people in Japan use electronic calculators and computers, these machines have not completely replaced the Japanese abacus, or *soroban* (SAWR uh bahn). The soroban has been in use for nearly 500 years. Each year, the Japanese hold contests to see who can add the fastest using the soroban. Contestants add twenty 11-digit numbers. A person skilled on the soroban can usually add and subtract faster than someone with a calculator.

Pointless Decimal Points?

In many European countries, decimals are written with a comma instead of a point. For example, the European wisent, an animal similar to the American bison, can weigh as much as 2205.58 pounds. In Europe, that weight would be written as 2205,58.

The European wisent can weigh as much as 2205,58 pounds.

Try This!

Do you know why we call the flat working surfaces in kitchens and other rooms counters? The ancient Greeks and Romans used counter boards when buying and selling items. They added and subtracted on the boards using stones or counters. Over time, the name was shortened from counter boards to counters.

Follow these steps to make your own counter board.

1 Draw three vertical lines on a sheet of paper to make four columns.

2 Arrange counters as shown to model the number 5713. The columns on the counting board are like the columns on a place-value chart. Reading from right to left, the columns show the number of ones, tens, hundreds, and thousands

3 Add 241 counters to show 5713 + 241.

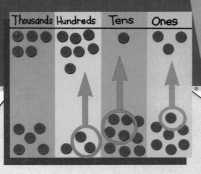

Try: 2632 + 117

7535 − 3324

Nothing to Sneeze At

Ancient people sometimes added and subtracted by making marks on trays covered with dust or sand.

Respond

With a partner . . .

find the weights of animals and write them in United States and European decimals.

Internet:
Houghton Mifflin Education Place
Explore the Math Center at
http://www.eduplace.com

Tenths and Hundredths

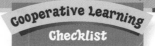

Getting Started

What You'll Need:
▶ tenths and hundredths squares
▶ crayons or markers
▶ recording sheet

Tenths and hundredths squares can help you understand decimals. A tenths square is divided into 10 equal parts. A hundredths square is divided into 100 equal parts.

Activity

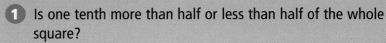

Exploring Tenths

Shade one part of your tenths square red.

The part represents $\frac{1}{10}$.

1 Is one tenth more than half or less than half of the whole square?

2 How many parts are not shaded? How many tenths does this represent?

The place-value chart shows how to write one tenth as a decimal.

Tenths can also be written as fractions. For example:

one tenth = 0.1 or $\frac{1}{10}$ nine tenths = 0.9 or $\frac{9}{10}$

3 Use the tenths squares on your recording sheet or make them. Shade each of these amounts:

a. $\frac{5}{10}$ b. 0.8   c. four tenths

d. Write $\frac{5}{10}$, 0.8, and four tenths from least to greatest.

e. Which represents $\frac{1}{2}$?

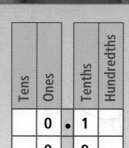

Tens	Ones	Tenths	Hundredths
0	. 1		
0	. 9		

Exploring Hundredths

Use a hundredths square. Shade one part of the square green.

4 How many hundredths does the green part represent?

5 How many hundredths are not shaded?

Hundredths in Decimal and Fraction Form

Tens	Ones	Tenths	Hundredths
	0 .	0	1
	0 .	9	9

The place-value chart shows how to write one hundredth as a decimal. Hundredths can also be written as fractions. For example:

one hundredth = 0.01 or $\frac{1}{100}$

ninety-nine hundredths = 0.99 or $\frac{99}{100}$

6 Use the hundredths squares on your recording sheet or make them. Shade each of these amounts.

    a. $\frac{34}{100}$ **b.** 0.50   **c.** sixty-eight hundredths

7 Write $\frac{34}{100}$, 0.50, and sixty-eight hundredths from least to greatest.

8 Which represents $\frac{1}{2}$?

9 Suppose you shade 8 tenths on a square and 19 hundredths on another square. What number does this represent?

Comparing Decimals and Fractions

Use your recording sheet or make decimal models.

10 Shade 0.7. Is 0.7 less than or greater than $\frac{1}{2}$? Explain.

11 Shade 0.48. Is 0.48 less than or greater than $\frac{1}{2}$? Explain.

12 Shade the squares to represent the decimals below. Write whether each number is closer to 0, $\frac{1}{2}$, or 1.

    a. 0.6   **b.** 0.17   **c.** 0.3   **d.** 0.92

13 Shade the squares to represent 0.5 and 0.07. Is 0.5 greater than or less than 0.07? How can you tell?

Show What You Know!

Write decimals from the box that are close to the numbers below.

0.2		0.57	
	0.38		0.87
0.9		0.49	
	0.05		0.4

1. 0   **2.** $\frac{1}{2}$ **3.** 1

4. What number would be represented if a square divided into tenths had no parts shaded?

5. What number would be represented if a square divided into hundredths had all small squares shaded?

6. Critical Thinking How are fractions and decimals alike?

Thousandths

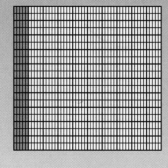

Cooperative Learning Checklist

☑ Work alone.
☑ Work with a partner.
☑ Work with a group.

Getting Started

What You'll Need:
▶ thousandths, hundredths, and tenths squares
▶ crayons or markers

Thousandths are parts that are even smaller than hundredths. You can use thousandths squares to help you understand decimals to the thousandths place.

There are 1000 small parts in the square. Each part is one thousandth of the square. Seventy-five of 1000 parts are shaded. You can use fractions or decimals to represent the shaded part.

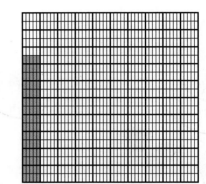

$$\frac{75}{1000} \quad or \quad 0.075$$

You can shade decimal models to learn more about thousandths.

Activity

Exploring Thousandths

Look at the shaded squares below.

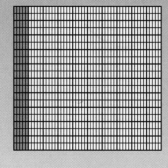 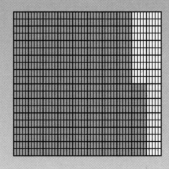 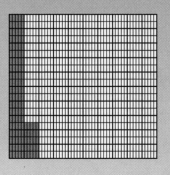

a.　　　　b.　　　　c.

1 How many thousandths are shaded in each square? Record your answers as fractions.

2 Which of these squares represents the greatest decimal?

Thousandths in Decimal and Fraction Form

Shade a thousandths square to represent each of the decimals:

3 0.120   **4** 0.925   **5** 0.475

6 0.005   **7** 0.250   **8** 0.090

9 Write each of the decimals above as a fraction.

10 Shade half of another thousandths square. This represents 0.500 or $\frac{1}{2}$.

11 Which of these decimals is greater than $\frac{1}{2}$: 0.200, 0.925, or 0.475?

Comparing Tenths, Hundredths, and Thousandths

12 Shade a tenths square to represent 0.2.

13 Shade a hundredths square to represent 0.20.

14 Shade a thousandths square to represent 0.200.

15 Compare the three squares. Describe the decimals 0.2, 0.20, and 0.200 with the words *greater than*, *less than*, or *equal*.

Show What You Know!

Write each set of decimals in order from least to greatest. Shade decimal models if you need to.

1. 0.105   0.015   0.150

2. 0.725   0.70   0.075

3. 0.065   0.605   0.6

4. 0.4   0.004   0.04

5. 0.11   0.10   0.101

6. 0.505   0.550   0.055

7. **Critical Thinking** Use models to explain why 0.300 is equal to 0.3.

8. **Number Sense** In what situations is it better to use a decimal? In what situations is a fraction better? Give an example of each.

Reading and Writing Decimals

Russian Olympic champion Svetlana Masterkova

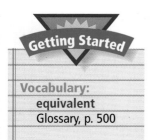
The gold medalist in the women's 1500-meter race in the track-and-field event at the 1996 summer Olympic games in Atlanta, Georgia, was Svetlana Masterkova. How do you read her winning time, 4.014 min?

You can use a place-value chart to help you read decimals.

Here's A Way! Read 4.014.

1 Say the whole number, "four."

2 Say "and" for the decimal point.

3 Say the decimal with the name of the last decimal place on the right, "fourteen thousandths."

Ones		Tenths	Hundredths	Thousandths
4	.	0	1	4

So, you read 4.014 min as "four and fourteen thousandths minutes."

Talk About It! What is the value of the digit 1 in 4.014?

Other Examples Sometimes two decimals that look different represent the same value. The decimals 0.4 and 0.40 in the chart below are **equivalent**.

Tens	Ones		Tenths	Hundredths	Thousandths
	0	.	4		
	0	.	4	0	

Standard Form	Word Form
0.4	four tenths
0.40	forty hundredths

Writing zeros to the right of the last digit in the decimal part of a number does not change the value. As you can see from the tenths and hundredths squares, 0.4 and 0.40 are equivalent.

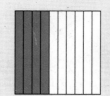

Show What You Know!

Write the value of the digit 6. Use a place-value chart to help.

1. 4.569　　　　2. 6.003　　　　3. 4823.6　　　　4. 7.986　　　　5. 24.06

Write the decimal in standard form.

6. four and eighteen thousandths　　　　7. seven and twenty-two hundredths

Write the decimal in word form.

8. 6.034　　　　9. 4.29　　　　10. 0.04　　　　11. 20.6

12. **Critical Thinking** Write a decimal that is equivalent to 12.7 and explain why it is equivalent. Do both decimals have the same word form?

Work It Out!

Write the value of the digit 3. Use a place-value chart to help.

13. 3.861　　　14. 465.023　　　15. 34.908　　　16. 0.53　　　17. 307.062

Write the decimal in standard form.

18. two hundred and eighty-three thousandths

19. twelve and five tenths

Write the decimal in word form.

20. 4.13　　　　21. 40,000.003

22. 0.631　　　　23. 63.09

Write an equivalent decimal.

24. 6.9　　25. 15.980　　26. 4.08　　27. 4387.9

Problem Solving

28. Sue, Gwen, and Anita ran in a 1500-meter race. Sue completed the event in 4.87 min, Gwen in 4.807 min, and Anita in 4.870 min. Which two girls finished the race in the same time?

More Practice Set 1.12, p. 464

Math Journal

Describe how place value to the right of the decimal point is similar to place value to the left of the decimal point. How is it different?

13 Comparing and Ordering Decimals

A piece of aragonite weighs 1.5 oz, and a piece of calcite weighs 1.45 oz. Both minerals cost the same. You want the heavier one. Which would you buy?

You can compare and order decimals by thinking about place value.

copper ore

aragonite

calcite

Here's A Way! Compare and order decimals.

Compare 1.5 oz and 1.45 oz.

1 Line up the digits by place value. Keep decimal points aligned.

1.5
1.45

2 Compare the digits. Begin with the digit in the greatest place on the left.

1.5
1.45

1 = 1

3 If the digits in the greatest place are equal, compare the digits in the next place to the right.

1.5
1.45   5 > 4

So 1.5 oz > 1.45 oz. The piece of aragonite weighs more.

Suppose you found another mineral that weighs 1.52 oz. How would you display the three minerals in order from least to greatest weight?

1 Line up the digits by place value. Write zeros so there are the same number of decimal places in each number.

1.50   1.5 = 1.50
1.45
1.52

2 Compare the digits in the greatest place on the left. If they are equal, compare the digits in the next place to the right.

1.50   1.50 > 1.45
same   1.45
1.52   1.50 < 1.52

1.45 < 1.50 < 1.52

So the mineral weights from least to greatest are 1.45 oz, 1.50 oz, and 1.52 oz.

Talk About It! How is comparing decimals like comparing whole numbers?

Show What You Know!

Compare. Write >, <, or =.

1. 0.42 ⬤ 0.398   2. 2.93 ⬤ 4.01   3. 4.90 ⬤ 4.09   4. 20.6 ⬤ 20.60

Order the numbers from least to greatest.

5. 34.19, 34.1, 35, 34.15

6. 4018, 4018.3, 1000.999, 4100

7. 0.03, 0.2, 1, 0.008

8. 2.99, 3, 2.099, 2.2

9. 30, 421, 652, 103; 3, 421, 652, 103; 342, 165, 210

10. **Critical Thinking** Since 8 > 4, is 8.0 > 4.00? Explain.

Use What You Know

Zeros written to the right of a decimal number do not change the value of the number.

5 = 5.0
0.5 = 0.50 = 0.500

5 tenths
50 hundredths
500 thousandths

Work It Out!

Compare. Write >, <, or =.

11. 7688 ⬤ 7599   12. 0.35 ⬤ 0.352   13. 503.1 ⬤ 530.9   14. 7.92 ⬤ 7.920

15. 0.3 ⬤ 0.07   16. 0.45 ⬤ 0.098   17. 12.4 ⬤ 12.40   18. 1.999 ⬤ 2

19. 61,034,521,625 ⬤ 61,426,881,203

20. 3,432,865,555 ⬤ 20,859,426,031

Order from least to greatest.

21. 0.35, 3.05, 0.33, 0.355   22. 7429, 7492, 7942, 7924   23. 5, 5.11, 5.01, 5.1

Problem Solving

Use the chart to solve each problem.

24. Which gem is the lightest?

25. Which gem is the heaviest?

26. Which gems weigh less than 4 carats?

27. Which gem weighs between 3.65 and 3.95 carats?

Weight of Gems

Gems	Weight (in carats)
Aquamarine	3.62
Diamond	4.23
Emerald	3.98
Sapphire	4.18
Topaz	3.75

28. Write the weight of the gems in order from least to greatest.

29. **Number Sense** Which gem is closest to 4 carats?

30. **Critical Thinking** When you compare whole numbers, a number with more digits is greater than a number with fewer digits. Is that true of decimal numbers? Justify your answer with an example.

More Practice Set 1.13, p. 464

LESSON 14 — Rounding Decimals

Mesa Arch, Canyonlands National Park

Canyonlands National Park in Utah is full of canyons of many-colored rocks. The park has a very dry climate. It receives an average rainfall of 10.34 in. per year. Round this value to the nearest whole inch.

You can use a number line to help you round decimals.

Here's A Way!   **Round 10.34 to the nearest whole number.**

Decimals can be rounded in the same way as whole numbers. To round 10.34 to the nearest whole number, place it on a number line.

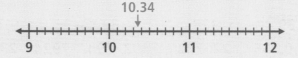

The number 10.34 is between 10 and 11, but is closer to 10. So, the average rainfall in Canyonlands National Park is rounded to 10 in.

Talk About It!   Suppose you want to round 10.34 to the nearest whole number without using a number line. What place do you need to look at to help you decide whether to round to 10 or 11? Explain your answer.

Other Examples   Sometimes you need to round a decimal to a given place. Other times, you may need to round it to the greatest place.

Round to the nearest whole number.	Round to the nearest hundredth.	Round to the greatest place.
5.3 ➡ 5	72.4<u>6</u>7	34.62 ➡ 30
0.30 ➡ 0	The number to the right is greater than 5 so round up.	8.099 ➡ 8
28.76 ➡ 29		28.76 ➡ 30

Show What You Know!

1. Use the number line to the right. Complete the sentence.

a. 3.7 is between 3 and 4 but closer to ■

b. 2.4 is between 2 and 3 but closer to ■

Round the number to the greatest place.

2. 588   3. $3.65   4. 38   5. 36,490   6. 8.42   7. 52.99

Round the decimal to the nearest whole number.

8. 356.5   9. 3.38   10. $45.16   11. 23.901   12. 0.338

Round to the underlined place.

13. 18.4̲17   14. 6.805̲1   15. 0.5̲92   16. 2.33̲3   17. 5.00̲1

18. **Critical Thinking** Give an example of when it might be better to use exact numbers rather than rounded. Justify your answer.

Work It Out!

Round the number to the greatest place.

19. $33.67   20. 56.39   21. 388   22. 6.645   23. $143.99   24. 734.9

Round the decimal to the nearest whole number.

25. 48.3   26. 6.978   27. 49.44   28. $23.12   29. 4.98

30. 354.55   31. 0.867   32. $60.86   33. 26.49   34. 26.51

35. **Number Sense** Write *rounded* or *exact* to describe the number.
    a. Yesterday, Philadelphia, Pennsylvania, received 0.73 in. of rain.
    b. The average annual precipitation in Phoenix, Arizona, is 7 in.
    c. Due to rain, only 109 people attended the play.

Round to the underlined place.

36. 60.0̲01   37. 42̲.371   38. 6.05̲1   39. 8.8̲18   40. 22.2̲1

Mixed Review

Write the product or quotient.

41. 7 × 4   42. 8 × 6   43. 45 ÷ 9   44. 12 ÷ 4   45. 6 × 6

46. 72 ÷ 8   47. 32 ÷ 4   48. 6 × 7   49. 8 ÷ 1   50. 5 × 8

More Practice Set 1.14, p. 465

15 Estimation: Adding and Subtracting Decimals

Every year thousands of people run in the Boston Marathon. The map below shows the route the runners follow. About how many miles long is a marathon route?

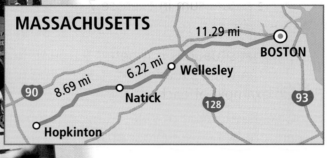

MASSACHUSETTS

11.29 mi

BOSTON

6.22 mi ○ **Wellesley**

90 8.69 mi ○ **Natick**

128

93

○ **Hopkinton**

You can estimate sums and differences of decimals by rounding.

Here's A Way!   Estimate 8.69 + 6.22 + 11.29.

1 Round each number to the nearest mile.

8.69 mi + 6.22 mi + 11.29 mi
↓   ↓   ↓
9   6   11

2 Add.

9 + 6 + 11 = 26

Estimate: 26 miles

It is about 26 miles from the start of the marathon to the finish.

Talk About It!   Use front-end estimation to find the estimate of 8.69 + 6.22 + 11.29. Compare it to the estimate you got by rounding. What do you notice?

Other Examples   You can estimate sums and differences by rounding to the greatest place.

4.7 + 3.25 + 9.8
↓   ↓   ↓
5 + 3 + 10

Estimate: 18

$34.72 − $9.76
↓   ↓
$30 − $10

Estimate: $20

Write the missing whole number.

1. The decimal 5.9 is between 5 and 6 but is closer to ■.

2. The decimal 8.4 is between ■ and ■ but is closer to ■.

3. The decimal 5.6 is rounded to ■.

4. The decimal 9.1 is rounded to ■.

Estimate by rounding to the greatest place.

5. 7.9 + 4.1 + 5.2   6. $9.35 − $4.99   7. 5.79 + 3.54   8. 10.6 − 7.3

9. **Critical Thinking** Is the actual sum in exercise 7 greater than or less than 10? How can you tell?

10. **Critical Thinking** In what situations is it better to round to the nearest whole number? In what situations is rounding to the greatest place better? Give an example of each.

Work It Out!

Write the missing whole number.

11. $6.32 is between $■ and $■ but is closer to $■.

12. 8.7 is rounded to ■.

13. 438 is rounded to ■ hundred.

14. 12.67 is rounded to ■.

Estimate by rounding to the greatest place.

15. 3.7 + 2.8

16. 8.5 − 5.1

17. $17.99 + $32.62

18. 47.6 + 2.10 + 25.5

19. 59.4 − 4.26

20. $5.55 − $3.22

21. 6841 − 1726

22. 93.9 + 201.7

23. $918.00 − $304.20

Problem Solving

Use estimation to solve each problem.

24. About how much farther do the runners travel on Route 135 than on Route 30?

25. About how far do the runners travel on Routes 135, 16, and 30 combined?

26. **Number Sense** Are the runners halfway through when they get to Route 16? Explain how you got your answer.

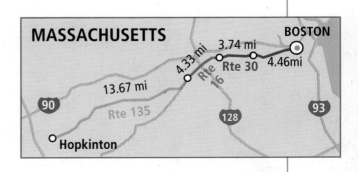

16 Adding Decimals

Barrel racing is a sporting event on horseback. A horse and rider race around three barrels as fast as possible. Suppose you finish your first ride in 15.752 s. You finish your second ride in 16.005 s, but get a penalty of 5 s added to your score for knocking over a barrel. How can you find your total time, including the penalty?

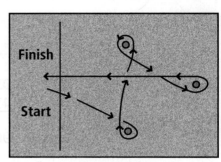

Finish

Start

Barrel Racing Pattern

Here's A Way! Find 15.752 s + 16.005 s + 5 s.

1 Line up the digits by place value.

```
   15.752 s
   16.005 s
+   5.000 s
```

5 = 5.000

2 Add.

```
    1
   15.752 s
   16.005 s
+   5.000 s
   36 757 s
```

3 Write the decimal point in the answer.

```
    1
   15.752 s
   16.005 s
+   5.000 s
   36.757 s
```

Your total time for the two runs, including the penalty, is 36.757 s.

Talk About It!   Is the answer reasonable? Explain how you decided.

Other Examples What addition property can you use to find each sum?

5.2 + 0

5.2 zero property

3.6 + 4.7 + 6.4

3.6 + 6.4 + 4.7 ➡ commutative property

10 + 4.7 ➡ associative property

14.7

Show What You Know!

Write the sum.

1. 6.09 + 4.231
2. $145.32 + $43.98
3. 6 m + 4.8 m
4. 0 + 544.9
5. 4.231 + 6.09
6. 15.008 + 5.736
7. 45.9 + 24.96 + 1.04 + 0.1
8. 196.75 + 78.53

9. **Critical Thinking** Which addition properties could help you use mental math to do exercise 7? What is the sum?

Use What You Know

Zero Property
The sum of zero and any number is that number.
2.8 + 0 = 2.8

Commutative Property
Changing the order of the addends does not change the sum.
2.1 + 5.9 = 5.9 + 2.1

Associative Property
Changing the grouping of the addends does not change the sum.
4.8 + (2.2 + 3.4) = 10.4
(4.8 + 2.2) + 3.4 = 10.4

Work It Out!

Write the sum. Use the properties when they help you add.

10.	11.	12.	13.
35.98 + 48.02	354.03 + 588.47	48.65 + 45.22	57.008 + 30.412

14.	15.	16.	17.
$318.78 + 56.40	45.996 + 30.006	3.373 + 6.891	$313.45 + 14.65

18. 21.87 + 82.1 + 34.25
19. 423.87 cm + 204.78 cm
20. 749.92 + 0
21. $338 + $521.08
22. 34.21 + 12.89 + 82.4
23. 423.98 + 423
24. 4.371 + 0.974 + 0.032 + 4.550
25. $26.88 + $34.32 + $.12 + $16.68

Problem Solving

26. Kendra completed her first barrel-racing ride in 15.540 s. She finished her second ride in 15.887 s. She knocked down a barrel and received a 5 s penalty. What was her total time for the two rides, including the penalty?

27. **Number Sense** Which two of the following numbers have a sum between 9.5 and 10?
    a. 8.089
    b. 1.005
    c. 1.493

28. **Patterns** Write the next three numbers in the pattern. 2.1, 3.2, 4.3, 5.4, ▪, ▪, ▪

More Practice Set 1.16, p. 465

Subtracting Decimals

Animal Speeds

Animal	Speed (mph)
Elephant	25
Black mamba snake	20
Spider	1.17
Tortoise	0.17
Three-toed sloth	0.15

The land animal that can run the fastest is the cheetah, which can run at 70 miles per hour (mph). Other animals move more slowly. How much slower is a spider's top speed than a cheetah's top speed?

You can use place value and your knowledge of decimals to find the difference between 70 mph and 1.17 mph.

Here's A Way! Subtract 1.17 mph from 70 mph.

You can subtract decimals by using place value the same way you did to add decimals.

1 Line up the digits by place value.

70 = 70.00

$$\begin{array}{r} 70.00 \\ -1.17 \end{array}$$

2 Subtract.

$$\begin{array}{r} 70.00 \text{ mph} \\ -1.17 \text{ mph} \\ \hline 6883 \end{array}$$

3 Write the decimal point in the answer.

$$\begin{array}{r} 70.00 \text{ mph} \\ -1.17 \text{ mph} \\ \hline 68.83 \end{array}$$

Is your answer reasonable?

The spider travels 68.83 mph slower than the cheetah.

Talk About It! How would an estimate help you know if the answer is reasonable? Give an example.

Other Examples When subtracting decimals, you may need to write zeros in the places to the right of the decimal point:

a. 8 − 4.287

$$\begin{array}{r} 8.000 \\ -4.287 \\ \hline 3.713 \end{array}$$

b. 5.923 − 0.3

$$\begin{array}{r} 5.923 \\ -0.300 \\ \hline 5.623 \end{array}$$

c. $402.83 − $6.00

$$\begin{array}{r} \$402.83 \\ -6.00 \\ \hline \$396.83 \end{array}$$

Show What You Know!

Write the difference.

1. 48.34
    − 16.52

2. 28.00 ft
    − 19.77 ft

3. 243.672
    − 58.008

4. $67.30
    − 9.99

5. 625.44
    − 36.26

6. $40 − 22.35   7. 65.9 − 4.88   8. 682.1 − 4.27

9. **Critical Thinking** Why is it important to line up the digits by place value when adding or subtracting?

Work It Out!

Write the difference.

10.   49.92
     − 29.90

11. $225.24
     − 56.88

12.   7.089 km
     − 0.046 km

13.   200.100
     − 45.823

14. 65.09 − 62.782   15. $356 − $89.67   16. 356.5 − 87.223

17. 54.45 − 13.08   18. 54.78 − 35.69   19. 132.573 − 10.745

20. 405 − 88.45   21. 536.3 − 488.354   22. 4537.101 − 4268.82

23. $55 − $40.98   24. 34.2 − 17.92   25. 23.03 − 19.086

Problem Solving   Using Data

Use the chart on page 36.

26. A fresh breeze of 24.2 mph will cause small trees with leaves to sway. Is this speed closer to that of the elephant or the black mamba snake?

27. The top speed of the three-toed sloth, at 0.15 mph, is close to that of the tortoise. Which is faster? How much faster?

Use a calculator to solve.

28. **Number Sense** What number could you add or subtract to change the 5 in the calculator display to a zero without changing the other digits?

29. How could you change the 7 to a 0 in the calculator display?

More Practice Set 1.17, p. 465

Mental Math: Subtraction

Every year in April, the city of San Antonio, Texas, holds a celebration called Fiesta. Suppose you buy a piñata for $3.99 to take home for a souvenir. You hand the cashier $5. What will your change be?

You can use mental math to solve a problem like this.

TEXAS

San Antonio

Here's A Way! Find $5.00 − 3.99.

1 Notice that $3.99 is 1 cent less than $4.00.

$$\$5.00 - \$4.00 = \$1.00$$

2 Since you subtracted 1 cent more than $3.99, add 1 cent back.

$$\$1.00 + \$.01 = \$1.01$$

Your change is $1.01.

Talk About It! How can you use mental math to find $20.00 − $16.99?

Other Examples This mental-math method works with other types of problems besides those dealing with money.

$8 - 2.9 = n$

$8 - 3 = 5$

So, $8 - 2.9 = 5.1$

> Add 0.1 to the difference because 3 is 0.1 more than 2.9

$8.5 - 2.9 = n$

$8.5 - 3.0 = 5.5$

So, $8.5 - 2.9 = 5.6$

> Remember, add 0.1 to the difference.

Use mental math to find the difference.

1. 50 − 29
2. 300 m − 199 m
3. 73 − 39
4. 4.2 − 3.9
5. $6.00 − $4.99
6. 8.2 cm − 1.9 cm
7. 4 − 1.9
8. 626 − 99

9. **Critical Thinking** Could you use this same method to find 45 − 28? Explain.

Work It Out!

Use mental math to find the difference.

10. 60 cm − 39 cm
11. 800 cm − 399 cm
12. $7.00 − $4.99
13. 6 lb − 1.9 lb
14. $7.00 − $2.99
15. $4.00 − $1.99
16. 75 − 49
17. 5.6 − 3.9
18. 327 − 99
19. 3268 − 999
20. 6411 − 299
21. $20.00 − $9.99

Face Painting at Fiesta

Problem Solving

22. At Fiesta you decide to purchase maracas that cost $5.99. How much change would you get from $10?

23. Caleb bought a T-shirt at Fiesta for $8.99. He gave the clerk $20. How much change did he get?

24. A container of juice costs $1.99, a bag of apples costs $.99, and a chicken dinner costs $5.99. Which of these items could you buy for $2? How much change would you get?

25. **Algebraic Reasoning** If 571 − n = 272, what number does n stand for?

26. **Create Your Own** Write a problem that can be solved using mental math by finding $8.00 − $3.99.

More Practice Set 1.18, p. 466

Math Journal

Explain the adding-one strategy for mental subtraction, and tell when you would use it.

Chapter 1 Test
for Pages 2-39

Test-Taking Tips
Remember to use estimation to check the reasonableness of your answer.

Problem Solving

Solve. Show your work. (page 8)

1. In your pocket you have the coins shown. How many different amounts of change can you make from them?

2. You are planning to mix 2 cans of yellow paint with 1 can of blue paint to make green paint. Yellow paint costs $12.99 a can. Blue paint costs $10.88. How much does it cost to mix 9 cans of green paint?

3. Visitors to the Science Museum on Saturdays in October included 757 students. The Science Museum had 192 more student visitors than the Art Museum on the same days. How many students visited the Art Museum?

4. You want to buy three books. The novel costs $6.95, the bicycle repair manual costs $5.98, and the biography costs $7.98. You have $20.00. How much more money do you need?

Concepts

Find the answer. (pages 6, 10, 12)

✗ **5.** Add 4.5 + 2.1 + 3.5 mentally. Explain how you did it.

✗ **6.** Explain how to use short word forms to help you find 8000 − 5000.

Will the actual answer be greater or less than the estimate? Explain.

7. 1532 + 3174 ➡ 4000

8. 582 − 312 ➡ 300

9. 1177 + 188 ➡ 1400

10. 2059 − 1130 ➡ 1000

Answer the question. Explain. (pages 22, 24)

11. Is 0.800 greater than 0.8?

12. What fraction is 0.03 equal to?

13. Is 0.72 less than 0.097?

Skills

Estimate to choose the correct answer. Write a, b, c, or d. (pages 10, 12, 32)

14. 3426 + 592
    a. 9346   b. 4018   c. 3018   d. 2834

15. 15 – 8.42
    a. 23.42   b. 7.42   c. 6.58   d. 17.58

Compare. Write <, >, or =. (page 28)

16. 4.5 ● 4.05   17. 604.6 ● 640.6   18. 5.2 ● 5.200

Round to the greatest place. (page 30)

19. 22.9   20. 5529   21. $29.88

Add or subtract. Show your work. (pages 14, 34, 36)

22. 8524   23. $46.88   24. 7.402   25. 56,800   26. 125.8
    + 3389   – 17.49   – 2.8   – 17,488   + 35.92

Add or subtract. Circle the answer if you used mental math. (pages 6, 14, 38)

27. 59 + 11   28. 56.2 + 88.753   29. 10,000 – 6000

30. 45,000 – 23,154   31. 13¢ + 39¢

 ## Performance Task

(pages 2, 3, 14)

Plan a used book sale to raise money for your school. You will sell three types of books for three different prices. Choose the type of book that you will sell for $.75, and the type of book you will sell for $1.00. The third type of book, a dictionary, will sell for $1.75. Make a sign for your customers listing the three types, their prices in numeric form and in word form.

• Write a receipt showing how much change Mrs. Juarez will get back if she buys the least expensive book, and pays for it with a five-dollar bill.

• Write a bill showing how much more money Mr. Ruby owes if he wants to buy the most expensive book and only has a one-dollar bill.

Cumulative Review

Reading and Writing Numbers (Chapter 1)
Write 7,320,502 in short word form, expanded form, and standard form.

> **Here's A Way!**
>
> Short word form:
>   7 million, 320 thousand, 502
>
> Expanded form:
>   7,000,000 + 300,000 + 20,000 + 500 + 2
>
> Standard form:
>   7,320,502

Write the number in short word form.

1. 40,978   2. 553,921

3. 8,200,000   4. 32,837,023

Write the number in standard form.

5. 33 thousand, 754

6. 450 thousand, 13

7. 45 million, 258 thousand

8. 9,000,000 + 10,000 + 3,000 + 100 + 70 + 6

9. Make up your own 8-digit number. Write it in standard form. Then write the short word form and expanded form.

Addition and Subtraction (Chapter 1)
Add and subtract these numbers: 493,607 and 242,678.

> **Here's A Way!**
>
> Addition
> ```
>       1  1   1
>     493,607
>   + 242,678
>     736,285
> ```
>
> Subtraction
> ```
>                15 9
>          2   5 10 17
>     4 9 3 , 6 0 7
>   − 2 4 2 , 6 7 8
>     2 5 0 , 9 2 9
> ```

Write the answer.

10. 5274
   + 1983

11. 7223
   − 3580

12. 19,061
   + 32,254

13. 36,820
   − 15,084

14. 676,915
   + 427,123

15. 373,998
   − 254,167

16. 900 + 200

17. 6000 + 8000

18. 8000 − 400

19. 197,564 − 78,120

20. 421,706 + 265,074

21. Why is the 7 in the tens place crossed out and 17 written above it?

```
      7 17
    4 8 7 7
  − 2 6 9 3
    2 1 8 4
```

Compare and Order Whole Numbers
(Chapter 1)

Order from greatest to least:
6,480,303; 3,182,453; 19,705,281

Line up the numbers by place value.

    6,480,303
    3,182,453
   19,705,281

Compare. Begin with the greatest place value on the left.
  1 ten million is the greatest place value, so 19,705,281 is the greatest number.
Continue comparing.
  6 > 3, so
  6,480,303 > 3,182,453
The numbers in order from greatest to least are 19,705,281; 6,480,303; and 3,182,453.

Order the numbers from greatest to least.

22. 6931; 18,374; 5076

23. 60,821; 60,281; 68,022

24. 96,502; 1,836,027; 1,382,175

25. 27,340,029; 72,438,141; 142,520,439

26. 579,306,481; 576,562,231; 579,197,202

27. 1,593,249,850; 15,923,429,850; 150,923,450

28. Give an example of two numbers that are both 6-digit numbers, but the greater number is determined by the hundreds place.

29. Give an example of two numbers that are both 8-digit numbers, but the greater number is determined by the hundred thousands place.

Problem Solving

Problem Solving Process
✓ Understand
✓ Plan
✓ Try It
✓ Look Back

Choose a Strategy You Have Learned
✓ Make a Table
  Act It Out
  Guess and Check
  Look for a Pattern
  Work Backward
  Make a List
  Work a Simpler Problem
  Draw a Picture
  Write an Equation

Choose one of the strategies you know to solve these problems. Show your work.

30. On a trip to the Grand Canyon, Jason's family drove 250 miles the first day. Every day after that they increased the distance they drove by 25 miles. How many miles did they travel in a week?

31. Suppose you want to save up some money to buy a school sweatshirt. If you save $1.00 the first week and then increase the amount you are saving by $.15 each week after that, how much will you have saved in 8 weeks?

Biking Across America

Geography Connection   **With Your Group**

Keep In Mind . . .

Your work will be evaluated on the following:

☑ If the distance traveled and cost of the trip is accurate

☑ If your equipment meets the needs of your group

☑ How clearly you explain your choices

☑ How well you work together to plan your trip

Your group is planning a bicycle trip across the United States. Use the map to choose the route you will follow.

Select the items you think your group will need from the list of biking equipment. You do not need to purchase every item on the list. Your group will have only $600 to buy equipment, so choose carefully!

In 1995, two boys from Wisconsin biked from New York to San Francisco in four months.

Map labels:

Walla Walla — 200.1 mi — Bend
Walla Walla — 346.4 mi — Great Falls
Walla Walla — 446.4 mi (to San Francisco)
Great Falls — 269.4 mi (to Idaho Falls)
Great Falls — 708.1 mi — Fargo
Fargo — 423.3 mi (toward Oshkosh)
Idaho Falls — 508 mi
Bend — 677.3 mi
San Francisco — 515.7 mi — Cedar City
San Francisco — 569.6 mi (to Yuma)
Oshkosh — 323.3 mi
Oshkosh — Sioux City
Sioux City — 500.3 mi
Sioux City — 492.6 mi
Cedar City — 461.8 mi — Colorado Springs
Colorado Springs — 446.4 mi
Colorado Springs — 361.8 mi — Terre Haute
Cedar City — 623.5 mi
Yuma — 600.4 mi — Carlsbad
Oklahoma City — 292.5 mi — Little Rock
Carlsbad — 400.2 mi
Carlsbad — 346.4 mi — San Antonio
Terre Haute — 477.2 mi
Little Rock — 400.2 mi — Chattanooga
Little Rock — 484.9 mi — Lexington
Shreveport — 361.8 mi — Tuscaloosa
Shreveport — 315.6 mi
Tuscaloosa — 269.4 mi
Tallahassee — 315.6 mi
Buffalo — 438.7 mi — Portland
New York — 284.7 mi — Portland
Buffalo — 215.5 mi
Buffalo — 354.1 mi — New York
Wheeling — 292.5 mi
Lexington — Virginia Beach
Virginia Beach — 207.8 mi
Chattanooga — 461.8 mi — Wilmington
Wilmington — 153.9 mi
Charleston — 315.6 mi

1

Plan It

- Choose the route you want to follow from those on the map.
- List the type and amount of equipment your group will need.

2

Put It Together

- Make a table that shows the cities along your route.
- In the table, record the distance between each pair of cities and find the total distance you will travel.
- Find the total cost of your equipment. It can not be over $600.

Calculator: If your group bought one of every item for each member, how much would it cost?

3

Wrap It Up

- Create a budget that shows the quantity and cost of each item bought, and the total cost.
- Write a paragraph that explains your choice of cities and equipment.

4

Discuss Your Results

- Did you meet the objectives listed in Keep In Mind?
- How is your route and budget similar to those of other groups?

Equipment List

Item	Price
Tire Pump	$22.00 ✓
Flat Repair Kit	$12.00 ✓
Bike Lock	$19.50 ✓
Bike Basket	$15.00 ✓
Odometer	$21.25 ✓
2 Riding Gloves	$14.99 ✓
Helmet	$28.50
2 Knee Pads	$32.50
2 Elbow Pads	$25.00 ✓
Compass	$10.00 ✓
State Map	$5.00 ✓
Water Bottle	$5.99 ✓
Bike Horn	$10.00 ✓

Internet

> Visit the **Math Center** at **Houghton Mifflin Education Pla**
http://www.eduplace.com

Math Power

Use What You Know

- multiplication patterns

$$4 + 2 = 6$$
$$4 - 2 = 2$$
$$4 \times 2 = 8$$

- how to write a mathematical sentence

- factor
- product

- the vocabulary

CHAPTER 2
Multiplication of Whole Numbers

Try This!

Create pictures using what you know about multiplication patterns and mathematical expressions.

What You'll Need

paper, grid paper, paper bag, scissors, colored pencils or markers

1

Cut eight small squares of paper. Number each square from 1–8. Decorate a paper bag and label it *n* for *number*. Put the squares of paper in the bag.

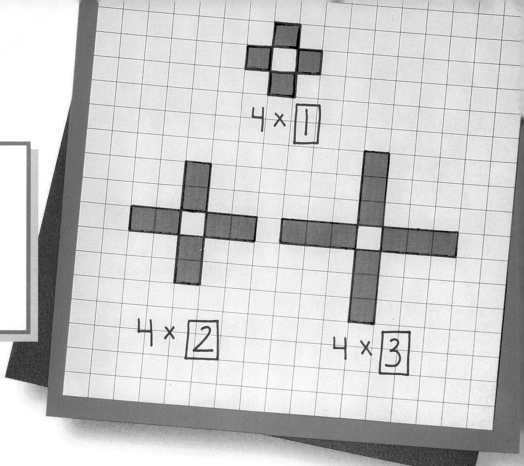

4 × 1

4 × 2   4 × 3

2

Write 4 × *n* on a piece of grid paper. Without looking, choose a number from the *n* bag. Now rewrite the expression substituting the number for the *n*.

3

Draw and color a design that shows the expression. Choose another number from the bag and repeat steps 2 and 3.

When would you need to use *n* instead of a number?

4 × 7   4 × 8

How would you describe the expression in words?

Ready to Go!

Expressions

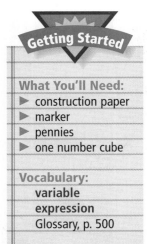

Getting Started

What You'll Need:
- ► construction paper
- ► marker
- ► pennies
- ► one number cube

Vocabulary:
variable
expression
Glossary, p. 500

In this lesson, you will explore using a variable in an expression. A **variable** is a letter like p, x, or n that can represent different values. If you roll a number cube three times, the value of your roll will vary. Use the variable p to represent the outcome of the rolls.

A symbol or combination of symbols that represents a mathematical quantity is called an **expression**. The value of these expressions depends on the value of the variables.

$$p + 8 \qquad p - 4 \qquad 879 + p$$

What is the value of each expression if $p = 4$? What if $p = 90$?

The Penny Slide

Activity

- Form two teams.
- Draw your gameboard on construction paper with expressions like the ones shown.
- Make a chart to record your scores.
- Label the cube: 4, 4, 5, 5, 6, 6.

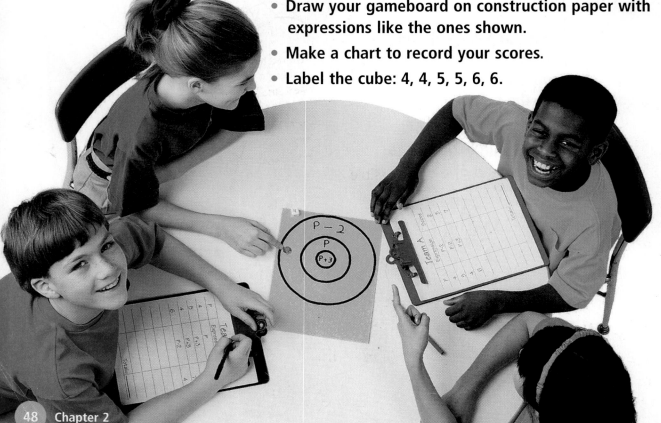

How to Play!

1

Roll the number cube. The number you roll is represented by the variable *p* for both teams in this round.

2

One player from Team A slides a penny onto the gameboard. Substitute the number rolled in Step 1 in the expression. Record the score.

3

One player from Team B slides a penny onto the gameboard. He or she finds and records the score.

4

Play five rounds. Roll a new number *p* for each round. At the end of five rounds, add the scores. Both teams compare scores for each round. What makes one score higher than another?

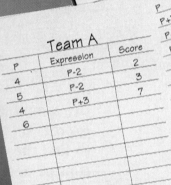

Team A		
P	Expression	Score
4	P-2	2
5	P-2	3
4	P+3	7
6		
		Total=

Team B		
	...ession	Score
		4
	P	8
	P+3	7
	P+3	4
	P-2	
		Total=

Repeat this activity by rolling the number cube to get another value for *p*. Then, try creating your own gameboard. Use different expressions, such as *p* + 12 or 20 − *p*.

Show What You Know!

Discuss each question. Explain your answer.

1. **Critical Thinking** What is the highest possible score for one turn?

2. **Number Sense** If Team A scored 2 in one turn, what was the value of *p*? Explain.

Algebraic Reasoning Write the value of the expression when *m* = 7; when *m* = 15.

3. *m* + 3   4. *m* − 1   5. 8 + *m*   6. 20 − *m*

7. *m* − 3   8. *m* + *m*   9. *m* − *m*   10. *m* + 0

More Practice Set 2.1, p. 466

Multiplication Expressions

LESSON 2

GORP

(1 Batch)

2 cups raisins
3 cups peanuts
2 cups dried apricots
4 cups rice cereal
1 cup coconut
2 cups chocolate or carob chips

Mix all ingredients. Store in airtight container.

What is GORP? It's Good Old Raisins and Peanuts. Suppose you are making different numbers of batches of GORP. How many cups of peanuts would you need for three batches? Five batches? Seven batches?

Use a multiplication expression with a variable to find the number of cups of peanuts.

Here's A Way! Find the value of the expression.

1 Choose a variable to represent the number of batches.

let **n** = number of batches

2 Write an expression.

3 cups per batch × number of batches

You can also write a multiplication expression with a dot: 3 · n

or

3 × **n**

3 Replace n with different numbers of batches. Find each value.

3 × **n**	3 × **n**	3 × **n**
3 × 3	3 × 5	3 × 7
9	15	21

cups of peanuts

Talk About It!
In a multiplication expression, is the order of the variable and the number important? Will 3 × n give you the same answer as n × 3?

Find the value of the expression when $n = 4$. When $n = 8$.

1. $n \times 3$ 2. $4 \times n$ 3. $7 \times n$ 4. $n \times 6$ 5. $10 \times n$ 6. $20 \times n$

7. $n \times 11$ 8. $n \times 25$ 9. $n \times 9$ 10. $n \times 21$ 11. $n \times 14$ 12. $n \times 22$

Write a multiplication expression to describe the situation.

13. A hiker usually hikes about 5 miles per hour. If h stands for the number of hours she will hike tomorrow, how far will she go?

14. Snake-bite kits cost $6 each. If n stands for the number of kits that a hiker buys, how much money will she spend?

15. **Critical Thinking** Suppose that exercise 14 had said that x stands for the number of snake-bite kits. Would that have changed your answers? Justify.

Write an expression for the weight of b chairs if each weighs 2 lb. Then solve.

16. 4 chairs   17. 7 chairs   18. 13 chairs   19. 17 chairs   20. 22 chairs   21. 10 chairs

22. 11 chairs   23. 30 chairs   24. 5 chairs   25. 33 chairs   26. 18 chairs   27. 3 chairs

Write an expression for the cost of n maps when each costs $4. Then solve.

28. 12 maps   29. 5 maps   30. 26 maps   31. 20 maps

32. **Mental Math** Which of exercises 28–31 did you solve using mental math? Explain.

Problem Solving   Using Data

33. Copy and complete the chart to the right. Use the recipe card to help you.

34. **Critical Thinking** How many cups of GORP does one recipe make?

35. **Mental Math** If a hiker uses 10 cups of carob chips, how many cups of GORP does she make?

Shopping List

GORP ingredients	Number of cups for n batches	Number of cups for 4 batches
Raisins	$2 \cdot n$	$2 \cdot 4 = ?$
Peanuts	$3 \cdot n$	?
Dried apricots	?	?
Rice cereal	?	?
Coconut	?	?
Chocolate or carob chips	?	?

More Practice Set 2.2, p. 466

Multiples and Least Common Multiple

Getting Started

Vocabulary:
multiple
common multiple
least common
multiple
Glossary, p. 500

In this lesson, you will explore using multiples. A **multiple** is a product of a given number and any whole number greater than zero.

A number that is a multiple of two or more given numbers is called a **common multiple**. The **least common multiple** (LCM) is the common multiple with the least value.

Find the LCM of 2, 3, and 4. You can solve the problem using the bars below to help you.

Here's A Way! **Find the least common multiple of 2, 3, 4.**

1 List the multiples.

Multiples of **2:** 2, 4, 6, 8, 10, 12, 14, 16, 18, 20 . . .

Multiples of **3:** 3, 6, 9, 12, 15, 18 . . .

Multiples of **4:** 4, 8, 12, 16, 20, 24 . . .

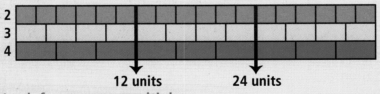

12 units   **24 units**

> If each red bar is 2 units, each yellow bar is 3 units, and each blue bar is 4 units, at what points do they all line up?

2 Look for common multiples.

Multiples of **2:** 2, 4, 6, 8, 10, 12, 14, 16, 18, 20, 22, 24 . .

Multiples of **3:** 3, 6, 9, 12, 15, 18, 21, 24 . . .

Multiples of **4:** 4, 8, 12, 16, 20, 24 . . .

3 Look for the common multiple that is the least.

The least number that is in all three lists is 12. So, 12 is the least common multiple of 2, 3, and 4.

Talk About It! When finding the LCM, why is it helpful to find the multiples of the greatest number first?

Write two common multiples for each set of numbers.

1. 3, 5   2. 8, 3   3. 3, 4, 6   4. 2, 5, 10   5. 4, 5   6. 2, 3, 10

7. What is the least common multiple for each of exercises 1–6?

8. **Critical Thinking** Does every pair of whole numbers greater than zero have a common multiple? Explain your answer.

Work It Out!

Write the first three common multiples.

9. 4, 5   10. 3, 6   11. 3, 7   12. 3, 8   13. 6, 5, 10

14. 2, 4, 5   15. 3, 6, 9   16. 8, 4, 2   17. 6, 4, 3   18. 2, 8, 10

Write the LCM for each set of numbers below.

19. 7, 9   20. 4, 10   21. 7, 10   22. 15, 3

23. 3, 4, 5   24. 3, 6, 7   25. 10, 4, 6   26. 5, 2, 9

91 cm
or ≈ 3 ft.

Problem Solving

27. During the month of June, a documentary on frogs was being shown at the local library. It was repeated every 6th morning and every 8th afternoon. When was the movie shown twice in the same day?

28. When sitting, the body of a Goliath frog is about 30.5 cm long. When it stretches its legs to jump, it is about 91 cm long. How long are the frog's legs?

29. **Critical Thinking** Is the least common multiple of a pair of numbers always the product of the numbers? Give examples to support your answer.

30. **Patterns** Use a calculator to complete the chart.

    Now, without using a calculator, predict the value of 12 × 37.

    $$3 \times 37 = ?$$
    $$6 \times 37 = ?$$
    $$9 \times 37 = ?$$

31. Use a calculator to find the first four multiples of 135.

More Practice Set 2.3, p. 467

LESSON 4

Mental Math: Multiples of 10, 100, and 1000

Use What You Know

You can use patterns to help you multiply greater factors.
Remember:

60×90

$6 \times 9 = 54$

$60 \times 9 = 540$

$60 \times 90 = 5400$

A fifth grader's heart normally beats 90 times in 1 minute. How many times does it beat in 1 hour?

You know that there are 60 minutes in an hour. Use mental math to find the product.

Here's A Way! Find 60×90.

① Multiply the non-zero digits.

$$60 \times 90$$

Think: $6 \times 9 = 54$

② Count the number of zeros in both factors. Write that number of zeros in the product.

$$60 \times 90 = 5400$$

1 zero + 1 zero   2 zeros

So, a fifth grader's heart normally beats 5400 times in 1 hour.

Talk About It! Can the product ever contain more zeros than the number of zeros in the factors?

Other Examples Look for two numbers whose product is a multiple of 10 when you multiply three factors such as 4, 6, and 5.

1 zero

$4 \times 6 \times 5$ ⟶ $4 \times 30 = 120$

30

Multiply the multiple of 10 by the third factor.

Use mental math to find the product.

1. 4 × 70   2. 5 × 900   3. 6000 × 6   4. 90 × 30

Find the value of the expression.

5. 12 × 10   6. 30 × 40   7. 60 × 20   8. 2 × 6000

9. **Critical Thinking** Which expressions in exercises 5–8 have the same product? Change the other expressions so that they have the same product as well.

Work It Out!

Use mental math to find the product.

10. 60 × 50   11. 80 × 200   12. 90 × 70   13. 2 × 5000

14. 5 × 7 × 4   15. 8 × 5 × 60   16. 2 × 38 × 5   17. 6 × 40 × 5

Use mental math to find the value of *n*.

18. 4 × *n* = 160   19. *n* × 80 = 4000   20. 700 × *n* = 14,000

21. *n* × 90 = 18,000   22. 600 × *n* = 3000   23. 10 × *n* = 10,000

24. *n* × 70 = 210   25. 40 × *n* = 8000   26. *n* × 300 = 6000

Problem Solving

27. An adult's heart pumps about 5 liters of blood every minute. About how much blood is pumped in an hour?

28. **Estimation** An adult's circulatory system includes about 90,000 miles of blood vessels! How many miles of blood vessels are at work in a 9-player softball team?

29. **Create Your Own** Write two multiplication problems. Use these factors: 100 and 200; 30 and 40.

More Practice Set 2.4, p. 467

Math Journal

Many calculators cannot show the answer to 6000 × 40,000,000 because the product has too many digits. How can you use mental math to find an answer if you don't have a calculator?

Estimating Products

6 strings

Musicians know that the 6 strings on electric guitars don't last forever. Will 200 strings be enough to restring 18 electric guitars?

You can use front-end estimation or rounding to find the answer.

Here's A Way! Estimate 6 × 18.

Front-end Estimation

1 Use the first digit in factors greater than 10.

$$\begin{array}{r} 18 \\ \times\ 6 \end{array} \longrightarrow \begin{array}{r} 10 \\ \times\ 6 \end{array}$$

Estimate: 6 × 10

2 Multiply.

$$6 \times 10 = 60$$

3 Look at the estimate. It is less than the actual product because the factor was rounded down. But, even if the product is doubled, it is still less than 200.

Rounding

1 Round factors greater than 10.

$$\begin{array}{r} 18 \\ \times\ 6 \end{array} \longrightarrow \begin{array}{r} 20 \\ \times\ 6 \end{array}$$

Estimate: 6 × 20

2 Multiply.

$$6 \times 20 = 120$$

3 Look at the estimate. If one or both factors were rounded up, the product is less than the estimate.

So, the two estimates, 60 and 120, show that 200 strings will be enough.

Talk About It! Why does front-end estimation give you a low estimate? How can rounding give you a low estimate? How can it give you a high estimate?

Estimate the product.

1. 7 × 67   2. 19 × 19   3. 74 × 43   4. 62 × 8   5. 81 · 18

6. 319 · 5   7. 59 · 9   8. 542 · 7   9. 20 × 18   10. 32 · 5

11. **Critical Thinking** Which product for exercises 1–10 is closest to 500? How did you decide?

Work It Out!

Use front-end estimation or rounding to estimate the product.

12. 5 × 78   13. 92 × 8   14. 6 × 702   15. 9 lb × 219   16. 825 · 4

17. 27 · 75   18. 46 · 46   19. 2 · 327   20. 14 × 52   21. 334 × 33

22. 68 × 43   23. 8 × 759   24. 6 · 52   25. 508 · 87   26. 862 · 174

27. **Write About It** How do you decide when to estimate? When might you start with an estimate, but go on to find an exact answer?

Problem Solving Using Data

28. About how many strings do you need to restring 125 banjos?

29. Would 300 strings restring 8 baroque lutes?

30. A group of three stringed instruments has 23 strings in all. What three instruments might be in this group?

31. Suppose you were restringing harps. If 5 harps need 40 new strings each, and 3 harps need 45 new strings each, would 400 strings be enough?

Strings	
Instrument	**Number of strings**
Russian balalaika	3 strings
Violin	4 strings
Dulcimer	4 strings
Bluegrass banjo	5 strings
Electric guitar	6 strings
Viola	6 strings
Greek sitar	7 strings
Mandolin	8 strings
Japanese koto	13 strings
German baroque lute	24 strings
Harp	47 strings

Mixed Review

Find the value of the expression when $t = 4$; when $t = 9$.

32. $t + 45$ 33. $700 - t$ 34. $71 - t$ 35. $t + t$

More Practice Set 2.5, p. 468

Problem Solving
Logical Reasoning

Logical Reasoning

Ask Yourself:

Can I eliminate possibilities?

Can I sort the information?

Corky, Jay, Tam, and Raina are in a skateboard race. One of their helmets has blue squiggles, one has green stripes, one has yellow circles, and one has red stars. Corky's helmet has red stars. Jay doesn't wear the one with blue squiggles. If Raina's helmet has green stripes, what helmet does Tam have on?

You Decide

- What information are you given? How can you use a chart?
- Corky's helmet has red stars. What do you know about the others?

	Blue Squiggles	Green Stripes	Yellow Circles	Red Stars
Corky	?	?	?	yes
Jay	no	?	?	?
Tam	?	?	?	?
Raina	?	yes	?	?

Work It Out!

Decide how to show the information. Then solve.

1. Mark, Ric, Sue, and Jo play in a band. Jo plays the flute and Ric does not play the tuba. Sue plays the drums. Who plays the bass?

2. Selma plays field hockey. Her jersey number has two digits and is less than 50. The sum of the digits is 9. If you multiply the two digits together, you get 14. What is Selma's jersey number?

3. Four friends are waiting in line. Stan is directly in front of Lisa. Juan is directly behind Aileen. Lisa was the last friend to get in line. In what order are the friends standing?

4. Matthew has fewer than 30 marbles. He can divide his marbles into 3 equal groups. When he divides them into 2 equal groups, 1 is left over. When he divides them into 5 equal groups, 1 is left over. How many marbles does he have?

Share Your Thinking

5. Explain how you solved problem 4.

Midchapter Review

for Pages 46–58

for Pages 46–58

Problem Solving

Solve. (pages 54, 58)

1. A theater has 22 rows of seats. There are 39 seats in each row. Does the theater have room to seat 567 students? How do you know?

2. A student's initials are T, C, and D. Her last name begins with C and her middle name doesn't begin with D. What letter does her first name start with?

3. Three even numbers have a least common multiple of 8. The sum of the three numbers is 14. What are the numbers?

Concepts

Write the letter of the best estimate. Explain your choices. (page 56)

4. 42×6	a. 24	b. 240	c. 2400	d. 24,000
5. 500×600	a. 300	b. 3000	c. 30,000	d. 300,000
6. 69×81	a. 5600	b. 560	c. 56,000	d. 560,000

Write the answers. (pages 50, 52)

7. Is 30 a common multiple of 2 and 5? How do you know?

8. A student swims one lap in 5 minutes. If l is the number of laps she swims, write an expression that shows how long the laps take.

Skills

Find the value of the expression when $t = 9$ and $v = 4$. (pages 48, 50)

9. $t + 8$ 10. $10 - v$ 11. $7 \cdot v$ 12. $t \cdot v$

Find the least common multiple for each group of numbers. (page 52)

13. 5, 7   14. 3, 10   15. 2, 6, 8   16. 1, 4, 9

Find each product. (page 54)

17. $40 \times \$70$ 18. 10×800 19. $9 \text{ ft} \times 7000$ 20. 200×300

Multiplication Around the World

Math World

Through history, people have used different math symbols and words to communicate with numbers. Read about them and try using one of the methods.

A Heap of Multiplication

HEAP

When you write a multiplication expression, you sometimes use a letter such as *p* or *h* as a variable. People in ancient Egypt used the symbol for their word *aha*, which meant "heap," to stand for an unknown number. The symbol for heap appears on the Rhind papyrus, an ancient scroll filled with math problems. The scroll is 3600 years old and got its name from the man who discovered it, Alexander Henry Rhind.

Notable Number Words

"Fourscore and seven years ago"
These words begin a famous speech by Abraham Lincoln known as the Gettysburg Address. *Fourscore* is another way of saying 80. *Score* means "a group of 20," so *fourscore* is four groups of 20, or 4 × 20. Throughout history, people have used words for numbers based on multiplication. In the language of the Toba people of Paraguay, the number word for 8 means two 4's, or 2 × 4. The number word for 40 used by the Igbo people of Africa, is made up of the words for 20 and 2. It means 20 × 2.

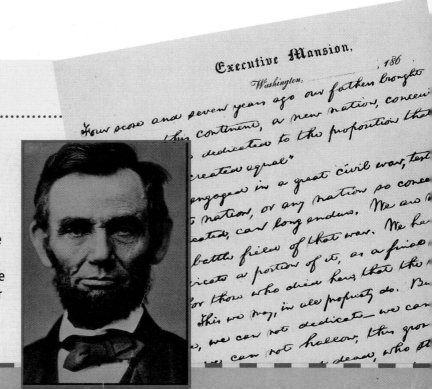

Try This!

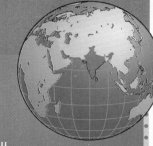

Buyers and sellers in the markets of southern India have a tradition of using their fingers and hands to communicate. Follow these steps to get an idea of how this language works:

1 Work with a partner. Decide who will buy and who sell.

2 The seller picks an object to "sell." Then both partners place their hands flat on top of the desk.

3 To agree on a price, you will create a multiplication sentence. The buyer chooses the first number of the sentence by pointing to the top, middle, or bottom of the seller's left little finger. The top is equal to 1, the middle to 10, and the bottom to 100. If you both agree, go to step four. If not, repeat this step until you do.

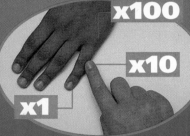

4 Now choose the second number. Each of the seller's fingers represents a number from 1 to 10. The seller raises the finger that will be the second number in the sentence. If the buyer agrees, the item is sold for the product of the two numbers. If you do not agree on a price., repeat this step until you do.

A Simpler Symbol?

About 300 years ago, some people in Europe started using this symbol for multiplication. This symbol was used to avoid confusion between the multiplication symbol × and the letter x used in expressions. What symbols do we use?

Respond

With a partner . . .
write another way of saying 120 and 160 using the word *score*. Make up some of your own.

Internet:
Houghton Mifflin Education Place
Explore the Math Center at
http://www.eduplace.com

Multiplying by 1-Digit Numbers

Pebbles the rover is programmed to help collect rocks on Mars. If Pebbles can collect 164 rocks in one day, how many rocks can it collect in 4 days?

Estimate first. Round, then multiply.

$$4 \times 164 = n$$
$$4 \times 200 = 800$$

Pebbles can collect about 800 rocks in 4 days. To find an exact answer, multiply with regrouping.

Pebbles the rover

Here's A Way! Find 4×164.

1 Multiply the ones. Regroup if necessary.

$$\begin{array}{r} \overset{1}{164} \\ \times \quad 4 \\ \hline 6 \end{array}$$

4 ones
$$\underline{\times\, 4}$$
16 ones

2 Multiply the tens. Add the tens. Regroup if necessary.

$$\begin{array}{r} \overset{2\;1}{164} \\ \times \quad 4 \\ \hline 56 \end{array}$$

6 tens
$$\underline{\times\, 4}$$
24 tens
→
24 tens
$$\underline{+\; 1 \text{ ten}}$$
25 tens

3 Multiply the hundreds. Add the hundreds.

$$\begin{array}{r} \overset{2\;1}{164} \\ \times \quad 4 \\ \hline 656 \end{array}$$

1 hundred
$$\underline{\times\, 4}$$
4 hundreds
→
4 hundreds
$$\underline{+\; 2 \text{ hundreds}}$$
6 hundreds

Pebbles can collect 656 rocks in 4 days. The estimate shows that the answer makes sense.

Talk About It! Why is it necessary to multiply with the ones first?

Find the product.

1. 87 × 5	2. 42 × 6	3. 39 × 3	4. 21 × 6	5. 278 × 4	6. 42 × 5
7. $850 × 6	8. 425 × 3	9. $425 × 3	10. 92 × 8	11. 63 × 3	12. 55 × 5

13. **Critical Thinking** How can you use addition to check the product of exercise 6?

Work It Out!

Find the product.

14. 68 × 5	15. 738 × 6	16. 402 × 3	17. $1.50 × 8
18. 392 × 4	19. 66 × 9	20. 725 × 5	21. $829 × 8
22. $829 × 7	23. 36 × 9	24. 289 × 5	25. 172 × 3
26. 67 · 6	27. 49 · 4	28. 720 · 7	29. 819 · 9
30. 7 · $115	31. 79 · 3	32. $28 · 4	33. 5 · 608
34. 310 · 6 lb	35. 8 · $485	36. 215 · 2	37. 215 · 4

38. **Number Sense** How can finding the answer to exercise 36 help you find the answer to exercise 37?

Problem Solving

39. NASA's Sojourner robot will have a mass of about 6400 kg on Mars. On Earth, its mass is about 3 times greater. What is Sojourner's mass on Earth?

40. Dante, an eight-legged robot, has been used to explore an erupting volcano in Antarctica. If 35 Dante robots were made in one month, and 45 in the next, would 620 legs be enough to make them all?

41. The volcano Mt. Erebus is 11,000 feet high. If Dante climbed about 3900 feet a day, would it take more than two days to reach the top? Justify your answer.

More Practice Set 2.7, p. 468

Multiplying by 2-Digit Numbers

How many hours a night do you sleep? If you answered 10 hours, that means you sleep 3650 hours a year! Many animals sleep even longer. If a giant armadillo can sleep up to 18 hours each day, how many hours can it sleep in a year?

Estimate to predict what the answer will be.

$$
\begin{array}{r}
365 \\
\times\ 18 \\
\end{array}
\Longrightarrow
\begin{array}{r}
400 \\
\times\ 20 \\
\hline
8000 \\
\end{array}
$$

3 zeros

3 zeros

To get the exact amount, find 18 × 365.

Here's A Way! Find 18 × 365.

❶ Multiply by the ones digit.

$$
\begin{array}{r}
365 \\
\times\ 18 \\
\hline
2920 \\
\end{array}
$$

$$
\begin{array}{r}
365 \\
\times\ 8 \\
\hline
2920 \\
\end{array}
$$

❷ Multiply by the tens digit.

$$
\begin{array}{r}
365 \\
\times\ 18 \\
\hline
2920 \\
+\ 365 \\
\end{array}
$$

❸ Add.

$$
\begin{array}{r}
365 \\
\times\ 18 \\
\hline
2920 \\
+\ 365 \\
\hline
6570 \\
\end{array}
$$

A giant armadillo sleeps 6570 hours a year. The estimate shows the answer makes sense.

Talk About It! You could also solve this problem with addition. Would you prefer to add or multiply? Why?

Other Examples Describe the steps you would follow to find each product.

a.
$$
\begin{array}{r}
569 \\
\times\ 85 \\
\hline
2845 \\
+\ 4552 \\
\hline
48,365 \\
\end{array}
$$

b.
$$
\begin{array}{r}
\$104 \\
\times\ 77 \\
\hline
728 \\
+\ 728 \\
\hline
\$8008 \\
\end{array}
$$

c.
$$
\begin{array}{r}
27 \text{ cm} \\
\times\ 64 \\
\hline
108 \\
+\ 162 \\
\hline
1728 \text{ cm} \\
\end{array}
$$

d.
$$
\begin{array}{r}
35 \text{ lb} \\
\times\ 90 \\
\hline
3150 \text{ lb} \\
\end{array}
$$

Find the product.

1. 264 ×38	2. $312 ×40	3. 109 ×17	4. 288 ×56

5. **Critical Thinking** For which of these exercises could you have used mental math? Explain your answer.

A lion sleeps about 15 hours per day.

Work It Out!

Find the product.

6. 49 ×23	7. $87 ×66	8. 422 ×51	9. 78 ×78	10. 548 ×25	11. 192 ×71

12. 308 · 12   13. 90 · 43   14. 780 · 26 ft   15. 700 · 20 ft   16. 240 · 13 ft

17. 15 · 22   18. 14 · 14 ft   19. 46 · 65   20. 44 · 65   21. 42 · 65

22. **Patterns** Look at exercises 19–21. What patterns do you see in the exercises and answers?

Use estimation to choose a factor from the box. Complete each sentence.

23. 23 × ■ = 1334   24. ■ · 64 = 1856   25. 3519 = 51 × ■

29	69	58
	47	23

Problem Solving   Using Data

26. About how many hours does a lion sleep each month?

27. How many hours does a koala bear sleep in March, April, and May?

28. What animal spends about half of every week sleeping?

29. Elsie sleeps about 1460 hours a year. What kind of animal is Elsie?

30. **Create Your Own** Write a word problem about one of the animals listed in the chart. Use multiplication and solve.

Good Night

Animal	Hours of sleep (per day)
Elephant	4
Gorilla	12
Koala bear	22
Lion	15
Pig	13
Rhino	9
Sloth	20

More Practice Set 2.8, p. 468

Problem Solving
Act It Out

Getting Started

What You'll Need:
▶ two different colors of cubes or tiles

A garden is 4 feet wide and 6 feet long. If you rake a 2-foot border around the outside edge of the garden, what is the area of the border?

You can act it out with a model to solve this problem.

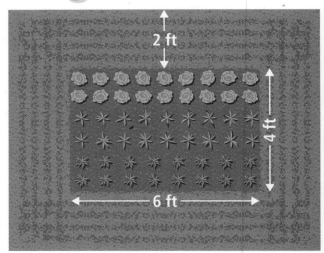

2 ft

4 ft

6 ft

Here's A Way! Use Act It Out to solve.

1 Understand

- What is the width of the garden? The border?
- How can you find the area of a rectangle?

2 Plan

- Use cubes or color tiles to make a model. Choose one color for the garden, and another color for the border.
- Can you use subtraction to find the area of the border?

3 Try It

- Build a rectangle to represent the garden. The number of tiles you use is the area.
- Add a 2-tile wide border around the edge.
- Find the area of the entire rectangle. Next, subtract the area of the garden alone.

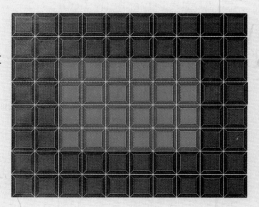

4 Look Back

The area of the border is 56 square feet. Are you surprised that the area of the border is greater than the area of the garden?

Use Act It Out to solve.

1. While painting your house, you stand on the second rung of a ladder. As you paint, you move up 8 rungs, down 5 rungs, up 2 rungs, and down 3 rungs. Where are you standing when you finish?

2. **Critical Thinking** Would a calculator help you solve problem 1? Explain.

Work It Out!

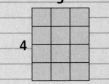
Use Act It Out or another strategy to solve each problem.

3. At a garden sale, you can buy 1 plant for $1.10 and 3 plants for $2.95. If you have $10, can you buy 10 plants? Justify your answer.

4. You and your sister are planting rows of seeds. You plant 14 seeds in the first row, 12 seeds in the second, and 30 seeds in the third. Your sister plants twice as many. How many seeds does each of you plant?

5. Square bricks are placed around a small tree. The area of the surface is 25. Which diagram represents the problem?

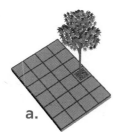

a.

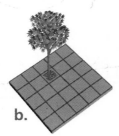

b.

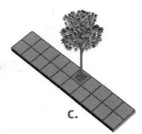

c.

6. You plant seeds for two hours. If you plant about 10 seeds every 5 minutes, and take one 5-minute break, how many seeds do you plant in all? Explain.

7. At a flower sale, your class sells 46 painted flower boxes. Sixteen more upper grade students buy boxes than students from the lower grades. How many from the upper grades buy a flower box?

8. Four out of 10 students in your class use bricks to make tree borders, while the others use stones. How many students use bricks in a class of 30?

Share Your Thinking

9. How does using a model help you to solve problem 6?

Multiplying by 3-Digit Numbers

Did you know that sharks have more than one row of teeth? The white shark pictured here has two rows of teeth. The whale shark can have as many as 311 rows. If each row in a whale shark's jaw has 115 teeth, how many teeth are there in all?

You can estimate to get a reasonable answer.

$311 \times 115 = \square$ $300 \times 100 = 30,000$

To get an exact answer, find 311×115.

Here's A Way! Find 115 × 311.

① Multiply by the ones digit.

```
  311
× 115
 1555
```

```
 311
×  5
1555
```

② Multiply by the tens digit.

```
  311
× 115
 1555
  311
```

```
 311
× 10
3110
```

③ Multiply by the hundreds digit. Then add.

```
   311
×  115
  1555
   311
+ 311
 35765
```

```
  311
× 100
31100
```

An adult whale shark can have as many as 35,765 teeth. The estimate shows this answer is reasonable.

Talk About It! In step 3, how do you know you are multiplying 311 × 100?

Other Example You do not need to show a product that is 0.

Paper and Pencil

```
  2112
× 308
 16896     8 × 2112
+ 6336
650,496    300 × 2112
```

Calculator

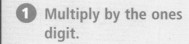

Show What You Know!

Find the product.

1. 453
   × 122

2. 608
   × 203

3. 765 mi
   × 400

4. $2.90
   × 469

5. 832 g
   × 601

6. **Critical Thinking** How are the two expressions below similar? How are they different?   321 · 46   321 · 146

Work It Out!

Find the product.

7. 332
   × 156

8. 405
   × 211

9. 500 lb
   × 172

10. $3.25
    × 200

11. 520 cm
    × 150

12. $450 · 631

13. 774 · 447

14. 628 kg · 152

15. 620 · 120

16. **Mental Math** In the above exercises, which products did you find using mental math?

Problem Solving

17. Scientists tracked one mako shark for 86 days. The shark traveled about 28 km per day. How many km short of 3000 km did it travel?

18. Sharks often travel up to 57 km per day. If one shark traveled 48 km each day for 31 days, and another shark traveled 57 km each day for 28 days, which traveled farther?

19. The piked dogfish is the most common shark. It is about 63 in. long. The largest shark, the whale shark, is about 11 times longer. How long is a whale shark?

20. The smallest shark is the spined pygmy shark. It is about 250 mm long. A large bull shark can be 13 times longer. Can a large bull shark be 30,000 mm long?

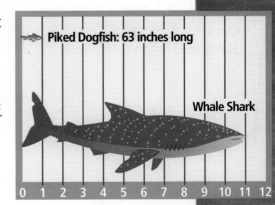

Piked Dogfish: 63 inches long

Whale Shark

0 1 2 3 4 5 6 7 8 9 10 11 12

Mixed Review

Find each sum or difference.

21. 289 + 758

22. 108 − 26

23. 8000 − 12

24. $15.32 + $81.91

25. $20.00 − $3.99

26. 4003 − 3004

27. 20,000 + 7283

28. 16 + 1029 + 643

More Practice Set 2.10, p. 469

Problem Solving
Using Strategies

You can read more about the Voyager 2 in the pages of *National Geographic World*

The Voyager 2 space mission was launched in 1977. Four years later, it took some incredible photos of Saturn's seven rings. These photos showed that the rings are made up of chunks of ice and rock. Some chunks are as big as buildings!

Problem Solving Process
✓ Understand
✓ Plan
✓ Try It
✓ Look Back

Choose a Strategy You Have Learned
✓ Make a Table
✓ Act It Out
  Guess and Check
  Look for a Pattern
  Work Backward
  Make a List
  Work a Simpler Problem
  Draw a Picture
  Write an Equation

This time line shows Voyager 2's mission from Earth to Neptune. About how many months was Voyager on its expedition?

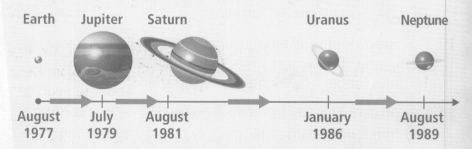

Earth	Jupiter	Saturn		Uranus	Neptune
August 1977	July 1979	August 1981		January 1986	August 1989

- What is the question you have to answer?
- Look at the timeline. How many planets did Voyager 2 pass? Can you show this information?
- Explain how making a table can help you to solve the problem.
- How long did each part of Voyager 2's trip take? How can you convert your answer into months?
- Solve the problem and describe the strategy you used.

Use any strategy to solve each problem. Show your work.

500 km

Enceladus

1. Saturn has at least 20 moons. One, Enceladus (en SEL uh duhs), has a diameter of 500 km. (The diameter is the distance from one side of a sphere to the other, measured on a straight line through the center.) Titan, Saturn's largest moon, has a diameter 10 times greater. What is the diameter of Titan?

2. Voyager 1 was launched 16 days after Voyager 2 took off on August 20, 1977. When was Voyager 1 launched? Can you tell the exact date? Justify your answer.

3. Earth rotates on its axis every 24 hours. Saturn rotates more quickly. It completes a rotation in 10 hours and 30 minutes. About how many times does Saturn rotate in 10 Earth days?

4. It takes 30 Earth years for Saturn to orbit the sun. How many Earth days is that? (Ignore leap years.)

5. Saturn's winds race at 1500 feet for each second. The strongest hurricanes on Earth roar at about 1800 inches for each second. Which is faster, a hurricane on Earth or Saturn's winds? How many times faster? Explain.

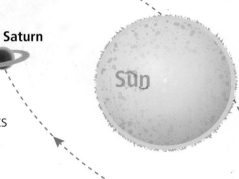

30 years

Saturn

Sun

6. Saturn's rings are labeled with the letters of the alphabet. Its C ring is 10,000 km wider than its D ring. Its C ring is also 6000 km narrower than its B ring. If its B ring is 25,500 km wide, what is the width of the D ring?

7. Many of Saturn's moons were discovered in different years. Pan was discovered in 1990. Janus was discovered 24 years before Pan. Pandora was discovered 14 years after Janus and 132 years after Hyperion. When was Hyperion discovered?

8. Telesto, Dione, Janus, and Prometheus are moons that lie at different distances from Saturn's center. Their distances are 295,000 km; 378,000 km; 151,000 km; and 139,000 km. Telesto's distance is 295,000. Dione's distance is not 151,000 km. If Prometheus is 12,000 km farther than Janus, what is Dione's distance?

Share Your Thinking

9. Choose one of the problems you solved. Explain your strategy.

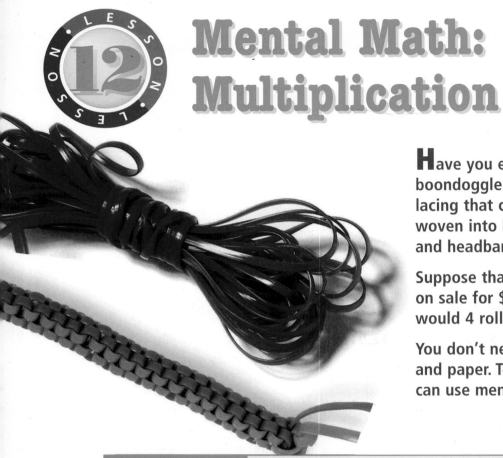

LESSON 12

Mental Math: Multiplication

Have you ever worked with boondoggle? It is colored plastic lacing that can be knotted and woven into key chains, necklaces, and headbands.

Suppose that green boondoggle is on sale for $2.99 a roll. How much would 4 rolls cost?

You don't need a calculator pencil and paper. To find the answer, you can use mental math.

Here's A Way! Find $2.99 × 4.

1 Notice that $2.99 is 1 cent less than $3.00, so multiply by $3.00.

$$4 × \$3.00 = \$12.00$$

> You have added $.01 for each of the 4 rolls. All together, you've added $.04.

2 Adjust your answer. Subtract the amount of money you've added.

$$\$12.00 - \$.04 = \$11.96$$

So, 4 rolls of boondoggle cost $11.96.

Talk About It! How can using mental math help you decide if you have enough money to make a purchase?

Other Examples You can use this mental math strategy to solve many multiplication problems.

$4 × \$1.51 = n$ $8 × 19 = n$

$4 × \$1.50 = \$6.00$ $8 × 20 = 160$

Then, $\$6.00 + \$.04 = \$6.04$.   Then, $160 - 8 = 152$.

Use mental math to find the product.

1. 3×99 2. $199 \cdot 4$ 3. $\$1.95 \times 3$ 4. $\$.26 \cdot 5$ 5. $7 \times \$3.99$

6. **Critical Thinking** In the exercises above, why might using a mental math strategy be faster than using pencil and paper?

Work It Out!

Use mental math to find the product.

7. 5×99 8. 99×7 9. 3×95 10. 4×101

11. $6 \cdot \$.99$ 12. $\$5.99 \cdot 2$ 13. 49×5 14. 8×26

15. $\$.49 \times 9$ 16. $10 \times \$.19$ 17. $\$2.51 \times 8$ 18. $10 \times \$3.99$

Problem Solving   Using Data

19. For a 20-in. necklace, you need 5 yd of boondoggle. How much will this cost?

20. A T-shirt design calls for four colors. How much will it cost to paint the shirt with metallic colors?

21. Arrange these items from least to most expensive:
    - 2 small bead kits
    - 6 bottles of gold fabric paint
    - 8 bottles of green fabric paint
    - 10 yd of boondoggle

22. If your class has $50 to spend, would you have enough to buy one of each item?

Craft Sale

Boondoggle	$2.99 a roll
	$ .19 a yard
Small bead kit (1500 beads)	$8.95
Large bead kit (3000 beads)	$15.95
Fabric paint: cherry red pearl purple forest green sun yellow	$1.99 each 3 for $4.99
Fabric paint: silver gold bronze copper	$2.49 each 3 for $6.49

Mixed Review

Find each sum or difference using mental math.

23. $31 + 49$ 24. $\$14.00 + \$76.00$ 25. $0.55 - 0.45$ 26. $18 - 0.05$

More Practice Set 2.12, p. 469

Math Journal

How can you use mental math to help you find the product of 3×98?

Chapter 2 Test

for Pages 44–73

Test-Taking Tips
Drawing a picture may help you to visualize a problem.

Problem Solving

Solve. Show your work. (pages 58, 66)

1. The flag of Mali has three equal, vertical stripes. The green stripe is to the left of the yellow stripe and does not touch the red stripe. Copy and color the flag.

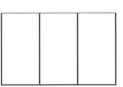

2. The flag of Kuwait is black, red, green, and white. The white shape is a rectangle. Green and red do not touch. Black and red touch in the lower left corner. Copy and color the flag.

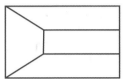

Choose the correct answer using data from the chart.
Write a or b. (page 56)

3. In Australia, about 6000 people would live in a 100-square-mile area.
   a. true
   b. false

4. In China, an estimated 19,800 people would live in a 45-square-mile area.
   a. true
   b. false

Country or Region	People per Square Mile (1994)
United States	72
United Kingdom	622
China	327
East Africa	90
Australia	6

Concepts

Use mental math. Explain how you found an answer. (page 72)

5. 2 × $1.98   a. $4.04   b. $3.98   c. $3.96   d. $3.90

6. $3.99 × 6   a. $18.99   b. $24.99   c. $24.94   d. $23.94

7. 7 × $4.05   a. $28.35   b. $23.85   c. $25.38   d. $25.83

Is the actual product greater than or less than the estimate? Explain how you know. (page 56)

8. 79 × 8 ➡ 640

9. 20 × 311 ➡ 6000

Multiply. Show your work. (pages 62, 64, 68)

| 10. 89 × 7 | 11. 127 × 4 | 12. 62 × 17 | 13. 77 × 22 |

| 14. 204 × 20 | 15. 713 × 248 | 16. 899 × 300 |

Estimate. Write the letter of the correct missing factor. (pages 50, 64, 68)

17. $12 \cdot n = 300$ a. 2

18. $804 \cdot n = 1608$ b. 7

19. $n \cdot 700 = 4900$ c. 10

20. $750 \cdot n = 7500$ d. 25

Find the products. Arrange them from least to greatest. (pages 54, 64, 68, 72)

21. a. 32 × 32   b. 93 × 7   c. 16 × 160   d. 24 × 100   e. 8 × 981

22. a. 555 × 55   b. 55 × 55   c. 55 × 5   d. 555 × 555   e. 555 × 5

 Performance Task

(pages 50, 64)

Plan a concert for your school. Where will the concert be held? Are any places in your school similar to the ones in the table? How many nights will the concert play? How many people can you seat per night? How much will you charge for tickets? After you have made these choices, answer the following questions:

• How much will your school earn if you sell out every night?

• How much will your school earn if about half of the tickets sell?

Keep In Mind . . .

Your work will be evaluated on the following:
☑ Realistic planning
☑ All questions answered
☑ Complete calculations
☑ Correct calculations

	Small Auditorium	Large Auditorium
	11 seats per row	18 seats per row
	9 rows of seats	20 rows of seats

Cumulative Review

Rounding Decimals (Chapter 1)
Round 16.87 to the nearest whole number.

Here's A Way!

Round 16.87 to the nearest whole number.

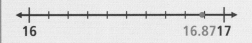

16   16.87 17

16.87 is between 16 and 17, but closer to 17.
So, 16.87 rounds to 17.

Round the decimal to the nearest whole number.

1. 14.1

2. 9.59

3. $34.70

4. 35.367

5. 4.861

6. 0.961

Round the number to the greatest place.

7. 676.3

8. $28.17

9. 126

10. 4.76

11. $504.82

12. 79.63

13. When rounding a decimal to the nearest whole number, how do you decide whether to round up or down?

Multiplication Expressions (Chapter 2)
Write a multiplication expression to describe the following situation: There must be 1 adult for every 5 students on the camping trip. How many students can go?

Here's A Way!

Choose a variable.
Let n = number of adults.
Write an expression for the number of students.
$$5 \times n$$
Use different values for n.
$$5 \times 7 = 35$$
If 7 adults go, then 35 students can go.

Write a multiplication expression. Then find the values.

14. Web sport belts cost $3 each. Let n = the number of belts. How much will these groups spend if each member buys a belt?
   a. a group of 6 friends
   b. a family of 4
   c. a class of 22

15. Wool ski socks cost $8 a pair. Let n = the number of pairs of socks. How much will it cost for each order?
   a. an order of 2 pairs
   b. an order of half a dozen pairs
   c. an order of 50 pairs

Write the value of the expression when $t = 3$; when $t = 9$.

16. $t + 5$

17. $92 - t$

18. $t - 0$

19. $4 \cdot t$

20. $50 + t$

21. $t + t$

Estimation (Chapter 2)
Estimate 5 × 27 using front-end estimation and rounding.

Here's A Way!

Front-end Estimation

Use the first digit in factors greater than 10.

       5 × 27

Estimate: 5 × 20

Multiply: 5 × 20 = 100

Rounding

Round factors greater than 10.

       5 × 27

Estimate: 5 × 30

Multiply: 5 × 30 = 150

Use front-end estimation or rounding to estimate the product.

22. 3 × 49
23. 62 × 4
24. 7 × 67
25. 496 × 5
26. 8 · 159
27. 26 × 19
28. 57 × 16
29. 63 × 245
30. 726 × 181

31. When are estimates done using front-end estimation and rounding the same?

Problem Solving

Problem Solving Process

✓ Understand
✓ Plan
✓ Try It
✓ Look Back

Choose a Strategy You Have Learned

✓ Make a Table
✓ Act It Out
  Guess and Check
  Look for a Pattern
  Work Backward
  Make a List
  Work a Simpler Problem
  Draw a Picture
  Write an Equation

Choose one of the strategies you know to solve these problems. Show your work.

32. Alec, Sabrina, and Tracy all wore costumes to the Fall Carnival. The costumes were a dragon, a robot, and a pumpkin. Alec wore the costume that most resembled a person. Tracy did not wear the vegetable costume. What costume did each person wear?

33. Suppose you want to make a large batch of spiced cider for a PTA meeting. Each gallon of cider will make 25 servings. The recipe calls for 3 cinnamon sticks for each gallon of cider. How many cinnamon sticks would you need to make 150 servings of spiced cider?

·CHAPTER·

2

I N V E S T I G A T I O N

Butterfly Farming

Science Connection   **With Your Group**

Keep In Mind . . .

Your work will be evaluated on the following:

☑ If your total amount shipped is accurate

☑ How clearly you explain the steps used by your group

☑ How clearly you show the information in your chart

☑ How your group divides the work among members

Did you know there are butterfly farms all over the world? These farms supply zoos, parks, and botanical gardens with butterflies.

The average butterfly lives about two months, so butterfly farms ship new supplies each month. Since butterflies are hard to ship, the farms send cocoons.

Your group will create a plan for a class butterfly farm. The farm can produce up to 3000 cocoons each year.

Number of Cocoons Shipped In One Box

| Blues 40 | Brushfoot 55 | Hairstreak 52 | Skippers 50 | Sulphers 45 | Swallows 88 |

1

Plan It

- Look at the table showing Last Year's Shipment. How many cocoons were sent? How many zoos and gardens ordered boxes?

- Look at this year's business plan. You will ship two types of butterflies to 16 zoos and 7 gardens. You can only ship one box of each. Your goal is to ship as close to 3,000 cocoons as possible.

- From the table above, choose two types of cocoons to ship in order to meet your goal.

LAST YEAR'S SHIPMENT

	10 Zoos	3 Gardens	
Blues (40 per box)	400	120	
Brushfoot (55 per box)	550	165	**TOTAL 1235**

2

Put It Together

- Create a business plan showing the cocoons you chose, and where they will be shipped.

- Multiply to find out how many cocoons will be shipped. For example, if you choose to ship one box of Blues to 11 zoos, multiply 11 X 40 to find the total number of cocoons.

Calculator If 17 zoos were sent a box of each of the butterflies, how many cocoons would be sent?

This Year's Shipment

	16 Zoos	7 Gardens	
Type of butterfly			
Type of butterfly			Total

4

Discuss Your Results

- Did you meet the points listed in the Keep in Mind?

- Did your group meet its goal? Compare your plan to the plans of other groups. Is there more than one kind of plan that meets the goal?

3

Wrap It Up

- Fill in each section of the business plan. Include your totals for both types of butterfly.

- How did you decide which cocoons to send?

Internet

> Visit the **Math Center** at **Houghton Mifflin Education Place.** http://www.eduplace.com

5 10 15
20 25 30
35 40 45

• how to count
  by 5's

3
4)12
−12
——
   0

• long division

  3 R3
4)15
−12
——
   3

• how to find
  remainders

CHAPTER

3

Division of Whole Numbers

Try This!

Use what you know about long division and remainders to play Divide by Four.

What You'll Need

pencil, grid paper, number cube, playing pieces

105 110 115 120

125

1

Make a grid 5 squares by 4 squares. Number the squares by 5's starting with 105. Use something small as your playing piece.

To start the game, each player rolls one number cube and moves that many squares. Player A divides the number landed on by 4. If the remainder is an odd number, Player A moves back that number of squares. If the remainder is an even number, Player A moves forward.

$$\begin{array}{r} 31\ R1 \\ 4\overline{)125} \\ \underline{-12} \\ 5 \\ \underline{-4} \\ 1 \end{array}$$

If the remainder is zero, Player A rolls the number cube and moves forward the number on the cube. Player B now plays. The game continues until one player has reached the last number in the grid.

Did the remainders have a pattern?

What kind of remainders would you have with larger numbers?

Ready to Go!

Division Expressions

Writing division expressions can help you solve division problems. When you write 15 ÷ 3, you are using a division expression.

You can write a division expression using a variable. For example, to find the number of dollars in x quarters, you can write $x \div 4$, or $\frac{x}{4}$.

Slide to Divide

Activity

- Make a gameboard on construction paper like the one shown.
- Write these numbers on separate index cards: 6, 12, 18, 24, 30.
- Try five rounds of Slide to Divide. Make a chart to record your score.

1. Draw the large triangle with a "T" inside.
2. Draw the "penny line" at the opposite end of the paper.
3. Write the expressions p in the smallest triangle at the top, $p \div 2$ on the left side of the "T," $p \div 3$ on the right side, and $p \div 6$ everywhere else.

Getting Started

What You'll Need:
- construction paper, 11 in. × 17 in.
- five index cards
- penny

Cooperative Learning
Checklist

- ☐ Work alone.
- ☑ Work with a partner.
- ☑ Work with a group.

How to Play!

1 Place index cards face down and mix them up. Choose a card. The number on the card will be p for this round.

2 A player from Team A slides the penny from behind the line into other parts of the board. To find the score, replace p in the expression that the penny lands on. Record the score.

3 One player from Team B slides the penny, determines his or her score, and records it. Return the index card to be used in the next round.

4 Continue play until one player's total score reaches at least 100.

Example: p is 12 and penny lands on $p \div 2$. The score is $12 \div 2$ or 6.

Player A

Round	p	Expression	Score	Total Score
1	6	$p \div 2$	3	3
2	18	$p \div 3$	6	9

Player B

Round	p	Expression	Score	Total Score
1	6	p	6	6
2	18	$p \div 6$	3	9

Show What You Know!

Discuss each question and explain your answer.

1. **Critical Thinking** What is the highest possible score for one round? Explain how you would get that score.

2. **Critical Thinking** If a player scored 15 points one round, what was p, and what expression did the penny land on?

3. Write an expression to describe the situation: You choose the number card 18. When you slide the penny, your score is 3. What expression did the penny land on?

4. Write a story problem using the expression $12 \div 2$.

5. Write the value of the expression when $w = 4$; when $w = 8$.

   a. $\dfrac{24}{w}$ b. $16 \div w$ c. $12 + w$ d. $\dfrac{32}{w}$ e. $\dfrac{40}{w}$

More Practice Set 3.1, p. 469

Estimation: Using Compatible Numbers

You have to read the book *Johnny Tremain* in six days. The book has 256 pages. About how many pages should you read each day?

You can use compatible numbers to make an estimate.
Compatible numbers are numbers that are easy to work with mentally.

Here's A Way! Estimate 256 ÷ 6.

1 Choose numbers close to 256 that are easy to divide by 6. Think of basic facts.

$$6\overline{)256}$$

$$6\overline{)240}$$

$$6\overline{)300}$$

The numbers 240 and 300 are **compatible numbers** with 6 because 6 divides 240 and 300 without a remainder.

2 Divide.

$$6\overline{)240} = 40$$

$$6\overline{)300} = 50$$

You will need to read between 40 and 50 pages a day.

Talk About It! How do basic facts help you choose 240 and 300 as compatible numbers with 6?

Other Examples When you estimate using compatible numbers, try to get a high and a low estimate.

a. 475 ÷ 3
- 300 ÷ 3 = 100
- 600 ÷ 3 = 200

b. 1763 ÷ 6
- 1200 ÷ 6 = 200
- 1800 ÷ 6 = 300

c. 34,659 ÷ 4
- 32,000 ÷ 4 = 8000
- 36,000 ÷ 4 = 9000

d. 2457 ÷ 7
- 2100 ÷ 7 = 300
- 2800 ÷ 7 = 400

Write the compatible numbers you would use to estimate. Then, estimate.

1. $5\overline{)237}$
2. $9\overline{)659}$
3. $6\overline{)2569}$
4. $7\overline{)1683}$
5. $8\overline{)43,071}$

6. $715 \div 2$
7. $275 \div 6$
8. $1623 \div 5$
9. $14,083 \div 4$
10. $42,654 \div 7$

11. **Critical Thinking** How can you tell whether your estimate is greater or less than the exact quotient?

Work It Out!

Choose the compatible numbers that help you estimate. Write a, b, or c.

12. $9\overline{)215}$	a. $9\overline{)900}$	b. $9\overline{)210}$	c. $9\overline{)180}$
13. $3967 \div 6$	a. $3900 \div 6$	b. $3600 \div 6$	c. $4000 \div 6$
14. $8\overline{)20,391}$	a. $8\overline{)24,000}$	b. $8\overline{)20,000}$	c. $8\overline{)15,000}$

Write the compatible numbers you would use to estimate. Then, estimate.

15. $2\overline{)481}$
16. $9\overline{)692}$
17. $7\overline{)3705}$
18. $6\overline{)7061}$
19. $8\overline{)39,092}$

20. $751 \div 4$
21. $397 \div 7$
22. $8552 \div 2$
23. $7834 \div 8$
24. $55,340 \div 8$

Problem Solving

25. What if you choose a book twice as long as *Johnny Tremain*? About how many pages would you need to read each day to finish the book in 6 days? Explain how you found your answer.

26. Suppose you choose a book to read that has 328 pages. About how many pages should you read each day to finish the book in 5 days?

27. You want to buy some books at the book fair. Each book costs $3.75. You only have $16. How many books can you buy?

28. You want to buy 3 books at the book fair. Each book costs $3.75. How much will you spend?

29. **Number Sense** When do you think it might be important to know whether your estimate is high or low? Why?

More Practice Set 3.2, p. 470

Dividing by a 1-Digit Divisor

Flashes Each Minute

Boston Light, the first lighthouse in America, flashes a white light six times per minute. If you saw a hundred flashes, about how long were you watching?

Here's A Way! Find 100 ÷ 6.

1 Estimate using compatible numbers.

$$6)\overline{100}$$

$$6)\overline{60} \qquad 10$$

$$6)\overline{120} \qquad 20$$

The quotient will be a 2-digit number between 10 and 20. So the tens digit is 1.

2 Write the tens digit. Multiply and then subtract.

$$
\begin{array}{r}
1 \\
6)\overline{100} \\
-\ 6 \\
\hline
4
\end{array}
$$

6 × 1 ten

3 Divide the ones. Multiply. Subtract.

$$
\begin{array}{r}
16 \\
6)\overline{100} \\
-\ 6 \\
\hline
40 \\
-\ 36 \\
\hline
4
\end{array}
$$

6 × 6 ones

4 Write the remainder if there is one. What does the answer mean?

$$
\begin{array}{r}
16\ \text{R4} \\
6)\overline{100} \\
-\ 6 \\
\hline
40 \\
-\ 36 \\
\hline
4
\end{array}
$$

You were watching for more than 16 minutes.

Talk About It! How was the remainder used to answer the question?

Divide.

1. 3)43
2. 4)98
3. 6)150
4. 5)398

5. 100 ÷ 7
6. 55 ÷ 2
7. 200 ÷ 8
8. 197 ÷ 3

9. **Critical Thinking** Can the remainder be greater than the divisor? Justify your answer.

Work It Out!

Divide.

10. 3)99
11. 7)83
12. 4)76
13. 5)213
14. 8)92

15. 63 ÷ 3
16. 82 ÷ 4
17. 93 ÷ 5
18. 280 ÷ 7
19. 239 ÷ 4

Look at exercises 20–22. Make a guess about what will happen to the quotients. Then, divide.

20. 126 ÷ 6
21. 252 ÷ 6
22. 504 ÷ 6

Estimate. If your estimate is less than 50, find the quotient.

23. 3)69
24. 5)87
25. 2)157
26. 8)326

27. 109 ÷ 7
28. 265 ÷ 3
29. 352 ÷ 5
30. 162 ÷ 6

31. **Number Sense** What does a quotient with a remainder tell you?

32. **Critical Thinking** Why do you need to record the remainder?

Problem Solving

33. **Estimation** About how long does it take for Boston Light to flash 1000 times?

34. **Number Sense** If another lighthouse flashes its light 8 times each minute, would it take more or less time to see 100 flashes from that lighthouse than from Boston Light? Why?

35. Usually, seagulls lay from 1 to 4 eggs each year. What is the least number of seagulls that could lay 150 eggs? What is the greatest number of seagulls that could lay 150 eggs?

36. **Critical Thinking** If a seagull laid 17 eggs in 4 years, would this be unusual? Why or why not?

More Practice Set 3.3, p. 470

Zeros in the Quotient

Have you noticed that you hear thunder after you see lightning when a storm is far away? By counting seconds, you can find how fast sound travels if you know how far away the lightning is. Suppose lightning flashes 9774 ft (about 2 mi) away and you hear thunder 9 seconds later. How many feet does sound travel in a second?

Here's A Way! Find 9774 ÷ 9.

1 Estimate using compatible numbers. The estimates tell you that the answer will be between 1000 and 2000.

$$\begin{array}{r} 1000 \\ 9\overline{)9000} \end{array} \qquad 9\overline{)9774} \qquad \begin{array}{r} 2000 \\ 9\overline{)18,000} \end{array}$$

2 Write the first digit in the quotient. Multiply and subtract.

$$\begin{array}{r} 1\_\_\_ \\ 9\overline{)9774} \\ -9 \\ \hline 7 \end{array}$$

9 × 1 thousand

3 Write the hundreds digit. Multiply and subtract.

$$\begin{array}{r} 10\_\_ \\ 9\overline{)9774} \\ -9 \\ \hline 7 \\ -0 \\ \hline 77 \end{array}$$

9 × 0 hundreds

4 Write the tens digit. Multiply and subtract.

$$\begin{array}{r} 108\_ \\ 9\overline{)9774} \\ -9 \\ \hline 7 \\ -0 \\ \hline 77 \\ -72 \\ \hline 54 \end{array}$$

9 × 8 tens

9 × 6 ones

5 Write the ones digit.

$$\begin{array}{r} 1086 \\ 9\overline{)9774} \\ -9 \\ \hline 7 \\ -0 \\ \hline 77 \\ -72 \\ \hline 54 \\ -54 \\ \hline 0 \end{array}$$

So, 9774 ÷ 9 is 1086. Then sound travels at 1086 feet each second.

Talk About It! Why must you write a zero as the second digit in the quotient?

Other Examples

a. $$\begin{array}{r} 70 \\ 9\overline{)630} \\ -63 \\ \hline 00 \\ -0 \\ \hline 0 \end{array}$$

b. $$\begin{array}{r} 702 \\ 8\overline{)5616} \\ -56 \\ \hline 16 \\ -16 \\ \hline 0 \end{array}$$

c. $$\begin{array}{r} 8050 \text{ R1} \\ 4\overline{)32,201} \\ -32 \\ \hline 20 \\ -20 \\ \hline 1 \end{array}$$

Estimate first, then divide.

1. $3\overline{)62}$ 　　　2. $2\overline{)1240}$ 　　　3. $9\overline{)2786}$ 　　　4. $5\overline{)40,530}$

5. $2472 \div 8$ 　　6. $3570 \div 7$ 　　7. $1047 \div 5$ 　　8. $20,124 \div 4$

9. **Critical Thinking** How does an estimate tell you how many digits will be in the quotient?

Work It Out!

Estimate first, then divide.

10. $2\overline{)81}$ 　　　11. $9\overline{)630}$ 　　　12. $3\overline{)181}$ 　　　13. $2\overline{)1212}$

14. $6\overline{)2405}$ 　　15. $8\overline{)5616}$ 　　16. $4\overline{)32,201}$ 　　17. $7\overline{)28,595}$

18. $742 \div 7$ 　　19. $320 \div 4$ 　　20. $1852 \div 9$ 　　21. $2045 \div 5$

22. $218 \div 2$ 　　23. $1844 \div 6$ 　　24. $35,007 \div 7$ 　　25. $12,092 \div 3$

Patterns

26. $1205 \div 4$ 　　27. $1206 \div 4$ 　　28. $1207 \div 4$ 　　29. $1208 \div 4$ 　　30. $1209 \div 4$

31. **Number Sense** Without dividing, decide which would have the greater quotient: $5372 \div 6$ or $5372 \div 5$. How do you know?

Problem Solving

32. Sound travels faster or slower depending on what substance it is traveling through. How far does sound travel through water each second?

33. Sound travels faster or slower depending on temperature. How far does sound travel in a second on a cold day? On a warm day? Does it travel faster on a cold day or on a warm day?

Substance	Distance	Seconds
water	30,072 ft	6
cold air	13,188 ft	12
steel	60,030 ft	3
warm air	7980 ft	7

34. How fast does sound travel in steel? About how many times faster or slower does sound travel through steel than through water?

35. Suppose an airplane is taking off 3 mi away, and it takes 14 s until you first hear it. Is it a warm or cold day? (Remember, 1 mi = 5280 ft.)

More Practice Set 3.4, p. 470

Problem Solving
Choose a Computation Method

Four friends are sharing equally the $40 cost for a party. Do you need a calculator to compute each person's share? Explain.

You Decide

* How can you use mental math to find out each share?
* Will it be easier to use a calculator? Why?

Work It Out!

Choose a computation method to solve these problems. Record which method you used.

1. 20 × 3   2. 200 − 99   3. 60 ÷ 6   4. 500 − 36

5. 2 × 7 × 5   6. 30 × 10   7. 0.17 + 2.58   8. 702 ÷ 26

9. $26.16 + $39.29   10. 7000 − 5000   11. 32,458 + 54,397

12. 36 × 47   13. 3 × 60.99   14. 74,005 + 20 + 10

15. 335 × 62 × 0 × 8   16. 5 + 50 + 5 + 5 + 50

17. **Share Your Thinking** How does estimation help you check for the reasonableness of answers? Explain your thinking.

18. Suppose the party begins at 7 P.M. You begin watching a movie at 8:35 P.M. The movie ends at 10:15 P.M. The party ends at the end of the movie. How long is the movie? How much longer is the party than the movie?

19. For entertainment, you and three friends tell jokes from a book of 500 jokes. Each of you tells different jokes. You tell 47 jokes, and your friends tell 23, 36, and 79 jokes each. How many jokes in the joke book are left untold?

20. **Create Your Own** Write two word problems.
    a. one mental math problem   **b.** one calculator problem

Sidebar

Choose a Computation Method

Ask Yourself:

Do I need an exact answer or an estimate?

Should I use a model, paper and pencil, mental math, or a calculator?

What operation should I use?

Midchapter Review

for Pages 82-90

for Pages 82-90

Problem Solving

Solve using a calculator or mental math. Write which you used. (page 90)

1. You and three friends sell wrapping paper as part of a fundraiser to earn money for school field trips. You sell $20.65 worth of paper and your friends sell $35.78, $16.73, and $45.87 worth. How much did you sell in all?

2. Suppose the principal tells your class that the middle school has about twice as many students as your elementary school. If your school has about 600 students, about how many attend the middle school?

Concepts

Find the answer. (pages 82, 84, 86, 88)

3. In what two different ways can you write a division expression for width divided by 4?

4. How do you use compatible numbers when estimating quotients?

5. What is the greatest remainder possible if the divisor is 6? Explain.

Skills

Write the value of the expression when $t = 2$; when $t = 6$. (page 82)

6. $\frac{18}{t}$ 7. $24 \div t$ 8. $\frac{6}{t}$ 9. $24 - t$ 10. $12 + t$ 11. $60 \div t$

Choose the numbers that are compatible. Write a, b, or c. (page 84)

12. $6\overline{)361}$ a. $4\overline{)300}$ b. $6\overline{)360}$ c. $5\overline{)370}$

13. $4821 \div 5$ a. $5000 \div 5$ b. $4800 \div 5$ c. $4600 \div 5$

Write your estimate. (page 84)

14. $8\overline{)361}$ 15. $832 \div 5$ 16. $3\overline{)7086}$ 17. $4\overline{)22,437}$

Divide. (pages 86, 88)

18. $3\overline{)213}$ 19. $6\overline{)242}$ 20. $5\overline{)187}$ 21. $7\overline{)763}$

Math *World*

Read about how one empire used division to make travel and communication easier. Then have fun playing a Chinese division game.

Special Delivery

Around 464 B.C., the Persian Empire stretched about 2400 miles, from present-day Libya to western India. That is about the same as the distance from San Francisco to Washington, D.C. To make trade and communication easier, the Persians built the Persia Royal Road, which was 1677 miles long. A series of messengers on horseback could carry a message from one end of the road to the other in nine days, a journey that normally took about three months. Along the road were 111 stations that provided fresh horses. Each messenger traveled at top speed for about 15 miles before changing horses.

This statue is shown in clothing similar to what a messenger would have worn.

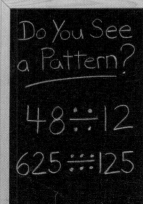

Do You See a Pattern?

$48 \div 12$

$625 \div 125$

Try This!

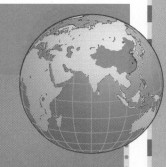

Fan Tan is a popular game in Chinese communities all over the world. It is often played with beans, but you can use counters. Two to four people can play this version of Fan Tan.

1 Assign each player a number from 0 to 3. Make a scoring chart by writing the numbers 0–3 across the top of a sheet of paper.

2 Write each number in the corner of a large sheet of paper. Place the paper on the desk or tabletop and have players sit by their assigned numbers.

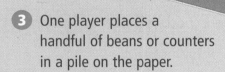

3 One player places a handful of beans or counters in a pile on the paper.

4 Another player uses the chopsticks or pencil to divide the beans into four equal piles. How many beans are left over?

5 If your assigned number equals the number of beans left over, you earn a point. Use the chart to record the results of each round. Keep playing until one player has 5 points.

Sign of the times

At one time, the symbol for division showed the number of digits in the numerator and the denominator. On the slate the division sentence 48 divided by 12 uses two dots above and below the line because there are two digits in 48 and two in 12. Why are there three dots in the division sentence 625 divided by 125?

Respond

Find the number of dots . . .

in the problem 38,450 divided by 25. Make up a problem that would have seven dots above the line.

Internet:
Houghton Mifflin Education Place
Explore the Math Center at
http://www.eduplace.com

Problem Solving
Guess and Check

A Texas sheriff's star and a Mexican peso cost $.72 total at a Texas souvenir stand near the Alamo. The star costs 3 times as much as the peso. What is the cost of each?

Here's A Way! **Use Guess and Check.**

1 Understand

- How can you use the price of the peso to find the price of the star?

2 Plan

- Start with a table to help you to organize.

- How would you label the rows and columns?

3 Try It

- Your first guess for the cost of the peso is $.10.

- Will your next guess be higher or lower?

- Guess and check until you solve the problem.

Cost of Peso	Cost of Star = 3 × cost of Peso	Cost of Peso + Cost of Star = $.72 ?
$.10	$.30	$.10 + $.30 = $.40 no; too low
$.20	$.60	$.20 + $.60 = $.80 no; too high
$.15	$.45	$.15 + $.45 = $.60 no; too low

4 Look Back

- If $.17 is too low and $.19 is too high, what is the price of the peso? What is the price of the sheriff's star?

- How did your guesses help you to find the correct answer?

Use Guess and Check to complete the problem.

1. At a snack shop near the Alamo, a group of 10 students bought either personal pizzas for $4 each or Texas burgers for $5 each. Together they spent $46. How many pizzas and burgers did they buy?

Pizzas Purchased	Cost of Pizzas at $4 Each	Burgers Purchased	Cost of Burgers at $5 Each	Cost of Pizzas + Burgers = $46 ?
7	$28	3	$15	$28 + $15 = $43 no

2. **Critical Thinking** The number 46 is even. An even number cannot be made by adding an odd and an even number together. The cost of the pizza is always even. What does this information tell you about the number of Texas burgers purchased?

Work It Out!

Use Guess and Check or any strategy to solve these problems.

3. Suppose you have $3.95 in coins. All your coins are dimes and quarters. The number of quarters you have is one less than the number of dimes. How many of each coin do you have?

4. Ms. Alverez took her 3 children on a tour of the Alamo. The product of her children's ages is 27. If the sum of the ages is 13, how old are they?

5. You have 14 coins to spend on an energy bar. The cost of the energy bar and the value of the coins is exactly $1.40. You only have quarters, dimes, and nickels. How many of each coin do you have?

6. Your friend bought 3 souvenir pens and 5 pencils for $2.25. You paid $2.95 for 5 souvenir pens and 3 pencils.
   a. How much is 1 pencil?   b. How much is 1 pen?

7. A display case at the souvenir store is 4 times as long as it is wide. Its length is 144 ft. How wide is it?

Share Your Thinking

8. How do unsuccessful guesses help you to find the answer?

9. How can using a table help you to make better guesses?

Dividing by Multiples of 10

FRANCE
SPAIN
★ Madrid
PORTUGAL
ANDALUSIA
A F R I C A

Use What You Know

To multiply using mental math, first find the product of the non-zero digits. Then place as many zeros at the end of the product as there are zeros in the factors.

$2 \times 3 = 6$
$20 \times 30 = 600$
1 zero + 1 zero = 2 zeros

Flamenco dancing comes from Spain. It is a very lively dance. If you danced the flamenco for an hour you would burn about 300 calories! How many calories would you burn in a minute of flamenco dancing?

You can use mental math to divide by multiples of 10.

Here's A Way! Find $300 \div 60$.

1 Find a related multiplication sentence.

$$300 \div 60 = n$$

$$60 \times n = 300$$

2 Find the related multiplication fact and solve.

$$60 \times n = 300$$

$$6 \times n = 30$$
$$6 \times 5 = 30$$

3 Use patterns to find the answer.

$$6 \times 5 = 30$$
$$60 \times 5 = 300$$
$$600 \times 5 = 3000$$

So, $300 \div 60 = 5$

You would burn about 5 calories for every minute of dancing!

Talk About It! Why does $300 \div 60 = n$ mean the same thing as $60 \times n = 300$?

Other Examples Use mental math to find the quotient.

a. $270 \div 90 = n$

$$90 \times n = 270$$

Think:
$9 \times n = 27$
$9 \times 3 = 27$

$$90 \times 3 = 270$$

So, $270 \div 90 = 3$

b. $36{,}000 \div 40 = n$

$$40 \times n = 36{,}000$$

Think:
$4 \times n = 36$
$4 \times 9 = 36$

$$40 \times 9 = 360$$
$$40 \times 90 = 3600$$
$$40 \times 900 = 36{,}000$$

So, $36{,}000 \div 40 = 900$

Use multiplication facts and mental math to find the quotient.

1. $3\overline{)90}$ 2. $50\overline{)250}$ 3. $4\overline{)2800}$ 4. $20\overline{)80,000}$

5. $420 \div 60$ 6. $5600 \div 8$ 7. $2400 \div 30$ 8. $4000 \div 50$

9. **Critical Thinking** A friend solved 20×30 by writing $2 \times 3 \times 10 \times 10 = 600$. Explain why this method helps you to find the product of 20 and 30.

Work It Out!

Use mental math to find the quotient.

10. $7\overline{)2100}$ 11. $70\overline{)2100}$ 12. $700\overline{)2100}$ 13. $90\overline{)540}$

14. $30\overline{)270}$ 15. $50\overline{)3500}$ 16. $20\overline{)1600}$ 17. $70\overline{)3500}$

18. $30\overline{)6000}$ 19. $9\overline{)8100}$ 20. $40\overline{)16,000}$ 21. $50\overline{)45,000}$

22. $120 \div 40$ 23. $1000 \div 5$ 24. $1800 \div 30$ 25. $4200 \div 60$

Patterns

26. $200 \div 50$ 27. $2000 \div 50$ 28. $20,000 \div 50$ 29. $20,000 \div 500$

Solve for the variable.

30. $3200 \div 400 = n$ 31. $8000 \div 20 = n$ 32. $72,000 \div 900 = n$

Problem Solving

33. During a long day of dancing, you burned 2400 calories. If dancing takes about 300 calories an hour, about how many hours did you dance?

34. If you went sightseeing for 4 hours, you would burn about 417 calories. About how many calories would you burn in one hour of sightseeing?

35. You've just eaten four desserts that totalled about 1600 calories! At least how many hours would you have to dance to burn it all off? At least how many hours of sightseeing?

36. **Estimation** Doing sit-ups for a minute burns about 14 calories. About how many calories would you burn if you did sit-ups for half an hour?

More Practice Set 3.7 p. 471

Estimating With 2-digit Divisors

The Sears Tower in Chicago has 4 major stairwells. Stairwell 3 has 1344 stairs. There are 21 stairs per floor. About how many floors are connected by Stairwell 3? You can estimate the answer.

Here's A Way! Estimate $1344 \div 21 = n$.

1 Find compatible numbers that help you divide. You can change one or both numbers.

$$1344 \div 21 = n \quad\Longrightarrow\quad 1400 \div 20 = n$$

2 Divide.

$$1400 \div 20 = 70$$

3 Interpret the answer.

About 70 floors are connected by Stairwell Number 3.

Talk About It! Is the estimate greater than or less than the exact answer? Justify your answer.

Other Examples To estimate, find compatible numbers.

a. $383 \div 50 = n \quad\Longrightarrow\quad 400 \div 50 = 8$

b. $3600 \div 96 = n \quad\Longrightarrow\quad 3600 \div 90 = 40$

c. $520 \div 58 = n \quad\Longrightarrow\quad 540 \div 60 = 9$

d. $763 \div 77 = n \quad\Longrightarrow\quad 800 \div 80 = 10$

e. $1827 \div 28 = n \quad\Longrightarrow\quad 1800 \div 30 = 60$

Stairwell 3

Estimate. Write the compatible numbers you use; then, write the estimate.

1. 17)203   2. 46)300   3. 58)2715   4. 41)221

5. 167 ÷ 20   6. 600 ÷ 59   7. 2679 ÷ 32   8. 7603 ÷ 89

9. **Critical Thinking** Find reasonable estimates for exercise 8 using different compatible numbers.

Work It Out!

Estimate using compatible numbers.

10. 40)390   11. 76)422   12. 23)844   13. 72)490

14. 23)2100   15. 32)7635   16. 50)231   17. 29)28,040

18. 853 ÷ 18   19. 1000 ÷ 45   20. 662 ÷ 90   21. 141 ÷ 62

22. 4230 ÷ 79   23. 2639 ÷ 60   24. 59,625 ÷ 29   25. 28,955 ÷ 34

26. **Number Sense** What compatible numbers would give an estimate of 800 for exercise 25?

27. **Create Your Own** Write a division problem that has an estimated quotient of 60. Then write the compatible numbers that you would use to find the estimate.

Problem Solving

28. An elevator travels 1442 feet to reach the top floor of the Sears Tower. It takes the elevator about 7 minutes if it is traveling at its slowest speed. How many feet does the elevator travel each minute at its slowest speed?

29. The total height, including the antenna, of the Sears Tower in Chicago is 1707 feet. The total height, including the antenna, of the Empire State Building in New York City is 1472 feet. How much taller is the Sears Tower than the Empire State Building?

30. The Sears Tower can hold approximately 16,500 people. About how many times more people is that than the number of students in your class? Show how you found your answer.

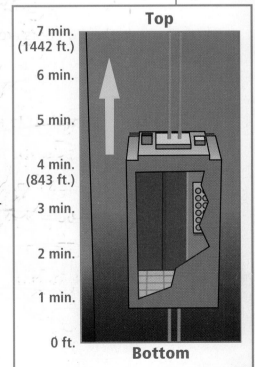

More Practice Set 3.8, p. 471

Dividing by 2-Digit Divisors

Giant kelp is the longest species of seaweed in the world. It is found in the Pacific Ocean and can grow up to 46 cm in one day. If a giant kelp plant is 731 cm long, what is the least number of days the kelp has been growing?

Here's A Way! Find $731 \div 46$.

1 Estimate using compatible numbers.

$$50\overline{)500} \quad 10$$

$$46\overline{)731}$$

$$50\overline{)1000} \quad 20$$

The quotient will be between 10 and 20. So the tens digit will be 1.

2 Write the tens digit. Multiply and then subtract.

$$
\begin{array}{r}
1 \\
46\overline{)731} \\
-46 \\
\hline
27
\end{array}
$$

46 × 1 ten

3 Divide the ones. Multiply and then subtract. Write the remainder.

$$
\begin{array}{r}
15\text{R}41 \\
46\overline{)731} \\
-46 \\
\hline
271 \\
-230 \\
\hline
41
\end{array}
$$

46 × 5 ones

The giant kelp plant could be about 16 days old!

Talk About It! How does an estimate help you know where to place the first digit in the quotient?

Other Examples Divide.

a.
$$
\begin{array}{r}
7\text{R}23 \\
93\overline{)674} \\
-651 \\
\hline
23
\end{array}
$$

93 × 7 ones

b.
$$
\begin{array}{r}
27 \\
35\overline{)945} \\
-70 \\
\hline
245 \\
-245 \\
\hline
0
\end{array}
$$

35 × 2 tens

35 × 7 ones

Divide.

1. 13)91
2. 18)97
3. 47)752
4. 22)145

5. 28)784
6. 12)612
7. 65 ÷ 15
8. 238 ÷ 26

9. 14)70
10. 914 ÷ 21
11. 884 ÷ 26
12. 45)385

13. **Critical Thinking** If a divisor has 2 digits, what is the greatest number of digits that the remainder can have? Justify your answer.

Work It Out!

Estimate and then divide.

14. 23)92
15. 14)98
16. 16)59
17. 25)73

18. 21)357
19. 62)564
20. 34)887
21. 15)675

22. 591 ÷ 19
23. 564 ÷ 12
24. 98 ÷ 16
25. 313 ÷ 11

26. 87 ÷ 29
27. 552 ÷ 92
28. 823 ÷ 14
29. 961 ÷ 17

30. **Number Sense** How could you change the dividend in exercise 25 so that the remainder would be 0?

Problem Solving

31. A giant kelp can grow 46 cm a day. If you find a giant kelp that is 414 cm long, what is the least number of days it could have been growing?

32. **Estimation** A giant kelp can grow to be about 200 ft high. If a story in a building is 12 ft high, about how many stories high is the giant kelp?

33. Some types of seaweed are used for food. Dried nori, which is used as the wrapper for sushi, sells for $.70 a sheet. How much would a dozen sheets cost?

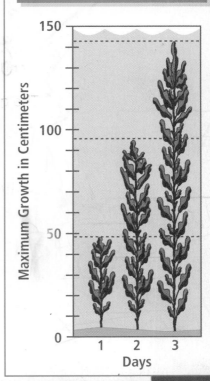

Growth of Giant Kelp

Maximum Growth in Centimeters

150

100

50

0

1   2   3

Days

More Practice Set 3.9, p. 471

LESSON 10

Dividing Greater Numbers

Use What You Know

1 yd = 36 in.

Traditional kimonos are made from bolts of silk. Silk is formed from the cocoons of silkworms. To make 10 kimonos would require a bolt of silk 4500 inches long. How many yards of silk fabric are needed to make 10 kimonos?

Here's A Way! Find 4500 ÷ 36.

1 Estimate using compatible numbers.

$$36\overline{)4500}$$

$$36\overline{)3600} \quad \substack{100}$$

$$36\overline{)7200} \quad \substack{200}$$

The quotient will be between 100 and 200. So the hundreds digit will be 1.

2 Write the hundreds digit. Multiply and subtract.

```
         1__
  36)4500
    -36
      9
```

36 × 1 hundred

3 Write the tens digit. Multiply. Subtract.

```
        12_
  36)4500
    -36
      90
     -72
      18
```

36 × 2 tens

4 Write the ones digit. Multiply. Subtract. Is there a remainder?

```
       125
  36)4500
    -36
      90
     -72
     180
    -180
       0
```

36 × 5 ones

No remainder. So, it takes 125 yards of silk fabric to make 10 kimonos.

Divide.

1. 12)480
2. 26)990
3. 50)2400
4. 48)5055

5. 5022 ÷ 81
6. 12,300 ÷ 37
7. 169 ÷ 16
8. 96,111 ÷ 41

9. **Critical Thinking** What does it mean when there is no remainder?

Work It Out!

Divide.

10. 18)216
11. 30)1117
12. 23)1242

13. 69)4308
14. 51)1736
15. 63)1260

16. 452 ÷ 22
17. 8417 ÷ 36
18. 642 ÷ 75

19. 2117 ÷ 29
20. 47,886 ÷ 29
21. 51,923 ÷ 32

Patterns

22. 4000 ÷ 35
23. 8000 ÷ 35

24. 12,000 ÷ 35
25. 16,000 ÷ 35

26. **Number Sense** 1680 ÷ 16 = 105. What does the zero in the quotient mean?

Problem Solving

27. The silkworm produces silk fiber and then winds the fiber around itself to form a cocoon. The cocoon contains about 600 yards of silk fiber. About how many feet of silk fiber are in a cocoon?

Silk Thread

28. Raw silk thread is sometimes made from 7 strands of silk fibers that are twisted together, each strand coming from a separate cocoon. About how many pieces of raw silk thread could you make with 768 silk fibers?

29. A formal silk kimono can cost $5850. A less formal one might cost $3375. How much more expensive is the formal one?

More Practice Set 3.10, p. 472

Order of Operations

When you are solving a problem that has more than one operation, you can get different answers if you do the operations in different orders. How can you know which operation to perform first? Follow these rules:

How would you find the value of $6 + 3 \times (6 - 4) - 1$?

Order of Operations

1. Do the operations in parentheses first.

2. Then multiply or divide from left to right.

3. Then add or subtract from left to right.

Here's A Way! Find the value of $6 + 3 \times (6 - 4) - 1$.

1 Do the operations in parentheses first.

$6 + 3 \times (6 - 4) - 1$

$6 + 3 \times 2 - 1$

2 Start from the left. Multiply or divide.

$6 + 3 \times 2 - 1$

$6 + 6 - 1$

3 Start from the left. Add or subtract.

$6 + 6 - 1$

$12 - 1$

11

Talk About It! What happens to the values of the expressions if you do not follow the order of operations?

Other Examples Find the value. Use the order of operations.

a. $3 + 6 \times 7$
$3 + 6 \times 7$
$3 + 42$
45

b. $27 - 18 \div 3 \times 4$
$27 - 18 \div 3 \times 4$
$27 - 6 \times 4$
$27 - 24$
3

Decide which operation you would do first. Write *add*, *subtract*, *multiply*, or *divide*.

1. $6 + 3 \times 2$
2. $6 - 3 \times 2$
3. $4 + 8 \div 2 \times 3$
4. $4 + 7 + 3 - 1$

5. $(4 + 9) \cdot 5$
6. $4 \cdot (9 - 5)$
7. $4 \times 9 \div (3 + 6)$
8. $4 \times (9 \div 3) + 6$

9. **Critical Thinking** Do exercises 7 and 8 have the same answer? Find the value of each.

Find the value.

10. $12 + 5 \times 7$
11. $3 + 21 \div 7$
12. $7 \times 9 - 2$

13. $18 \div (5 - 3)$
14. $(30 - 20) \div 5$
15. $30 - 20 \div 5$

Find the value.

16. $7 - 4 + 9$
17. $4 \times 9 \div 6$
18. $50 - 25 - 4$

19. $15 - 4 \times 3 + 8$
20. $49 \div 7 + 2 \times 3$
21. $15 - 3 + 4 \times 4$

22. $7 + (4 - 2)$
23. $12 \div 6 + 10$
24. $(12 \div 6) + 10$

25. $(7 - 1) + 7 \times 5$
26. $1 + (30 - 15) \div 5$
27. $27 \div (3 \times 1) - 7$

28. Copy the number sentence. Where would you put parentheses to make the number sentence true?

   a. $42 \div 2 \times 3 = 7$
   b. $5 \times 6 + 3 \div 3 = 15$
   c. $7 + 28 \div 4 + 3 = 11$

Write an exercise that demonstrates order of operation and has the following answer.

29. 9
30. 10
31. 6
32. 2
33. 15
34. 0

Number Sense For each exercise, replace the variables with the numbers 1, 3, 5, and 10 to make the sentence true.

35. $j \times (h - p) + n = 16$
36. $(k - t) \times (m - u) = 28$

37. $(w - y) \times (a \div z) = 20$
38. $(m + r) \div s + v = 12$

More Practice Set 3.11, p. 472

LESSON 12
Divisibility: Looking for Patterns

Getting Started

What You'll Need:
▶ calculator
▶ recording sheet

Vocabulary:
divisible
Glossary p. 500

Cooperative Learning Checklist

☑ Work alone.
☑ Work with a partner.
☐ Work with a group.

A number is divisible by . . .	when . . .	Examples		
2	The ones digit is an even number.	8	14	546
3	The sum of the digits is divisible by 3.	15	180	80,301
5	The ones digit is 5 or 0.	35	340	4055
10	The ones digit is 0.	20	360	19,350

Suppose you divide two numbers and the remainder is zero. Then the first number is **divisible** by the second number. For example, $10 \div 2 = 5$, we say 10 is divisible by 2.

Divisibility rules can help you decide if one number is divisible by another. The chart above shows divisibility rules for 2, 3, 5, and 10.

Activity

Multiples of Fours

Look for a pattern for numbers that are divisible by 4.

1. Use a calculator to see which numbers in the chart are divisible by 4. Record your results.

2. Look at the numbers that are divisible by 4. Circle the numbers formed by the digits in the tens and ones places. What pattern do you notice? Example: 424 becomes 4⟨24⟩

3. Use the pattern to predict which of the following numbers will be divisible by 4. Write *yes* or *no*.
   a. 836   b. 1714   c. 29,357   d. 418,660

Number	Divisible by 4?
424	yes
7,103	no
45,922	?
104	?
3,016	?
226,934	?
98,112	?

Now look for a pattern in numbers that are divisible by 6.

4 Look at the first three entries of this chart. Which numbers are divisible by 2? By 3? By both 2 and 3? By 6?

5 What pattern do you notice for numbers divisible by 6?

6 Use the pattern to complete the chart.

Number	Divisible by		
	2?	3?	6?
122	yes	no	no
234	yes	yes	yes
1,257	no	yes	no
71	?	?	?
15,016	?	?	?
28,458	?	?	?
7,383	?	?	?

Divide by Nine

Discover a pattern for divisibility by 9.

7 Complete the chart.

8 Look at the Sum of Digits column. Circle the numbers that are divisible by 9. What pattern do you notice? For example: 108 becomes $1 + 0 + 8 = 9$.

9 Use the pattern to predict which of the following numbers will be divisible by 9. Write *yes* or *no*.
   a. 703   b. 3780   c. 14,148   d. 721,682

Number	Sum of Digits	Divisible by 9?
108	$1 + 0 + 8 = 9$	yes
648	$6 + 4 + 8 = 18$	yes
249	$2 + 4 + 9 = 15$	?
53,784	?	?
5,113	?	?
99,873	?	?
4,725	?	?

Show What You Know!

1. **Critical Thinking** Use the patterns that you discovered to write divisibility rules for the number 4, 6, and 9.

2. **Critical Thinking** Without using a calculator, write two numbers that are divisible by 4, 6, and 9. Explain why you chose them.

3. **Share Your Thinking** Is the rule for divisibility by 10 the same as using the rules of divisibility for 2 and 5?

Greatest Common Factor

In the last lesson you learned about divisibility. For example, you know that 12 is divisible by 1, 2, 3, 4, 6, and 12. These numbers are called factors. **Factors** are numbers that divide another number evenly. You can draw arrays to find the factors of any number.

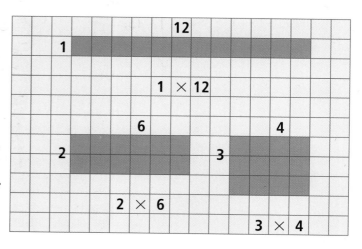

Activity

Use arrays to find factors.

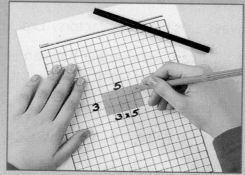

Find the factors of 15.

1. On squared centimeter paper draw all the arrays that cover 15 square units. Outline the arrays, and label the lengths and widths.

2. Write the multiplication expression for each array.

3. Write the factors of 15. Explain why those numbers are factors of 15.

Find the factors of 18.

4. Draw all the arrays that cover 18 square units. Outline the arrays and label the lengths and widths.

5. Write the multiplication expression for each rectangle.

6. Write the factors of 18.

7. Explain how multiplication facts help you to find factors of 18 or of any other number.

Find the greatest common factor.

Compare your results. Use the arrays for 12 on page 108.

8 What factors are the same for 12, 15, and 18? These factors are their **common factors**.

9 What is the greatest number that is a **common factor** of 12, 15, and 18? This is called the **greatest common factor (GCF)** of 12, 15, and 18.

Show What You Know!

Discuss each question and explain your answer.
Determine if 4 is a factor of each number. Write *yes* or *no*.

1. 21   2. 28   3. 36   4. 45

5. **Critical Thinking** Is a number always divisible by its factors? Explain.

6. **Critical Thinking** Use your results. Can an odd number have an even factor? Can an even number have an odd factor? Why or why not?

Write the factors of the number. Circle the common factors in the group.

7. 12, 16   8. 15, 27   9. 7, 14, 28   10. 24, 30, 32

11. Write the greatest common factor (GCF) for each set of numbers in exercises 7–10.

12. **Write About It** How can you find all the factors of a number?

Mixed Review

Write the product or quotient. Use mental math where you can.

13. 90 × 20   14. 500 ÷ 25   15. 53 × 162   16. 840 ÷ 12

More Practice Set 3.13, p. 472

Prime and Composite Numbers

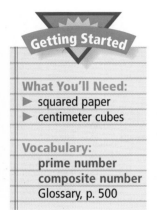

Getting Started

What You'll Need:
▶ squared paper
▶ centimeter cubes

Vocabulary:
prime number
composite number
Glossary, p. 500

You can use arrays to find the prime factors of numbers.

A **prime number** is a number greater than 1 that has only two whole number factors—itself and 1. 7 is a prime number. You can only draw one array to show the factors of a prime number.

A **composite number** is a number that has more than two factors. 9 is a composite number. You can draw more than one array to show the factors of a composite number.

Is 6 a prime or composite number?

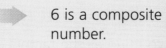

Here's A Way! Draw arrays to find the factors of 6.

1 Draw an array made of factors of 1 and the number itself.

• Start with the factors 1 and 6.

2 See if you can make other arrays with the same number of blocks.

• Draw an array for the next two factors, 2 and 3.

3 Count all the factors. ➡ 6 has 4 factors

• If there are exactly two factors, the number is prime. ➡ 6 is not prime

• If there are more than two factors, the number is composite. ➡ 6 is a composite number.

Talk About It! In the array for 1 and 6, how many rows are there? How many are in each row? In the array for 2 and 3, how many rows are there? How many are in each row?

Show What You Know!

Draw arrays and write whether the numbers are _prime_ or _composite_.

1. 9   2. 19   3. 15   4. 17

5. 18   6. 21   7. 13   8. 26

9. 24   10. 37   11. 57   12. 36

13. **Critical Thinking** How many arrays could you draw for
    exercises 2, 4, 7, and 10?

**Write the factors for the number. Decide whether the
number is prime or composite. Write _prime_ or _composite_.**

14. 2   15. 3   16. 4   17. 5

18. 10   19. 29   20. 68   21. 47

22. **Critical Thinking** Do you need to draw all the arrays to decide
    if a number is prime or composite? Explain.

23. **Critical Thinking** What is the least number of factors an even
    number greater than 2 may have? What is that even number?

Work It Out!

**Draw arrays to find the factors for the number. Decide whether the number
is prime or composite. Write _prime_ or _composite_.**

24. 33   25. 17   26. 11   27. 20   28. 23

Find all the factors, draw arrays if necessary. Write _prime_ or _composite_.

29. 22   30. 44   31. 35   32. 31   33. 39   34. 38

35. **Critical Thinking** How can you use the divisibility rules to help you
    find factors?

Mixed Review

Divide or multiply. Use mental math where you can.

36. 300×60 37. $243 \div 74$ 38. $810 \div 90$ 39. $594 \div 36$

Math Journal

Can you say that the greater the number, the greater the number of
factors? Explain. Give examples.

15 Prime Factorization

Vocabulary:
base
exponent
prime factorization
Glossary, p. 500

Any composite number can be shown as the product of prime factors. This is called **prime factorization**.

A factor tree can help you find the prime factorization of a number. How do you factor 56?

Here's A Way! **Use prime factor trees.**

1 Begin the factor tree. Choose a pair of factors for the number.

56
7 × 8

2 Look at the factors. If one or both of the factors is a composite number, continue factoring.

56
7 × 8
7 × 2 × 4

Seven is a prime number. Continue factoring 8.

3 Continue factoring until all factors are prime. 56

56
7 × 8
7 × 2 × 4
7 × 2 × 2 × 2

Two is prime. Continue factoring until all the factors are prime. Then stop.

4 List the factors in order from least to greatest.

The prime factorization of 56 is $2 \times 2 \times 2 \times 7$.

5 Another way to write this is with exponents. Exponents show how many times a number is used as a factor.

exponent

$2 \times 2 \times 2 \times 7$ can be written as $2^3 \times 7$

base

Talk About It! How can a factor tree help you decide if a number is prime or composite?

Copy and complete the factor trees. Write the prime factorization. Use exponents if possible.

1.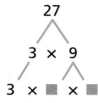
  27
  3 × 9
  3 × ■ × ■

2.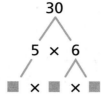
  30
  5 × 6
  ■ × ■ × ■

3.
  45
  5 × ■
  ■ × ■ × ■

Write the prime factorization. Use a factor tree.

4. 41   5. 24   6. 47   7. 54   8. 72

9. **Critical Thinking** What if you begin factoring 40 with 2×20 and another student begins with 5×8. Will you both get the same prime factorization? Justify your answer.

Write the letter of the prime factorization for each number. Write the prime factorization. Use exponents if possible.

10. 18   a. $2 \times 9 \times 1$ b. $3 \times 2 \times 3$ c. $2 \times 2 \times 3$

11. 12   a. $3 \times 2 \times 2$ b. $2 \times 3 \times 3$ c. $2 \times 3 \times 4$

12. 32   a. $2 \times 2 \times 2 \times 4$ b. $2 \times 2 \times 8 \times 1$ c. $2 \times 2 \times 2 \times 2 \times 2$

Write *prime* or *composite* for the number. If the number is composite, find the prime factorization using a factor tree.

13. 17   14. 16   15. 63   16. 23   17. 43

18. 91   19. 85   20. 52   21. 79   22. 120

23. **Patterns** You can write $10 \times 10 \times 10$ as 10^3. Find the product. Now find 10^4 and 10^5. Describe the pattern.

Mental Math Write the number that has this prime factorization.

24. $3 \times 5 \times 3$ 25. $2 \times 2 \times 7 \times 5$ 26. $2 \times 2 \times 2 \times 11$ 27. $2 \times 3 \times 5 \times 7$

More Practice Set 3.15, p. 473

Math Journal

How can an exponent help you describe the factors of a number?

LESSON 16

Problem Solving
Using Strategies

You can read more about garbage in the pages of *Kids Discover*

Americans produce tons of trash and garbage each year. On average, each American contributes 28 pounds of trash and garbage per week!

E ach day, Americans dispose of about 150,000 tons of packaging materials, like boxes and wrappers. This trash would fill about 10,000 semi-trailer trucks. The number of trucks lined end-to-end would stretch for 120 miles! About how many of these trucks would it take to stretch 1 mile?

- What is the question you have to answer?

- What information do you need? Is there some information that you don't need?

- If there were 10 trucks per mile, how many would be required for 120 miles?

- If there were 100 trucks per mile, how many would be required for 120 miles?

- Look at the table. Which of the two numbers in the first column is closer to the number you are seeking?

- Explain a strategy that can help you solve the problem. Then solve it.

Problem Solving Process
- ✓ Understand
- ✓ Plan
- ✓ Try It
- ✓ Look Back

Choose a Strategy You Have Learned
- ✓ Make a Table
- ✓ Act It Out
- ✓ Guess and Check
- Look for a Pattern
- Work Backward
- Make a List
- Work a Simpler Problem
- Draw a Picture
- Write an Equation

Trucks per Mile	Trucks per 120 Miles	Higher or lower than 10,000?
10	1200	lower
100	12,000	higher

Work It Out!

Use any strategy to solve each problem. Show your work.

1. On the average, each American disposes of about 4 pounds of garbage each day. There are about 260 million Americans. About how many pounds of garbage does each American dispose of in a year?

2. One way to reduce the space occupied by trash is to use a trash compactor. A compactor squeezes a large bag of trash into a smaller package. If it takes a family 5 days to throw out enough trash for 1 bag of compacted trash, about how many bags of compacted trash will the family create in 1 month?

3. In December of 1981, the garbage workers of New York City went on strike for 17 days. In that time, over 200,000 tons of garbage littered the streets. If about the same amount of garbage accumulated each day, estimate how many tons of garbage were added to the streets each day.

4. Estimate how much garbage New York City disposed of in 1981, if the same amount of garbage accumulated each day.

5. One way to reduce the amount of trash is to recycle. Some recycling centers pay $.25 per pound for aluminum and $.50 per pound for plastic. Suppose your class received $32.50 for recycling aluminum and plastic. Your class collected more pounds of plastic than aluminum. How many pounds of aluminum and plastic did your class recycle? Is there more than one right answer?

Pounds of Aluminum	Amount Aluminum Is Worth	Pounds of Plastic	Amount Plastic is worth	Total Amount From Recycling
4	$1	2	$1	$2
40	$10	20	$10	$20

6. Find out the population of your town or city. Use that number to calculate the number of pounds of garbage that your town or city makes in a week.

Share Your Thinking

7. Which problems required you to use division?

More Practice Set 3.16, p. 473

Chapter 3 Test

for Pages 80–115

Test-Taking Tips
When time allows,
go back and check
your answers.

Problem Solving

Solve using Guess and Check or another strategy. Show your work. (page 94)

1. A special San Diego Zoo tour package costs $10 more for adults than for children. If the total cost for 1 adult and two children is $37, what is the price for an adult? The price for a child?

2. On a field trip to the zoo, a group of 12 students each bought either a large bag of popcorn or a regular bag of popcorn. The large bags cost $3 each and the regular bags cost $2 each. If the total cost was $32, how many of each size were bought?

Concepts

Find the answer. (pages 84, 86, 88, 96, 104, 106, 110)

3. Will the exact quotient be greater than or less than the estimate? Explain how you know.
   a. $6392 \div 8 \longrightarrow 800$ b. $29,498 \div 4 \longrightarrow 7000$

4. A friend asks you to check his answer. $4691 \div 5 = 937$ R6. How can you tell that there is a mistake without working it out?

5. What multiplication sentence means the same as $2100 \div 70 = n$? Explain.

6. Write the order of the operations you would follow to find the value of $9 \times (3 + 7) \div 3 + 1$.

7. Use a divisibility rule to decide whether 95 is prime or composite. Explain how you used the rule.

Estimate. (pages 84, 98)

8. $6\overline{)293}$ 9. $3\overline{)1687}$ 10. $49\overline{)1764}$ 11. $23\overline{)92,083}$

12. $286 \div 4$ 13. $2936 \div 8$ 14. $8702 \div 21$ 15. $16,690 \div 72$

Divide. Circle the quotient if you used mental math. (pages 86, 88, 96, 98, 100, 102)

16. $5\overline{)226}$ 17. $9\overline{)2700}$ 18. $8\overline{)1665}$ 19. $7\overline{)3787}$

20. $16\overline{)912}$ 21. $27\overline{)3795}$ 22. $42\overline{)1216}$ 23. $70\overline{)28,000}$

24. $135 \div 3$ 25. $963 \div 4$ 26. $60,000 \div 20$ 27. $21,822 \div 38$

Find the value of the expression. (page 104)

28. $7 + 1 \times (6 - 4)$ 29. $8 + 2 \times (10 - 5)$ 30. $18 \div (2 + 1) - 6$

Write the greatest common factor for the group of numbers. (pages 106, 108)

31. 4, 12   32. 3, 8   33. 9, 24   34. 20, 25, 30

Write the letter of the prime factorization for the number. (pages 110, 112)

35. 54
   a. 9×6
   b. $3 \times 3 \times 6$
   c. $3 \times 3 \times 3 \times 2$

36. 72
   a. $8 \times 3 \times 3$
   b. $2 \times 2 \times 2 \times 3 \times 3$
   c. $2 \times 2 \times 2 \times 3 \times 3 \times 3$

 Performance Task

(pages 108, 112)

Create factor trees to help you find the greatest common factor of 40, 64, and 96. Identify and explain what you created.

• Be sure to find the prime factorization of each number.

• Select the common factors in each prime factorization. Find their product to find the greatest common factor.

Keep In Mind . . .

Your work will be evaluated on the following:

☑ Clearly drawn factor trees

☑ Correct prime factorizations

☑ Common factors shown

☑ Correct calculation of GCF

Cumulative Review

Estimating (Chapter 1)
Estimate 4645 + 273 + 1635.

Here's A Way!

Front-end estimate: add or subtract digits in the greatest place.
4645 + 273 + 1635 ➡ 5000
Adjust using the next greatest place.
600 + 200 + 600 = 1400
Adjusted estimate: **6400**

Write the estimate.

1.	620	2.	5274	3.	1448
	515		638		1589
	+ 46		+ 2270		+ 2057

4.	3682	5.	9821	6.	$84.86
	− 3457		− 5237		− 30.52

7. Is the exact sum for exercise 2 greater than or less than 7000? How can you tell?

Multiples of 10, 100, 1000 (Chapter 2)
Find 80 × 40 using mental math.

Here's A Way!

Multiply the non-zero digits.
8 × 4 = 32
Count zeros in the factors (2).
Write that number of zeros at the end of the product.
80 × 40 = **3200**

Use mental math to find the product.

8. 30 × 90   9. 200 × 70   10. 80 × 50

11. 400 × 60   12. 40 × 200   13. 9 × 8000

14. In exercise 10, the answer has more zeros than the sum of the number of zeros in the original factors. Explain why.

Division (Chapter 3)
Find 2391 ÷ 18.

Here's A Way!

```
      132 R15
18)2391
   − 18    ➡ 18 × 1 hundred
     59
   − 54    ➡ 18 × 3 tens
     51
   − 36    ➡ 18 × 2 ones
     15
```

Divide.

15. 9)183   16. 7)243

17. 6)1254   18. 12)990

19. 9)3624   20. 41)16,277

21. 493 ÷ 8   22. 1527 ÷ 3

23. 6930 ÷ 33   24. 98,100 ÷ 57

25. Is the answer to exercise 15 closer to 20 or to 21? Explain why.

Division Expressions (Chapter 3)
Write an expression to describe the following situation.

Suppose you and 3 friends plan to share equally a box of baseball cards. How many cards will each person get?

Here's A Way!

Choose a variable.
   b = total number of baseball cards
Write an expression for the number of cards each person will get.
   $b \div 4$
Use different numbers for b.
   $24 \div 4 = 6$
If there are 24 cards, then each person will get 6.

Write a division expression. Then find the values.

26. Suppose you want to have 9 tomato plants in each row of a garden.

Let t = the total number of tomato plants you have in all. How many rows can you make if you have
   a. 18 plants?   b. 36 plants?   c. 90 plants?

27. Suppose you have 36 cookies to sell at a bake sale.

Let c = the number of cookies on each plate. How many plates of cookies do you have to sell if each plate holds
   a. 6 cookies?   b. 2 cookies?   c. 4 cookies?

Write the value of the expression when $r = 2$; $r = 6$.

28. $\frac{24}{r}$ 29. $12 \div r$

30. $9 \cdot r$ 31. $40 - r$

32. $r + 15$ 33. $r + r$

34. Write a situation that could be described by the expression $40 \div n$.

Problem Solving

Problem Solving Process
   ✓ Understand
   ✓ Plan
   ✓ Try It
   ✓ Look Back

Choose a Strategy You Have Learned
   ✓ Make a Table
   ✓ Act It Out
   ✓ Guess and Check
      Look for a Pattern
      Work Backward
      Make a List
      Work a Simpler Problem
      Draw a Picture
      Write an Equation

Choose one of the strategies you know to solve these problems. Show your work.

35. A large bag of pretzels costs 4 times as much as a small bag of peanuts. The total cost of a bag of pretzels and a bag of peanuts is $2.00.
   a. What is the cost of pretzels?
   b. What is the cost of peanuts?

36. Suppose you start an exercise program by exercising 10 minutes a day. If every week you increase your daily exercise time by 5 minutes, how long will it take until you are exercising 40 minutes a day?

Crack the Code

Language Connection   **With Your Group**

There are many kinds of codes used around the world. Cryptographers, people who put messages in code, use different combinations of letters, numbers, and mathematical ideas to create codes.

Your group will create a number code. Then you will try to crack a coded message from another group.

Keep In Mind . . .

Your work will be evaluated on the following:

☑ How you use your math skills to create and decipher codes

☑ If your factoring chart is clear and correct

☑ The accuracy of your coded sentence

☑ How well your group organizes and divides the work

4725	4662	315
2499	2499	
2583	231	
4662	693	
4662	315	

TOP SECRET

E = 5
E = 1 × 5
E = 15
E = 315

1

Plan It

- List the letters of the alphabet. Leave five lines blank between each letter.
- Below each letter, write a number. A will be 1, B will be 2, C will be 3, and so on.

2

Put It Together

- Factor each number. For prime numbers, show the number and 1. For example, C = 3, so write 1 × 3.
- Remove the multiplication sign to get the code number. For C, the code number will be 13.
- To make your code different from other groups, multiply each code number by a number between 11 and 25. For example, if you picked 11, C would become 13 × 11, or 143.

GROUP NUMBER IS 21

T h e
4725 | 4662 | 315

m e s s a g e
2373 | 315 | 2499 | 2499 | 231 | 357 | 315

w a s
2583 | 231 | 2499

b e h i n d
252 | 315 | 4662 | 693 | 567 | 462

t h e
4725 | 4662 | 315

3

Wrap It Up

- Write a sentence from a book in your group's code. Separate each number that represents a letter with a slash.
- Exchange your coded sentence with another group. See which group can decode the other group's sentence first.

Hint: You will not have a remainder when you divide the letter number by the secret code number.

4

Discuss Your Results

- Did you meet the objectives in Keep In Mind?
- What other mathematical ideas could be used to create a code?

Internet

> Visit the **Math Center** at **Houghton Mifflin Education Place.** http://www.eduplace.com

Use What You Know

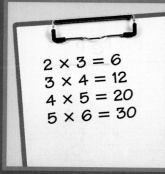

$2 \times 3 = 6$
$3 \times 4 = 12$
$4 \times 5 = 20$
$5 \times 6 = 30$

- multiplication facts

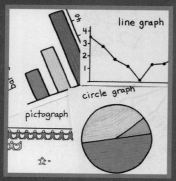

line graph

circle graph

pictograph

- different ways to record information

- range
- line plot

- the vocabulary

CHAPTER 4

Collecting, Organizing, and Using Data

Try This!

If you roll two number cubes and multiply the numbers that you roll, above which number on the line plot will the product most often be found?

What You'll Need

number cubes, pencil, paper

1

Use a number line to make a line plot. Label the number line 1–9. Label one number cube 2, 2, 2, 3, 3, 3. Label the other cube 1, 1, 2, 2, 3, 3.

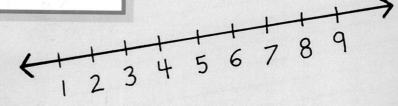

1 2 3 4 5 6 7 8 9

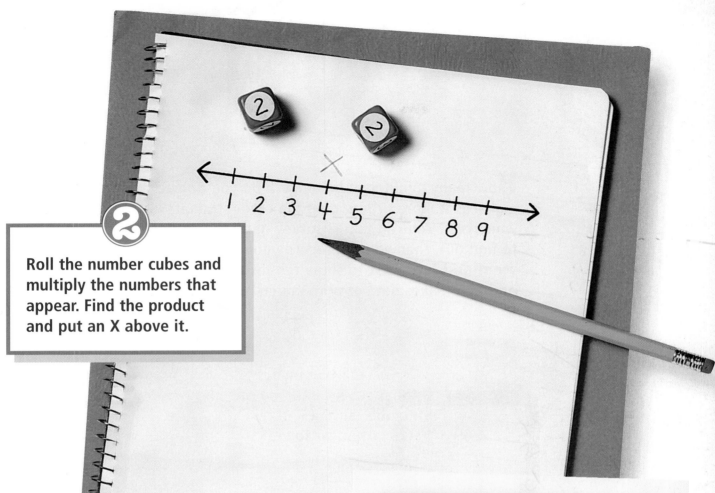

2

Roll the number cubes and multiply the numbers that appear. Find the product and put an X above it.

3

Repeat step 2, rolling the cubes a total of 20 times. Compare your line plot with another group's. Describe the shape of the data on your line plot using words like higher, lower, wider, and curve. Write a paragraph telling how the line plot gives you a picture of what happened.

Why was using the line plot helpful?

Could you have used a different kind of graph to record your information?

Ready to Go!

LESSON 1

Stem-and-Leaf Plot

Cooperative Learning Checklist

☐ Work alone.

☑ Work with a partner.

☑ Work with a group.

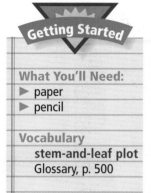

Getting Started

What You'll Need:
▶ paper
▶ pencil

Vocabulary
stem-and-leaf plot
Glossary, p. 500

How many minutes of homework do you do each night? Is it more or less than the other students in your class? You can take a survey of all the students to find out. Then you can record your data on a **stem-and-leaf plot** to show the results. This kind of graph makes data easy to understand.

Activity

Record the tens digits on the left side of the line. This is the stem.

Record each ones digits on the right side of the line. These are the leaves.

Stem-and-Leaf Plot

Stem	Leaf
0	2, 5
1	0, 5
2	0
3	0, 0, 0, 0, 5
4	5
5	0, 0
6	0, 0, 0, 0, 0, 0, 0, 0, 0, 0
7	
8	
9	
10	
11	
12	0, 0, 0, 0, 5
13	
14	
15	0, 0

1

Create a survey asking students how many minutes of homework they do each night. Give the survey to the students in your class. Look at the number of minutes each student answered.

60, 30, 2, 60, 35, 10, 60, 120, 15, 20, 60, 120, 30, 150, 60, 30, 45, 50, 50, 120, 60, 5, 60, 60, 120, 30, 60, 125, 150, 60

2

Record the number of minutes on a stem-and-leaf plot. First split the numbers into tens and ones. In the first column, record the tens and line them up as the stem. In the second column, write the ones, one after another. These are the leaves.

60, 30, 2, 60, 35, 10, 60, 120, 15, 20, 60, 120, 30, 150, 60, 30, 45, 50, 50, 120, 60, 5, 60, 60, 120, 30, 60, 125, 150, 60

Stem-and-Leaf Plot

0	
1	
2	
3	
4	
5	
6	

3

You may now want to organize your data by putting the number of minutes in order from least to greatest.

4

How can you tell from the plot which was the most common number of minutes students spent doing homework? Which was the least common? How many students in your class do more minutes of homework than you do? How many do less?

Show What You Know!

1. How does the stem-and-leaf plot show that two or more students study the same number of minutes?

2. How can you tell from the plot how many students were surveyed?

3. How many students do 120 minutes of homework a night?

4. How many more students in the survey do over 45 minutes of studying a night than under 45 minutes?

5. **Critical Thinking** How does the stem-and-leaf plot help you compare data quickly?

6. **Critical Thinking** How does the stem and leaf plot help you organize data?

Mean, Range, and Mode

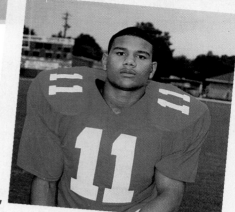

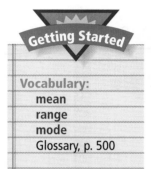
Vocabulary:
mean
range
mode
Glossary, p. 500

In 1996, Antoneyo of Central High School, Tuscaloosa, Alabama, was a star running back. The table shows the number of yards he gained in the first five football games.

You can use mean, range, or mode to describe the data. The **mean** is one number that represents all the numbers. The **range** is the difference between the greatest and least numbers. The **mode** is the number that occurs most often.

Game	Yards Gained
1	152 yards
2	108 yards
3	207 yards
4	124 yards
5	64 yards

Source: Coach Buzz Buzby, Central High School

Here's A Way! Use mean, range, and mode to describe data.

Find the mean, or average, number of yards gained.

1 Find the sum of all the numbers. $152 + 108 + 207 + 124 + 64 = 655$

2 Count how many numbers you added. Divide your sum by this number. $655 \div 5 = 131$

The mean number of yards Antoneyo ran was 131 yd.

Find the range in number of yards gained.

1 Find the greatest and least numbers.

greatest: **207**   least: **64**

2 Subtract the least number from the greatest number.

$207 - 64 = 143$

The range of Antoneyo's yards gained in a game is 143 yd.

Find the mode of a group of data.

Suppose in the 5 games, a player ran with the ball 12, 14, 15, 14, and 14 times. The mode of this group of numbers is 14.

Sometimes no numbers appear more than once. Then there is no mode.

Talk About It! Would you use the mean or the range to tell how well a player did? Justify your answer.

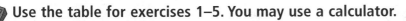

Show What You Know!

Use the table for exercises 1–5. You may use a calculator.

1. Find the mean number of minutes that Carey played in a game.

2. If you were finding the mean number of minutes Billy played in a game, by what number would you divide? Why?

3. What is the mode for the number of minutes Carey played?

4. Who had the greatest range in number of minutes played?

5. **Critical Thinking** Describe a real-life instance in which you might want to know the range.

Minutes Played Each Game

Player	Game				
	1	2	3	4	5
Stephen	13	11	12	10	17
Billy	10	not at game	8	11	7
Carey	8	13	13	6	5

Work It Out!

Use the table for exercises 6–12. You may use a calculator.

The costs of four types of footballs at different stores are shown. Find the mean and the range of the cost of each football.

6. Spiral
7. Cowboy
8. Eagle
9. Champ

10. If Quick's store lowers the price of the Champ to $49, will the range of prices for the Champ change? Explain your answer.

11. Is the mean or the mode greater for the Champ? How much greater?

12. **Patterns** Without adding and dividing, how can you tell that Ideal's and Quick's have the same average prices for footballs?

Cost of Footballs

Ball	Stores		
	Dane's	Ideal's	Quick's
Spiral	$30	$34	$23
Cowboy	$44	$51	$34
Eagle	$19	$23	$48
Champ	$51	$48	$51

Mixed Review

Compare. Write >, <, or =.

13. 8633 ● 8544
14. 3.99 ● 4
15. 89,990 ● 9888
16. 11,032 ● 11,320
17. 0.53 ● 0.532
18. 13.13 ● 30
19. 9.72 ● 9.270
20. 12.80 ● 12.08

More Practice Set 4.2, p. 473

LESSON 3 Median

Getting Started

Vocabulary:
median
Glossary, p. 500

Suppose you walk dogs as a job after school. The five dogs that you walk are shown below. How can you describe the typical weight of the dogs?

5 lb   15 lb   25 lb   45 lb   180 lb

The mean weight of the dogs is 54 lb. But, the mean does not describe the typical weight of the dogs, because three weigh much less than 54 lb and one weighs much more.

Another way to think about the typical weight is to order the weights from least to greatest and then find the middle number, or **median**.

Here's A Way!   **Find the median of 5, 15, 25, 45, and 180.**

1 Write the numbers in order from least to greatest.

   5   15   25   45   180

2 Find the middle number.

   5   15   25   45   180

The middle number is 25, so the median weight of these five dogs is 25 lb.

Talk About It!   How many weights were greater than the median? How many were less than the median?

Other Examples When there are two middle numbers, the median is the average of the two numbers.

   26   28   29   31   37   71   ◀   29 + 31 = 60   60 ÷ 2 = 30

The median of this group of numbers is 30.

Show What You Know!

 Use the information below to find the mean, median, and range.

Weight of Dog Food Bags	
Chew Bits	🐕🐕🐕
Barkies	🐕🐕🐕
Pup-Up	🐕
K9 Crunch	🐕🐕🐕🐕
Doggie's	🐕🐕🐕🐕🐕
Key	🐕 = 4 lb 🐕 = 2 lb

$1.99 $1.05 $1.49 $5.95 $2.89 $4.69

1. mean   2. median   3. range   4. mean   5. median   6. range

7. **Critical Thinking** In which exercise above does the median give a better idea of a typical member of the group? Why?

Work It Out!

Find the median.

8. 12, 13, 6, 9, 4   9. 23, 18, 29, 16, 25   10. 6, 2, 12, 9, 12, 7

11. At a dog show, dogs were rated on a 1 to 10 scale. The votes were: 5, 5, 3, 6, 8, 5, 4, 1, 5, 4, 2, 6, 5, 10, 7, 7, 4, 8, 6, 5. In the line plot below, the scale is shown as a number line. Each x represents a vote. A line plot is a way to order data. Use the line plot to find the mode and median of the data.

```
                        x
                        x
                        x
              x    x    x
              x    x    x   x    x
x    x    x   x    x    x   x    x        x
+----+----+----+----+----+----+----+----+----+
1    2    3    4    5    6    7    8    9    10
```

12. How did you find the mode? the median?

Problem Solving

13. In exercise 11, what is the average rating?

14. **Create Your Own** Make up a set of 5 numbers with a mean of 20, a median of 10, and a range of 50. You can repeat some numbers.

More Practice Set 4.3, p. 474

Math Journal

If your quiz scores in math were: 94, 98, 95, 100, 67, 93, 97, would you want your teacher to use the mean or median for your typical score? Why?

Problem Solving
Is the Answer Reasonable?

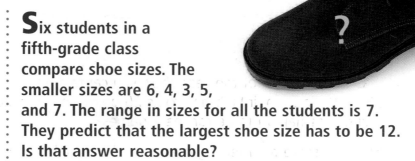

Six students in a fifth-grade class compare shoe sizes. The smaller sizes are 6, 4, 3, 5, and 7. The range in sizes for all the students is 7. They predict that the largest shoe size has to be 12. Is that answer reasonable?

You Decide

- How do you find the range of a group of numbers?
- What shoe sizes do you know in the problem? What is their range?
- What is the smallest shoe size? How can you use it to find the largest shoe size?

Work It Out!

Is the Answer Reasonable?

Ask Yourself:

Did I answer the question?

Did I calculate correctly?

Is the answer labeled with the right units?

Does my answer need to be rounded to a whole number to make sense?

Decide whether the predicted answer makes sense.

1. On the first 4 tests, your scores are 80, 60, 70, and 90. You predict that if your score on the next test is greater than 90, your average will increase. Does your prediction make sense? Explain.

2. Seven students make up a problem about their median height in inches. The answer to the problem is 55 in., but then 1 student leaves. The 6 heights are 50, 54, 47, 61, 58, and 56 in. They decide they must find a student whose height is exactly 55 in. for their answer to be correct. Is their decision reasonable? Explain.

3. On a class trip, the teacher offers to hold some money for 4 students. She collects a total of $5.50 from them. Shawn gives her $1.50, Darrin $1.25, and Ruth $2.25. She also holds some money for Erika. Shawn says the range of the amounts the 4 students give is $1.00. Is this answer reasonable? Explain.

Share Your Thinking

4. Why is checking whether your answer is reasonable a good decision-making strategy?

Midchapter Review

for Pages 122-130

Solve. Show your work. (pages 128, 130)

1. In the first 6 basketball games of the year, the team captain has scored 10, 7, 8, 4, 9, and 8 points. If he scores 25 points in the next game, what will his median score be for the 7 games?

2. What will his median score be after 7 games if he scores only 2 points in the next game? How can you explain this?

Concepts

Use the data showing shoe price changes to answer the questions.
(pages 126, 128)

Month	Store					
	A	B	C	D	E	F
December	$29	$45	$33	$37	$42	$30
February	$26	$42	$29	$35	$40	$26

3. Find the median and range of the 6 stores' December prices.

4. Did the median price drop from December to February? If yes, how much did it drop? Did the range of prices drop from December to February? If yes, how much?

5. What was the mean price in December? In February?

6. Store E alone raises the price to $42 in March. Does the median price change? The mean price? The range of prices?

Skills

Use the data to answer the questions. (pages 126, 128)

7. Find the mean and range for this set of data showing minutes playing soccer.

M	T	W	Th	F	Sat	Sun
48	50	37	60	20	90	17

8. Find the median for this set of data showing prices of video games.

$109	$119	$115
$125	$179	$142

Math *World*

Collecting, organizing, and using data has been an important part of most cultures. How many ways can you think of to keep track of important data?

Recording With Pictures

Native Americans sometimes used buffalo skins and paint to record their history. The buffalo skin on this page, painted in 1797, is a record of a battle between two tribes. We can learn from the painting how many warriors were in the battle, how many were on horseback, and what kind of weapons they used. People who study history find records like this just as important as written records.

The Story of Storage

Throughout history, groups of people have used different ways to solve the problem of recording and storing data. Among the devices people have used are knotted cords, tally sticks, and handwritten ledger books. Today, computers store large amounts of data.

1 A.D.	500 A.D.	1000 A.D.

Inca quipu, 600

British Exchequer tallies, 1200

Early calculating machine, 1600s

Try This! Record and Compute Data the Old Way

Before computers, many businesses recorded what they bought and sold in a ledger book. This page from a ledger book is a record of items purchased from China in the 1800s. Could you keep records this way?

1. On a piece of lined paper, make columns like the ones on the student's page.

2. On the first line in the third column, write a date. Since these are items already purchased, use a date from last year.

Code	Item
1	Clothing
2	Furniture
3	Food
4	Other

3. Choose ten items to record on your ledger page. In the first column, write the correct code for your item from the list on the page.

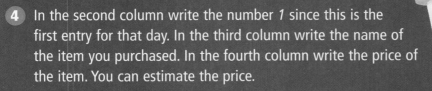

4. In the second column write the number 1 since this is the first entry for that day. In the third column write the name of the item you purchased. In the fourth column write the price of the item. You can estimate the price.

5. Repeat step 4 for one more item. Then add the amounts and write the total in column five. Complete the ledger with the remaining eight items you have chosen, buying two items a day.

May 9, 1997				
1	Wooden Desk	250		
4	2	Video Game	70	320
	June 1, 1997			
3	1	Apples		2
1	2	Winter Coat	80	82

1500 A.D.   2000 A.D.

Ledger books, 1800

CD-ROM, 1990

Computer Punch Card, 1965

Respond

With a partner . . .
create a way to record data without using words or numbers.

Internet:
Houghton Mifflin Education Place
Explore the Math Center.
http://www.eduplace.com

Estimation: Reading Graphs

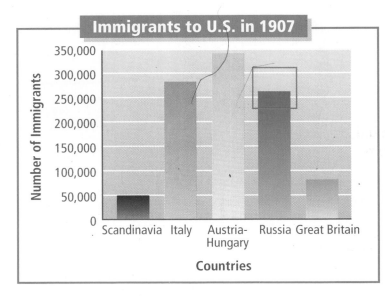

Immigrants to U.S. in 1907

Number of Immigrants

350,000
300,000
250,000
200,000
150,000
100,000
50,000
0

Scandinavia Italy Austria-Hungary Russia Great Britain

Countries

Your family may have come to the United States from another country. If they came between 1892 and 1954, they may have arrived at Ellis Island in the harbor of New York City.

The year in which the greatest number of immigrants came through Ellis Island was 1907. About how many people arrived from Russia that year?

Here's A Way! **Estimate numbers from the graph.**

1 Find the bar that represents Russia.

2 Look at the vertical scale. Find the two numbers that the top of the bar is between.

The top of the bar is between 250,000 and 300,000.

| 300,000 |
| 275,000 |
| 250,000 |

3 Find the number that is halfway between these two numbers.

Since 275,000 is the halfway number, estimate its location.

4 Decide whether the top of the bar is below, at, or above the halfway point. If the top of the bar is:

- at the halfway point, use that number for your estimate

- below the halfway point, make your estimate less

- above the halfway point, make your estimate greater

Since the bar that represents Russia is below 275,000, make your estimate less. A reasonable estimate for Russian immigrants in 1907 is 260,000.

Talk About It! Why is 260,000 a reasonable estimate?

Show What You Know!

Use estimation to answer the question.

1. About how many people came from Vietnam? Ireland?

2. From which country did about 40,000 people come? about 27,000?

3. From which countries did fewer than 30,000 people come?

4. **Critical Thinking** Discuss how you would estimate the number of immigrants from China in 1993.

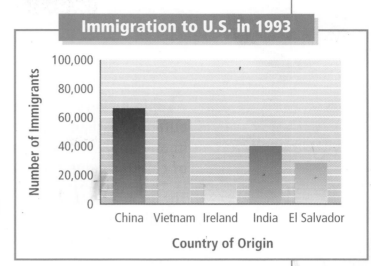

Immigration to U.S. in 1993

Number of Immigrants — Country of Origin: China, Vietnam, Ireland, India, El Salvador

Work It Out!

Write the answer. Use estimation.

5. Which states received more than 60,000 immigrants in 1993?

6. Which two states together had about 100,000 immigrants?

7. About how many immigrants went to each of the five states?

8. **Critical Thinking** About how many immigrants in all were admitted in the five states? Explain your method of finding the estimate.

9. **Number Sense** Suppose the numbers on the vertical scale are missing. What information would you get just from looking at lengths of the bars?

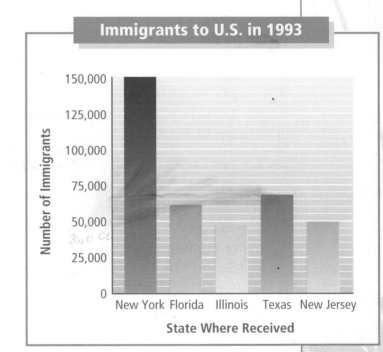

Immigrants to U.S. in 1993

Number of Immigrants — State Where Received: New York, Florida, Illinois, Texas, New Jersey

Problem Solving

10. During 1993, about 260,000 immigrants were admitted through California. How many more numbers would have to be added to the scale of the graph above to include California?

More Practice Set 4.5, p. 474

6 Line Graphs

Getting Started

What You'll Need:
▶ squared paper

Vocabulary:
horizontal axis
vertical axis
Glossary, p. 500

Apple picking is a favorite autumn pastime in New England. In one apple orchard, free samples of cider are given to visitors.

The table shows the number of samples given each hour on a certain day.

You can represent this data in a line graph. A line graph shows how data can change over time.

Time	Number of Cups of Free Cider
9:00 A.M.	0
10:00 A.M.	25
11:00 A.M.	50
12:00 P.M.	75
1:00 P.M.	150
2:00 P.M.	200
3:00 P.M.	225
4:00 P.M.	250

Here's A Way! Represent data in a line graph.

1 Draw the vertical and horizontal sides of the graph. These are called **axes**.

2 Decide on a title. Then decide what the labels for the vertical axis and the horizontal axis should be.

3 Number the vertical axis starting at 0. Let each space represent 25. Mark the spaces evenly.

4 Write the times starting at 9 A.M. on the horizontal axis. Let each space represent an hour. Mark the spaces evenly.

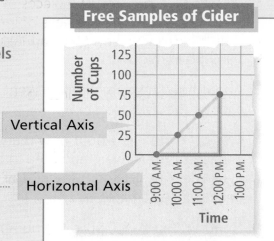

5 Now begin placing points on the graph. For example, find 12 P.M. on the horizontal axis. Follow the vertical line up 3 spaces to 75.

6 Connect the points with line segments.

Talk About It! Why must the numbers on an axis increase by the same amount?

Copy the graph on page 136. Use it to answer each question.

1. Finish drawing the axes on the graph, and label the marks. Use the table on page 136. Place the remaining points on the graph. Connect the points with line segments.

2. Between which points does the line rise most steeply? What does this tell you about the number of cups given away during that hour?

3. Were more cups of free cider given away in the morning or the afternoon?

4. **Critical Thinking** Can you use the line graph to find out how many cups of free cider had been given away by 1:30 P.M.?

Use the graph to answer each question.

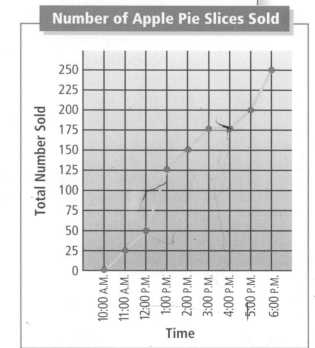

Number of Apple Pie Slices Sold

5. Each point represents two pieces of information. What two pieces of information does the first point on the graph represent? The last point?

6. By what time were 125 slices sold?

7. Does the graph show an increase or a decrease in the number of slices sold?

8. How many more pieces of pie were sold by 5:00 P.M. than by 4:00 P.M.?

9. Between which 2 hours were no slices sold?

10. Between which 2 hours were the greatest number of slices sold?

11. **Critical Thinking** How are the graph on page 136 and this graph alike? How are they different? Explain.

12. **Critical Thinking** Would you use a line graph to show different types of pie sold? Justify your answer.

More Practice Set 4.6, p. 474

Interpreting Graphs

Weather data is recorded at the National Weather Service.

You can compare two sets of temperature data on a double-bar graph and a double-line graph.

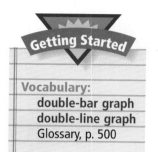

Getting Started

Vocabulary:
double-bar graph
double-line graph
Glossary, p. 500

Here's A Way! Compare graphs.

Highs & Lows for June 10, 1996

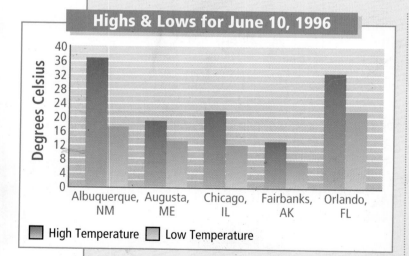

High Temperature   Low Temperature

Daily Temperatures

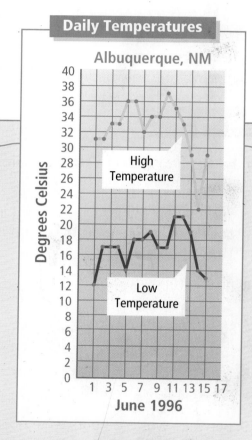

Albuquerque, NM

A **double-bar graph** uses a bar for each set of data. In the double-bar graph shown, you can compare the highest and lowest temperature on a given day in many cities.

A line graph is useful for showing changes over time. A **double-line graph** allows you to compare two sets of data such as high and low temperatures for one city during a given period.

Talk About It! What information can be found on both graphs?

Show What You Know!

Use the correct graph on page 138 to answer each question. Tell which graph you used.

1. What were the hottest and coldest days in Albuquerque during the first half of June?

2. How much warmer was the high temperature in Chicago than in Fairbanks on June 10?

3. Which city had the greatest difference between its high and low temperatures on June 10?

4. **Critical Thinking** When would you use a double-bar graph to compare two sets of data? When would you use a double-line graph?

Dear Grandma,
We are enjoying our visit to Albuquerque. It is really hot, so we spent the day swimming.

Love,
Jason

Mrs. Edith Oakley
11 Green St.
Denver, CO 80232

Work It Out!

Use the graph to answer each question below.

5. Which cities had low temperatures below 10°C?

6. Which cities had high temperatures above 22°C?

7. Which city had the greatest range in temperature? The least range?

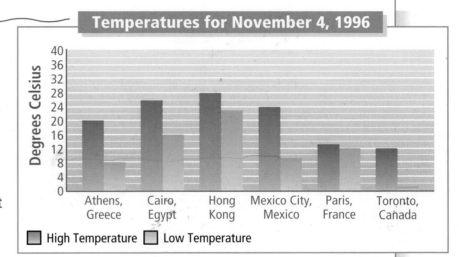

Temperatures for November 4, 1996

8. What was the median for the high temperatures for the cities?

9. Is there a mode among either the high or low temperatures? If so, what is the mode?

Problem Solving

10. What is the difference between the warmest and coldest temperatures shown on the graph? Between which two cities do you see this range?

11. How do the high and low temperatures for Hong Kong compare to the high and low temperatures of the other cities?

Mixed Review

Write the answer.

12. 651 × 3   13. 328 ÷ 6   14. 402 × 5   15. 198 ÷ 4   16. 204 ÷ 9

More Practice Set 4.7, p. 475

Circle Graphs

You have seen data presented in different graphs. In this lesson, you will take a survey and display the results in a **circle graph**.

Favorite Lunch	
pizza	𝍩𝍩 ////
burger	𝍩𝍩 /
cheese sandwich	𝍩𝍩 /
other	///

Activity

1

Survey your classmates.

- Choose a category such as sports, TV shows, or music. Each group should choose a different category. List three or four choices that fit in your category. For example, if your category is sports, you might choose ice hockey, baseball, and soccer. You may want to include "other" as one of the choices.

- Have each classmate write his or her favorite choice on a sheet of paper.

- Collect the data and find the total for each choice.

2

Record the votes.

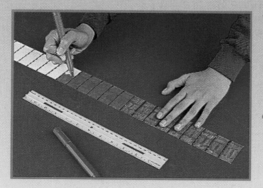

- On a long paper strip, mark a 1-in. section for each student you surveyed. For example, if you surveyed 24 classmates, you need 24 sections. Cut off any extra paper.

- Shade the strip to show how many classmates voted for each choice. Shade all the votes for one choice in the same color, next to each other. Choose another color for the next choice.

3

Create a circle graph.

- When all the choices are shaded, bend the strip into a circle. Tape the ends together.
- Place the strip on a clean sheet of paper. Carefully trace around the inside of the circle. Then find the center by folding the circle in half two different ways. Draw a line segment from the center to each point where two colors meet on the strip.
- Color the sections of the circle to match the colors on the strip. Write what each color represents.

4

Compare your results.

Trade your circle graph with another group and discuss the graph you have now.

a. How is the other group's circle graph different from the one you made? How is it similar?

b. What can you tell from this graph about your classmates' favorite choices?

c. What are two pieces of information you can get from the graph?

Favorite Type of Book

3 Biography
3 Other
12 Adventure
6 Mystery

Circle graphs show all the parts of a whole.

Show What You Know!

Use the circle graphs to answer the question.

1. Which type of book did most students choose?

2. How does the number of students who chose Mystery compare to the number who chose Biography?

3. **Number Sense** How can you find the total number of students surveyed?

4. How does the fraction of students who chose Adventure compare to the fraction who chose Mystery?

5. What fraction of students chose Other?

6. Which type of book was chosen by $\frac{1}{4}$ of the students? How many students does this represent?

7. **Critical Thinking** How can you use fractions to describe the data on the circle graph that you made?

Favorite Type of Book

$\frac{1}{8}$ Biography
$\frac{1}{8}$ Other
$\frac{1}{2}$ Adventure
$\frac{1}{4}$ Mystery

You can show the same information using fractions.

More Practice Set 4.8, p. 476

Problem Solving
Look for a Pattern

You are training for your town's bicycle race. On your first day of training, you ride 44 miles. On your second, you ride 45. On your third, you ride 47, and on your fourth, you ride 50.

If this pattern continues, how many miles will you ride on the fifth day?

Days	Miles
Day 1	44
Day 2	45
Day 3	47
Day 4	50
Day 5	?

Here's A Way! Use Look for a Pattern to solve the problem.

1 Understand

- You need to find the number of miles on Day 5.

2 Plan

- Look for the pattern in the way the numbers are increasing.
- How much greater was the number of miles on Day 2 than on Day 1? How much greater was the number of miles on Day 3 than on Day 2?

3 Try It

- Continue the pattern until you reach the number of miles on Day 5.

Days	Miles
Day 1	44
Day 2	44 + 1 = 45
Day 3	45 + 2 = 47
Day 4	47 + 3 = 50
Day 5	50 + 4 = ?

4 Look Back

- On Day 5, you will ride 54 miles.
- Does the answer make sense? Explain.

Show What You Know!

Use Look for a Pattern to solve the problem.

1. The longer you look, the fewer seashells you seem to find on the beach. On the first day of your 6-day vacation, you collect 30 shells. You collect 22 on the second day, 15 on the third day, and 9 on the fourth day. If the pattern continues, how many shells will you collect during your vacation?

2. **Critical Thinking** Describe the pattern in the way you collect shells.

Work It Out!

Use Look for a Pattern or any other strategy to solve the problem.

3. You want to buy some stickers for your collection. They are on sale for $.25 each. For every 3 stickers you buy, you get 1 free. You spend $1.50. How many stickers do you get?

4. You price 2 mountain bikes. Together they cost $420. The difference between the prices of the bikes is $30. How much does each bike cost?

5. You are collecting autographs of friends and relatives. The first week, you collect just 1 autograph. You collect 10 the second week, 19 the third week, and 28 the fourth week. If you continue at this pace, after how many weeks will you have at least 100 autographs?

6. Future Burgers is giving prizes to some of its customers as they enter the store. The prizes are awarded according to a pattern. The first, the sixth, and the eleventh person each receives a prize. If the pattern continues, will the twenty-sixth customer to enter the store receive a prize?

7. The owners of Future Burgers plan to give away prizes until 200 people have entered the store. How many prizes will they need?

8. You number the pages of your nature scrapbook. There are 100 pages. How many times do you write the digit 6?

9. You have 7 wooden figures that fit one inside the other. The height of the smallest figure is 1 in. The heights of the next figures are 2 in., 4 in., 7 in., and 11 in. If this pattern continues, what are the heights of the remaining figures?

Share Your Thinking

10. How can identifying the pattern in problem 5 make it possible to find the solution?

Problem Solving
Using Strategies

You can read more about marine archeology in the pages of *Kids Discover*.

People have invented different ways to explore the oceans. Trained scuba divers go deeper than 300 ft. With a JIM suit for protection, they can dive to 2000 ft. To go farther down, a special undersea craft such as a submarine, bathyscaph, or crewed submersible is needed.

Problem Solving Process
✓ Understand
✓ Plan
✓ Try It
✓ Look Back

Choose a Strategy You Have Learned
✓ Make a Table
✓ Act It Out
✓ Guess and Check
✓ Look for a Pattern
  Work Backward
  Make a List
  Work a Simpler Problem
  Draw a Picture
  Write an Equation

An experienced diver plans to make 5 dives during an all-day trip. Her first dive is to a depth of 130 ft. The next 3 dives are to depths of 120, 100, and 70 ft. If she continues this pattern, to what depth will she go on her final dive?

- What problem are you asked to solve?
- How can looking for a pattern in the depths of the dives help you solve the problem?
- What is the pattern?
- How can you continue the pattern to find the solution?

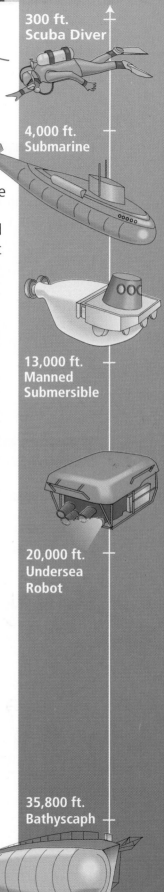

300 ft.
Scuba Diver

4,000 ft.
Submarine

13,000 ft.
Manned
Submersible

20,000 ft.
Undersea
Robot

35,800 ft.
Bathyscaph

Work It Out!

Use any strategy to solve each problem. Show your work.

1. A diver goes to the Great Barrier Reef in 1986. He returns in 1988, 1992, and 1998. If this pattern continues, when will his next trip be?

William Beebe and Otis Barton with their bathysphere, 1934

2. In 1934, two men used a bathysphere to descend to a depth of 3028 ft under the ocean. By 1960, the record descent was 35,840 ft to the deepest part of the Pacific Ocean. How much deeper was the record descent than the dive made in 1934?

3. Mt. Everest, the highest mountain on Earth, reaches 29,028 ft above sea level. The deepest part of the Pacific Ocean is 35,840 ft below sea level. Which is farther from sea level? About how great is the difference between the two in miles?
   (Hint: A mile is 5280 ft.)

4. The time you can safely stay underwater is based on how deep you dive. You can safely stay at a depth of 80 ft for 30 min; at 90 ft for 25 min; at 100 ft for 20 min; and so on. If the pattern continues, how long can you safely stay at a depth of 130 ft?

5. At 8:55 A.M. a diver returns to the surface following a dive. Because of the depth of his dive, he cannot safely dive again for at least 5 hours and 40 min. What is the earliest time he can dive again?

6. Elephant seals typically dive to a depth of 1000 ft to 2000 ft in search of food. If an elephant seal dives twice in 1 hour for 20 min each time, how many seconds altogether is it underwater?

7. A diver has 2 air tanks with her. Altogether, she has enough air to stay underwater for 90 min. One tank has 20 min more air supply than the other. How long is the air supply in each tank?

Share Your Thinking

8. When solving a problem, how can the strategy Make a Table help you when you use Guess and Check or Look for a Pattern?

145

Chapter 4 Test
for Pages 122–145

Test-Taking Tips
First work the problems you feel sure you can do. Then go back to the others.

Problem Solving

Solve using Look for a Pattern or another strategy. Show your work.
(pages 130, 142, 144)

1. The station where Helen buys gas is offering this deal: fill up 3 times and get a free drinking glass. Helen has already collected 3 glasses. She wants a total of 8. How many more times must she fill up?

2. Your family wants you to help more around the house. They agree to pay you a small amount for your work. You tell them you want $.01 the first day, $.02 the second day, $.04 the third day, $.08 the fourth day, and so on. How many days will you have to work to collect at least $20.00? How much will they owe you for your work on the 15th day?

Concepts

Use the bar graph to answer questions 3–4. (page 134)

3. About how many more visitors did Spain have than Italy? How many more did France have than Spain?

4. What is the median number of visitors to the 4 countries?

Use the double line graph to answer questions 5–6. (pages 136, 138)

5. About how many miles per hour faster was the land speed record than the record on water in 1930?

6. Between which years did the water speed record increase the most? By about how many miles per hour?

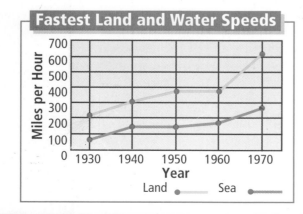

Fastest Land and Water Speeds

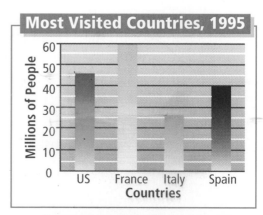

Most Visited Countries, 1995

Choose the answer that gives the correct mean, median, and range for each set of numbers. Write a, b, c, or d. (pages 126, 128)

Super Bowl Games	
Year	Winning Scores
1992	37
1993	52
1994	30
1995	49
1996	27

Species in U.S. Zoos	
Zoo	Number of Species
Denver	600
New Orleans	500
Houston	605
San Diego	800
St. Louis	665
Cinncinatti	760

Smallest Populations	
Country	1996 Pop.
Vatican City	1000
Nauru	10,000
Tavalu	10,000
Palau	17,000
San Marino	24,000

7. a. 37, 37, 52
   b. 39, 39, 52
   c. 39, 37, 25
   d. 37, 39, 25

8. a. 655, 635, 300
   b. 635, 655, 300
   c. 605, 655, 800
   d. 605, 635, 800

9. a. 10,000; 12,400; 23,000
   b. 13,500; 12,400; 24,000
   c. 10,000; 10,000; 24,000
   d. 12,400; 10,000; 23,000

 Performance Task

(page 134)

Look around your classroom and make a list of 30 items you see. Choose attributes, such as color or size, by which you can classify the items. Then make a tally sheet and assign each item to the appropriate category. Record your results on a bar graph.

- Label your graph with the categories into which you are sorting the items.

- Explain what the graph shows.

Keep In Mind . . .

Your work will be evaluated on the following:

☑ Classified items

☑ Fully recorded data

☑ Complete, correct graph

☑ Clear explanation

Cumulative Review

Prime and Composite Numbers
(Chapter 3)

Is the number 8 prime or composite?

Here's A Way!

Draw a rectangle made of factors of 1 and the number.

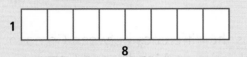

1
8

See if you can make other rectangles with the same number of blocks.

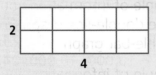

2
4

If there are exactly 2 factors, the number is *prime*. If more, the number is *composite*.
Count the factors.
  8 has 4 factors.
  8 is a composite number.

Write whether these numbers are prime or composite.

1. 11   2. 7

3. 10   4. 21

Write the factors for the number. Tell whether the number is prime or composite.

5. 28   6. 13

7. 9   8. 17

9. Describe a method you can use, other than drawing rectangles, to determine whether a number is prime or composite.

10. How could recognizing prime numbers help you simplify fractions?

Dividing by Multiples of 10 (Chapter 3)
Divide: 240 ÷ 60

Here's A Way!

Find a related multiplication fact.

6 × 4 = 24 ➡ basic fact
60 × 4 = 240
240 ÷ 60 = 4

Use mental math to find the quotient.

11. $80\overline{)4000}$

12. $30\overline{)150}$

13. $50\overline{)40,000}$

14. $60\overline{)4800}$

15. $20\overline{)10,000}$

16. $90\overline{)3600}$

17. How does knowing how to divide by multiples of ten help you divide 1241 by 59?

Interpreting Double-bar and Double-line Graphs (Chapter 4)

Compare two related sets of data.

This double-line graph shows high and low price changes over time.

This double-bar graph shows high and low prices on one day.

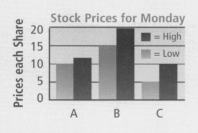

Use the graphs in Here's a Way! to answer each question. Tell which graph you used.

18. How much higher was the high price than the low price for Company A on Tuesday?

19. Which company had the same high price as Company A's low price on Monday?

20. When was Company A's high price the same as its low price on Tuesday?

21. What is the difference between Company A's high price on Monday and its high price on Friday?

22. What is the difference between Company A's high price on Monday and Company B's high price on Monday?

23. Give an example of information you could learn from the double-line graph, but not from the double-bar graph.

24. Give an example of information you could learn from the double-bar graph, but not from the double-line graph.

25. Give an example of information you could learn from either graph.

Problem Solving

Problem Solving Process
- ✓ Understand
- ✓ Plan
- ✓ Try It
- ✓ Look Back

Choose a Strategy You Have Learned
- ✓ Make a Table
- ✓ Act It Out
- ✓ Guess and Check
- ✓ Look for a Pattern
- Work Backward
- Make a List
- Work a Simpler Problem
- Draw a Picture
- Write an Equation

Choose one of the strategies you know to solve these problems. Show your work.

26. You are starting an exercise program. The first week, you will exercise for 20 minutes each weekday. Your goal is to increase your exercise time each week by 5 minutes per weekday until you are up to 5 hours of exercise per week. In how many weeks will you reach your goal?

27. An uncle gives his favorite niece a savings bond every year for her birthday. He increases the amount by $25 each year. If he gave her a $75 savings bond on her 8th birthday, how much will he give her for her 16th birthday?

The Age of Music

Music Connection   With Your Group

In 1877, Thomas Edison made the first musical recording. It was of his own voice singing "Mary Had a Little Lamb." By the 1960s, music of all kinds could be found on records and tapes. Now people can listen to their favorite music on compact and laser discs.

In this investigation, you will compare the types of music listened to by people of different ages. To find the data, you will conduct a survey.

1 Plan It

- As a group, make a list of different types of music.

- Each member of your group will ask six people under 30 years old and six people over 30 years old what type of music they prefer. Each member should use a tally sheet to record data.

2 Put It Together

- Make a music survey chart like the one pictured to record your group's data.

- Show your data on a double-bar graph. Compare the number of people under 30 to the number of people over 30 who prefer the same music. Do this for each type of music.

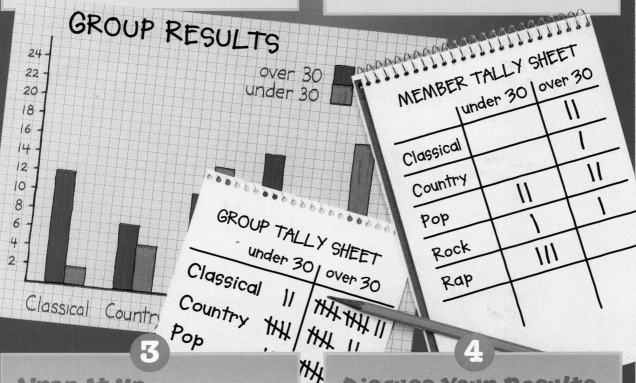

GROUP RESULTS

over 30
under 30

MEMBER TALLY SHEET	under 30	over 30
Classical		II
Country		I
Pop	II	II
Rock	I	I
Rap	III	

GROUP TALLY SHEET	under 30	over 30
Classical		II
Country	︱︱︱︱	︱︱︱︱ ︱︱︱︱ II
Pop		

3 Wrap It Up

- What does the information in the graph tell you?

- Write a report that tells how you collected your data and explains the information on the graph.

4 Discuss Your Results

- Did you meet the objectives listed in Keep In Mind?

- How might your results be different if you surveyed three age groups?

Internet

> Visit the **Math Center** at Houghton Mifflin Education Place. http://www.eduplace.com

Measurement and Geometry

Math Power

Use What You Know

- how to make geometric figures

- how to make measurements

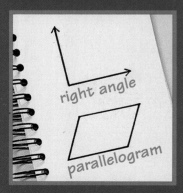

right angle

parallelogram

- geometry terms

Try This!

Make a maze by using what you know about geometry.

What You'll Need

quarter-inch grid paper, inch ruler, pencil, paper

1 On quarter-inch grid paper, draw the geometric figures described on this notebook, leaving paths between the figures.

- 1 in. by 2 in. rectangle
- 1 in. by $1\frac{1}{2}$ in. rectangle
- $\frac{1}{2}$ in. by $\frac{1}{2}$ in. square
- $1\frac{1}{4}$ in. by $1\frac{1}{4}$ in. square
- 3 triangles with right angles
- 2 parallelograms with two sides that measure $\frac{3}{4}$ in. and two sides that measure 1 in.

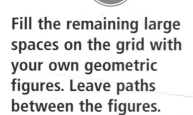

Fill the remaining large spaces on the grid with your own geometric figures. Leave paths between the figures.

Label a starting place and an ending place. Decide which path will lead through your maze. Then, draw lines to block the other paths.

Why was it helpful to measure the first figures?

Could you have used circles in your maze?

Ready to Go!

153

Measurement Sense

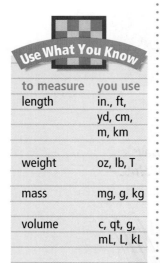

Use What You Know

to measure	you use
length	in., ft, yd, cm, m, km
weight	oz, lb, T
mass	mg, g, kg
volume	c, qt, g, mL, L, kL

Cooperative Learning Checklist

- ☐ Work alone.
- ☑ Work with a partner.
- ☑ Work with a group.

Getting Started

What You'll Need
- ▶ recording sheet
- ▶ measurement tools
- ▶ markers
- ▶ paper

How many ways can you measure an object? You can measure its length, its weight, or how much it holds. The measurements you can make depend on what you want to find out and the kind of measuring tools you have.

Measure for Measure

Activity

- Make a table, like the one below, for 10 objects. Or, use your recording sheet.
- Choose another group to compare tables at the end.
- Complete the first column of the table with the other group.
- Measure four of the objects using the tools.
- Compare your results.

How to Play!

1

Both groups decide on 10 objects that may have many measures. Write them in the Object column of each group's table.

2

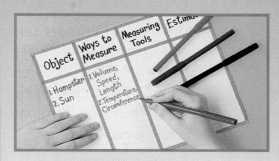

Each group thinks up as many ways as possible to measure the objects. Write these in the Ways to Measure column.

3

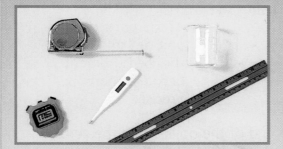

Write the tools you will need in the Measuring Tools column. Estimate the measurement of the object. Write your estimate in the column.

4

To see which group's estimate is closest, choose four of the objects to measure. Use the tools you have available. Compare your results.

Show What You Know!

Discuss each question and explain your answer.

1. **Critical Thinking** Did you get the same results as the other group? How were they the same? How were they different? Explain.

2. Write three things you would need to measure in order to:
   a. plan a field day   **b.** follow a muffin recipe   **c.** build a birdhouse.

155

Measuring to $\frac{1}{8}$ Inch

The inch is the most common unit used in the United States for measuring the length of small objects. The ladybug is 1 in. long to the nearest inch. You can use an inch ruler to measure the ladybug more precisely.

How long is the ladybug measured to the nearest $\frac{1}{8}$ in.?

Here's A Way! Measure the insect to the nearest $\frac{1}{8}$ in.

1 Make sure the zero mark is lined up with one end of the object you are measuring.

2 Find the mark that the other end of the object is closest to.

To the nearest $\frac{1}{8}$ in., the ladybug is $\frac{5}{8}$ in. long.

As the parts of the unit get smaller, the measurement becomes more precise.

Talk About It! Why must you line up one end of the object with the zero mark on the ruler?

Other Examples Measure to the nearest:

a. $\frac{1}{2}$ in.

The butterfly is $2\frac{1}{2}$ in. long to the nearest $\frac{1}{2}$ in.

b. $\frac{1}{4}$ in.

The butterfly is $2\frac{1}{4}$ in. long to the nearest $\frac{1}{4}$ in.

c. $\frac{1}{8}$ in.

The butterfly is $2\frac{3}{8}$ in. long to the nearest $\frac{1}{8}$ in.

1. Estimate the length of the walking-stick insect.

2. Measure the length of the walking-stick insect to the nearest:
   a. inch   b. $\frac{1}{2}$ in.   c. $\frac{1}{4}$ in.   d. $\frac{1}{8}$ in.

3. **Critical Thinking** Which two answers in exercise 2 are the same? Explain why.

4. **Number Sense** How many $\frac{1}{8}$ in. are in $\frac{1}{2}$ in.? Explain.

Walking-stick Insect

Work It Out!

Estimate and measure.

5. Estimate the length of this bee to the nearest inch.

6. Estimate the flower width to the nearest inch.

7. Measure the length of the bee to the nearest $\frac{1}{2}$ in. and $\frac{1}{4}$ in. Which is closer to your estimate?

8. Measure the width of the flower to the nearest $\frac{1}{2}$ in. and $\frac{1}{4}$ in. Which is closer to your estimate?

9. Measure the length of two of the bees (left) to the nearest $\frac{1}{8}$ in. Are both of the bees the same length?

10. Measure the width of one of the bees to the nearest $\frac{1}{8}$ in.

11. Measure the width of a honeycomb cell to the nearest $\frac{1}{8}$ in. Will the bee you measured fit into the cell you measured?

More Practice, Set 5.2, p. 476

Math Journal

- Give an example of when you can use an estimate instead of measuring.
- Give an example of when you need to measure.

Estimation: Length

LESSON 3

Sometimes when you need to measure you may not have a ruler available. You can estimate a length using another length you already know.

How long are the book and the desk?

Here's A Way! Estimate the length.

Small Objects	Large Objects

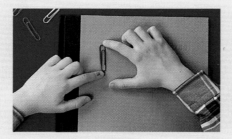 

1 For small objects, use a unit of measure that is smaller than the object.

You can use the length of a paper clip since it is smaller than the book and is about one inch.

2 Measure the object using your unit of measure.

The book is about 9 in. long.

1 For large objects, use a different measuring unit than for small objects.

You can use the length of a sheet of paper since it is smaller than the desk and is about one foot.

2 Measure the object using your unit of measure.

The desk is about 3 ft. long.

Talk About It! Can you estimate to find the answer in all measurement problems? Justify your answer.

Show What You Know!

Estimate and measure.

1. The distance from the tip of your thumb to the closest joint is about 1 in. Use this information to estimate the length of your foot. Then measure. How do the two measurements compare?

2. Use your height to estimate the height of your classroom. Compare your result with your partner's. Are they close? Why?

3. **Write About It** When would you need to estimate using inches, feet, or yards instead of estimating with measuring units such as a paper clip or your height?

Work It Out!

Estimate the measures and explain your answers.

4. The chalkboard is 12 ft long and 6 ft tall. About how long is the wall? About how tall is the wall?

5. How many more of the same size chalkboards could you fit on this classroom wall?

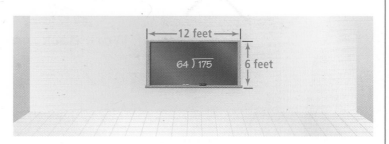

6. The room is 40 ft wide. About how wide is each desk chair?

7. Suppose a table is 6 ft long and 2 ft wide. How many of the chairs would fit around the table?

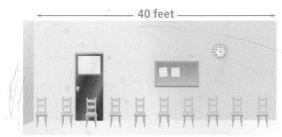

Choose the unit of measure you would use to estimate. Write *inch* or *foot*.

8. the length of a dollar bill

9. the height of a table

10. the length of the school hallway

11. the distance across a plate

12. the length of a basketball court

13. the width of a computer screen

14. the width of a computer disk

15. the height of a desk chair leg

16. **Critical Thinking** Describe three situations when an estimated measure would not give you the precision you need.

LESSON 4

Problem Solving
Work Backward

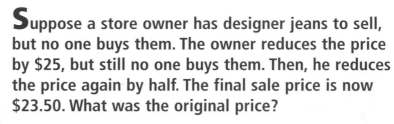

Suppose a store owner has designer jeans to sell, but no one buys them. The owner reduces the price by $25, but still no one buys them. Then, he reduces the price again by half. The final sale price is now $23.50. What was the original price?

Some problems can be solved by working backward.

Here's A Way! Work Backward to solve the problem.

1 Understand

- The store owner reduced the price twice.

- What did the store owner do the first time he reduced the price? The second time?

2 Plan

- Focus on one step at a time, starting with the last step.

3 Try It

- The final sale price is the first reduction divided by 2. What operation is the inverse (opposite) of division?

- Focus on each step separately until the problem is solved.

- The first reduction is the original price less $25. What operation is the inverse of subtraction?

4 Look Back

- The original price was $72.

- How did using the inverse operation help you work backward?

Use the Work Backward strategy to solve the problem.

1. You have been saving for a shirt that costs $29. If you save $4 per week for the next 3 weeks, you will have enough to buy the shirt. How much money do you have now?

2. **Critical Thinking** How did you use Work Backward to solve problem 1?

Work It Out!

Use Work Backward or any strategy to solve the problem.

3. Your friend has earned some money doing chores. You ask how much she made. She says that half went into the bank. Then, she and her 2 sisters split the rest evenly. She shows you a $5 bill and says that each of her sisters has one, too. How much did she earn doing chores?

4. You have just bought a used CD for $5 and sold it again for $6. Then you go to another music store and buy the same CD for $7. Later, you sell it for $8. How much money did you make or lose in buying and selling the CDs?

5. Suppose you went to a souvenir stand. You buy 2 T-shirts and 1 sweatshirt for $30. A sweatshirt costs 3 times as much as a T-shirt.
   a. What is the price of a T-shirt?
   b. What is the price of a sweatshirt?

6. Suppose it takes your friend 15 minutes to ride his bike to your house from his home. You and your friend want to skate together for an hour. What time should your friend leave his house to go skating with you and be back home by 5:00 P.M.?

7. A store is having a big sale. On Tuesday, all sale items have the price marked down $5. On Wednesday, all remaining items have the price marked down by $10 more. On Thursday, whatever is left sells for half of the Wednesday price. If you buy a jacket on Thursday for $18, what was the original price?

Share Your Thinking

8. Why do you think "Work Backward" is a good name for the strategy? Justify your answer.

Using Customary Measures

LESSON 5

A chicken soup recipe calls for 6 pints of broth but your measuring cup only holds one cup. How many cups of broth do you need? Show 6 pints as cups.

Units of Measure		
Length		
12 inches = 1 foot		
3 feet = 1 yard		
5280 feet = 1 mile		
Capacity		
8 fluid ounces = 1 cup		
2 cups = 1 pint		
2 pints = 1 quart		
4 quarts = 1 gallon		
Weight		
16 ounces = 1 pound		
2000 pounds = 1 ton		

Here's A Way! Write pints as cups or quarts.

Write pints as cups.

1 Cups are smaller than pints.

2 cups = 1 pint

2 Multiply to write the larger unit as a smaller one.

6 pints = __ cups
6 pints = (6 × 2) cups
So, the recipe uses 12 cups of broth.

You can also write pints as quarts.

1 Quarts are larger than pints.

2 pints = 1 quart

2 Divide to write the smaller unit as a larger one.

6 pints = __ quarts
6 pints = (6 ÷ 2) quarts
So, the recipe uses 3 quarts of broth.

Talk About It! Why divide when writing a larger unit as a smaller one?

Other examples You can also express equivalent measures as fractions.

a. 1 inch is equal to what fraction of a foot? 12 inches = 1 foot So, an inch is $\frac{1}{12}$ foot.

b. 1 ounce is equal to what fraction of a cup? 8 ounces = 1 cup. So, an ounce is $\frac{1}{8}$ cup.

Show What You Know!

1. 3 gal = __qt

2. 12 pt = __qt

3. 10 oz = __lb

4. 1 lb = __oz

5. 2 mi = __ ft

6. 4000 lb = __T

7. **Critical Thinking** Write the answer to 32 oz ÷ 4 in pounds.

Midchapter Review

for Pages 154–162

Problem Solving

Solve. Show your work. (page 160)

1. Today the balance in your checking account is $69.55. During the last week you made a deposit of $20.00 and wrote two checks for $17.30 and $29.95. What was your balance a week ago?

2. Before going to the 2:45 P.M. movie, you need to practice the piano 1 hour and then clean your room for 20 minutes. Allow half an hour to walk to the theater. At what time should you begin piano practice?

Concepts

Find the answer. (pages 154, 156, 158)

3. Write 3 things that you would need to measure in order to wrap a gift with paper and ribbon.

4. When is an estimated measurement accurate enough, and when do you need to actually measure an object?

5. How could you estimate whether a desk will fit through a door?

6. Why are standard measuring tools used?

Skills

Measure the length of each object to the nearest $\frac{1}{4}$ in. and $\frac{1}{8}$ in. (page 156)

7.

8.

Choose the unit of measure you would use to estimate. Write *inch* or *foot*. (page 158)

9. the height of a drinking glass

10. the length of a sleeping bag

Choose the correct number of sides. Write a, b, c, or d. (page 162)

11. A heptagon has   **a.** 5 sides   **b.** 6 sides   **c.** 7 sides   **d.** 9 sides

12. A pentagon has   **a.** 5 sides   **b.** 6 sides   **c.** 7 sides   **d.** 8 sides

Math World

How many different things do you measure each day? Read about how people have used measurement and geometry in different ways.

The Art of Math

In the 1930s, many artists around the world started using geometric figures in their art. Max Bill, an artist from Sweden, often used mathematical formulas to create his geometric designs. This oil painting by Bill is called *Field of 32 Parts in 4 Colors*. It is 32 triangles in four colors. The painting is symmetrical. However, each triangle on the left does not have the same color as its mirror image on the right.

The Correct Time

In 1845, workers at the U.S. Naval Observatory in Washington, D.C., started dropping a ball every day exactly at noon. This gave people the correct time each day. The observatory still keeps time for the United States by tracking the position of stars and the rotation of the Earth. The master clock at the observatory is able to keep the correct time to one millionth of a second.

U.S. Naval Observatory in Washington D.C.

Try This! Counting the Seconds

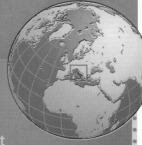

The scientist, Galileo, lived in Italy around 1600. He discovered that a swinging weight, or pendulum, could give nearly accurate time. Make your own pendulum that keeps time by seconds.

1 With a partner, measure a piece of string about 4 ft long. Tie a knot in one end.

2 From the knot, measure 36 inches. Tie a weight to the string at this point.

3 Hold the string by the end with the knot and let it swing like a pendulum. The time it takes to swing in one direction should be one second.

1 second

4 With your partner, time how long it takes the pendulum to swing back and forth ten times. Swing it gently to get the motion started. If the pendulum slows down, do not swing it to make it go faster. It should take twenty seconds to complete ten swings.

Warrior Weights

Throughout history, people have used a standard, or common, unit of weight when trading goods with other people. A statue of an Ashanti warrior was used as a standard unit of weight in parts of Africa. Now, most countries use the kilogram.

Respond

Create your own . . .

picture using geometry and measurement. Make a field of 18 parts with 3 colors.

Internet:

Houghton Mifflin Education Place

Explore the Math Center at
http://www.eduplace.com

Measuring Polygons

Cooperative Learning
Checklist

☑ Work alone.
☑ Work with a partner.
☑ Work with a group.

In this lesson you will measure figures to learn the difference between a regular figure and an irregular figure.

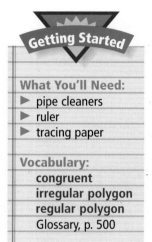
Activity

Polygons Around You

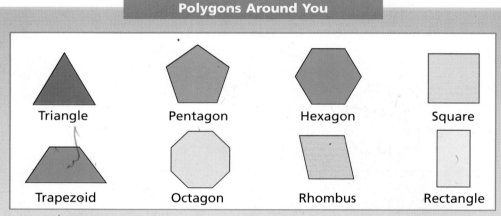

Triangle   Pentagon   Hexagon   Square

Trapezoid   Octagon   Rhombus   Rectangle

Polygons are all around you.

• Look for polygons in your classroom.

• Use the chart of polygons to help you list all the polygons you see in your classroom. Record the number of sides for each polygon.

Regular and Irregular Polygons

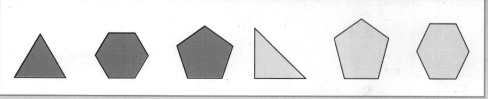

Three of the polygons shown are **regular.** The other three polygons are **irregular.**

• Study the two groups of figures. Discuss any differences you see.

• Use your observations and guess what a regular polygon is. Record your answer.

Experimenting with Angles

Use the polygons shown in the previous activity.

- Put a piece of tracing paper over the regular hexagon. Trace along one side with a pencil. Measure each of the other sides using this line. What do you notice?

- Next, trace one of the angles of the regular hexagon. Measure each of the other angles using this angle. What do you notice?

- Repeat these steps for the regular triangle and the regular pentagon. What do you notice about the length of the sides and the measure of the angles?

Is It Congruent?

Some polygons have congruent angles, congruent sides, or both. **Congruent** means equal in measure.

- Measure the sides and angles of the irregular polygons using the steps described in the previous activity.

- List the figures that have all congruent
    a. sides   b. angles   c. sides and angles

- Is it possible to form a hexagon whose sides are congruent, but whose angles are *not* congruent? Try to form one using pipe cleaners.

Show What You Know!

Discuss each question and explain your answer.

1. **Critical Thinking** What two requirements must be met for a polygon to be regular? Compare your answer with what you discussed in the second activity.

Tell whether the polygon is regular or irregular. Explain.

2.   3.   4.   5.

Write the name of the polygon. Tell if it is regular or irregular.

6.   7.   8.   9.   10.

Diagonals in Polygons

Cooperative Learning
Checklist
☐ Work alone.
☑ Work with a partner.
☐ Work with a group.

The corner of a polygon is called a **vertex**. A **diagonal** is a line segment that joins two vertices but is not a side of the polygon. In this lesson you will discover patterns in the numbers of diagonals in polygons.

Getting Started

What You'll Need:
► recording sheet
► ruler

Vocabulary:
diagonal
vertex
   (pl. vertices)
Glossary, p. 500

Activity

1

There are two diagonals in quadrilateral *ABCD*. One diagonal is drawn. Line segment *AC* is a diagonal because it joins two vertices but is not a side.

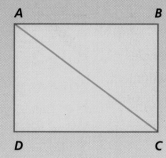

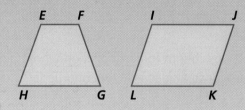

Discuss these questions with your partner. Record your answer.

● What line segment would you need to draw to show the other diagonal?

● How many diagonals does each quadrilateral have?

● Does every quadrilateral have the same number of diagonals? Explain.

● Does a triangle have diagonals? Explain your reasoning.

2

Differences in Diagonals

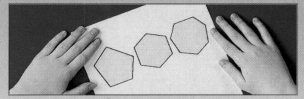

Look at the three figures here or on the recording sheet.

- Do these figures have more diagonals or fewer diagonals than a quadrilateral?

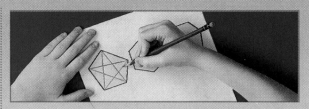

- Copy the figures and draw all the possible diagonals for each polygon.
- Copy and complete the first five rows of the table below.

Show What You Know!

Discuss each question and explain your answer.

1. **Critical Thinking** Look at the number of diagonals in the table. Describe the pattern that you see.

2. Using the pattern you discovered, predict the number of diagonals in an octagon. Check your answer by drawing an octagon or using the one on the recording sheet. Record the number in the table.

3. Predict the number of diagonals for a nonagon. Check by drawing a nonagon or using the one on the recording sheet. Record this number on the table.

4. **Mental Math** How could you use your pattern to predict the number of diagonals in a dodecagon, which is a figure with 12 sides?

Figure	Number of sides	Total number of diagonals
triangle	3	?
quadrilateral	4	?
pentagon	5	?
hexagon	6	?
heptagon	7	?
octagon	?	?
nonagon	?	?

Mixed Review

Subtract.

5. 70.45
   − 17.28

6. 0.512
   − 0.087

7. 16.902
   − 2.068

8. 72.4
   − 6.93

Math Journal

How can you determine the possible number of diagonals from one vertex of a polygon with 20 sides?

Perimeter

Getting Started

Vocabulary:
  perimeter
  Glossary, p. 500

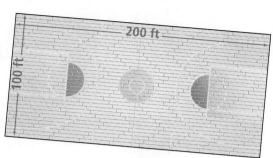

The President's Challenge compares the mile times of students throughout the United States. Some students run the mile by doing laps around a gym. The distance around the gym or around any figure is the **perimeter**. What is the length of one lap?

To find the length of a lap, you need to find the perimeter of the gym.

Here's A Way! **Find the perimeter of the gym.**

1 Find the length of each side.

The sides of the gym are 100 ft, 200 ft, 100 ft, and 200 ft.

2 Find the sum of the sides.

100 ft + 200 ft + 100 ft + 200 ft = 600 ft

So the students would run 600 ft in each lap.

Talk About It! If students run outside the lines of the gym, would they run more or less than 600 ft per lap? Explain.

Other Examples To find the perimeter of the pentagon, add the lengths of the sides.

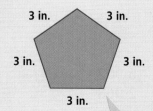

3 in.   3 in.

3 in.   3 in.

3 in.

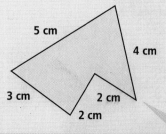

5 cm

4 cm

3 cm   2 cm

2 cm

3 in. + 3 in. + 3 in. + 3 in. + 3 in. or 15 in.	5 cm + 4 cm + 2 cm + 2 cm + 3 cm or 16 cm

Find the perimeter of each polygon.

1.

5 ft   4 ft
3 ft

2.
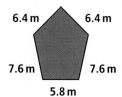
6.4 m   6.4 m
7.6 m   7.6 m
5.8 m

3.
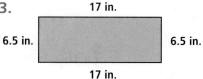
17 in.
6.5 in.   6.5 in.
17 in.

4. **Critical Thinking** If a figure is a regular polygon, how many sides do you need to know to find the perimeter? Explain.

Work It Out!

Find the perimeter.

5.
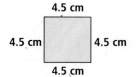
4.5 cm
4.5 cm   4.5 cm
4.5 cm

6.
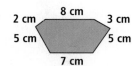
8 cm
2 cm   3 cm
5 cm   5 cm
7 cm

Compare regular and irregular polygon perimeters.

7. Draw an irregular pentagon with a perimeter greater than 30 cm.

8. **Number Sense** Draw a square with a perimeter of 30 cm.

9. **Patterns** Find the perimeter for each square.

   a. side = 1.4 in.   **b.** side = $3\frac{1}{2}$ cm   **c.** side = 24 cm

10. How is the length of the side of a square related to its perimeter?

Problem Solving

11. On a nice day, a gym teacher might want students to run the President's Challenge mile around the schoolyard rather than the gym. If the schoolyard is 20 ft longer and 20 ft wider than the course around the gym, how much longer is each lap?

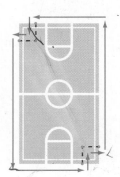

12. Suppose the gym teacher uses orange cones to mark out two 10-ft squares from opposite corners of the gym floor. Then, she asks half the students to run from cone to cone and half to run the perimeter. Will one group run farther than the other? Justify your answer.

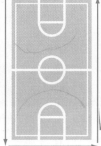

More Practice Set 5.8, p. 477

Perimeter and Polygons

In this lesson, you will discover rules to help you find the perimeter of regular and irregular polygons.

Activity

Getting Started

What You'll Need:
▶ recording sheet
▶ centimeter ruler

Use What You Know

A regular polygon has congruent sides and congruent angles.

Perimeter of a Square

5 cm

5 cm   5 cm

5 cm

1 Write an addition sentence to show how to find the perimeter of the square.

5 cm + 5 cm + 5 cm + 5 cm

2 Complete the multiplication sentence below to show how to find the perimeter of the square.

4 × ▮ cm = 20 cm

pentagon

heptagon

hexagon

Perimeter of a Regular Polygon

3 Measure a side of each regular polygon on the left.

4 Write a multiplication rule for the perimeter of each regular polygon in Chart A. Complete the rest of the chart.

5 Write a multiplication sentence for the perimeter of these polygons:
  a. a regular decagon with a side measuring 9 cm
  b. a regular octagon with a side measuring 4 cm

Chart A

Regular Figure	Addition Expression	Multiplication Expression	Perimeter (cm)
square	5 cm + 5 cm + 5 cm + 5 cm	?	20 cm
pentagon	?	?	?
hexagon	?	?	?
heptagon	?	?	?

Chart B

Object	Length of Side (cm)				Perimeter (cm)
	1	2	3	4	
Rectangle	?	?	?	?	?
Book	?	?	?	?	?
Desk	?	?	?	?	?

2 cm

6 cm   6 cm

2 cm

6 The rectangle to the right above is not a regular polygon. Why?

7 Complete the first row in Chart B.

8 Measure the cover of this book and the top of your desk. Complete the next two rows in Chart B

9 Measure and record three other rectangular objects in your classroom.

10 Look at Chart B. What do you notice about the lengths of the sides in a rectangle?

11 Do you need to know the measurement of all four sides of a rectangle to find the perimeter? Explain.

12 Write a rule for finding the perimeter of a rectangle.

13 Use your rule to find the perimeter of the rectangles:
a. width 5 in., length 6 in.
b. width 3 ft, length 2 ft

Show What You Know!

1. **Critical Thinking** How can multiplication help you find the perimeter of a figure?

2. How can you multiply by 4 to find the perimeter of a square?

3. A regular hexagon has a perimeter of 48 cm. How long is each side?

Find the perimeter. Use mental math when you can.

4. a regular decagon: side = 5 cm

5. a regular octagon: side = 7 cm

6. a regular heptagon: side = 4 cm

7. a regular nonagon: side = 9 cm

Math Journal

Explain the difference between finding the perimeter of a rectangle and finding the perimeter of a regular polygon. Include examples in your explanation.

Circumference

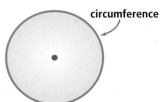

Cooperative Learning
Checklist

☑ Work alone.
☑ Work with a partner.
☐ Work with a group.

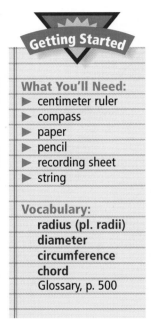

Getting Started

What You'll Need:
▶ centimeter ruler
▶ compass
▶ paper
▶ pencil
▶ recording sheet
▶ string

Vocabulary:
radius (pl. radii)
diameter
circumference
chord
Glossary, p. 500

You have learned how to measure the different parts of a polygon. Now, find out how to measure the different parts of a circle. The three circle measurements you will need are shown below.

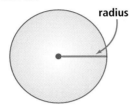

radius

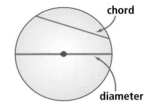

chord

diameter

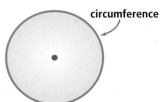

circumference

▶ the **radius** is a line segment from the center of the circle to any point on the circle

▶ a **chord** is a line segment that connects two points on the circle

▶ the **diameter** is a chord that goes through the center of the circle

▶ the **circumference** is the distance around the circle

Activity Use your recording sheet or your own paper.

Construct a Circle

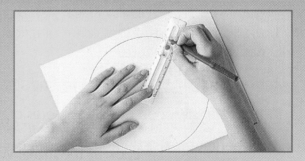

● Draw a dot and place the center of the compass over it. The dot is now the center point of the circle. Set the compass to the radius you want.

● Move the compass in a circle around the center point.

Draw 4 more circles and label each one.

1 radius: 2 cm   **2** radius: 3 cm   **3** radius: 4 cm   **4** radius: 5 cm

Compare Radius and Diameter

5 Measure the radius at three different places on the circles you drew. Does the radius change?

6 Measure the diameter at three places on each circle. Does the diameter change? Record the diameter of each circle.

7 About how many times greater is a circle's diameter than its radius?

Measure Circumference

- Place a string around each circle you drew.

- Measure the string length with your ruler.

- Record the circumference of each circle. About how many times greater is the circumference than the diameter?

Compare Diameter and Circumference

8 Predict the diameter and circumference of a circle with a radius of 6 cm.

9 Draw a circle with a radius of 6 cm and measure the diameter of the circle.

10 The exact circumference is Pi (π) times as long as its diameter. Pi is about 3.14. Multiply the diameter by 3.14 to find the circumference. $C = \pi \cdot d$

Show What You Know!

Discuss each question and explain your answers.

1. **Critical Thinking** Look at the table. Write a rule about the relationship between the diameter and the radius.

A whole number estimate for Pi (π) is 3. Find the circumference of a circle with the given radius using the estimate for Pi (π).

2. radius = 6 cm   3. radius = 7 cm   4. radius = 8 cm   5. radius = 9 cm

6. **Algebraic Reasoning** You know how a diameter and circumference are related. How can this help you know how a radius and circumference are related?

Elapsed Time

NASA launched a space shuttle at 3:55 A.M. It reached orbit at 4:04 A.M. How long did the shuttle take to reach orbit?

You can subtract to find the answer.

Here's A Way! Find the difference in times.

1 Write the subtraction as hours and minutes.

4:04   4 h 4 min
3:55   − 3 h 55 min   cannot subtract

2 If necessary, change hours to minutes and then subtract. Regroup if needed.

60 min = 1 h

    4 h 4 min   3 h 64 min
  − 3 h 55 min   − 3 h 55 min
                             9 min

It took the space shuttle 9 minutes to reach orbit.

Talk About It! What other method could you have used to solve this problem?

Other Examples The shuttle landed in Houston at 1:01 P.M. It started landing procedures at 11:59 A.M. How long did it take to land? Find the total time needed for the landing.

Find the time until noon ⟶ 11:59 A.M. to noon is 1 min.

Find the time after noon ⟶ Noon to 1:01 P.M. is 1 h 1 min.

Add to find total elapsed time: 1 h 1 min + 1 min = 1 h 2 min.

So it took the shuttle 1 h 2 min to land.

Find how much time will pass. Explain your method.

1. from 4 P.M. to 6:45 P.M.

2. from 6:30 P.M. to 8:20 P.M.

3. from 11:15 A.M. to 1:30 P.M.

4. from 11:30 A.M. to 3:10 P.M.

5. What exercises above can you solve using mental math?

6. 2 h 15 min
   + 3 h 30 min

7. 3 h 20 min
   + 5 h 50 min

8. 1 h 25 min
   −   40 min

9. **Create Your Own** Write a word problem that is solved by changing hours to minutes as in exercise 8.

Work It Out!

Add or subtract.

10. 8 h 25 min
    + 15 h 45 min

11. 7 h 20 min
    − 3 h 40 min

12. 6 h 10 min
    − 2 h 55 min

13. 11 h 10 min
    − 10 h 45 min

14. 4 h 38 min
    + 6 h 47 min

15. 1 h 39 min
    +   57 min

16. **Critical Thinking** When do you need to change hours to minutes? When do you need to change minutes to hours?

Problem Solving

17. Alan Shepard was the first American astronaut in space. His total flight lasted 15 min and he landed at 9:49 A.M. on May 5, 1961. When did he take off?

18. On July 20, 1969, the crew on the Apollo 11 mission landed on the moon at 4:17 P.M. Suppose they made final landing checks for 2 h 7 min 30 sec. Then it took them twice as long as that to get into their spacesuits to make the first moonwalk. When was the first step on the moon?

19. Getting into their spacesuits took 24 min 30 sec longer than their first moonwalk. When did the first moonwalk end?

Mixed Review   Write the answer.

20. 64 × 35

21. 72 ÷ 48

22. 83 × 29

23. 309 ÷ 18

24. 285 × 45

More Practice Set 5.11, p. 477

Problem Solving
Is the Answer Reasonable?

Is the Answer Reasonable

Ask Yourself:

Did I answer the questions?

Did I calculate correctly?

Is the answer labeled with the right units?

Does the answer need to be rounded to a whole number to make sense?

Suppose your class and two other classes are going on a field trip to a museum. There are 91 of you in all, including teachers. In the museum is a small planetarium that seats 26 people at one time. How many times will the museum have to show the star show for all of you to see it?

Your friend tells you that the museum will have to show the star show $3\frac{1}{2}$ times for everyone to see it. Is that reasonable?

You Decide

- Did your friend correctly calculate the number of show times?
- Is the answer labeled in the right units?
- Does the answer make sense?
- Does the answer need to be rounded to a whole number to make sense? Why or why not?

Is the answer reasonable? Explain.

1. The guide in the planetarium tells you that there are 200 stars shown. Then she says that there are about 2 stars in the planetarium for each of you. Is she right?

2. The museum charges $2.50 admission for students and teachers. So, the museum will collect a total of $2275 from your group. Does that amount seem reasonable?

3. A rocket simulator at the planetarium can seat 3 people at one time. One of the students says it will take 31 rides for everyone to have a chance. Is this correct? Explain how the student found the answer.

4. At lunchtime, you and three friends buy lunch together for $12.15. One of your friends pays the total and then uses a calculator to determine the amount you each owe her. She says you each owe $3.038. Is that right?

5. One of the exhibits in the museum displays 5 old cars. Each of them could go only 20 miles per hour. Your friend says that modern cars go 100 times that fast. Is your friend right?

6. Together, you and your friend spent $16.98 on souvenirs at the planetarium. You spent $5.76 and your friend spent the rest. She says she spent about twice as much as you did. Does that make sense?

7. Your friend bought a 576-page book about space exploration. Your friend says about one-quarter, or 90 pages, describes planets. Does what he says make sense?

8. The museum is open from 10 A.M. to 5:30 P.M. on weekdays. A museum tour lasts 45 minutes. Tour guides get 1 hour for lunch. So, a guide can lead 8 tours a day. Is that right?

9. **Create Your Own** Write a problem for a classmate to solve and then give a possible answer. Let your classmate decide whether the answer is reasonable or unreasonable.

Share Your Thinking

10. What are some clues that an answer is unreasonable?

Time Zones

Suppose that the California Angels are playing the New York Yankees. If the game starts at 1:30 P.M. in California and is televised live, what time will fans see the game in New York?

You can use the time-zone map to solve the problem.

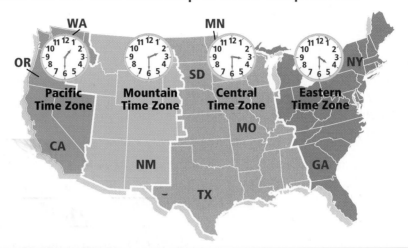

| **Here's A Way!** | **Find the time in New York.** |

1 Decide if you need to add or subtract hours.

- When going from west to east, it gets later, so you add.
- When going from east to west, it gets earlier, so you subtract.

When you cross from California to New York, you cross time zones from west to east. So you will add hours.

2 Count the number of time-zone lines crossed between places.

Since three time zone lines are crossed between California and New York, there is a 3-hour time difference between California and New York.

3 Find the correct time.

Add 3 hours. When it is 1:30 P.M. in California, it will be 4:30 P.M. in New York.

Talk About It! What happens when you cross time zones from west to east? from east to west?

Use the map on page 180 if you need help. Write the time in Chicago when it is:

1. 5:00 A.M. in New York City, New York.

2. 6:15 P.M. in Atlanta, Georgia.

3. 11:30 A.M. in Portland, Oregon.

4. 9:14 P.M. in Rapid City, South Dakota.

5. **Critical Thinking** How can a 5-hour flight leave New York at 2:00 P.M. and arrive in San Francisco at 4:00 P.M.?

Work It Out!

Copy and complete. What time is it in the other three cities?

Atlanta	Santa Fe	Los Angeles	Chicago
4:45 A.M.	6.	7.	8.
9.	9:00 P.M.	10.	11.
12.	13.	12:00 A.M.	14.
15.	16.	17.	3:37 A.M.

18. Do you think it is earlier or later in Texas when it is 6:00 P.M. in Washington, D.C.? Why?

Problem Solving

19. A game between the San Francisco Giants and the Atlanta Braves ended at 6:36 P.M. in Atlanta, Georgia. What time did the game end in California?

20. Baseball fans in Santa Fe, New Mexico, watched a game between the Minnesota Twins and the Seattle Mariners. The game started at 4:00 P.M. in Seattle. What time did the fans in Santa Fe see the start of the game?

21. Suppose that the St. Louis Cardinals must be in Los Angeles, California, by 9:00 A.M. to get ready for a game with the Los Angeles Dodgers. What time must the Cardinals leave St. Louis if it takes $3\frac{1}{2}$ hours to fly to Los Angeles, California?

More Practice Set 5.13, p. 478

Using a Calendar

Akira Matsushima rode a unicycle for 3260 miles. He started on July 10, 1992, in Newport, Oregon, and finished on August 22, 1992, in Washington, D.C. How many weeks and days did Akira ride?

You can use the 1992 calendar to solve this problem.

Here's A Way! Count the number of weeks and days.

1 Use a calendar to count the number of complete weeks until you get to the last full week.

Akira left on a Friday. Count 6 weeks from July 10 to August 21.

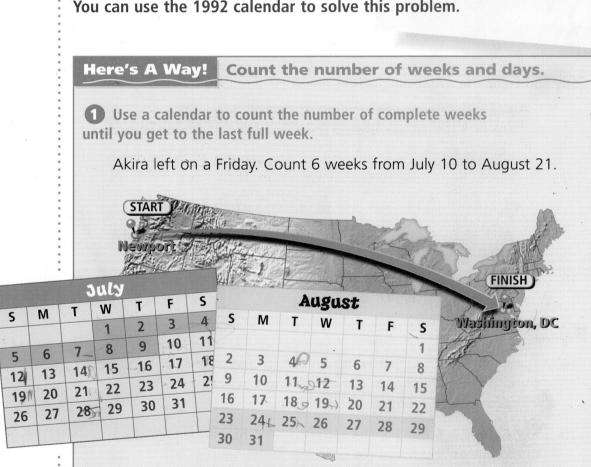

2 Count the number of days after the last week. Include the last day.

After the 6 full weeks, Akira rode 1 more day to August 22.
It took Akira 6 weeks and 1 day to ride his unicycle 3260 miles.

Talk About It! Could you count days to Saturday first and then the weeks? Would it change your answer? Explain.

1. If Akira had started his trip 2 weeks earlier, would he have ridden on the Fourth of July?

2. Suppose Akira was delayed and started his trip 2 weeks and 4 days later. Would he have ridden on the first Monday in September?

3. **Number Sense** What day of the week would Akira have arrived in Washington, D.C., if he had left on a Wednesday instead of a Friday and traveled the same number of days?

4. **Critical Thinking** How would you find the number of hours of Akira's trip if you knew what time he started and ended his trip? Would you have to add or subtract hours because of time zones?

Work It Out!

5. If Akira's trip had taken 1 week and 3 days longer, when would he have arrived in Washington, D.C.?

6. If Akira had left on July 1 and traveled the same number of days, when would he have arrived in Washington, D.C.?

7. **Critical Thinking** How can you answer question 5 without counting each week and day?

Problem Solving

September

S	M	T	W	T	F	S
		1	2	3	4	5
6	7	8	9	10	11	12
13	14	15	16	17	18	19
20	21	22	23	24	25	26
27	28	29	30			

October

S	M	T	W	T	F	S
				1	2	3
4	5	6	7	8	9	10
11	12	13	14	15	16	17
18	19	20	21	22	23	24
25	26	27	28	29	30	31

8. November 3, 1992, was Election Day. How long before Election Day did Akira arrive in Washington, D.C.?

9. Suppose Akira turned around in Washington, D.C., on August 23 and went back to Newport, Oregon. If the return trip took just as long, on what day and date would he have arrived back in Newport?

Temperature

There are two types of scales used to measure temperature: the Fahrenheit (°F) and Celsius (°C) scales. A cold day in Fairbanks, Alaska, is 0 degrees, Fahrenheit or Celsius. But on a hot day in Phoenix, Arizona, it can reach 100 degrees. Is it 100°C or 100°F?

You can read the thermometer shown to answer this question.

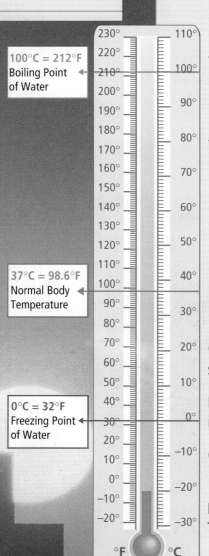

100°C = 212°F
Boiling Point of Water

37°C = 98.6°F
Normal Body Temperature

0°C = 32°F
Freezing Point of Water

Here's A Way! Decide: 100°C or 100°F.

1 Look at the thermometer and find 100°C.

Notice that water boils at 100°C.

2 Look at the thermometer and find 100°F.

Notice that your normal body temperature, 98.6°F, is near 100°F.

3 Decide which is more reasonable for a hot day.

• Boiling water (100°C) is much hotter than a hot day.
• You can take a bath in water that is 100°F, close to your body temperature.

So on a hot day in Phoenix, Arizona, it can reach 100°F.

Talk About It! What are some other situations you could use to compare 100°F and 100°C?

Other Examples It is 15 degrees outside. Ice forms on the street. Is the temperature 15°F or 15°C?

Look at the thermometer. Find the freezing point of water in both scales.

Celsius: 0°
15°C is above freezing.

Fahrenheit: 32°F
15°F is below freezing.

For ice to form, the temperature must be at or below freezing. Therefore, the temperature is 15°F.

Copy the graph at the right on squared paper. Record each thermometer reading. Then, mark a point for each thermometer reading on the graph. Connect the points.

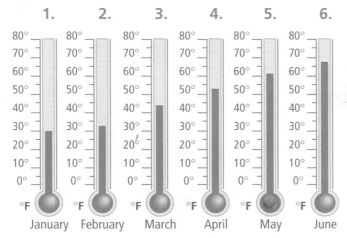

1. 2. 3. 4. 5. 6.

January February March April May June

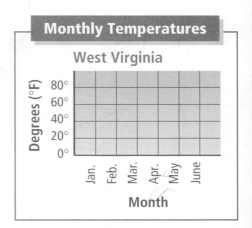

Monthly Temperatures

West Virginia

Write the letter of the more reasonable temperature.

7. melted butter
   a. 30°C
   b. 98°C

8. a small campfire
   a. 200°F
   b. 200°C

9. a glass of juice
   a. 15°F
   b. 50°F

10. Critical Thinking What would the temperatures have been in exercise 1–6 if they were recorded on a Celsius scale?

Is it unusual

11. if it is 8°C in Tampa, Florida, in December?

12. if it is 42°F in Trinity, Texas, in July?

13. if it is 20°C in New Orleans, Louisiana, in August?

Problem Solving

14. What is the difference between the hottest recorded temperature and the coldest recorded temperature in Texas in °F?

15. Which two places on the thermometer have a difference of 14°F between their temperatures? What is the approximate difference in these two temperatures in degrees Celsius?

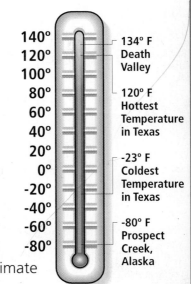

134° F Death Valley

120° F Hottest Temperature in Texas

-23° F Coldest Temperature in Texas

-80° F Prospect Creek, Alaska

More Practice Set 5.15, p. 478

LESSON 16

Problem Solving
Using Strategies

You can read more about gold miners in the pages of *Kids Discover.*

Gold miners work in mines in search of gold. In the world's deepest mine, the mine shaft is 12,000 feet deep. As miners go deeper into the shaft, the temperature increases. Sometimes miners work in temperatures near 130°F.

Suppose the temperature at the top of the gold mine shaft is 45°F. At 1000 feet down the shaft, you are halfway down and the temperature has doubled. At the bottom, the temperature has increased another 23 degrees. How hot is it at the bottom?

- What is the question you have to answer?

- How does the temperature change from the top of the mine shaft to the bottom?

- Do you need to know how deep the shaft is to answer the question?

- Look at the diagram. What information do you know about the change in temperature?

- Explain a strategy that can help you to solve the problem. Then solve it.

Problem Solving Process
✓ Understand
✓ Plan
✓ Try It
✓ Look Back

Choose a Strategy You Have Learned
✓ Make a Table
✓ Act It Out
✓ Guess and Check
✓ Look for a Pattern
✓ Work Backward
  Make a List
  Work a Simpler Problem
  Draw a Picture
  Write an Equation

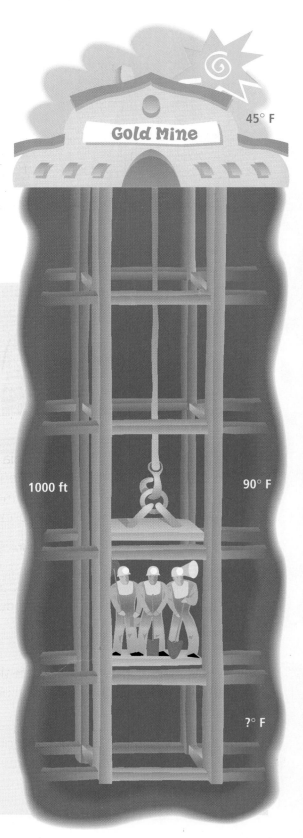

Gold Mine
45° F
1000 ft
90° F
?° F

Use any strategy to solve each problem. Show your work.

1. If you work in a mine, you wear a battery-powered flashlight. You turn it on for the 20-minute ride down, and turn it off when you get back to the top. Your battery lasts 6 hours. Suppose you have been working in the shaft for 3 hours 15 minutes. How much longer can you work before you should go back to the elevator?

2. Miners use beams of wood to stabilize the tunnels as they dig. Suppose that miners use 24 beams for a tunnel that is 72 ft long. How long is the tunnel if the miners need 36 beams?

3. How many beams of wood are needed for a 99-ft long tunnel?

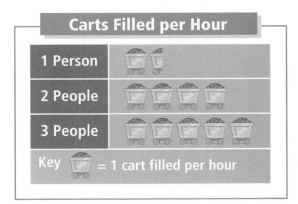

Carts Filled per Hour

1 Person	
2 People	
3 People	
Key	= 1 cart filled per hour

4. This miner's cart is used to haul away rocks that are dug up in the mine. Suppose one miner fills $1\frac{1}{2}$ carts in an hour when working alone. When two miners work together, they can fill 4 carts in an hour. When three miners work together, they get in each other's way and can only fill 5 carts in one hour. Suppose 9 miners are working in a tunnel for 2 hours. How should they work together to get the most carts filled?

5. Gold was discovered in California in 1848, and many people moved there. By the end of 1849, the population of California increased to almost 100,000, more than 6 times the population in 1848. What was the approximate population in 1848?

6. In 1987, Nevada produced more gold than all the other states combined. Utah produced less than half of what California produced, but not the least amount. List the states in order from least production to greatest production.

Share Your Thinking

7. How does knowing many strategies make it easier to solve problems?

Chapter 5 Test

for Pages 152–187

Test-Taking Tips
If you are having difficulty with one problem, go on to the next. Then go back to the difficult one.

Problem Solving

Solve using Work Backward or another strategy. Show your work. (page 160)

1. At a craft sale, a wood carving of a raccoon sold for $35. At noon the original price was reduced by half, and then, just before the carving was sold, the price was reduced by another $5. What was the original price of the wood carving?

2. There was 1 cookie left at the end of the club meeting. During the meeting, 9 students ate 2 cookies each. Before the meeting, the club sponsor and 2 students ate 1 cookie each. How many cookies were there originally?

Concepts

Tell whether you would estimate each measurement in inches or feet. Explain why. (page 158)

3. the length of a car

4. the height of a basketball hoop

5. the length of your pencil

6. the distance from the floor to the top of your desk

Tell how many sides each polygon has. Write the prefix that you used for your answer. Draw an example of each. (page 162)

7. octagon

8. pentagon

9. hexagon

10. decagon

Draw an example of each polygon. Label the side measures. (page 166)

11. a regular pentagon

12. an irregular triangle

13. a trapezoid

14. a regular triangle

Draw an example of each polygon. Show all possible diagonals. (page 168)

15. triangle

16. parallelogram

17. hexagon

Measure each line segment to the nearest $\frac{1}{8}$ inch. (page 156)

✗18. _____

✗19. _____

Choose the correct perimeter. Write a, b, c, or d. (pages 170, 172)

20. a regular decagon with sides of 4 in.
   a. 32 in.   b. 24 in.   c. 36 in.   d. 40 in.

21. a rectangle with length of 12 in. and width of 11 in.
   a. 46 in.   b. 132 in.   c. 23 in.   d. 1 ft 11 in.

Stop

Estimate the circumference for each circle described. (page 174)

✗22. a circle with a radius of 10 in.

✗23. a circle with a diameter of 12 in.

Write the answers. (pages 176, 180, 182, 184)

24. 1 h 32 min + 7 h 43 min

25. 23 h 4 min − 10 h 35 min

26. If it is 4:30 A.M. on the East Coast, what time is it on the West Coast? (see map, p. 180)

27. If it is midnight in Chicago what time is it in California? (see map, p. 180)

28. How many weeks and days is it from May 16 to July 21?

29. Is a normal body temperature closer to 100°C or 100°F?

 Performance Task

(page 176)

Find the shortest path from point A to point J. Calculate the time it would take to travel this path.

- List all the points you would pass through on your path.

- Explain how you decided which path would be shortest.

Keep In Mind . . .
Your work will be evaluated on the following:
☑ Finding the shortest path
☑ Correct calculations
☑ Complete answer
☑ Clear explanation

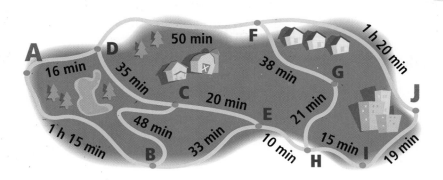

Cumulative Review

Finding the Mean, Median, and Range
(Chapter 4)
Find the mean, median, and range for these numbers: 97, 85, 94, 88, 91.

Here's A Way!

The mean is the average. Add the numbers and divide by the number of addends.

$$97 + 85 + 94 + 88 + 91 = 455$$
$$455 \div 5 = 91$$

The median is the middle number when numbers are ordered:

97, 94, **91,** 88, 85

The range is the difference between the greatest and least numbers.

$$97 - 85 = 12$$

Use the table showing points scored in girls' basketball games to answer the questions.

Game	1	2	3	4	5
Jenell	24	14	18	20	16
Margo	18	4	8	14	10
Chris	2	0	4	8	6
Tanya	12	10	6	14	20
Rosa	6	10	4	12	18

1. What is the mean number of points scored by all players during game 4?

2. What is Rosa's point score range?

3. What is the median score for game 1?

4. How can you tell, without calculating, if Rosa or Margo has the higher average?

Diagonals in Polygons (Chapter 5)
Find the diagonals in a hexagon.

Here's A Way!

Triangle 3 sides		0 diagonals
Quadrilateral 4 sides	+2	2 diagonals
Pentagon 5 sides	+3	5 diagonals
Hexagon 6 sides	+4	n diagonals

The difference in number of diagonals between one polygon and the next increases by 1.
A hexagon has 9 diagonals.

5. How many diagonals does an octagon have?

6. How many diagonals does a nonagon have?

7. How many diagonals does a decagon have?

8. How can you tell how many diagonals a polygon has without drawing the figure?

9. Why doesn't a triangle have any diagonals?

Comparing and Ordering Decimals
(Chapter 1)
Compare 1.6 and 1.56.

Here's A Way!

Line up the numbers   1.6
by place value.   1.56
Compare digits. Begin on the left.
If the digits are equal, compare the
digits in the next place to the right.
   6 > 5, so 1.6 > 1.56

Compare. Write <, >, or =.

10. 0.53 ● 0.5   11. 1.6 ● 0.98

12. 3.09 ● 3.9   13. 0.157 ● 0.2

Order from least to greatest.

14. 0.04, 1.13, 1.3, 0.008

15. 2100, 2100.01, 210.98, 2100.1

16. If 3 < 5, then why isn't 0.3 < 0.05?

Multiply by 1-, 2-, and 3-Digit Numbers
(Chapter 2)
Multiply 346 × 23.

Here's A Way!

    346
×   23
   1038   Multiply by the ones digit.
    692   Multiply by the tens digit.
   7958   Add.

Find the product.

17. 542 × 7   18. 34 × 76

19.   145   20.   708
    ×   56   × 128

21. How is multiplying by a 3-digit number the same as multiplying by a 2-digit number? How is it different?

Problem Solving

Problem Solving Process
✓ Understand
✓ Plan
✓ Try It
✓ Look Back

Choose a Strategy You Have Learned
✓ Make a Table
✓ Act It Out
✓ Guess and Check
✓ Look for a Pattern
✓ Work Backward
  Make a List
  Work a Simpler Problem
  Draw a Picture
  Write an Equation

Choose one of the strategies you have learned to solve these problems. Show your work.

22. Tickets to last night's concert were sold out in 2 hours. Seventeen more tickets were sold in the first hour than in the second. If 267 tickets were sold in all, how many were sold during the second hour?

23. A local business donated 50 computers to the elementary school. The principal has chosen 9 classrooms to receive computers. Some classrooms will get 6 computers and others will get 5. How many classrooms will get 6 computers? How many will get 5?

CHAPTER 5

INVESTIGATION

Fort Mose

Keep In Mind . . .

Your work will be evaluated on the following:

☑ If your measurements and geometric figures are correct

☑ How clearly you explain the design for your fort

☑ How well you combine measurement and design

☑ How well your group uses the ideas on the list

History Connection   With Your Group

Before the United States became a nation, many countries claimed land in North America. Those countries built forts to defend their land. Fort Mose (MOZE) was one of those forts.

Fort Mose was built in 1738 to help defend Saint Augustine, Florida, a Spanish settlement. Enslaved African Americans moved to Fort Mose because the Spanish promised them freedom. It is believed that Fort Mose was the first free African-American settlement in America. Your group will design a similar fort.

1

Plan It

- Each group member lists ideas on how Fort Mose was used for defense.

- As a group, decide what measuring tool you will use to measure the walls of the fort and buildings.

2

Put It Together

- Use the list of buildings on the notepad to construct your fort.

- Measure and draw the walls of the fort and its moat on a large sheet of paper or poster board. Show the river on your drawing.

- Measure and draw the buildings on construction paper. Cut them out and place them within the walls of the fort.

Calculator If 1 inch on your drawing equals about 16 feet, what was the length of the walls of Fort Mose?

Measurements of Fort and Buildings

- Surrounding Area: Use a piece of paper that is about 15 in. × 15 in.

- Three walls are 13 in. long. The fourth side is along a river and has no wall.

- The moat surrounds the three walls. Make it $\frac{3}{8}$ in. wide.

- The chapel is a rectangle $1\frac{7}{8}$ in. × $1\frac{1}{8}$ in.

- The watchtower is a hexagon. Each wall measures $\frac{1}{2}$ in.

- The guardhouse is a trapezoid. One side is 1 in., another is $\frac{1}{2}$ in., and the remaining two sides are each $\frac{3}{4}$ in.

- Make three rectangular houses. The first house measures $1\frac{5}{8}$ in. × 1 in., the second is $1\frac{3}{8}$ in. × $\frac{7}{8}$ in., and the third is $1\frac{1}{4}$ in. × $\frac{7}{8}$ in.

3

Wrap It Up

- Refer to your list and locate on your drawing any other items you would need for defense.

- Write a paragraph telling how your design is a good defense.

4

Discuss Your Results

- Did you meet the objectives in Keep In Mind?

- Is your fort easier or harder to defend than other forts in the class? Why?

Internet

> Visit the **Math Center** at Houghton Mifflin Education Place. **http://www.eduplace.com**

6

Multiplication of Decimals

Math Power

Use What You Know

- how to use a calculator

8.5 > 6.9

3.04 < 3.4

5.5 = 5.50

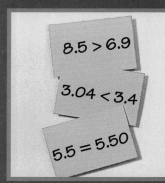

- how to order decimals

- decimal place
- product

- the vocabulary

Try This!

Multiplying with decimals can be tricky. Use a calculator and decimals to play a game that shows the least and greatest products.

What You'll Need

calculator, pencil and paper

Score Sheet		1st Factor	2nd Factor	Product
Game 1	Try 1	341	3.1	1057.1
	Try 2	341	.31	105.71
Game 2	Try 1			
	Try 2			
Game 3	Try 1			
	Try 2			
Game	Try 1			

1

Each player makes a score sheet like the one pictured. One player thinks of a 3-digit number. All players write the number in the 1st Factor column of their score sheets.

For Game 1, choose the digits 1 and 3 from the Multiplier Digits list to the right. Write the digits in any order in the 2nd Factor column of your score sheet. Place a decimal point anywhere in the number. For example, the Multiplier could be 3.1, 0.13, or 31.

Multiplier Digits

Games 1 and 2 ....1 and 3
Games 3 and 4 ....4 and 6
Games 5 and 6 ....7 and 8

Use a calculator to multiply the factors. In game 1, each player has two tries to make the greatest product. The greatest number wins. In Game 2, each player has two tries to make the smallest product. Use the same first factor and repeat Step 2. Continue playing until you have used all the multipliers listed.

How did you decide where to place the decimal to make the product smaller?

Would your product be different if the 1st Factor had a decimal in it?

Ready to Go!

Multiplication of Decimals

Cooperative Learning
Checklist
☐ Work alone.
☑ Work with a partner.
☐ Work with a group.

You can represent equivalent decimals on squared paper. In this lesson, you'll use this idea as you explore multiplying whole numbers and decimals.

To find 3 × 0.4, shade 3 groups of 4 tenths or 12 tenths.

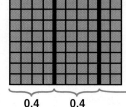

0.4   0.4   0.4
3 × 0.4 = 1.2

To find 2 × 0.08, shade 2 groups of 8 hundredths or 16 hundredths.

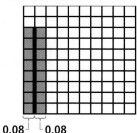

0.08 0.08
2 × 0.08 = 0.16

Use What You Know

You know that
0.1 = 0.10.

You can show this with tenths squares and hundredths squares.

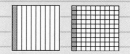

1 tenth = 10 hundredths

Decimal Spin

Activity

• Label a spinner: 0.1, 0.02, 0.03, 0.04, 0.5, 0.05, 0.6, 0.8.
• Each player creates a score sheet like the one shown.
• Play five rounds. Then, add and compare your scores.

How to Play!

1

Each player makes a score sheet like the one shown. With your partner, pick five whole numbers from 1 through 9. Write these numbers on your charts.

Round	Whole Number	x	Spinner Number	Product	Model Shown Correctly yes/no
1	8	x	0.1	0.8	
2	5				
3	2				
4	7				
5	6				
				Total = _____	

Player A

Player B | **Product** | **Model Shown Correctly**

2

Take turns spinning. When it is your turn, multiply the whole number by the spinner number. Shade hundredths squares to show the product. Have your partner check your work. If there is a mistake, work together to draw a correct model or write the correct product.

3

Play four more rounds. Add the products to get your scores. Which player has the greater score? How was the greater score reached?

Play again using different numbers for each round. Create a new spinner that includes the labels 0.001 and 1 thousandth.

Show What You Know!

Discuss each question and justify your answer.

1. **Critical Thinking** Is your score greater when you multiply by 1 hundredth or 1 tenth? How do you know?

2. **Number Sense** After 2 rounds, the score is 0.48. How might this score have been reached?

Find each product. Shade tenths and hundredths squares to help you.

3. 3×3 tenths   4. 6×2 hundredths   5. 4 tenths $\times 5$

6. 9×0.02 7. 0.06×7 8. 0.03×7 9. 0.02×5 10. 0.3×4

11. 0.01×4 12. 0.08×9 13. 0.7×6 14. 0.3×6 15. 0.9×6

Multiplying by 10, 100, and 1000

Glaciers, like the one shown here, are huge masses of ice that move over time. The Shirase Glacier in Antarctica moves about 6.71 m every day. How far does it move in 100 days?

Patterns help you multiply decimals. Notice how the decimal point moves to the right.

$$10 \times 6.71 = 67.1$$
$$100 \times 6.71 = 671.0$$
$$1000 \times 6.71 = 6710.0$$

You can also use mental math to find the product.

Use What You Know

You have used patterns to multiply whole numbers by 10, 100, and 1000.

$10 \times 35 = 350$
$100 \times 35 = 3500$
$1000 \times 35 = 35,000$

100×35 can also be written as 100×35.0.

Here's A Way! Use mental math to find 100×6.71.

1 Count the number of zeros in the whole number factor.

100×6.71

↑

2 zeros

2 Multiply the nonzero digits. After the last digit in the product write as many zeros as there are in the whole number factor.

$6.71 \times 1 = 6.71$

write 2 zeros ➡ 6.7100

3 For every zero in the whole number factor, move the decimal point in the product one place to the right.

671.00

2 places to the right

Remember, 671.00 is the same as 671.

The Shirase Glacier moves about 671 m in 100 days. How can you decide if this answer is reasonable?

Talk About It! How does knowing patterns help you multiply a decimal by 10, 100, and 1000?

Show What You Know!

Use What You Know

Use mental math to find the two factors whose product is 10, 100, or 1000. Then, multiply by the third factor.

4 · 9 · 25

Mental Math Find the products.

1. 10 × 6.928
   100 × 6.928
   1000 × 6.928

2. 10 × 42.5
   100 × 42.5
   1000 × 42.5

3. 10 × 1.07
   100 × 1.07
   1000 × 1.07

4. **Critical Thinking** In exercise 3, what happens to the value of the digit 7 when you multiply by 10? By 100? By 1000?

Work It Out!

Use mental math to find the product.

5. 10 × 5.65

6. 100 × 3.11

7. 100 × 9.723

8. 1000 · 4.2

9. 100 · 60.5 cm

10. 0.15 · 10

11. 100 × $.99

12. 685.4 × 100

13. 1000 × 40.7 km

14. 10 · 0.06

15. 100 · 0.06

16. 1000 · 0.06

17. **Patterns** Look at exercises 14–16. What pattern do you notice? Using this pattern, what is the next product?

Use mental math and the commutative property to find the product.

18. 5 · 2 · 9.4

19. 7.81 · 25 · 4

20. 20 · 0.6 · 50

21. 50 · 1.3 · 2

Problem Solving

22. The Byrd Glacier in Antarctica moves about 2.05 m a day. How far does it move in 1000 days?

23. The fastest glacier ever recorded was the Black Rapids Glacier in Alaska. It moved more than 29.9 m a day. About how far would it move in 100 days?

24. Every year, about 16,000 icebergs break off Greenland's glaciers. Will more than 1 million break off in a century? Explain.

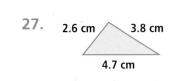

glacier

icebergs

16,000 break off every year

Mixed Review

Name the polygon. Find the perimeter of each.

25.
```
    5.8 cm
5.8 cm    5.8 cm
    5.8 cm
```

26.
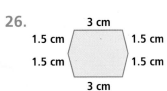
```
      3 cm
1.5 cm    1.5 cm
1.5 cm    1.5 cm
      3 cm
```

27.
```
2.6 cm    3.8 cm
     4.7 cm
```

199

Estimation: Products

Students at the Phillis Wheatley School in Roxbury, MA, painted a mural on their gymnasium wall. Suppose one group needed 4 quarts of paint for a section of the mural. If each quart cost $8.47, would $38 be enough to buy the paint?

You can estimate to find an answer.

Here's A Way! Estimate 4 × $8.47.

1 To find a low estimate, round down to a whole dollar. Multiply.

$$4 \times \$8.47 \longrightarrow 4 \times \$8 = \$32$$

Will the actual amount be greater or less than the estimate?

2 To find a high estimate, round up to the next dollar. Multiply.

$$4 \times \$8.47 \longrightarrow 4 \times \$9 = \$36$$

The actual price will be between $32 and $36.

Since the actual price will not be as high as your high estimate, $38 will be enough.

Talk About It! How do you know that the actual price will be less than $36?

Other Examples Use this strategy for decimals that are not money amounts.

Estimate: 5 × 7.6

Round Down $\longrightarrow$ 5 × 7 = 35   Round Up $\longrightarrow$ 5 × 8 = 40

So, the product of 5 × 7.6 is between 35 and 40.

Write the missing numbers.

1. 6.33 × 4 Estimate: between ▪ and ▪

2. $7.22 × 3 Estimate: between $▪ and $24

3. 5 × 2.8 Estimate: between ▪ and ▪

4. 8 × $3.57 Estimate: between $24 and $▪

5. **Critical Thinking** Look at exercise 4. Can you buy 8 drop cloths with $35 if each cloth costs $3.57? Explain.

Work It Out!

Write the missing numbers.

6. 2 × $3.85 Estimate: between $6 and $▪

7. 7 × 5.49 Estimate: between ▪ and 42

8. $5.63 × 9 Estimate: between $▪ and $▪

9. 8 × 8.31 Estimate: between ▪ and ▪

10. 7.4 × 5 Estimate: between ▪ and ▪

Problem Solving

Estimate to decide if you can make each purchase.

11. four 1-in. brushes with $18?

12. three 2-in. brushes with $25?

13. 6 rolls of masking tape for $18?

14. 12 mixing trays for $12?

15. eight $\frac{1}{2}$-in. brushes with $24?

16. five 1-in. brushes with $26?

Art Supplies	
$\frac{1}{2}$-in brush	$3.58
1-in brush	$5.24
2-in brush	$7.88
masking tape	$2.72
mixing tray	$0.77

Mixed Review Add and Subtract.

17. 5.2
    + 0.3

18. 5.2
    − 0.3

19. 9.5
    − 2.3

20. 9.0
    − 2.3

21. 7.3
    − 0.9

22. 9.5
    + 2.3

23. 7.2
    + 0.8

24. 7.2
    − 0.8

25. 4.1
    + 0.8

26. 4.0
    − 0.9

More Practice Set 6.3, p. 478

Decimals and Whole Numbers

1.3 cm

Scientists estimate that a hair on your head can grow as much as 1.3 cm in a month. How much can it grow in 3 months?

You can use decimal models to find 3 × 1.3 cm. This model shows that 3 × 1.3 = 3.9.

Another way to solve this problem is to multiply.

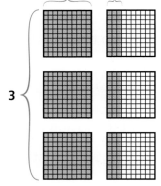

1   0.3

3

Here's A Way!   Find 3 × 1.3 cm.

1 Round to estimate the answer.

Round down.   Round up.

1.3 ➤ 1   1.3 ➤ 2

3 × 1 = 3   3 × 2 = 6

> The answer is between 3 cm and 6 cm.

2 Multiply. Follow the same steps you use for whole numbers.

$$\begin{array}{r} 1.3 \\ \times\ \ 3 \\ \hline 39 \end{array}$$

3 Write the decimal point in the product. Use the estimate to decide where to write it.

$$\begin{array}{r} 1.3 \\ \times\ \ 3 \\ \hline 3.9 \end{array}$$

> The answer is between 3 and 6, so write the decimal point to show the answer as ones and tenths.

In 3 months, a hair on your head would grow 3.9 cm.

Talk About It!

- How did the estimate help you place the decimal point in the product?
- What is the total number of decimal places in the factors 1.3 and 3? What is the total number of decimal places in the product?

Show What You Know!

Write the product. Use squared paper if you need to.

1. 3 × 2.2   2. 6 × 5   3. 12.7 × 9   4. 81 × 4 ft   5. 4 × 2.2   6. 10.7 × 3

7. 2.7   8. 4.7   9. 9.9   10. 2.4   11. 32.4   12. 0.5
   $\times\ 2$ $\times\ 4$ $\times\ 9$ $\times\ 5$ $\times\ 3$ $\times\ 2$

13. **Critical Thinking** When can you leave the decimal point out of a number?

hair magnifications

20 X

100 X

50 X

Work It Out!

Find the product. Use squared paper if you need help.

14. 5.9   15. 2.8   16. 9.5   17. 10.3 oz   18. 2.9
    $\times\ 6$ $\times\ 2$ $\times\ 1$ $\times\ 4$ $\times\ 2$

19. 8 · 7.7   20. 4.9 · 6 km   21. 19.1 × 8   22. 15.5 · 3 L   23. 12.1 · 3

Problem Solving

24. Hair can be measured in microns. One micron is $\frac{1}{1000}$ of a millimeter.

    One hair could be about 75.5 microns thick. How wide would this hair look if it were magnified 10 times by a microscope?

25. Most people shed about 1600 eyelashes every year. About how many do you shed each month?

Critical Thinking Which of the following hairs will appear thickest? Why?

26. a 92.4 micron hair viewed at 100 times magnification

27. a 63.4 micron hair viewed at 10 times magnification

28. a 50.1 micron hair viewed at 1000 times magnification

More Practice Set 6.4, p. 479

Math Journal

What are the steps involved in multiplying a decimal by a whole number?

Zeros in the Product

Use What You Know

Properties for multiplying:

Associative:
$(4.31 \times 2) \times 8 = 68.96$
$4.31 \times (2 \times 8) = 68.96$

Commutative:
$6 \times 0.008 = 0.048$
$0.008 \times 6 = 0.048$

Distributive:
$7 \times 5.9 = 41.3$
$7 \times (5 + 0.9) = 41.3$
$(7 \times 5) +$
$\quad (7 \times 0.9) = 41.3$

The average woman walks at a speed of about 0.04 miles a minute. At this speed, how far would a woman walk in 2 minutes?

You can multiply to find the answer.

Here's A Way! Find 2×0.04.

1 Write the short word form. Multiply.

$$\begin{array}{r} 0.04 \\ \times \quad 2 \\ \hline \end{array}$$

4 hundredths
$\times 2$
8 hundredths
(2 decimal places)

2 Write the product as a decimal.

8 hundredths ➡ 0.08

Remember, write a zero in the ones place for decimals less than 1.

In 2 minutes, a woman would walk about 0.08 miles.

Talk About It! Why must you write a zero in the tenths place of the product?

Other Examples The short word form can help you find other decimal products.

1. $$\begin{array}{r} 0.09 \\ \times \quad 3 \\ \hline 0.27 \end{array}$$

9 hundredths
$\times 3$
27 hundredths

2. $$\begin{array}{r} 0.021 \\ \times \quad 5 \\ \hline 0.105 \end{array}$$

21 thousandths
$\times 5$
105 thousandths

Write the exercise in short word form. Multiply. Write the product as a decimal.

1. 0.02
    × 4

2. 0.001
    × 9

3. 1.08
    × 3

4. 2.004
    × 2

5. 2.04
    × 2

6. 5 · 3.02   7. 3.01 · 6   8. 8 · 4.44   9. 4 · 2.22   10. 7.005 · 2

11. **Critical Thinking** How can you use the distributive property to find the product for exercise 10? Write an expanded expression and solve.

Work It Out!

Solve. Use the short word form or estimation to write the decimal point.

12. 8.02
     × 3

13. 0.07
     × 5

14. 2.003
     × 8

15. 21.003
     × 3

16. 21.03
     × 3

17. 2.05 · 5   18. 2.05 · 10   19. 6 · 0.003   20. 6 · 0.03   21. 6 · 0.3

22. **Patterns** What is the pattern in the products for exercises 19–21? If you continued the pattern, what would the next product be?

Write the letter of the equivalent product.

23. 6 × 4.73   a. 6 × (4 × 0.73)

24. (6 × 4) × 0.73   b. (6 × 0.7) + (6 × 0.03)

25. 6 × 0.73   c. 0

26. 3 × 6.047 × 0   d. 4.73 × 6

Problem Solving

27. **Estimation** Plennie Wingo set a world record by walking backward from California to Turkey! On her 534-day trip, she averaged 14.98 miles per day. About how far did she travel?

28. Shin Don-mok sprinted 50 meters in 17.44 seconds, running on his hands. Suppose he had wanted to beat a record of 18 seconds. Did he succeed? How much better than 18 seconds was his time?

29. Johann Hurlinger walked on his hands 10 hours a day for 55 days, averaging 1.58 miles each hour. How far did he travel? How many decimal places does the calculator show?

More Practice Set 6.5, p. 479

Problem Solving
Make a List

Pick Your Products

Your school carnival features a game called Pick Your Products. Players pick one numbered ball from each bucket. Then they find the product of the two numbers. Players win if the product is between 50 and 55.

How many pairs of winning numbers are there? Making a list can help you to find out.

Here's A Way! Use Make a List to solve the problem.

1 Understand

- You can use a tree diagram to find pairs of winning numbers.

2 Plan

- How can you organize your information to keep track of all possible combinations?

Bucket A	Bucket B	Product
8	6.7	53.6
	6.1	48.8
	5.8	46.4
9	6.7	60.3
	6.1	54.9
	5.8	52.2

3 Try It

- Complete your tree diagram to show all possible pair of numbers.

- Check the products to find winning pairs.

4 Look Back

- The pairs that win are 8 × 6.7, 9 × 5.8, and 9 × 6.1.

- How did the tree diagram help you to keep track of the pairs?

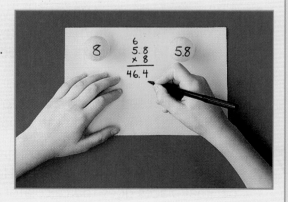

Use Make a List to help you solve the problem.

1. The Rainbow Dancers will perform at the carnival. Each dancer wears a shirt and a pair of pants. The color choices are red, blue, and green. How many different outfits are possible?

2. **Critical Thinking** How do you know when your list is complete?

Work It Out!

Use Make a List or another strategy to solve each problem. Show your work.

3. Fun House tickets cost 25¢ each. You have 3 dimes, 3 nickels, and 6 pennies. You want to buy a ticket using as many coins as possible. Which coins should you use?

4. Another game at the carnival is called Spin 6. Using this spinner, players spin 3 times and add their scores. If the total score is 6, they win. How many sets of 3 different numbers can win? (1, 2, 3 and 1, 3, 2 count as the same set.)

5. Red, yellow, and purple crepe paper streamers decorate one booth. There are 12 streamers of each color. Each streamer is 6 feet long. How many yards of crepe paper were used to decorate the booth?

6. You won three prizes playing Ping Pong Products. If you first picked an 8, then a 9, and a 9 again from bucket A, what were your corresponding picks from bucket B?

7. Is this T-shirt sign accurate? Will most combinations of 2 shirts cost less than $10?

8. You have $8.50 for the carnival. You spend half of it on games. If burgers cost $1.50 each, can you buy a burger for yourself and two friends?

Share Your Thinking

9. How does using an organized list help you keep track of information in problem 7?

10. How can the Make a List strategy help you when you make a table?

Problem Solving
Choose a Computation Method

Suppose a magazine contest asked readers to tell how many stars are in the Milky Way Galaxy. If you wanted to enter, would you use an estimate or compute an exact answer?

You Decide

- Could you actually compute the exact number of stars in the Milky Way Galaxy? Explain.
- How could you estimate the number of stars in the photo?
- How could you check your answer?

Work It Out!

Tell whether you would estimate or calculate an exact answer. Explain your decision and solve.

1. Can you buy 3 star charts with $10 if each is $3.98?

2. In 1994, the Columbia spacecraft completed a 354-hour mission. Did the mission last more than 14 days?

3. A student uses a calculator to find the product of 50.4 and 8.15. Is the answer shown reasonable?   `41.076`

4. If you work 20 hours a week for $6.15 an hour, after 4 weeks, will you have enough money to buy a $500.00 telescope?

Share Your Thinking

5. Explain whether the following phrases suggest estimation or exact calculation: About how much? Is it enough? Is it reasonable?

More Practice Set 6.7, p. 480

Midchapter Review

for Pages 194–208

Problem Solving

Solve using Make a List or another strategy. Show your work. (pages 202, 206)

1. A restaurant sells pizzas plain or with any combination of mushrooms, onions, and peppers. How many different types of pizzas are there in all?

2. Pizza sells for $1.55 per slice, and $10.95 per large pizza (8 slices). How much less does a large pizza cost than 8 separate slices?

3. A slice of pizza includes 14.2 g of cheese. How much cheese is on an 8-slice pizza?

Concepts

Write the letter of the best estimate. Explain your choices. (page 200)

4. 6.71×8
   a. between 6 and 8   b. between 8 and 671   c. between 48 and 56

5. $5 \times \$4.43$
   a. between $40 and $50   b. between $20 and $25   c. between $4 and $5

Write the multiplication expression shown by the model. (page 196)

6.

Skills

Find the product. Use squared paper if it helps. (pages 198, 202)

7.	8.	9.	10.
99.3	10	0.3	0.7
× 100	× 19.72	× 1000	× 3

Math *World*

When using money or measurements, decimals are very important. Read about the different ways decimals are used around the world.

A Big Improvement

About 1000 years ago, the Chinese government printed the world's first paper money. The bills were bigger than the front cover of this book but were easier to carry than heavy coins. The bill shown here was equal to 1000 coins. Each coin weighed about 3.5 grams. How much would 1000 coins weigh?

Spare Change

Today, most countries use a base–ten money system. In Nigeria, for example, the basic unit of money is the naira (NY ruh). This is like our dollar because it uses a base–ten system. The naira is equal to 100 kobos (KAW baws') and our American dollar is equal to 100 pennies. Nigeria also has a $\frac{1}{2}$ kobo. The United States used to have a similar coin called the half cent, which was last made in 1857. A half-cent was worth $.005. A $\frac{1}{2}$ kobo coin is worth 0.005 naira.

How much would 100 $\frac{1}{2}$ kobo coins be worth?

Try This!

EXPLORE ANCIENT UNITS OF MEASURE

The first units of length used in Egypt were based on the body parts of a pharaoh. The smallest Egyptian unit was the digit, which means *finger*. In this activity, you will create a unit of measurement like the one used in ancient Egypt.

Unit	Length (cm)
Digit (finger)	?
Palm (4 digits)	?
Cubit (7 palms)	?
Rod (100 cubits)	?

1. Copy this chart on a piece of paper.

2. Measure the width of your index finger. Record this in the chart.

3. Multiply the width of your finger by 4 to find the approximate length of a palm in centimeters. Write this in the chart.

4. Use multiplication to fill in the rest of the chart.

5. You can use your chart to estimate lengths. Look around the room. What do you see that is about 3 palms long? What do you see that is about 4 cubits long? Measure these things using your new measuring system. If you need to, estimate your answers.

Seeing Dollar Signs

Did you know the $ symbol started as the symbol for a Mexican coin? The English Americans who founded the United States based the dollar on the peso (PAY soh), a Spanish coin used in Mexico. It made sense to use the abbreviation for pesos, *ps*, for dollars, too. Over time, *ps* turned into $.

Respond

With a partner . . .
create a new coin. Draw what it will look like and tell how much it is worth.

Internet:
Houghton Mifflin Education Place
Explore the Math Center. at
http://www.eduplace.com

211

Placing the Decimal Point

How do you decide where to place the decimal point in a product? You have used two strategies:

Getting Started

What You'll Need:
▶ calculator
▶ lined paper
▶ recording sheet

- estimate by rounding up and down
- write the decimals in short word form to find the product

There is a rule you can follow when multiplying decimals. This activity will help you discover that rule.

Activity

1

Write Multiplication Sentences

- Make a chart like the one shown here, or use your recording sheet.
- Copy the multiplication sentences.
- Write five more multiplication sentences in the first column. Use decimals in your new sentences.

Multiplication Sentence	Number of decimal places in the factors	Number of decimal places in the product
7 x 6.4 = 44.8	1	
0.7 x 6.4 =	2	
.07 x 6.4 =	3	
9 x 5.22 =		
0.2 x 3.02 =		
7 x 1.25 =		

② Multiply Decimals

- Complete the chart.
- Count the number of decimal places in the factors. Write the number in column 2.
- Count the number of decimal places in the product. Write the number in column 3.
- Use a calculator to find each product.

③ Find the Rule

- Compare columns. Describe the pattern you find.
- Use the pattern to write a rule for placing the decimal point in a product.

Show What You Know!

Predict the number of decimal places in the product. Discuss and explain your answer. Then find the product with a calculator. Were your predictions correct?

1. 6.8 × 3
2. 0.068 × 3
3. 0.68 × 3
4. 9.3 × 4.6

5. 0.93 × 4.6
6. 5.4 × 72
7. 5.4 × 7.2
8. 5.4 × 0.72

9. 9.5 × 7
10. 0.54 × 65
11. 0.54 × 6.5
12. 8.4 × 25

13. **Critical Thinking** You multiply 1.5 by 1.2 and find 1.80 is the product. How would the product be shown on a calculator?

14. **Critical Thinking** Explain how you could use the mental math rule for multiplying by 100 and your rule for multiplying decimals to find 100 × 0.05.

Estimate to find the expressions that have 3 decimal places in the product.

15. 7.2 × 0.09
16. 5.8 × 0.1
17. 6.7 × 4.2
18. 0.25 × 0.3
19. 6.8 × 13.2

20. 5 × 0.009
21. 3.1 × 11.3
22. 0.2 × 0.8
23. 0.123 × 4
24. 0.123 × 8

25. **Mental Math** Choose two of the expressions in exercises 15–24 to solve using mental math. Explain your choice.

26. **Number Sense** How can you use the answer to exercise 23 to find the answer to 24?

Multiplying Decimals

1 pound of cheese costs $2.78. So, 156.4 pounds cost 156.4 × $2.78.

cheese $2.78 lb

Use What You Know

A pattern develops when multiplying a number by decimals. Below, notice how the decimal point moves to the left:

346 × 0.1 = 34.6
346 × 0.01 = 3.46
346 × 0.001 = 0.346

A group of people in Wilmington, California, set a world record by making a 2000-foot-long burrito. They used 156.4 pounds of cheese. If the cheese costs $2.78 a pound, what was the total price? Use the rule for placing the decimal point.

The number of decimal places in the product equals the sum of the number of decimal places in the factors.

Here's A Way! Find 156.4 × $2.78.

1 Multiply. Follow the same steps you follow for whole numbers.

```
      156.4
  × $2.78
    12512
    10948
    3128
  434792
```

2 Count the decimal places in the factors and move the decimal point.

```
      156.4      1 place
  × $2.78      2 places
    12512
    10948
    3128
  434.792
```

The decimal point moves 3 places to the left.

3 Round the product to the nearest cent.

$434.792

↓

$434.79

At that price, cheese for the world's longest burrito would cost $434.79.

Talk About It! Why does it make sense to round $434.792?

Other Examples Notice how the number of decimal places in the product is equal to the number of decimal places in the factors.

1.
```
   $1.03
  ×    5
   $5.15
```
2 places

2.
```
     2.4
  × 0.12
      48
      24
   0.288
```
3 places

3.
```
    0.32
  × 0.3
   0.096
```
3 places

Write the product. Round dollar amounts to the nearest cent.

1. $1.89
   × 3.4

2. 5.4
   × 82

3. 9.25
   × 17.1

4. $5.40
   × 0.3

5. $2.10
   × 0.2

6. 5.5 lb · 0.01

7. 18.4 · 0.25

8. 0.2 · 7.3

9. 1.4 · $9.20

10. **Critical Thinking** What do you notice about the size of the product when one factor is a decimal less than 1?

Work It Out!

Write the product. Round dollar amounts to the nearest cent.

11. 1.24
    × 0.1

12. $3.89
    × 0.7

13. 5.4 km
    × 4.7

14. 12.3
    × 2

15. $8.92 · 1.2

16. 4.5 L · 67

17. 4.5 L · 0.67

18. 0.5 · 12.8

19. 1.5 × 4.05

20. $12.99 × 0.4

21. 6.24 × 0.01g

22. 4.2 × $2.65

23. **Mental Math** Which exercises did you solve using mental math? Explain.

Problem Solving   Using Data

24. **Estimation** If beans cost $.69 a pound, would $450 be enough to buy beans for the whole burrito?

25. If tortillas cost $.02 each and there are 21 tortillas in one pound, how much would tortillas for the whole burrito cost?

26. **Create Your Own** What giant food would you make? Create 2 problems that can be solved by multiplying decimals.

World's Longest Burrito
2,012.9 feet long

| 738.5 lb of tortillas |
| 761.3 lb of refried beans |
| 156.4 lb of cheese |
| 580.8 lb of other ingredients |

Total weight
2,237 lb

Mixed Review

Evaluate the expressions when $s = 3$; $s = 6$.

27. $18 \div s$

28. $36 \div s$

29. $11 \cdot s$

30. $20 \cdot s$

More Practice Set 6.9, p. 480

Math Journal

How is multiplying decimals the same as multiplying whole numbers? How is it different?

Problem Solving
Using Strategies

You can read more about moths in the pages of *Scienceland.*

Entomologists, scientists who study insects, know that moths are far more common than butterflies. However, because butterflies are active during the day, you probably see them more often than moths, which are active at night.

Problem Solving Process
- ✓ Understand
- ✓ Plan
- ✓ Try It
- ✓ Look Back

Choose a Strategy You Have Learned
- ✓ Make a Table
- ✓ Act It Out
- ✓ Guess and Check
- ✓ Look for a Pattern
- ✓ Work Backward
- ✓ Make a List
- Work a Simpler Problem
- Draw a Picture
- Write an Equation

Some entomologists study these kinds of moths: atlas moth, emperor moth, hercules moth, polyphemus moth, and silkworm moth.

The five different moths have these wingspreads: 13.5 cm, 12 cm, 28 cm, 30.5 cm, and 15 cm. Can you use the following clues to match each kind of moth with its wingspread?

The emperor moth has the smallest wingspread. The hercules moth has a wingspread greater than 25 cm, but does not have the largest wingspread. The silkworm moth has a larger wingspread than the polyphemus moth, but a smaller wingspread than the atlas moth.

- What is the question you have to answer?
- What information do you know about moths?
- How can you show the information?
- Explain a strategy that can help you to solve this problem. Then solve.

Work It Out!

Use any strategy to solve each problem. Show your work.

1. The emperor moth can have a 4.7 in. wingspread. You want to create a display with one row of 5 life-sized models of emperor moths. There is 0.5 in. of space between each moth and at the edges of the display. What is the length of the display case?

4.7   0.5

2. The swallowtail butterfly's wingspread can range from 2.5 to 3.5 in. If an entomologist displays 8 swallowtails with wingtips touching, what is the greatest possible length of the display? the shortest length?

3. Cicadas are insects that grow underground. Some types stay underground for 17 years. Suppose one group of 17-year cicadas hatched in 1970 and another group hatched in 1987. If this pattern continues, what are the next 3 years you would expect them to hatch?

4. The hawk moth can fly up to 53 km each hour. It moves its wings in a figure 8. At this rate, would it take a hawk moth more or less than 3 hours to fly 200 km?

5. During the summer, monarch butterflies live in Canada and the northern United States. In winter, they fly south to Mexico. They fly about 160 km in one day, 320 km in two days, and 480 km in 3 days. About how far do they fly in 8 days?

6. Caterpillars have 16 legs. After changing into butterflies, they have 6 legs. If an entomologist is working with caterpillars and butterflies and sees 9 heads and 104 legs, how many of each type are there? Is more than one answer possible?

7. An entomologist has 3 moths, 3 butterflies, and 3 cicadas. She wants to put 3 insects in a display case. How many combinations can she display?

Share Your Thinking

8. How did making a list help you to solve problem 7?

9. Which problems did you solve using Draw A Picture? Justify your answer.

Problem Solving
Using Strategies

On May 25, 1986, more than 5 million people joined hands for a record-breaking charity event called Hands Across America. The chain stretched from New York City to the wharf of the Queen Mary in Long Beach, California.

New York, NY

Long Beach, CA

Problem Solving Process
✓ Understand
✓ Plan
✓ Try It
✓ Look Back

Choose a Strategy You Have Learned

✓ Make a Table
✓ Act it Out
✓ Guess and Check
✓ Look for a Pattern
✓ Work Backward
✓ Make a List
  Work a Simpler Problem
  Draw a Picture
  Write an Equation

Participants in the chain were asked to contribute $10 to $35 each. Suppose a family of 4 contributed $100. Each person contributed an amount that was a multiple of $5.

- Dad paid $20.
- Mom paid $35.
- The son paid twice as much as the daughter. How much did the son pay?
- What is the question you have to answer?
- What was the total amount contributed?
- How much did the parents contribute?
- How can you organize the information?
- How can you find out how much money each child donated?
- What strategy did you use? Justify your strategy.

Use any strategy to solve each problem. Show your work.

1. An average adult arm span is 1.69 meters. Suppose it takes 178 people to form a chain along the wharf of the Queen Mary in Long Beach, California. About how long is the wharf?

2. Complete the chart using these clues:

   • More people participated in Arizona than in Tennessee.

   • More people participated in Arkansas than in New Mexico.

   • Twice as many people joined hands in New Jersey as in Tennessee.

Hands Across America in Five States

State	Number of Participants
?	100,000
New Mexico	238,000
?	150,000
?	200,000
?	240,000

3. The Hands Across America chain stretched across 16 states and 550 cities. On average, about how many cities did the chain pass through in each state? Is this a reasonable answer?

4. If every one of the 5 million participants contributed $10, how much money was raised? How much was raised if participants gave an average contribution of $22.50?

5. At about 3:15 P.M. eastern daylight time, the chain broke apart. Americans across the country had held hands and sung hopeful songs for 900 seconds. At what time did the chain begin in California? (California is in the Pacific time zone, which is 3 hours earlier than eastern daylight time.)

6. What do you think is the average arm span for a fifth grader? How many fifth graders would it take to form a chain 100 miles long?

what is the average fifth-grader's arm span?

7. How did acting it out help you solve problem 6?

Chapter 6 Test

for Pages 194–219

Test-Taking Tips
Use estimation to help you place the decimal in the product. Round factors to estimate.

Problem Solving

Solve. Show your work. (pages 202, 206, 208, 216, 218)

1. A store sells clear glass marbles with two different colors swirled inside. The colors can be purple, red, blue, green, or yellow. How many different color combinations are there?

2. An artist creates clay beads that can be baked in the oven. Here is one bead: How long is a bracelet that uses 16 of these clay beads?

1.2cm

3. If 3 oz of clay is enough to make 27 beads, will 12 oz be enough to make 100 beads?

2.5cm
1.5cm

4. A string of 4 larger beads is 9.6 cm long. How long is a string of 20?

5. The artist uses 20 of these beads to make a necklace 40 cm long. He used two colors in an alternating pattern. Which colors did he use?

1.8cm

6. A necklace follows this pattern: red, black, yellow, black. It uses 40 beads. How long is the necklace?

Concepts

Estimate the product. Write a, b, c, or d. Explain how you placed the decimal point. (pages 212, 214)

7. 3.2×4.7 a. 1504   b. 150.4   c. 15.04   d. 1.504

8. 4.05×8.1 a. 3.2805   b. 32.805   c. 328.05   d. 3280.5

9. 7.25×1.6 a. 11.6   b. 116   c. 1.16   d. 0.116

Complete each estimate. Explain. (pages 200, 202)

10. 4.327×6 ➡ between 24 and ▪

11. 8×9.407 ➡ between ▪ and ▪

Multiply. Show your work. (pages 212, 214)

12.	6.4	13.	8.21	14.	9.08	15.	32	16.	8.22
	× 0.1		× 5.4		× 4.5		× 0.17		× 2.2

17.	$21.70	18.	7.36	19.	0.98	20.	$47.50
	× 32.4		× 7.3		× 5.4		× 0.4

Write the letter of the correct product. (pages 204, 212, 214)

21. 32 × 4.5   a. 1.44

22. 3.2 × 4.5   b. 0.144

23. 0.32 × 4.5   c. 1440

24. 0.32 × 0.45   d. 144

25. 32 × 45   e. 14.4

Write the letters of the equivalent multiplication expressions in each set.
(pages 212, 214)

26. a. 2.4 × 4.8   b. 2.8 × 4.2   c. 8.8 × 4.4   d. 1.2 × 9.6

27. a. 3.21 × 3   b. 18.72 × 5   c. 7.8 × 1.2   d. 0.78 × 12

 Performance Task

(pages 202, 204, 212, 214)

Draw a map of a town or city area, either a place you know or a place you create. Label eight or more locations. Mark the distance between locations. Estimate the mileage. Assume that each long city block is about 0.2 mile.

• Use your map to plan the route of a 4-mile walk.

• Mark your starting place.

• List the places you would pass on the walk.

• Explain how you know your route is about 4 miles long.

Keep In Mind . . .
Your work will be evaluated on the following:
☑ Clearly labeled map
☑ Plan for 4-mile walk
☑ Locations passed
☑ Explanation of calculations

Cumulative Review

Add and Subtract Decimals (Chapter 1)
Add and subtract: 15.61 and 11.957

Here's A Way!

Line up the decimal points.

$$
\begin{array}{r}
\scriptstyle 1 \\
15.610 \\
+\ 11.957 \\
\hline
27.567
\end{array}
\qquad
\begin{array}{r}
\scriptstyle 15\ 10 \\
\scriptstyle 4\ 16\ 11\ 10 \\
15.6\,1\,0 \\
-\ 11.9\,5\,7 \\
\hline
3.6\,5\,3
\end{array}
$$

Write the answer.

1. $56.1 - 9.513$ 2. $127.12 + 0.987$

3. $40 - 1.85$ 4. $75.64 + 723.097$

5. $\begin{array}{r} 34.6 \\ +\ 2.904 \\ \hline \end{array}$ 6. $\begin{array}{r} 871 \\ -\ 20.642 \\ \hline \end{array}$

7. Make up a decimal subtraction problem in which you must regroup 7 tenths as 6 tenths and 10 hundredths.

Estimating Quotients (Chapter 3)
Estimate $367 \div 7$ using compatible numbers.

Here's A Way!

Choose numbers close to 367 that are easy to divide by 7.

$$7)\overline{350} \qquad 7)\overline{420}$$

Divide:
$350 \div 7 = 50 \qquad 420 \div 7 = 60$
$367 \div 7$ is between 50 and 60.

Give a high and low estimate for each.

8. $4)\overline{27,325}$ 9. $6)\overline{578}$

10. $9)\overline{7124}$ 11. $8)\overline{39,541}$

12. $478 \div 6$ 13. $7412 \div 9$

14. $12,589 \div 5$ 15. $4197 \div 7$

16. Explain how you choose compatible numbers when estimating a quotient.

Divisibility Rules for 4, 6, and 9
(Chapter 3)
Is 288 divisible by 4, 6, or 9?

Here's A Way!

A number is divisible by 4 if the number in the ones and tens place is divisible by 4,
by 6 if it is divisible by 2 and 3,
by 9 if the sum of its digits is divisible by 9.
288 is divisible by 4, 6, and 9.

Tell whether the following numbers are divisible by 4, 6, or 9.

17. 327   18. 9642

19. 13,516   20. 5276

21. 125,348   22. 981

23. Write a 4-digit number that is divisible by 6 and 9, but not by 4.

24. Write a 3-digit number that is divisible by 4 and 6, but not by 9.

Elapsed Time (Chapter 5)

How much time will pass from 5:30 P.M. to 9:15 P.M.?

Here's A Way!

Subtract as hours and minutes. First, change hours to minutes.

9 h 15 min	➡	8 h 75 min
− 5 h 30 min		− 5 h 30 min
		3 h 45 min

Find how much time will pass.

25. from noon to 4:15 P.M.

26. from 3:25 P.M. to 6:00 P.M.

27. from 7:50 A.M. to 11:20 A.M.

28. from 11:45 A.M. to 2:15 P.M.

29. How did you calculate in exercises 25 and 28?

Multiplying Decimals by 10, 100, and 1000 (Chapter 6)

Multiply 4.52 × 100.

Here's A Way!

Count the zeros in 100: 2 zeros. Multiply the non-zero digits. Write the zeros counted at the end of the product: **4.52 × 1 = 4.5200**
For every zero, move the decimal in the product one place to the right:

452.00   100 × 4.52 = 452

Use mental math to find the product.

30.	34.72 × 10	31.	6.71 × 10

32. 0.512 × 1000   33. 12,452.7 × 100

34. How can you use mental math to find 50 × 4.734 × 2?

35. Where would you place the decimal point in 253 to make the answer correct?

$$1000 \times 253 = 2530$$

Problem Solving

Problem Solving Process
- ✓ Understand
- ✓ Plan
- ✓ Try It
- ✓ Look Back

Choose a Strategy You Have Learned
- ✓ Make a Table
- ✓ Act It Out
- ✓ Guess and Check
- ✓ Look for a Pattern
- ✓ Work Backward
- ✓ Make a List
-   Work a Simpler Problem
-   Draw a Picture
-   Write an Equation

Choose one of the strategies you have learned to solve these problems. Show your work.

36. A supermarket is having a sale. For every 4 cans of tuna you buy, you get 1 can free. Each can costs $1.25. If you have $16 to spend, how many cans can you buy?

37. A girl read 24 pages of her book in one night. The second night she read 29 pages, the third night she read 35 pages, and the fourth night she read 42 pages. If she continues this pattern, how many days will it take her to read the 308-page book?

The Space Mission Weights

Science Connection | **With Your Group**

Objects can weigh more or less on other planets because the pull of gravity is greater or less than on Earth. One of the things scientists consider when setting the spacecraft's trajectory, or flight path, is the weight of the ship. If the weight is not correctly determined, the spacecraft can be pulled off course.

Your group will compute the weight of equipment and crew members on other planets. Then, you will create flight teams for four planets.

Planet	Weight Factor	Research Equipment	Individual Weights					
			1	2	3	4	5	6
Earth	1.00	650 pounds	210	187	163	145	132	120
Mercury	0.38	247 pounds						
Venus	0.91	591.5 pounds						
Mars	0.38	247 pounds						
Jupiter	2.54							
Saturn	1.07							
Uranus	0.88							
Neptune	1.14							
Pluto	0.05							

1

Plan It

- Create a table like the one pictured.
- To compute the weight of the equipment and crew members for other planets, multiply the weight factor by the Earth weight. Divide the work among your group.

2

Put It Together

- Create flight crews for Venus, Mars, Neptune, and Pluto. Each crew will have four members. Each member must be included on at least two flight teams. Use the weights listed on the chart.
- The total weight of each crew cannot be more than the research equipment weight for that planet.
- Record each attempt to create teams.

Calculator The space shuttle weighs 4,491,000 pounds at liftoff. How much would it weigh on Jupiter?

	Earth	Venus	M
equipment	650	591.5	
crew member 2	187		
crew member 3	132		
crew			

3

Wrap It Up

- Make a table showing the four flight teams. Include the total weight for equipment and crew members.
- Write a paragraph explaining your failed attempts.

4

Discuss Your Results

- Did you meet the objectives listed in Keep In Mind?
- How are your teams different from teams created by other groups? How are they the same?

Internet

> Visit the **Math Center** at **Houghton Mifflin Education Place.**
http://www.eduplace.com

Math Power

Use What You Know

- how to use a calculator

1.2 > 0.98

2.2 < 2.25

3.40 = 3.4

- how to order decimals

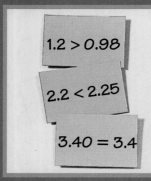

1.5 × 8 = 12
2.34 × 6 = 14.04
3.5 × 4 = 14

- how to multiply decimals

Division of Decimals

Try This!

How would you find how much food to buy for a large group of people? Use a calculator and what you know about multiplying decimals to find out.

What You'll Need

calculator, paper, pencil, food containers

1

Read the labels on 5 containers of food. Find how many ounces are in each container. Use amounts that have decimals. Make a chart that lists the type of food and the number of ounces in each container.

NET WT 11 OZ (312g)

Now, read the nutrition labels and find how many servings are in each container of food. Make a third column in your chart for this number.

Type of Food	Amount in Container	Number of Servings in Container	Ounces per Serving
Frozen Pizza	21.5 ounces	4	5.38 ounces
Bagels	17.1 ounces	6	2.85 ounces
Dry Potato Mix	13.3 ounces	17	0.78 ounces
Macaroni and Cheese	7.25 ounces	3	2.42 ounces
Crackers	3.3 ounces	8	0.66 ounces

Use a calculator to find how many ounces make one serving. Divide the amount in the container by the number of servings. Round to the nearest hundredth. Add this number to your chart. Make a grocery list that shows how many ounces you would need for 16 servings of each item.

How did you find how much you would need of each item?

Which container of food gives the smallest servings?

Ready to Go!

227

Dividing by a Whole Number

You can draw hundredths squares to model decimals. A 10 by 10 square represents 1. Each shaded small square represents one hundredth of the whole square, or 0.01.

Ten shaded small squares represent ten hundredths, or one tenth of the whole square. This is written as 0.1.

The diagram to the right represents ten hundredths or one tenth.

How can you use models to find $2.6 \div 2$?

Activity

1

Draw a model of 2.6 on squared paper.

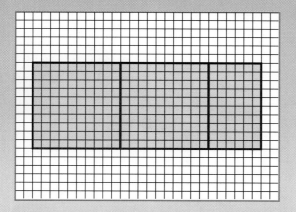

a. How many whole hundredths squares will you draw?

b. How many extra tenths will you draw?

2

Look at the shape of the model. Erase the pencil lines inside your model.

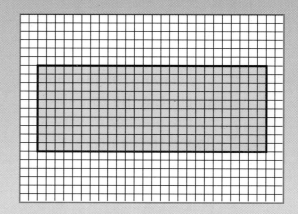

Your model shows 26 tenths.

3

Now draw a vertical line dividing 26 tenths into two equal parts to represent 26 ÷ 2.

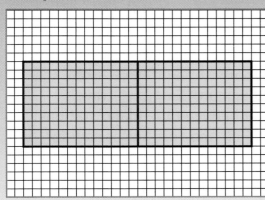

a. How many tenths are in each part?

b. What decimal does each part represent?

c. Write a division sentence to describe dividing 26 tenths into two equal parts.

Show What You Know!

Use hundredth squares. Draw a model to find the quotient.

1. 1.6 ÷ 2   2. 1.8 ÷ 3   3. 2.4 ÷ 5   4. 1.5 ÷ 6

5. 1.8 ÷ 2   6. 2.8 ÷ 2   7. 1.4 ÷ 2   8. 3.6 ÷ 3

9. **Critical Thinking** How is 2.7 ÷ 3 similar to 27 ÷ 3? How is it different?

10. **Critical Thinking** How does knowing how to divide whole numbers help you divide decimals?

11. **Create Your Own** Write a problem about dividing 5.6 into 8 equal parts. Solve the problem and write a division sentence to show the answer.

12. **Patterns** Use a calculator to help you find the pattern in each row. Find the quotients in a row and describe the pattern.
   a. 450 ÷ 5   b. 45 ÷ 5   c. 4.5 ÷ 5   d. 0.45 ÷ 5
   e. 320 ÷ 4   f. 32 ÷ 4   g. 3.2 ÷ 4   h. 0.32 ÷ 4

Mental Math: Dividing by 10, 100, and 1000

In the 1850s, it might have taken a covered wagon 10 days to travel 201.8 mi between the Idaho stations of Fort Hall and Fort Boise. How far could a wagon travel in one day?

You need to divide to find the answer. Patterns can help you divide decimals. Notice how the decimal point is moved in this pattern:

$$201.8 \div 10 = 20.18$$
$$201.8 \div 100 = 2.018$$
$$201.8 \div 1000 = 0.2018$$

You can also use mental math to find the answer.

Here's A Way!   Find 201.8 ÷ 10.

1 Count the number of zeros in the whole-number divisor.

$$201.8 \div 10$$

one zero

2 Divide with the appropriate non-zero digits.

$$201.8 \div 10$$

Think: 201.8 ÷ 1 = 201.8

3 For every zero counted in the whole-number divisor, move the decimal point one place to the left.

$$201.8 \longrightarrow 20.18$$

A wagon could travel about 20.18 miles each day. Is your answer reasonable? Explain.

Talk About It!   What happens to the decimal point when you divide a number by 10?

Other Examples   Mental math can help you find other quotients.

1. $1.45 \div 100 = 0.0145$ ← Decimal point moved two places to the left.

two zeros

2. $345 \div 1000 = 0.345$ ← Decimal point moved three places to the left.

three zeros

Show What You Know!

Use mental math to divide.

1. 27.2 ÷ 10   2. 7384 ÷ 10   3. 8229 ÷ 1000   4. 204 ÷ 100   5. 324 ÷ 100

6. 67.52 ÷ 10   7. 8.1 ÷ 100   8. 555 ÷ 100   9. 800 ÷ 1000   10. 1 ÷ 100

11. **Critical Thinking** When you divide decimals by 10, why do you move the decimal point to the left and not to the right?

Work It Out!

Use mental math to divide.

12. 5.4 ÷ 10   13. 4.1 ÷ 100   14. 7.4 ÷ 10   15. 6.7 ÷ 10

16. 0.28 ÷ 100   17. 0.87 ÷ 10   18. 0.87 ÷ 100   19. 19.4 ÷ 100

20. 97.132 ÷ 100   21. 65 ÷ 10   22. 6500 ÷ 1000   23. 0.65 ÷ 10

24. 6.5 ÷ 10   25. 7.7 ÷ 100   26. 13.3 ÷ 10   27. 13.3 ÷ 100

28. **Number Sense** How can you use the quotient of exercise 26 to find the quotient of exercise 27?

29. **Patterns** Which two exercises above have the same answer? Look for a pattern. Write two more expressions that have the same answer.

Problem Solving

30. In 1860, a rider with the Pony Express could travel about 2896.8 km in 10 days. About how far could a rider travel in 1 day?

31. Each rail of the North American transcontinental railroad was held in place by ten spikes. There were 400 rails in 1 mile. How many spikes were in each mile?

32. Railroad trackage increased from 35,000 miles in 1865 to 254,000 miles in 1916. About how many times more track was this?

Math Journal

How is dividing decimals by 10, 100, and 1000 similar to dividing whole numbers by 10, 100, and 1000? How is it different?

Equivalent Metric Measures

Today, movie platters are used in theaters instead of reels. A movie platter can hold about 7400 m of film. Your friend told you that a full-length movie uses about 2.5 km of film. Will one platter hold an entire movie?

You need to compare 7400 m and 2.5 km to solve the problem. First, write equivalent measures.

Movie Platters

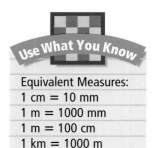

Use What You Know

Equivalent Measures:
1 cm = 10 mm
1 m = 1000 mm
1 m = 100 cm
1 km = 1000 m

Here's A Way! Write equivalent measures, then compare.

You can multiply or divide to find equivalent measures.

Write kilometers as meters.

1 Multiply to write the larger unit as a smaller one.

> Remember that 1 km = 1000 m. So multiply the number of kilometers by 1000 to find the number of meters.

2.5 km = ■ m

2.5 km = (2.5 × 1000) m
2.5 km = 2500 m

2 Compare the two numbers.

2500 m < 7400 m

Write meters as kilometers.

1 Divide to write the smaller unit as a larger one.

> Remember that 1000 m = 1 km. So you can divide the number of meters by 1000 to find the number of kilometers.

7400 m = ■ km

7400 m = (7400 ÷ 1000) km
7400 m = 7.4 km

2 Compare the two numbers.

2.5 km < 7.4 km

Since 2.5 km is less than 7400 m, a platter can hold all the film.

Talk About It! When finding an equivalent measure, how do you decide whether to multiply or divide? Explain.

Equivalent Measures

Length
1000 millimeters (mm) = 1 meter (m)
100 centimeters (cm) = 1 meter (m)
10 decimeters (dm) = 1 meter (m)

Capacity
1000 milliliters (mL) = 1 liter (L)
1 milliliter (mL) = 1 cubic centimeter (cm³)

Mass
1000 milligrams (mg) = 1 gram (g)
1000 grams (g) = 1 kilogram (kg)

Write the missing number.

1. 10 cm = ■ mm
2. 0.1 cm = ■ mm

3. 3.8 cm = ■ mm
4. 6 m = ■ cm

5. 0.1 m = ■ cm
6. 3.8 m = ■ cm

7. 5000 mm = ■ m
8. 100 mm = ■ m

Complete. Write >, <, or =.

9. 200 cm ● 2000 mm
10. 18 km ● 180,000 m
11. 7.28 m ● 728 mm

12. **Critical Thinking** How is writing centimeters as meters like writing cents as dollars?

Work It Out!

Write the letter of the equivalent measure.

13. 6.724 m
    a. 6724 cm
    b. 67.24 cm
    c. 672.4 cm

14. 27 mm
    a. 270 m
    b. 0.27 m
    c. 0.027 m

15. 500 cm
    a. 5000 mm
    b. 50 mm
    c. 5 mm

Write the missing number.

16. 8.91 m = ■ cm
17. 248 mm = ■ m
18. 6.6 km = ■ m

19. 27 km = ■ m
20. 0.0092 m = ■ mm
21. 8.79 cm = ■ mm

Complete. Write >, <, or =.

22. 848 mm ● 72.4 cm
23. 2.045 m ● 2545 mm
24. 19.5 cm ● 1 m

25. **Number Sense** If you write 12 meters as millimeters, will the number of millimeters be greater or less than 12? Explain.

26. **Problem Solving** Movie film today is usually 35 mm wide. Some theaters use special film that is 7 cm wide. Is the special film wider or narrower than the standard size?

Mixed Review Write the mean, median, and range for each set.

27. 16, 12, 16, 18, 18
28. 11, 25, 24, 10, 15
29. 2, 8, 50, 42, 63

More Practice Set 7.3, p. 481

Estimating with Money

Use What You Know

Compatible numbers are numbers that are easy to use with mental math. Use compatible numbers in place of actual numbers to estimate.

In 1905, about how much did one bottle of grape juice cost?

You can use compatible numbers to help you to find the cost.

$1.51 for 6 bottles

Here's A Way!   Estimate $1.51 ÷ 6.

① Write the cost as cents.

$1.51 ÷ 6

151¢ ÷ 6

$1.00 = 100¢

② Find compatible numbers that are close to the numbers you are dividing.

120¢ ÷ 6

151¢ ÷ 6

180¢ ÷ 6

③ Divide to estimate the quotient.

120¢ ÷ 6 = 20¢

180¢ ÷ 6 = 30¢

So, one bottle of juice costs between 20¢ and 30¢.

Talk About It!   Using only 120 to estimate, how do you know that the actual answer is greater than 20¢?

Tell what compatible numbers you would use to estimate. Then estimate the quotient.

1. 4)$1.28
2. $19.98 ÷ 4
3. $23.15 ÷ 5
4. $28.05 ÷ 6
5. 8)$.51

6. 7)$3.27
7. $29.10 ÷ 5
8. $3.19 ÷ 3
9. 9)$30.55
10. $5.99 ÷ 7

11. **Critical Thinking** Do you think the actual quotient in exercise 10 is greater than or less than 80 cents? Explain.

Work It Out!

Write the letter of the most reasonable estimate.

12. $4.13 ÷ 6
 a. $.07   b. $.70   c. $7.00

13. $.78 ÷ 4
 a. $.02   b. $.20   c. $2.00

14. $215.25 ÷ 5
 a. $.40   b. $4.00   c. $40.00

15. $2.15 ÷ 7
 a. $.03   b. $.30   c. $3.00

Tell what compatible numbers you use to estimate. Then estimate the quotient.

16. 4)$22.60
17. $3.99 ÷ 3
18. 2)$9.01
19. 7)$5.60

20. 8)$650
21. $5.82 ÷ 3
22. 5)$4.08
23. 4)$1.75

24. $43.89 ÷ 6
25. 7)$3.27
26. $43.05 ÷ 9
27. 3)$2.84

Problem Solving   Using Data

Use the chart and compatible numbers to answer.

28. About how much did three dozen eggs cost in Los Angeles in 1905?

29. About how much did one egg cost in New York City in 1995?

30. In which city did the price of eggs increase the most between 1905 and 1995?

31. In what city and in what year did eggs cost about $.07 each?

Price of one dozen eggs

Year	New York, New York	Denver, Colorado	Los Angeles, California
1905	$0.32	$0.26	$0.31
1995	$1.41	$0.82	$1.67

More Practice Set 7.4, p. 481

Problem Solving
Is the Answer Reasonable?

Suppose you are going on a canoe trip. There are 63 campers in all on your trip. Each canoe can hold four people. How many canoes will you need? You will need to use the remainder to help you find the answer.

Is the Answer Reasonable?

Ask Yourself:

Did I answer the question?

Did I calculate correctly?

Is the answer labeled with the right units?

Does my answer need to be rounded to a whole number to make sense?

You Decide

- What does the remainder stand for? Should you write the remainder as a whole number or a fraction?
- How can you use the remainder to solve the problem?
- How many canoes do you need in all?

Work It Out!

Describe how to use the remainder to help solve each problem.

1. A group of 8 campers brought a package of 20 energy bars on their canoe trip. They shared all the bars equally. How many energy bars did each person get?

2. There are 43 people traveling by car to a campsite. If each car will hold 5 people, how many cars will they need?

3. Trail maps cost $3. You have $20. How many maps can you buy?

 4. **Create Your Own** Write a problem about camping that uses the remainder to answer the problem. Solve your problem, then trade with a classmate.

Share Your Thinking

5. What are the different ways you can use a remainder? How do you decide?

Midchapter Review

for Pages 226–236

for Pages 226–236

Problem Solving

Solve. Show your work. (page 236)

1. Suppose you can read 4 books in a week and you want to read 50 books. How many weeks would it take to read all 50?

2. A school auditorium has 228 seats with 9 seats in each row, except for one longer row. How many seats are in the long row?

Use data from the chart to solve. (pages 228, 234)

3. A student bought $2\frac{1}{2}$-inch letters to sew onto a baseball jacket. She spent $6.32. How many letters did she buy?

4. Another student bought 7 iron-on letters. He spent $8.33. What size letters did he buy?

Iron-On Letter Prices	
1 inch	$ .49 each
2 $\frac{1}{2}$ inch	$ .79 each
4 inch	$ 1.19 each

Concepts

Write the letter of the best answer. Explain your choices. (page 230)

5. 24.76 ÷ 100   a. 2.476   b. 0.2476   c. 247.6   d. 2,476,200

6. 85.2 ÷ 10   a. 852   b. 8520   c. 8.52   d. 0.852

Skills

Divide. Use a model when it helps. (page 228)

7. $2\overline{)2.5}$ 8. $3\overline{)6.3}$ 9. $4\overline{)8.8}$ 10. $5\overline{)0.5}$

Use mental math to divide. (page 230)

11. 7.1 ÷ 10   12. 56.8 ÷ 100   13. 8.07 ÷ 10   14. 4.3 ÷ 1000

Write the letter of the correct equivalent measure. (page 232)

15. 1.5 cm   a. 0.0015 km

16. 1.5 km   b. 0.015 m

17. 1.5 m   c. 1500 m

Math World

Read about different ways decimals are used

around the world. Then, make some metric

measurements of things in your classroom.

At age 30, Fanny (right), won four gold medals and held seven world track records.

Golden Seconds

In the Olympic games, officials use decimals when timing races to be more accurate. In the 1948 Summer Olympics, Francina "Fanny" Blankers-Koen, from the Netherlands, won the gold medal in the first 200-meter run for women. She finished in 24.4 seconds, which was 0.7 seconds faster than the second-place runner. In the 200-meter run, how many meters did she run per second?

An Early Decimal System

It is believed that the Chinese developed one of the earliest decimal systems. They used a system of numbers to represent calculations done with wooden sticks. The sticks were used on a counting board that looked like a checkerboard. It had columns for 1000, 100, 10, 1, 0.1, 0.01, and so on.

Try This! Metric Estimations

The centimeter, kilometer, and millimeter are probably the most commonly used metric measurements. The decimeter (DEHS uh meet er), which is $\frac{1}{10}$ of a meter, is rarely used.

Find the length in decimeters of items in your classroom. Why do you think the decimeter is not often used?

1 Measure your desk in millimeters. Change millimeters to centimeters by dividing by 10.

2 Change centimeters to decimeters by dividing by 10 again. Change decimeters to meters by dividing by 10 again.

3 Make a table and list the measurements of the desk and four more items in the classroom. Include in the table measurements in millimeters, centimeters, decimeters, and meters.

4 One hectometer is 100 meters. If you lined your desks up end to end, how many desks would you need to measure about one hectometer?

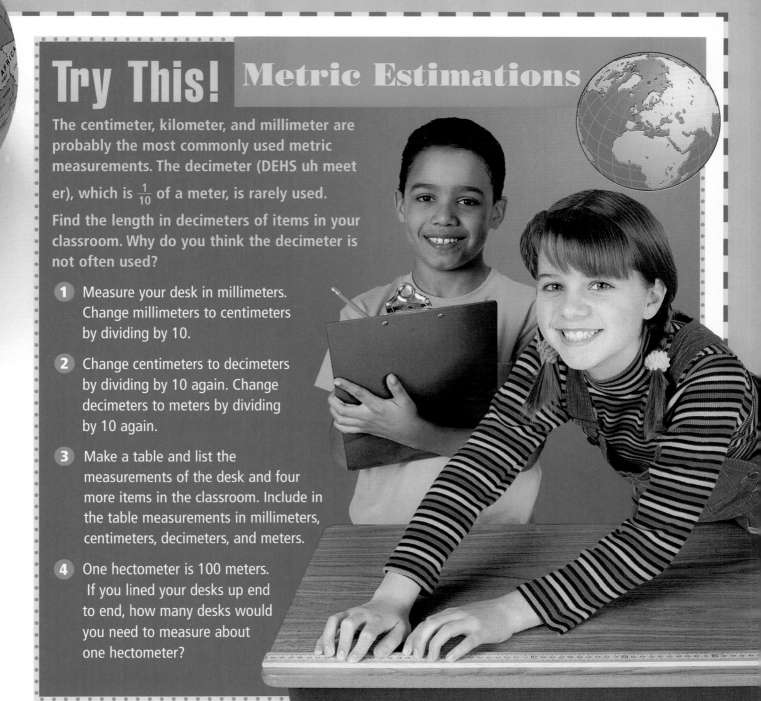

The Making of Metric

In the 1700s, the government of France asked the French Academy of Sciences to come up with a system of measurement that could be used easily by all people. This system, known as the metric system, established the meter as the basic unit of length.

Respond

With a partner...
create your own system of measurement. Name the different units.

Internet:
Houghton Mifflin Education Place
Explore the Math Center at
http://www.eduplace.com

239

LESSON 6

Placing the Decimal Point

Portobelo

PANAMA

One of the heaviest rainfalls in history occurred in 1911 in Portobelo, Panama. In just five minutes, 2.5 in. of rain fell. About how much rain fell each minute?

You can model dividing 2.5 by 5 by shading squares.

2.5   2.5 ÷ 5

The models show you that $2.5 \div 5 = 0.5$.
So, about 0.5 in. of rain fell each minute.

You can also divide decimals without using models.

Here's A Way! **Find 2.5 ÷ 5.**

① Estimate to place the decimal point in the quotient.

$$5)\overline{2.5}$$

If you divide 2.5 into 5 parts, each part will be less than 1.

So, about 0.5 in. of rain fell each minute.

② Divide as you would with whole numbers.

Write the decimal point in the quotient above the decimal point in the dividend.

$$\begin{array}{r} .5 \\ 5)\overline{2.5} \\ -2\ 5 \\ \hline 0\ 0 \end{array}$$

Talk About It! How can your estimate help you decide if your answer is reasonable?

Other Examples Notice where the decimal point is placed in the quotient. Look for zeros in the quotients, too.

a.
$$\begin{array}{r} 2.06 \\ 4)\overline{8.24} \\ -8 \\ \hline 24 \\ -24 \\ \hline 0 \end{array}$$

b.
$$\begin{array}{r} 1.04 \\ 4)\overline{4.16} \\ -4 \\ \hline 16 \\ -16 \\ \hline 0 \end{array}$$

c.
$$\begin{array}{r} 0.38 \\ 3)\overline{1.14} \\ -9 \\ \hline 24 \\ -24 \\ \hline 0 \end{array}$$

Write the quotient. Estimate to place the decimal point.

1. 5)5.05   2. 3)52.2   3. 7)$28.49   4. 8)6.08   5. 2)33.2   6. 3)3.21

7. **Critical Thinking** What do you know about the quotient if the divisor is greater than the dividend?

Work It Out!

Write the quotient. Estimate or think about a related multiplication sentence to place the decimal point.

8. 2)6.08   9. 8)9.84   10. 4)1.008   11. 6)67.8   12. 9)76.05   13. 3)0.84

14. 7)35.14   15. 5)0.10   16. 3)0.09   17. 7)29.05   18. 6)24.6   19. 4)28.16

20. 12.6 ÷ 3   21. 12.6 ÷ 6   22. 10.8 ÷ 9   23. 3.48 ÷ 6   24. 1.26 ÷ 9   25. 1.8 ÷ 2

26. **Patterns** Find the quotients. Describe the pattern.
    a. 224 ÷ 4 = ▪   b. 22.4 ÷ 4 = ▪   c. 2.24 ÷ 4 = ▪   d. 0.224 ÷ 4 = ▪

Problem Solving   Using Data

Use the chart to answer.

27. Did more than an inch of rain fall each minute during the storm on August 1, 1977 in Muduocaidang, China?

28. Which location had a rainfall that lasted for exactly 9 hours?

29. About how many inches of rain fell each hour during the storm in Muduocaidang, China?

30. How much more rain fell in Reunion Island than in the Texas rainfall?

Some Record-Breaking Rainfall

Duration	Amount in Inches	Date	Place
130 min	19	May 31, 1935	D'Hanis, Texas
540 min	42.79	February 28, 1964	Belouve, Reunion Island, Indian Ocean
600 min	55.12	August 1, 1977	Muduocaidang, China

Mixed Review

Tell which numbers are prime or composite.

31. 3   32. 5   33. 9   34. 31

More Practice Set 7.6, p. 482

Decimal Quotients

You know that 4 quarters equal 1 dollar. You can use a fraction to represent this fact: a quarter is $\frac{1}{4}$ of a dollar.

How can you use a decimal to represent the value of a quarter?

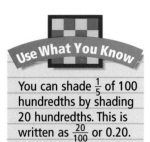

Use What You Know

You can shade $\frac{1}{5}$ of 100 hundredths by shading 20 hundredths. This is written as $\frac{20}{100}$ or 0.20.

Here's A Way!   **Find 1 ÷ 4.**

1 Divide the numbers. Follow the same steps you follow for whole numbers.

$$
\begin{array}{r}
25 \\
4\overline{)1.00} \\
-8 \\
\hline
20 \\
-20 \\
\hline
0
\end{array}
$$

Write an equivalent decimal for the dividend.
1 = 100 hundredths

2 Estimate to place the decimal point.

25 ➡ .25

You divided 1 into 4 equal parts, so each part is less than 1.

$$
\begin{array}{r}
.25 \\
4\overline{)1.00} \\
-8 \\
\hline
20 \\
-20 \\
\hline
0
\end{array}
$$

The value of a quarter can be shown as $.25.

Talk About It!   Why might you need to write an equivalent decimal for the dividend?

Other Examples   Notice the placement of the decimal point in each example.

a. $4 \div 5$
$$
\begin{array}{r}
0.8 \\
5\overline{)4.0} \\
-40 \\
\hline
0
\end{array}
$$

b. $7 \div 4$
$$
\begin{array}{r}
1.75 \\
4\overline{)7.00} \\
-4 \\
\hline
30 \\
-28 \\
\hline
20 \\
-20 \\
\hline
0
\end{array}
$$

c. $\$10 \div 8$
$$
\begin{array}{r}
\$1.25 \\
8\overline{)\$10.00} \\
-8 \\
\hline
20 \\
-16 \\
\hline
40 \\
-40 \\
\hline
0
\end{array}
$$

Write the quotient. Estimate to place the decimal point.

1. 4)2   2. 4)$10   3. 8)6   4. 5)$11   5. 4)$2   6. 6)$48

7. 15 ÷ 4   8. 54 ÷ 5   9. 7 ÷ 8   10. 75 ÷ 8   11. 20 ÷ 8   12. 70 ÷ 5

13. **Critical Thinking** Can you write a rule for placing the decimal point in the exercises above?

Work It Out!

Write the quotient.

14. 5)2   15. 8)2   16. 6)$9   17. 6)21   18. 5)27

19. 5)8   20. 8)5   21. 5)41   22. 4)38   23. 4)$38

24. 4 ÷ 8   25. $20 ÷ 8   26. $2 ÷ 8   27. 54 ÷ 9   28. $29 ÷ 4

Problem Solving

29. How do you write the value of three nickels as a decimal?

30. Adam has four coins with a total value of $.30. What are the coins? Is there more than one combination possible? Explain.

31. Al, Eva, Duke, and Joy each have a coin. The coins are a nickel, a dime, a penny, and a silver dollar. Al had the dime, and Eva did not have the penny. If Duke did not have the nickel or the silver dollar, and Joy's coin was $.99 more than Duke's, what coin did Joy have?

32. **Estimation** At a coin show, you can buy 3 rare coins of equal value for $3.00. If you want 5 coins of equal value and you have $5.00 to spend, will you have enough money?

33. Suppose you have 17 dimes and spend 3 of them. Then, after buying 2 rare coins at the same price, you have $.10. If the coins are of equal value, what is the price of each?

 Create your own word problem for each of these expressions. Then solve.

34. $1.25 ÷ 5   35. 6 ÷ 3   36. 3 ÷ 6

Mixed Review

Write the product or the quotient.

37. 5.14 × 0.2   38. 0.08 · 0.3   39. 26 ÷ 10   40. 0.78 × 1.5   41. 0.33 × 1.4

More Practice Set 7.7, p. 482

Problem Solving
Work a Simpler Problem

A family of spot-nosed guenons (guh NOHNS) at the San Diego Zoo eats almost 2 lb of food daily. There are 4 bags of food left. They weigh 4.5 lb, 2.3 lb, 6.6 lb, and 2.2 lb. How many days will this supply last?

You can make this problem easier to solve by rewriting it using simpler numbers.

Here's A Way! **Use Work a Simpler Problem.**

1 Understand

- How much food do the guenons eat each day? How much is left?
- What do you need to find out?

| 2.2 lb | 2.3 lb | 4.5 lb | 6.6 lb |
| Raisins | Sunflower Seeds | High Fiber Biscuits | High Protein Biscuits |

2 Plan

- Can you make the problem easier with simpler numbers?
- How will you solve your simpler problem?

3 Try It

- Round the decimals to the nearest whole numbers to make them simpler.
- Add the numbers and divide by the amount of food used each day.
- Use the same steps to solve the original problem.

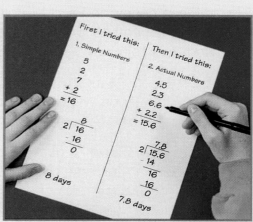

4 Look Back

- The answer is 7.8 days.
- How does your answer to the simpler problem help you to tell if your actual answer makes sense?

Use Work a Simpler Problem to help you solve the problem.

1. As a public relations assistant at the zoo, you will earn $378.50 per week. Working at the souvenir shop, you will earn $10.80 per hour for a 37.5 hour week. Which job will pay more? How much more? Justify your answer.

Possible Jobs

Job Title	Actual Numbers	Simpler Numbers
Public Relations Assistant	$378.50 per week	$400 per week
Shop Manager	$10.80 per hour for 37.5 hours a week	?

2. **Critical Thinking** When you use simpler numbers, what is an advantage of using rounded numbers?

Work It Out!

Use Work a Simpler Problem or any other strategy to solve the problem.

3. A fence will be built around a well at the zoo. One plan uses fencing for 6 sides. Each side will use 1.9 m of fencing. Another plan is for a square with sides that are 3.1 m long. Which plan needs more fencing?

4. There are 64 birds housed in the bird exhibit at the local zoo. There are 6 more females than males. How many birds are male?

5. You and three friends are standing single file in line for zoo tickets. How many different ways can you and your friends arrange yourselves in line?

6. Find the sum of the first 25 odd numbers, beginning with 1. (Hint: Find the sum of the first 2, 3, 4, and then 5 odd numbers, then generalize.)

7. You are jogging around a square-shaped area that has 8.7 m of fencing on each side. How many times will you have to run around the square in order to reach your goal of 150 m?

8. Tickets to the local zoo cost $5.25 each. Your parents give you and four friends $25.50 toward the cost of the tickets. You each chip in the same amount to make up the rest of the money needed. How much do you each chip in?

Share Your Thinking

9. Discuss problem 8 with a classmate. Compare and explain the strategies you used.

You can read more about the leaning tower in the pages of *Current Science.*

LESSON 9

Problem Solving
Using Strategies

For almost 800 years, the Bell Tower in Pisa, Italy, has been leaning. Recently, engineers have found a way to keep it from falling over. They have even found a way to reverse the tilting.

Thanks to metal braces similar to those that straighten children's teeth, and with the help of lead weights, the tower is slowly moving to a more upright position. So far, it has been straightened by 3.75 cm.

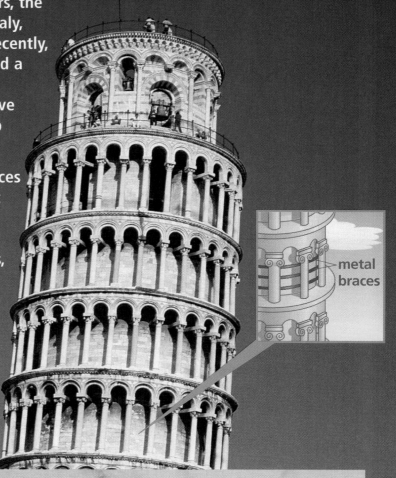

metal braces

Problem Solving Process
✓ Understand
✓ Plan
✓ Try It
✓ Look Back

Choose a Strategy You Have Learned
✓ Make a Table
✓ Act It Out
✓ Guess and Check
✓ Look for a Pattern
✓ Work Backward
✓ Make a List
✓ Work a Simpler Problem
  Draw a Picture
  Write an Equation

Suppose you want to know exactly how many centimeters the tower will have straightened over a ten-year period. If the tower moves upright at an average of 1.9 cm a year for 3 years, 2.3 cm a year for 2 years, 0.7 cm a year for 4 years, and 2.0 cm a year for 1 year, how much will it have straightened?

- What information do you already know about the tower?
- What do you want to find out?
- Can simpler numbers help you solve this problem? How?
- Explain how you will solve this problem. Then solve it.

Use any strategy to solve the problem. Show your work.

1. You visit the Leaning Tower of Pisa at 9:08 A.M. You plan to drive to Rome, which is about 220.5 miles away. If you drive an average of 55 miles each hour, will you reach Rome by 12:45 P.M.? Explain.

2. For your vacation to Italy, you save $1 the first week, $3 the next, $5 the next, $7 the next, and so on. Suppose you continue saving according to this pattern for the next 11 weeks. How much will you have saved in 15 weeks?

3. In 1990, the increasing tilt of the tower was measured to be an average of 1.9 cm per year. Using this average, about how long would it take for the tower to tilt another 20 cm?

4. Galileo Galilei, who was born in 1564, performed many of his gravitational experiments from atop the Leaning Tower of Pisa. He died when he was 78 years old. How many years has it been since his death?

Pisa

220.5 miles

Rome

5. Suppose the Leaning Tower of Pisa straightens up 2.1 cm each of the next 2 years, then increases by only 1.4 cm in the third year. Suppose further that this pattern continues for 16 years. How much will the Leaning Tower have straightened?

6. Suppose the first measurements to record the straightening of the tower took place on June 2, 1991. If the metal braces were put into place 120 days before this, on what date were they put onto the tower?

7. After straightening by 3.5 cm, suppose the tower begins to tilt again. If it tilts 0.2 cm a year, how long will it take before the straightening that has occurred is completely reversed?

8. With the help of braces, suppose the tower of Pisa straightens 1.5 inches in one year. If it continues to straighten 1.5 inches each year, how many years will it take for it to straighten 1.5 ft?

Share Your Thinking

9. Explain how you solved problem 8.

10. In problem 2, add the savings for the first and fifteenth weeks. Then, add the savings for the second and fourteenth weeks. What do you notice? Can you continue the pattern?

LESSON 10 Fractions and Decimals

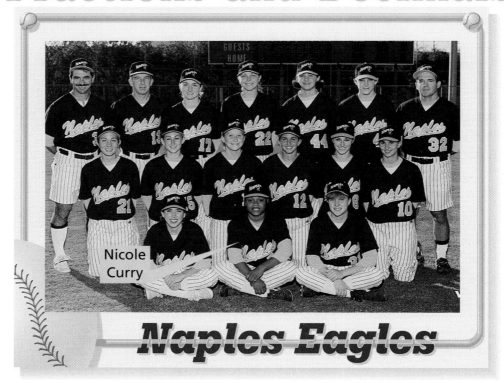

Naples Eagles

Nicole Curry's powerful swing helped her team win the Florida championship. That season, she was at bat 83 times with 37 hits.

What was Nicole's batting average? $\frac{37}{83}$ ⟹ number of hits / number of times at bat

Batting averages are written as decimals to the thousandths place. You can write her batting average as a decimal by dividing the number of hits by the number of times at bat.

Here's A Way!   Write $\frac{37}{83}$ as a decimal.

1 To write the fraction as a decimal, divide the numerator by the denominator. Use a calculator.

$$\frac{37}{83} = 37 \div 83$$

$$= 0.4457831$$

2 Round the decimal to the nearest thousandth.

0.44**5**7831 ⟹ 0.446

thousandths place

Nicole's batting average was 0.446 for the season.

Talk About It!   How can you tell by looking at the fraction $\frac{37}{83}$ that Nicole's batting average is less than 0.500?

Show What You Know!

Write each fraction as a decimal to the hundredths place. Use a calculator and write zeros or round answers to the nearest hundredth if necessary.

1. $\frac{4}{5}$ 2. $\frac{8}{15}$ 3. $\frac{6}{27}$ 4. $\frac{11}{12}$ 5. $\frac{3}{4}$ 6. $\frac{3}{5}$ 7. $\frac{5}{26}$ 8. $\frac{5}{27}$

9. **Critical Thinking** Can two fractions be equivalent to the same decimal? Explain.

Work It Out!

Write each fraction as a decimal. Use a calculator. Round answers to the nearest hundredth if necessary.

10. $\frac{5}{4}$ 11. $\frac{4}{10}$ 12. $\frac{5}{12}$ 13. $\frac{1}{7}$ 14. $\frac{3}{2}$ 15. $\frac{8}{11}$ 16. $\frac{4}{11}$ 17. $\frac{2}{11}$

18. $\frac{8}{9}$ 19. $\frac{5}{6}$ 20. $\frac{7}{11}$ 21. $\frac{3}{9}$ 22. $\frac{2}{15}$ 23. $\frac{3}{19}$ 24. $\frac{6}{1}$ 25. $\frac{9}{19}$

26. Copy and complete the chart below.

Problem Solving

27. Use the chart to put the players in order by their batting averages, from least to greatest. Then find the difference between the top two averages.

Player	Hits	At Bats	Hits ÷ Times at Bat	Batting Average
Nicole Curry	37	83	37 ÷ 83	0.446
Michelle Moschel	28	64	28 ÷ 64	?
Marissa Moschel	9	30	?	?
Kristine Turner	32	82	?	?
Mindi Harris	37	96	?	?

28. Nicole, Michelle, Marissa, and Kristine are at practice. Their t-shirts are orange, blue, green and red. Nicole wears the orange shirt. Michelle does not wear the green or red shirt. If Marissa does not wear the red shirt, what color shirt does Kristine wear?

29. Order the fractions below from least to greatest. Begin by writing each fraction as a decimal to the nearest hundredth. Use a calculator. Then find the two decimals whose difference is 1.29.

$\frac{7}{8}$ $\frac{9}{4}$ $\frac{46}{50}$ $\frac{21}{9}$ $\frac{89}{72}$ $\frac{48}{50}$

30. **Mental Math** Use mental math to find each batting average.
   a. 4 hits in 10 at bats   b. 38 hits in 100 at bats

Math Journal

Write the steps you can follow to find your own batting average.

Chapter 7 Test

for Pages 226-249

Test-Taking Tips
When you're finished, go back and check that your answers are reasonable. Show your work.

Problem Solving

Solve. Show your work. (pages 244–247)

1. You and 2 friends decide to combine your money to buy 3 video games that cost $24.95 each. So far, you have $71.10 saved. How much more do you each have to contribute to buy the 3 games?

2. There are 294 steps that go to the top of the Tower of Pisa. At one time, people were allowed to climb to the top. If you could climb at a rate of 2.5 seconds per step, how long would it take to reach the top?

3. A customer buys 5 CDs that each cost the same amount. She pays with a $100 bill and receives $20.25 in change. How much did each CD cost?

4. You have a piece of wood 12.25 ft long. You need 4 pieces that are each 3.3 ft long. Do you have enough wood to cut the pieces you need?

5. During 1 week, a student kept a television log. From Monday to Friday, he watched 10.75 hours of television. About how many hours a day did he watch?

6. A student decided to cut down on her television watching. In 10 days, she watched 4.8 hours of television. On average, did she watch more than an hour a day?

Concepts

Choose the letter of the correct quotient. Explain how you placed the decimal point. (pages 240, 242)

7. $7\overline{)21.42}$
   a. 0.0306
   b. 0.036
   c. 3.06
   d. 30.6

8. $252.6 \div 6$
   a. 42.1
   b. 4.21
   c. 0.421
   d. 0.0421

9. $5\overline{)0.025}$
   a. 0.005
   b. 0.05
   c. 0.5
   d. 5

Use compatible numbers to estimate. Tell what numbers you used. (page 234)

10. $74.45 \div 8

11. $5\overline{)\$3.42}$

12. $358.79 \div 6

13. $9\overline{)\$4.61}$

14. $1.63 \div 4

15. $3\overline{)\$2.89}$

16. $193.20 \div 2

17. $7\overline{)\$71,390}$

Skills

Divide. Show your work. (page 242)

18. $8\overline{)6}$ 19. $12 \div 10$ 20. $5\overline{)4}$ 21. $24 \div 5$ 22. $8\overline{)12}$

Write each fraction as a decimal. Use a calculator and round answers to the nearest hundredth. (page 248)

23. $\frac{1}{6}$ 24. $\frac{5}{9}$ 25. $\frac{7}{12}$ 26. $\frac{9}{25}$

Write the letter of the correct quotient. (pages 240, 242)

27. $22.86 \div 9$ a. 2.54

28. $0.762 \div 3$ b. 25.4

29. $1016 \div 4$ c. 0.254

30. $177.8 \div 7$ d. 254

Performance Task

(pages 240, 242)

By recycling, the Carson family saved $95.45 this year. Ms. Carson plans to give an equal share of the money to each of her 7 children to spend on their vacation. Decide how much money each child will receive.

- Model with play money to show your solution.

- Write an equation that shows how to solve the problem.

- Explain how the results will be different if Mr. and Ms. Carson each take a share of the money.

Keep In Mind . . .

Your work will be evaluated on the following:

☑ Careful calculations
☑ Good modeling
☑ Correct equation
☑ Clear explanation

Cumulative Review

Reading Graphs (Chapter 4)
Estimate the number of English-speaking people in the world.

Here's A Way!

On the bar graph at right, find the two numbers closest to the top of the bar.

Does the end of the bar fall below, at, or above the halfway mark?

The bar for English speakers falls between 400 and 500 million. It ends above the halfway mark.

So, the number of English speakers is between 450 and 500 million.

Languages Spoken Worldwide, 1996

Millions of Speakers

Use the graph to answer each question.

1. Estimate the number of Hindi speakers.

2. Which language was spoken by fewer than 300 million people?

3. Which languages were spoken by at least 350 million people?

4. About how many more people spoke English than Spanish?

5. Explain how you would estimate the number of Russian speakers.

Calendar (Chapter 5)

March 1998
S M T W T F S
1 2 3 4 5 6 7
8 9 10 11 12 13 14
15 16 17 18 19 20 21
22 23 24 25 26 27 28
29 30 31

April
S M T W T F S
1 2 3 4
5 6 7 8 9 10 11
12 13 14 15 16 17 18
19 20 21 22 23 24 25
26 27 28 29 30

Find out how many weeks and days there are from March 25 to April 17.

Here's A Way!

Count up the number of weeks until you have counted the last full week.
There are 3 full weeks from March 25 to April 17.

Count the number of days after the last full week.
There are 2 more days.

Use the calendar for March and April 1998 to answer each question.

6. How many weeks and days are there from March 1 to March 17?

7. If you began a 5-week trip on March 26, what date would the last day of your trip be? What day of the week will it be on May 1?

8. How many weeks and days are there from March 13 to April 29?

9. How could you find which day of the week will be 3 weeks and 3 days from April 3?

Multiplying Decimals (Chapter 6)

Find 21.4 × 3.1.

Here's A Way!

Multiply.
Follow the same steps you follow for whole numbers.

$$\begin{array}{r} 21.4 \\ \times\ 3.1 \\ \hline 214 \\ 642 \\ \hline 66.34 \end{array}$$

21.4   1 decimal place
× 3.1   1 decimal place

There are 2 decimal places in the product.

Write the product. Round dollar amounts to the nearest cent.

10. $\begin{array}{r} 6.3 \text{ km} \\ \times\ 2 \\ \hline \end{array}$

11. $\begin{array}{r} 1.06 \\ \times\ 8.1 \\ \hline \end{array}$

12. $\begin{array}{r} 5.42 \\ \times\ 9.6 \\ \hline \end{array}$

13. $7.25 × 4.3   14. 0.27 × 0.6

15. $4.69 × 3.2

16. Why would you round dollar amounts to the nearest cent in decimal products?

Divide Decimals (Chapter 7)

Find 16.1 ÷ 7.

Here's A Way!

Divide.
Estimate to place the decimal point in the quotient.
16 ÷ 7 is about 2.

$$\begin{array}{r} 2.3 \\ 7\overline{)16.1} \\ -14 \\ \hline 21 \\ -21 \\ \hline 0 \end{array}$$

Write the quotient.

17. $6\overline{)1.62}$ 18. $2\overline{)0.902}$ 19. $3\overline{)0.063}$

20. $4\overline{)20.56}$ 21. $5\overline{)10.3}$ 22. $7\overline{)3.304}$

23. 6.12 ÷ 9   24. 21.944 ÷ 8

25. Explain how you placed the decimal point in exercise 22.

Problem Solving

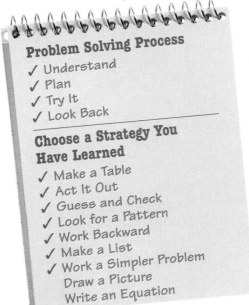

Problem Solving Process
✓ Understand
✓ Plan
✓ Try It
✓ Look Back

Choose a Strategy You Have Learned
✓ Make a Table
✓ Act It Out
✓ Guess and Check
✓ Look for a Pattern
✓ Work Backward
✓ Make a List
✓ Work a Simpler Problem
  Draw a Picture
  Write an Equation

Choose one of the strategies you know to solve these problems. Show your work.

26. At the end of the month there is $127.59 in a savings account. During the month, deposits of $13.00 and another of half that amount were made. How much was in the account before the deposits?

27. You have 6 coins in your pocket worth $.85. There are quarters, dimes, and nickels. How many of each type of coin do you have?

CHAPTER 7

INVESTIGATION

Out of the Past

History Connection   **With Your Group**

In 1950, a gallon of milk and a loaf of bread cost about $.98. How much do you think they cost today?

Your group will gather prices of different food items. Then, you will compare current prices to prices from the 1950s.

Keep In Mind . . .

Your work will be evaluated on the following:

☑ If your price averages are accurate

☑ How well you organize your chart

☑ How clearly your graph compares prices from the past and present

☑ How well your group cooperates to collect data

254

1 Plan It

- Divide all the items on the list from 1950 among your group members.

- Find today's prices for these items in a local store. Choose 3 to 5 different brands for each item. Use the same size containers as those listed—pounds, dozens, and quarts. Keep careful records.

Fine Foods Market
Bill for December, 1950

Apples – 12 pounds	$1.56
Bread – Six 1-pound loaves	$.84
Butter – 4 pounds	$2.92
Cheese – 8 pounds	$4.08
Coffee – 5 pounds	$4.00
Eggs – 9 dozen	$5.40
Milk – 16 quarts	$3.36
Rice – 13 pounds	$2.21

2 Put It Together

- Find the price for each pound, dozen or quart of each item on the 1950 receipt. To do this, divide the total amount spent on each item by the number of pounds, dozens, or quarts bought.

- Find the average prices for today. For each item, add the cost of each pound, dozen, or quart for the brands collected. Then, divide by the number of brands for that item.

- Create a chart for your data.

3 Wrap It Up

- Make a double-bar graph to show your data. Which prices changed the most? The least?

- Write a report telling why you think the prices have changed.

Item	1950	Today
apples	$.13 each lb.	
bread		

☐ –1950 ■ –Today

$ .95
.90
.85
.80
.75
.70
.65
.60
.55
.50
.45
.40
.35
.30
.25
.20
.15
.10
.05

4 Discuss Your Results

- Did you meet the objectives in Keep In Mind?

- Do you think families in 1950 got better buys on food than families today? Why or why not?

ShopMore Supermarket

Wheat Farms bread
2.29/pound
Store Brand bread
1.49/pound
Stone Hill bread
2.75/pound

Internet

> Visit the **Math Center** at **Houghton Mifflin Education Place.**
http://www.eduplace.com

255

Geometry

Try This!

Many geometric figures can be divided into smaller figures. Use what you know to make geometric figures.

What You'll Need

grid paper, scissors, glue

Cut two 10 × 10 grids into four congruent triangles.

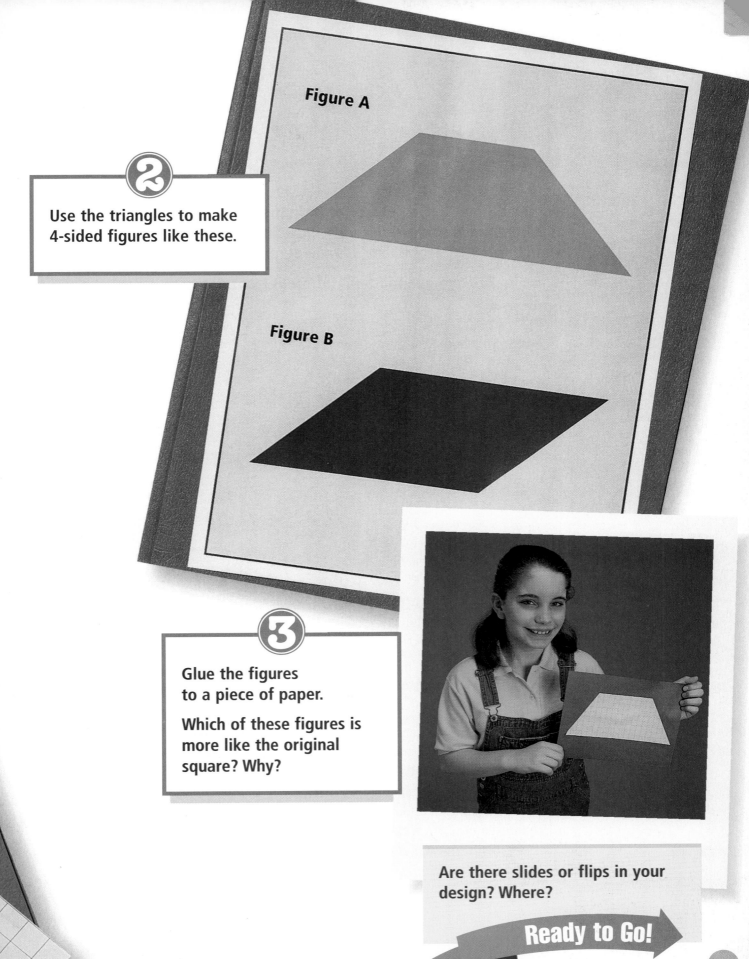

Figure A

Figure B

2

Use the triangles to make 4-sided figures like these.

3

Glue the figures to a piece of paper.

Which of these figures is more like the original square? Why?

Are there slides or flips in your design? Where?

Ready to Go!

257

Quadrilaterals

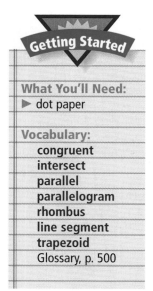

A quadrilateral is a polygon with four sides. There are many different kinds of quadrilaterals, including rectangles, squares, rhombuses, trapezoids, and parallelograms.

What makes one quadrilateral different from another?

Activity

Line Segments in Quadrilaterals

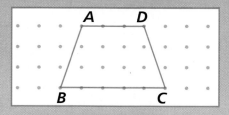

1 Copy this figure.

a. The sides of quadrilaterals are **line segments.** Line segment *BC* is part of a line with endpoints *B* and *C.* Line segment *BC* is written $\overline{BC}$. How would you write names for the other sides of *ABCD*?

b. $\overline{BC}$ **intersects** $\overline{CD}$, meaning the two line segments meet. What other segments intersect?

c. Two lines that extend in the same direction and never intersect are **parallel.** Line segments can also be parallel, for example $\overline{AD}$ and $\overline{BC}$, written $\overline{AD} \parallel \overline{BC}$. What other segments in *ABCD* are parallel?

Congruent Sides and Angles

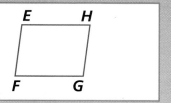

1 Copy this figure.

a. Is $\overline{EF} \parallel \overline{GH}$?

b. When two line segments have the same length they are **congruent.** The symbol for congruent is ≅. Is $\overline{EF} \cong \overline{GH}$? Is $\overline{EH} \cong \overline{FG}$? Is $\overline{EH} \cong \overline{GH}$?

c. When two angles have the same measure, they are congruent. The symbol for angle is ∠. Quadrilateral *EFGH* has two pairs of congruent angles. One pair is ∠*EFG* ≅ ∠*EHG*. What is the other pair of congruent angles? To name an angle, put the vertex in the middle.

Parallelograms

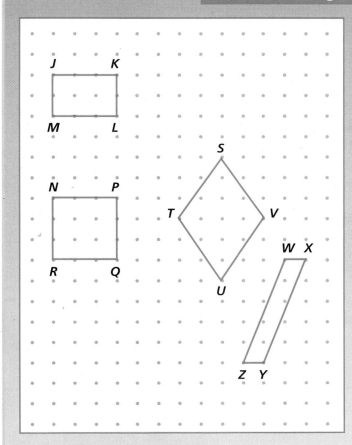

1 Copy these figures.

A quadrilateral with two pairs of parallel sides is a **parallelogram.**

a. Which figures are parallelograms?

b. How many pairs of congruent sides does each parallelogram have?

c. Which figures have at least one pair of congruent angles?

A **rhombus** has two pairs of parallel sides and its four sides are congruent.

d. Is a square a rhombus?

e. What other figure is a rhombus?

Figure *ABCD*, on p. 258, is a **trapezoid.**

f. How is it like the other quadrilaterals? How is it different?

Show What You Know!

Write *yes* or *no*.

1. Which of the following are parallelograms?
   a. rectangle   **b.** square   **c.** trapezoid   **d.** rhombus

2. Is a square also a
   a. rectangle?   **b.** trapezoid?   **c.** rhombus?

3. Write About It What do all quadrilaterals have in common?

Slides and Flips

Cooperative Learning Checklist

☑ Work alone.
☑ Work with a partner.
☐ Work with a group.

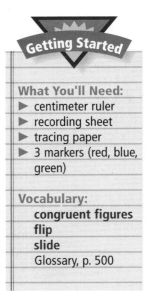

Getting Started

What You'll Need:
► centimeter ruler
► recording sheet
► tracing paper
► 3 markers (red, blue, green)

Vocabulary:
congruent figures
flip
slide
Glossary, p. 500

M.C. Escher was a mathematician and artist who used **congruent figures** to make his drawings. Congruent figures are figures that have the same size and shape.

In this drawing, Escher used slides of the horse. A **slide** is a motion in which every point of the figure moves the same distance and in the same direction. You can use slides and flips to make congruent figures. A **flip** is a motion made by turning a figure over a flip line.

Make slides and flips with this triangle, slide arrow, and dotted flip line.

Activity

Slides

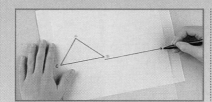
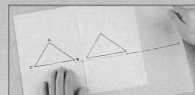
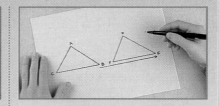

1. Copy the triangle and the slide arrow above onto paper or use the recording sheet. Then make a tracing of the triangle and darken the back of the tracing.

2. Slide the tracing to the end of the arrow. Draw over the tracing of the triangle. Label the new image *DEF* as shown.

3. Compare triangles *ABC* and *DEF*. Do they appear to be congruent? Find and color:
   a. one pair of congruent line segments red.
   b. one pair of congruent angles blue.

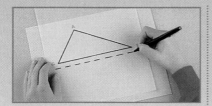 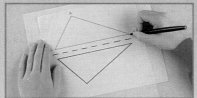 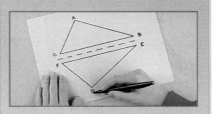

1 Copy and trace the triangle and dotted flip line on page 260 as in the first activity.

2 Flip the tracing over. Match the flip lines. Draw over the tracing.

3 Remove the tracing. Label the image *DEF*.

4 Compare triangles *ABC* and *DEF*. Do they appear to be congruent? Use the tracing to check.

5 Find and color:

  a. one pair of congruent line segments red.

  b. one pair of congruent angles blue.

  c. any pair of parallel line segments green.

Comparing Flips and Slides

1 Draw a triangle on a clean sheet of paper.

2 Slide the triangle and draw the figure following the instructions for a slide.

3 Flip the triangle and draw the figure following the instructions for a flip.

4 Are the figures you drew congruent to your original triangle? How can you check?

Show What You Know!

1. **Critical Thinking** How are slides and flips similar? How are they different?

2. **Critical Thinking** If you slide or flip a triangle using a tracing, are all the sides and angles congruent? Is the same true if you trace and slide a rectangle? A trapezoid?

Use the figure and its slide and flip images.

3. Name two angles congruent to ∠*DCE*.

4. Name two segments congruent to $\overline{CE}$.

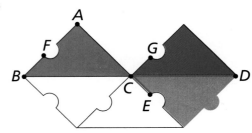

More Practice Set 8.2, p. 482

Measuring and Drawing Angles

Cooperative Learning
Checklist

☑ Work alone.
☑ Work with a partner.
☐ Work with a group.

Most public buildings have ramps for easier access. It is important that the angle between the ground and the ramp is not too great or the ramp will be too steep to use.

Architects measure angles to do their work. You can use a protractor to measure angles.

Getting Started

What You'll Need:
▶ protractor
▶ recording sheet
▶ ruler

Vocabulary:
acute angle
obtuse angle
perpendicular
ray
Glossary, p. 500

Activity

Using your Protractor

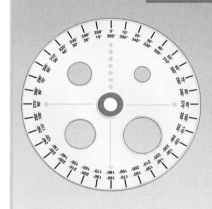

1 The unit of measure for an angle is a degree (°). The tool used for measuring angles is a protractor. It has two scales: one you read clockwise from 0° to 360°, the other you read counter-clockwise from 0° to 360°.

   a. How many degrees does each mark on the protractor represent?

   b. What is the greatest angle you can measure with a protractor?

Measuring Angles

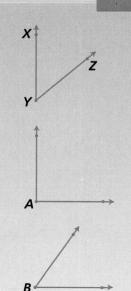

A **ray** is a part of a line with one endpoint. Angle *XYZ* is formed by rays *YX* and *YZ*. You can name an angle by its vertex. For example, angle *XYZ* is angle *Y*.

To measure an angle follow these steps:

1 Place the center point of the protractor at the vertex of the angle. Turn the protractor until 0° lines up with one of the rays.

2 Read the degrees along the other ray. The measure of ∠*XYZ* is 50°.

3 Copy and measure angles A and B or use section A of your recording sheet. If you need to, extend the rays. Write each angle measure. Which angle is a right angle?

Drawing Angles

You can also use a protractor to draw an angle with a given measure.

1 Draw a ray. Place the center point of the protractor on the end of the ray and the 0° mark along the ray.

2 Mark a point at the measure you want.

3 Draw the second ray. Label the angle.

4 Draw angles of 35° and 120° on your own paper or in section B of your recording sheet.

Naming Angles

An angle that has a measure less than 90° is an **acute angle.** An angle that has a measure greater than 90° but less than 180° is an **obtuse angle.** An angle that has a measure of 90° is called a **right angle.** The rays that form a right angle are **perpendicular.**

1 Draw an obtuse angle on your own paper or in section C of your recording sheet. Write its measure.

2 Draw an acute angle. Write its measure.

Show What You Know!

Write *true* or *false*. Explain your reasoning.

1. The largest angle measure is 360°.

2. All angles less than 180° are either acute or obtuse.

3. **Critical Thinking** If the minute hand of a clock is on 12, at what four times during a 24-hour period do the hands form a right angle?

4. Draw clock faces to show each pair of perpendicular rays in exercise 3.

5. What is the angle measure of the hands of a clock at 6:00 P.M.?

6. **Write About It** Besides a clock with hands, name and draw pictures of some everyday objects that change angle measure as they move.

More Practice Set 8.3, p. 483

Turns

quarter turn

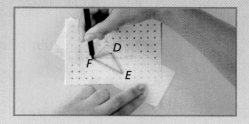

half turn

When a figure is rotated around a point we call it a **turn**.

The picture shows two turns. It is the same picture of the student showing a quarter turn and a half turn.

Activity

Make a Turn Image

1 Draw the figure on dot paper.

2 Trace the figure. Darken the area on the back of the figure.

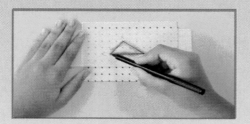

3 Place your pencil point on the turning point. Turn the tracing.

4 Draw over the tracing. Remove the tracing. Label the second figure *DEF*. Are the two triangles congruent? Explain.

5 Copy and complete each statement.

a. $\angle BAC \cong$ ■   b. $\overline{BC} \cong$ ■   c. $\angle ABC \cong$ ■   d. $\overline{AC} \cong$ ■

Quarter, Half, and Three-quarter Turns

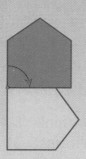
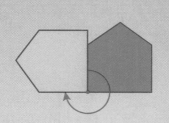

1. Trace the green pentagon above. Turn your tracing a quarter turn so it fits over the yellow pentagon.

2. Repeat for a half turn.

3. Repeat for a three-quarter turn.

4. Draw quarter, half, and three-quarter turn images of the figure on the right.

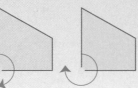

Degrees of a Turn

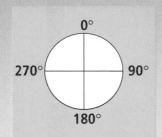

Copy this circle 3 times on your paper.

1. Lay your pencil on the vertical line of one of the circles. Point the pencil toward the zero. Begin at zero and go clockwise, shading the part of the circle that represents a quarter turn.

2. Write the number of degrees in the shaded fraction of the circle.

3. Repeat the steps above for a half-turn and a three-quarter turn.

Show What You Know!

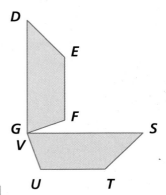

Discuss each question and explain your answers.

1. **Critical Thinking** Look at the congruent figures. Is *STUV* the result of a slide, flip, or turn? How do you know?

2. **Critical Thinking** How can you use multiplication or division to find the number of degrees in a turn? Think about $\frac{1}{4}$ $\frac{1}{2}$ $\frac{3}{4}$ turns and 360°.

Complete each statement based on the figure and the turn at the right.

3. $\angle DGF \cong$ ■
4. $\overline{VS} \cong$ ■
5. $\angle VUT \cong$ ■
6. $\overline{EF} \cong$ ■

More Practice Set 8.4, p. 483

Symmetry

What You'll Need:
▶ recording sheet

Vocabulary:
half-turn
 symmetry
line of symmetry
line symmetry
Glossary, p. 500

Look at the chair. When you close your book, do you think the halves match? Because the halves match, the chair has **line symmetry**. The line between the halves is the **line of symmetry**.

Think about turning the chair upside down. Will it look exactly the same? A figure has **half-turn symmetry** if, after a half turn, it looks exactly the same as before the turn. The quadrilateral at the left has half-turn symmetry, but the chair does not.

How can you find lines of symmetry? How can you tell if a figure has half-turn symmetry?

Here's A Way! Identify symmetry in figures.

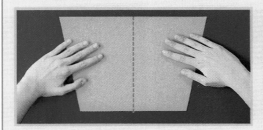

1 Fold the figure in half.

2 Compare the two sides. If the two sides match, the fold line is a line of symmetry.

The trapezoid has one line of symmetry

3 Turn the figure halfway around. If it looks exactly the same, it has half-turn symmetry.

The trapezoid does not have half-turn symmetry.

Talk About It! How does turning the trapezoid help you see whether the trapezoid has half-turn symmetry?

Show What You Know!

1. **Critical Thinking** Look at the figures below. If you cut along a line of symmetry in each one, would you get congruent figures? Explain.

A. B. Z C. D. C E.

2. Which of these figures have line symmetry? Do any have more than one line of symmetry? Copy the table or use the recording sheet to record your findings.

Figure	Number of Lines of Symmetry	Half-Turn Symmetry (yes/no)
A	?	?
B	?	?
C	?	?
D	?	?
E	?	?

3. **Write About It** Find objects in your classroom that have symmetry.
   a. Make a list of 5 objects that have line symmetry.
   b. Make a list of 5 objects that have half-turn symmetry.
   c. Which objects are on both lists?

Work It Out!

Copy the figures above.

4. Draw the half-turn image over the top of each figure on your recording sheet.

5. Which of the above figures have half-turn symmetry? Complete the second column of the chart.

Write *yes* or *no*. If *yes*, draw a figure to support your answer. Can a figure have:

6. more than 2 lines of symmetry?

7. line symmetry and half-turn symmetry?

8. line symmetry but not half-turn symmetry?

9. half-turn symmetry but not line symmetry?

10. **Critical Thinking** Look at a clock with hour and minute hands. The clock has a line of symmetry from the 12 to the 6. At what other times do the hands on a clock form a line of symmetry?

11. **Write About It** In your own words, what is line symmetry and half-turn symmetry?

Problem Solving
Logical Reasoning

Logical Reasoning

Ask Yourself:

Can I eliminate any possibilities?

Can I sort the information?

Suppose you must group these figures by their characteristics. How will you show that a figure belongs in two groups? How will you show that a figure does not belong in a group?

You can use a Venn Diagram to help you solve this problem.

You Decide

- How can a Venn Diagram help you to group the shapes into the two categories?
- How can the diagram help you to use the word *or* to show how shapes are related? How can it help you to use the words *not* and *and?*

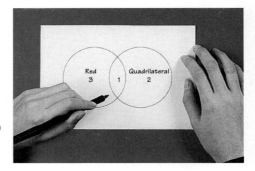

Work It Out!

Use Venn Diagrams and the figures above to answer the questions.

1. Which figures are green or circles?

2. Which pair of figures has the same shape and color?

3. Which quadrilateral is
   a. not red
   b. not a rectangle

4. Which figures are
   a. yellow or circles?
   b. yellow and circles?

5. Which figures are triangles and green?

6. Which figures are yellow or green but not quadrilaterals?

7. Which figures are not quadrilaterals?

8. Which figures are red and not circles?

Share Your Thinking

9. *Or* means the shape had one of the characteristics. *Not* means the shape had none of the characteristics. How many characteristics does the word *and* suggest the shape has?

Midchapter Review

for Pages 256–268

Solve. Show your work. (pages 258, 268)

1. Use these numbers: 1, 12, 14, 36, 49. Which of the numbers are even and multiples of 7? Which are odd or multiples of 7?

A   B   C   D

2. Which of the figures above are quadrilaterals or striped? Which are not quadrilaterals and not striped?

Concepts

a   b   c   d   e

(pages 258, 264, 266) **Use the figures above. Write the letter of each figure that**

3. is a rhombus.

4. has line symmetry.

5. has half-turn symmetry.

(page 260) **Use the figures below.** *QRST* **is the slide image of** *ABCD*. **Name a pair of**

6. congruent angles.

7. congruent sides.

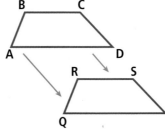

Skills

Use a protractor to draw these angles. (page 262)

8. an acute angle

9. an obtuse angle

10. a right angle

Math World

Geometry

Around the World

Geometry is everywhere. Explore how geometry was used in ancient art. Then, use an Egyptian method to create a square corner.

Shadowless Days

The length of your shadow depends on the angle of the sun overhead. Your shadow is shortest around noon, when the sun is at its highest point in the sky. In countries located very near the equator, there are two days each year when the sun passes directly overhead. Around noon on these days, shadows vanish! Try standing a small object on its end. Shine a flashlight on it to see how the shadow changes when you move the flashlight.

Hawaiian Rock Art

Some of the best examples of petroglyphs, or rock paintings, can be found on volcanic rock in the Hawaiian islands. People from ancient cultures often used geometric patterns in their paintings. Triangles and straight lines were used to make this painting of two people. People who have studied the petroglyphs think that the rock paintings were special symbols for birthdays, children, and families.

Try This!

EGYPTIAN RIGHT - ANGLE TOOL

Builders in ancient Egypt used cords with 12 evenly-spaced knots to make square corners. Make and use your own knotted cord to see how this is done.

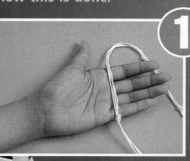

1 Work with a partner. Use a string at least 12 in. long. Decide what unit of measurement you will use to space the knots. For example, you might use the width of four fingers. Tie 12 evenly-spaced knots in the string.

2 Use a thumbtack to attach one end of the string to a piece of heavy cardboard. Make a triangle by using three sections of the string in the first line of the triangle, four in the second line, and five in the third line.

3 Use a protractor to measure the angle where the three-section and four-section lines connect.

4 Now make a triangle with three sides of equal length. What is true about the angles in this triangle? How many different triangles can you make?

Geometry Mystery

Over 2000 years ago, the Nazca people of Peru scratched huge drawings in the desert surface. The drawings, like the one here, cover miles of the desert floor. It is not known how or why the Nazca people made these drawings.

Respond

Make your own . . .
petroglyph using geometric shapes.

Internet:
Houghton Mifflin Education Place
Explore the Math Center at
http://www.eduplace.com

Triangles

Four kinds of triangles are **equilateral, scalene, isoceles,** and **right.**

 An equilateral triangle has three congruent sides and angles.

 A scalene triangle has no congruent sides or angles.

 An isoceles triangle has at least two congruent sides and angles.

 A right triangle has one angle that is 90°.

I.M. Pei designed this building using equilateral triangles.

How can you identify triangles? What is the sum of the angles in a triangle?

Here's A Way! Use a protractor and a ruler.

You can think of ∠*GEF* as ∠*E* since *E* is the vertex of the angle.

1 Measure and record the angles of the triangle.

• ∠*E* = 66°   ∠*F* = 66°   ∠*G* = 48°

2 Measure and record the lengths of the sides of the triangle.

• *EF* = 4 cm   *FG* = 5 cm   *GE* = 5 cm

Triangle 1 is isosceles since it has two congruent sides and angles.

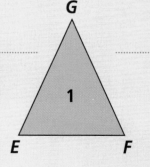

3 Find and record the sum of the angles in Triangle 1.

• 66° + 66° + 48° = 180°

The sum of the angles in Triangle 1 is 180°.

Talk About It! Is an equilateral triangle also an isosceles triangle? Explain.

Show What You Know!

Use Triangle 2 to answer the following questions.

1. Copy the chart below. Measure and record the angles and sides of the triangle. Write whether the triangle is equilateral, scalene, or isosceles.

2. **Critical Thinking** Explain your decision for exercise 1.

3. **Write About It** Describe the difference between an isosceles triangle and an equilateral triangle.

E   2

G

Triangle	Angle Measures	Measure			Sum of Angle measures ($\angle E + \angle F + \angle G$)	Length (cm)		
		$\angle E$	$\angle F$	$\angle G$		$\overline{EF}$	$\overline{FG}$	$\overline{GE}$
1	66°, 48°, 66°	66°	66°	48°	?	?	?	?
2	?	?	?	?	?	?	?	?
3	?	?	?	?	?	?	?	?

Work It Out!

G

3

F

E

4. Measure and record the angles and sides of Triangle 3. Write whether the triangle is equilateral, scalene, or isosceles.

5. Are any of the triangles you measured right triangles?

6. Complete the Sum of Angle measures column in the chart above. Describe the pattern that you see.

 7. Write the missing angle measure for each triangle. Tell whether the triangle is isosceles, equilateral, or scalene.
 a. triangle *RSK* $\angle R = 70°$ $\angle S = 35°$ $\angle K = $ ■
 b. triangle *MSW* $\angle M = 45°$ $\angle S = 90°$ $\angle W = $ ■
 c. triangle *LTV* $\angle L = 22°$ $\angle T = 64°$ $\angle V = $ ■

8. Can a triangle have more than one right angle? Explain.

9. Name three things that all triangles have in common.

10. **Write About It** For each of the triangles, compare the angle measures with the lengths of the sides. What pattern do you see?

Ordered Pairs

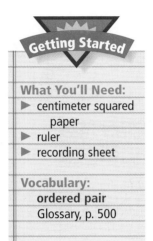
When you want to describe the position of a figure on a grid, you can give its horizontal and vertical location, such as row and column. For example, the checker on the board is at the third column, second row.

An **ordered pair** of numbers is used to describe a location on a coordinate grid. The order of the numbers is important. The position (3,2), third column, second row, is different from (2,3), second column, third row.

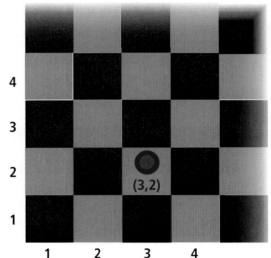

How can you locate points on a grid?

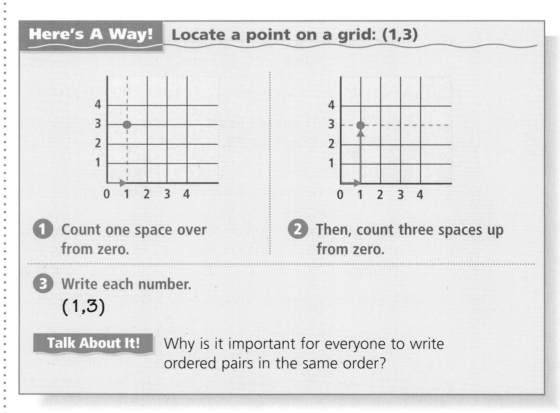

Here's A Way! Locate a point on a grid: (1,3)

1 Count one space over from zero.

2 Then, count three spaces up from zero.

3 Write each number.
(1,3)

Talk About It! Why is it important for everyone to write ordered pairs in the same order?

Draw a grid like the one below. Plot the points on the grid. Label them with the ordered pair.

1. (2,1)
2. (4,1)
3. (5,2)
4. (4,3)

5. (2,5)
6. (1,2)
7. (2,3)
8. (2,2)

Connect the pair of points on the grid using a ruler.

9. (4,3) to (2,5)
10. (2,1) to (4,1)
11. (2,2) to (5,2)

12. (1,2) to (2,2)
13. (2,3) to (2,5)
14. (4,3) to (2,3)

15. (2,1) to (1,2)
16. (4,1) to (5,2)
17. (2,2) to (2,3)

Work It Out!

18. Copy the chart below and write the ordered pair for each vertex of triangle *ABC*.

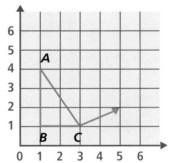

Figure	Ordered Pairs Vertex		
	A	*B*	*C*
ABC	?	?	?
△ *ABC* image	?	?	?

19. Copy triangle *ABC* above on graph paper. Draw a slide image of triangle *ABC* using the slide arrow. Record in your chart the ordered pair that names each vertex of the second figure.

20. Circle the first number in each ordered pair of triangle *ABC* and the first number in each ordered pair of the second figure. Describe the pattern you see.

21. Underline the second number in each ordered pair of triangle *ABC* and the second number in each ordered pair of the second figure. Describe the pattern you see.

Similar Figures

Getting Started

What You'll Need:
► geoboard
► geoboard dot paper
► protractor
► recording sheet
► tracing paper
► squared paper

Vocabulary:
similar
Glossary, p. 500

Cooperative Learning Checklist

☑ Work alone.
☑ Work with a partner.
☐ Work with a group.

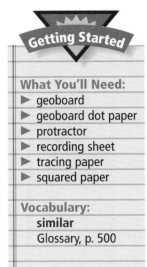

There are many objects around you that have the same shape but not the same size. Look at this window designed by Frank Lloyd Wright. It has many of the same shapes in it but they are different sizes. Figures with the same shape but different sizes are called **similar**.

There are many ways to make similar figures.

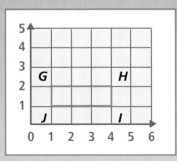

Activity

1

Use your geoboard.

• Make the figure shown on a geoboard. Then make a figure with the same shape, but smaller.

   a. Compare the angles and the sides of the two figures. What do you notice?

2

Use ordered pairs.

• Copy the chart below and write the ordered pair for each vertex of the rectangle *GHIJ*.

• Multiply the numbers in each ordered pair by 2. Write the new ordered pairs. For example, vertex G (1,2) becomes (2,4).

• Copy rectangle *GHIJ* on graph paper. Draw the new rectangle on your paper. Using tracing paper to compare, how does the new rectangle compare with the original?

Figure	Ordered Pairs Vertex			
	G	H	I	J
1	?	?	?	?
2	?	?	?	?

3

Make larger similar figures.

- Repeat the steps in Activity 2 with the hexagon, but multiply each number of the ordered pair by 3.

Figure	Ordered Pairs Vertex					
	P	Q	R	S	T	U
1	?	?	?	?	?	?
2	?	?	?	?	?	?

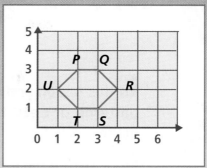

4

Make smaller similar figures.

- Copy the chart below and write the ordered pair for each vertex of the triangle.

- Divide each number in each ordered pair by 2. Write the new ordered pairs. Predict how the measure of the sides and angles will change.

- Copy triangle *ABC* on grid paper and draw the new triangle. How do the triangles compare?

Figure	Ordered Pairs Vertex		
	A	B	C
1	?	?	?
2	?	?	?

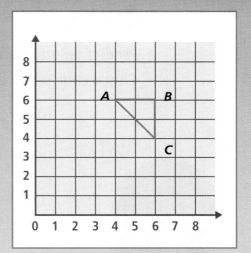

Show What You Know!

1. **Critical Thinking** Describe what happens when you double only the first number in each ordered pair of a figure.

2. **Critical Thinking** Describe what happens when you add 3 to both numbers in each ordered pair?

3. **Critical Thinking** How are similar figures the same as congruent figures? How are they different?

More Practice Set 8.9, p. 484

LESSON 10

Making Cubes

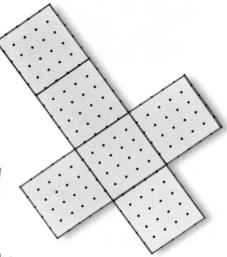

Cooperative Learning Checklist

☑ Work alone.
☑ Work with a partner.
☐ Work with a group.

In this lesson you will explore patterns, or **nets,** that can be used to make cubes.

Work with a partner to see if a flat pattern can be folded to form a cube!

Getting Started

What You'll Need:
▶ dot paper
▶ ruler
▶ scissors
▶ tape

Vocabulary:
net
Glossary, p. 500

Fold the Cube!

Activity

- Predict whether a net will become a cube.
- Check your predictions.

How To Play!

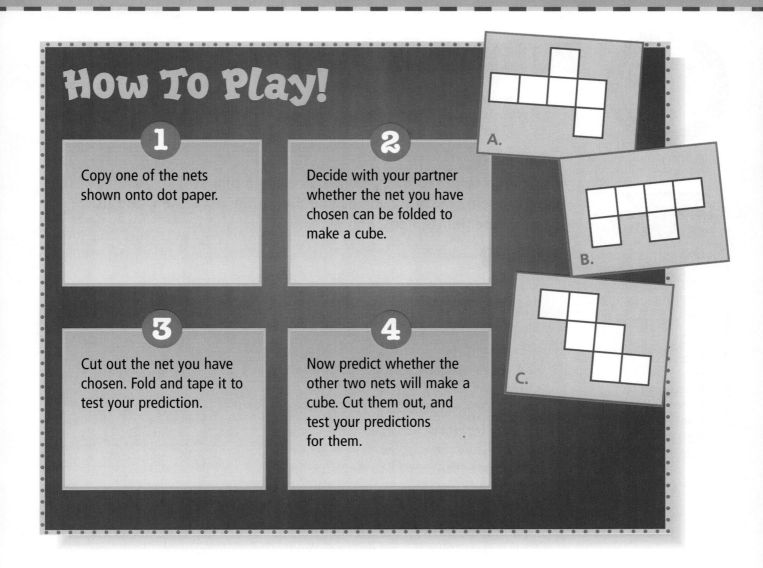

1 Copy one of the nets shown onto dot paper.

2 Decide with your partner whether the net you have chosen can be folded to make a cube.

3 Cut out the net you have chosen. Fold and tape it to test your prediction.

4 Now predict whether the other two nets will make a cube. Cut them out, and test your predictions for them.

A.

B.

C.

Show What You Know!

1. **Critical Thinking** Without cutting and folding, which of the following nets do you think will make a cube? Test your predictions by copying and folding all the nets below. Label each net before you cut it out.

   a. 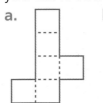   b. 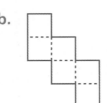   c. 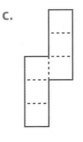   d. 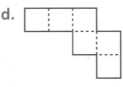   e.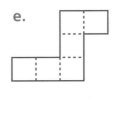

2. Explain why some of the nets did not make cubes.

3. **Write About It** Would this net make a cube? How can you tell?

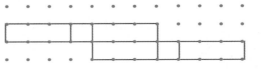

Points, Lines, and Planes

Cooperative Learning
Checklist

☐ Work alone.
☑ Work with a partner.
☐ Work with a group.

Parts of a cube represent points, lines, and planes. Can you identify them? Make a cube as you did in the last lesson, and use it to explore points, lines, and planes.

Getting Started

What You'll Need:
▶ recording sheet
▶ scissors
▶ tape

Vocabulary:
intersect
line
line segment
plane
point
Glossary, p. 500

Activity

1

Examine the cube. It contains models of points, lines, and planes.

a. A corner of a solid is a vertex, or **point**. How many points are shown on the cube?

b. A **line** extends forever in both directions. A **line segment** is part of a line. A straight edge of a solid is an example of a line segment. How many line segments does your cube have?

c. The faces on your cube are polygons. They represent parts of planes. **Planes** are flat surfaces that extend forever in all directions. What kind of polygons are the faces of your cube? How many different planes are represented by your cube?

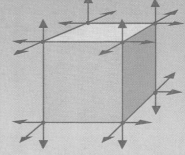

2

Planes sometimes cross or intersect each other.

a. Look at your desk. Where are the planes? Where on the desk do two planes intersect?

b. Look at your cube. Where on the cube do two planes intersect? What do you call a place where two planes intersect?

c. Where on the desk do three planes intersect?

d. Find where three planes meet on the cube. What do you call a place where three places intersect?

e. Describe other places in your classroom where three planes intersect.

Lines and planes extend forever.

a. Do you think the tulip fields in the photo make a better model of a plane than the classroom ceiling? Why or why not?

b. If a plane extends forever in all directions, what can you say about a line? About a point?

1. **Critical Thinking** How many planes are represented by the faces of a pyramid?

2. **Critical Thinking** How many planes meet at each of the vertices?

3. Can you measure a plane in geometry? Explain your answer.

4. **Write About It** What examples can you find on this page that model three planes meeting to form a line? Can you find other examples of three planes meeting? Can you describe a place where more than three planes meet?

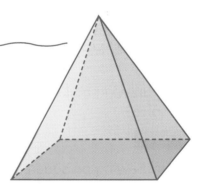

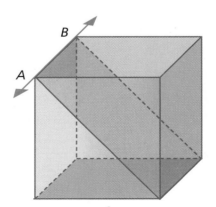

Problem Solving
Draw a Picture

Suppose you have a paper route in Middletown, shown on the map. You start your route from home, then go 2 blocks north, 2 blocks east, 1 block north, 2 blocks east, 3 blocks south, and 1 block west. How many blocks from home are you at the end of the route? In which direction are you heading?

You can make this problem easier to solve by drawing a picture.

Here's A Way! **Draw a Picture to solve the problem.**

1 Understand

- You know the *direction* and *distance* of each stop on the paper route.
- You need to know the number of blocks you are from home and the direction you are heading at the end of the route.
- How will a drawing make this problem easier to solve?

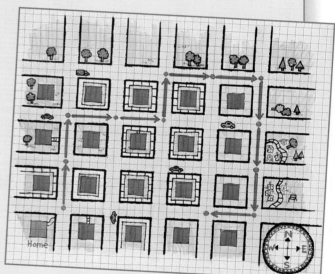

2 Plan

- Make your drawing on squared paper.
- How will you show the number of blocks and the distance you travel?

3 Try It

- Draw a dot to stand for your house.
- Draw a line along the squares to show the route: Start at your house. Draw a line that shows you going 2 blocks north, 2 blocks east, 1 block north, 2 blocks east, 3 blocks south, and 1 block west.

4 Look Back

- The drawing shows that the route ends 3 blocks east of your house.
- How did drawing a picture help you to solve the problem?

Use the strategy Draw a Picture to solve the problem.

1. Some large cars and some small cars are parked on Main Street in Middletown. Large cars are 11 ft long and small cars are 8 ft long. There are exactly 3 ft of space between each car. Main Street is 100 ft long. The front of the first car is at the beginning of Main Street. The end of the last car is 3 ft from the end of Main Street. How many large and small cars could be parked there?

2. **Critical Thinking** Does the order in which the large and small cars are parked matter? Explain.

Work It Out!

Draw a Picture or use any other strategy to solve the problem.

3. Middletown is having a Founder's Day Banquet. A fifth-grade teacher is taking 12 students to the celebration. Square tables that can seat one person on each side will be moved together in a line, to make one long table for the teacher and students. What is the least number of tables needed to seat the students and their teacher?

4. Four towns are along a 75-mile stretch of road. In order, the towns are Middletown, Anchorage, Prospect, and Crestwood. Middletown to Anchorage is the same distance as Prospect to Crestwood and $\frac{1}{3}$ of the distance from Anchorage to Prospect. How far is it from Middletown to Anchorage?

5. An apartment complex in Middletown has 4 buildings. Building F is taller than Building G but not as tall as Building H. Building J is shorter than Building F. Which picture represents the problem?

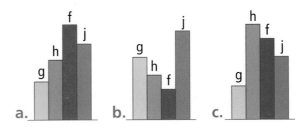

a.   b.   c.

6. Use all the numbers 5, 2, 8, 6, and 3 exactly once with any operations you would like to write an expression that equals 12.

7. Which problems did you solve by using the strategy drawing a picture? How did this strategy help?

8. How is Draw a Picture like Make a Table or Make a List?

Problem Solving
Using Strategies

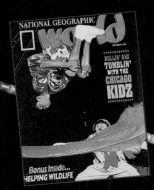

You can read more about the **Chicago Kidz** in the pages of *National Geographic World*.

The Chicago Kidz—a group of teenage boys— tumbled with Ringling Bros. and Barnum & Bailey Circus from 1992 to 1996. They wowed audiences by leaping over lines of volunteers, forming human pyramids, and performing a gymnastics Dutch rope-jumping routine. The Kidz practiced every day and attended school in the circus' traveling "Little Red School House."

Problem Solving Process
✓ Understand
✓ Plan
✓ Try It
✓ Look Back

Choose a Strategy You Have Learned
✓ Make a Table
✓ Act It Out
✓ Guess and Check
✓ Look for a Pattern
✓ Work Backward
✓ Make a List
✓ Work a Simpler Problem
✓ Draw a Picture
  Write an Equation

Suppose you want to arrange the boys in a human pyramid. You put Allen, Melvin, Robert, and Timothy on the bottom; Donald, Richard, and Terrell on the second level; Justin and Sergio in the third level; and Greg alone on top. How many different ways can you arrange the boys on the bottom?

- What information do you already know?
- What do you want to find out?
- Explain a strategy to solve this problem. Then solve it.

Use any strategy to solve the problem. Show your work.

1. Suppose the Kidz are performing in a town that is 250.5 miles from your home. You can drive to the town at an average of 45 miles each hour. If you leave your house at 8:25 A.M., can you get to the 1 P.M. show in time? Why or why not?

2. A group of clowns made a human pyramid with one clown on the top row. On the bottom level there were 16 clowns. On the level above that there were 13, and on the level above that, there were 10. If this pattern continues, how many levels of clowns will there be in all? How many clowns are in the whole pyramid?

3. Two circus tickets cost $17.50 altogether. One ticket is an adult's which is $5 more than the other ticket which is a child's. How much does the child's ticket cost?

4. Suppose that when Allen was 15 years old, he was 3 years younger than Melvin. Donald was Allen's age and 2 years younger than Timothy. Timothy was 3 years older than Richard, Terrell, Sergio, and Justin. Greg, the youngest, was 6 years younger than Melvin. How old were the other Kidz when Allen was 15 years old?

5. Before their exciting performances, the Kidz practice long hours. Suppose 4 of the Kidz want to practice a tumbling act that requires 2 performers. Each of the 4 Kidz wants to practice one time with each of the others. How many times will the 4 Kidz practice the act?

6. Suppose the Kidz show began at 6:45 and ended at 9:00. If there was a 20-minute intermission, how long was the show?

7. Pick a number from 1 to 9. Multiply the number by 27, and then subtract 12. Divide the difference by 9, and the remainder will always be the same number. What is that number?

8. Discuss problem 5 with a classmate. Compare and explain the strategies you used.

Chapter 8 Test

for Pages 256–285

Problem Solving

Solve. Show your work. (pages 268, 282, 284)

1. A photographer wants to take a picture of the five starters on a basketball team. They have to be standing in size order from shortest to tallest. The first forward is 2 inches shorter than the second forward. The point guard is 3 inches taller than the second guard, but 1 inch shorter than the first forward. The center is not shorter than the second forward. In what order should the team be standing?

2. Each of six rectangular tables is 5 feet long and 2 feet wide. When moved together in a certain way, they will make one large table that is 10 feet long and 6 feet wide. Show how the tables are arranged.

Concepts

Use the figures to answer questions 3–9. (pages 260, 264, 274, 276)

3. Which angle in slide image *EFGH* is congruent to angle *BCD* in figure *ABCD*?

4. Which side of flip image *MNOP* is congruent to side *JK* in figure *JILK*?

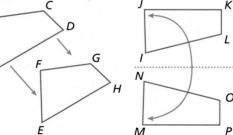
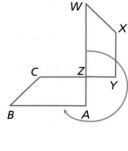

5. Which angle in the turn image is congruent to angle *WXY*?

6. How many degrees was figure *WXYZ* turned?

7. Write the ordered pair that names each point in *LMNP*.

8. By what number was each ordered pair in *LMNP* multiplied to get figure *TUVW*?

9. Are figures *LMNP* and *TUVW* congruent? Are they similar?

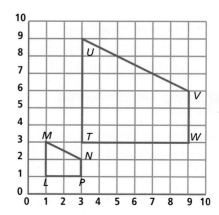

Write the measure of each angle. Use a protractor. (page 262)

10.

11.

12.

Write the measure of each missing angle. (page 272)

13.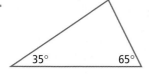

14.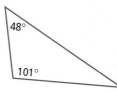

15.

Write the missing angle measure for each triangle. (page 272)

16. △BCD: 80°, 55°, ■   17. △YOU: 90°, 28°, ■

18. △CAR: 37°, 74°, ■   19. △MAD: 115°, 33°, ■

Choose the correct answer. Write a, b, c, or d. (page 272)

20. Which set of angles forms an isosceles triangle?
    a. 35°, 40°, 105°   b. 59°, 60°, 61°   c. 45°, 45°, 90°   d. 50°, 60°, 70°

21. Which set of angles forms a scalene triangle?
    a. 25°, 50°, 105°   b. 40°, 40°, 100°   c. 60°, 60°, 60°   d. 25°, 25°, 130°

22. Which set of angles forms an equilateral triangle?
    a. 45°, 45°, 90°   b. 60°, 60°, 60°   c. 50°, 60°, 70°   d. 15°, 30°, 135°

Performance Task

(pages 268, 282, 284)

A necklace is made in a repeating pattern of five beads: square, round, square, round, square. If every third square bead is red, predict how many red squares will be in a necklace 30 beads long?

• Show what the bead pattern looks like.

• Explain how you use the pattern to predict the number of square red beads.

Keep In Mind . . .
Your work will be evaluated on the following:
☑ Clearly drawn model
☑ Correct bead pattern
☑ Number of square red beads
☑ Explanation of strategy

Cumulative Review

Greatest Common Factor (Chapter 3)
Find the greatest common factor of 12 and 16.

Here's A Way!

List the factors of 12: ①, ②, 3, ④, 6, 12

List the factors of 16: ①, ②, ④, 8, 16

Circle the factors that are the same.
4 is the greatest common factor.

Find the greatest common factor for each set of numbers.

1. 10 and 25
2. 4 and 30
3. 6, 8, and 12
4. 5, 9, and 12
5. 20, 30, and 40
6. 8, 24, and 40

7. Is the greatest common factor of two numbers ever the greatest factor of one of the numbers? Give an example and explain.

Measuring Lengths (Chapter 5)
Measure the pin to the nearest $\frac{1}{8}$ inch.

Here's A Way!

Line up the zero mark on your ruler with one end of the object.
What line on the ruler is closest to the other end?
The pin is 1 in. long to the nearest $\frac{1}{8}$ inch.

Measure the length of each object to the nearest $\frac{1}{2}$ in. and $\frac{1}{8}$ in.

8.    9.    10.

11. Which gives a more precise measurement: to measure to the nearest $\frac{1}{2}$ inch or to the nearest $\frac{1}{8}$ inch? Explain.

Multiplying Decimals (Chapter 6)
Find 5×2.7.

Here's A Way!

Estimate to place the decimal point.
$5 \times 2 = 10$, and $5 \times 3 = 15$.
The answer will be between 10 and 15.
Multiply. $2.7 \times 5 = 13.5$
13.5 is between 10 and 15.
The answer is reasonable.

Find the product.

12.   5.3
    $\times$ 3

13.   16.3 cm
    $\times$ 7

14.   6.8
    $\times$ 2

15.   6.7 mm
    $\times$ 9

16. 15.8×5
17. 9.2×8
18. 25.6×1
19. $3.5 \text{ km} \times 4$

20. How does estimating help you place the decimal point in the product?

Dividing Whole Numbers (Chapter 7)

Find 3 ÷ 8.

Here's A Way!

Add zeros as needed. Divide.

$$3 \div 8 \longrightarrow 8\overline{)3.000} \; = 0.375$$

Find the quotient.

21. $5\overline{)4}$ 22. $8\overline{)6}$ 23. $4\overline{)10}$

24. $8\overline{)29}$ 25. $15 \div 6$ 26. $27 \div 5$

27. $\$5 \div 4$ 28. $39 \div 6$

29. Can you tell without dividing how many places will be in the quotient? Explain.

Classifying Triangles (Chapter 8)

Is the triangle equilateral, isosceles, or scalene?

Here's A Way!

Use the definitions.

Equilateral triangle:
3 congruent sides,
3 congruent angles

5 cm
4 cm
3 cm

Isosceles triangle: 2 congruent sides,
2 congruent angles

Scalene triangle: no congruent sides
no congruent angles

The triangle is scalene because each side has a different length.

Find the missing angles for each triangle below. Using the definitions, tell whether each triangle is equilateral, isosceles, or scalene.

30. 25°, 45°, ■   31. 60°, 60°, ■

32. 49°, 82°, ■

33. Can an isosceles triangle also be a right triangle? Explain.

Problem Solving

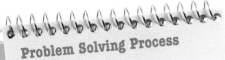

Problem Solving Process
✓ Understand
✓ Plan
✓ Try It
✓ Look Back

Choose a Strategy You Have Learned
✓ Make a Table
✓ Act It Out
✓ Guess and Check
✓ Look for a Pattern
✓ Work Backward
✓ Make a List
✓ Work a Simpler Problem
✓ Draw a Picture
Write an Equation

Choose one of the strategies you know to solve these problems. Show your work.

34. A game is played with a number cube labeled 1 to 6. You roll the cube twice and score a point if the sum of the two rolls is 9 or greater. How many ways are there to score a point?

35. Mr. Brown has been on a diet for 3 months. He weighed 185 pounds when he began. After 1 month he weighed $183\frac{1}{2}$ lb; after 2 months, 182 lb; after 3 months, $180\frac{1}{2}$ lb. If he continues to lose at the same rate, how much will he weigh after 7 months?

Native American Patterns

History Connection   **With Your Group**

Many Native Americans use geometric designs to decorate traditional clothing. The shoulder bag on the next page shows quadrilaterals and triangles as well as slides, flips, turns, and symmetry.

Find in the shoulder bag pattern the geometric ideas listed on the next page. Draw them on a piece of paper. Now, work with your group to design your own shoulder bag.

Keep In Mind . . .

Your work will be evaluated on the following:

☑ If the geometric figures are identified accurately

☑ How well you use your knowledge of slides, flips, turns, and symmetry

☑ How clearly the geometric figures are shown in your design

☑ If each group member contributed to the pattern

1

Plan It

- Cut the grid from six sheets of half-inch grid paper.
- Tape the papers together to make one long sheet of paper.

Geometric Ideas

- a quadrilateral
- a triangle
- a slide
- a flip
- a turn
- an example of line symmetry
- an example of half-turn symmetry

2

Put It Together

- Have one group member draw on the paper the first geometric figure listed.
- The next group member will draw the next figure listed. Try to use each geometric figure at least twice.
- Continue this process until the shoulder bag pattern is complete.

3

Wrap It Up

- If you wish, add designs that use other geometric shapes.
- Color the entire design.

4

Discuss Your Results

- Did you meet the objectives listed in Keep In Mind?
- Can you find examples of the geometric figures in another group's design?

Internet

> Visit the **Math Center** at Houghton Mifflin Education Place.
> http://www.eduplace.com

Fractions and Mixed Numbers

Use What You Know

$\frac{1}{2}$

$\frac{1}{4}$ $\frac{1}{4}$

- how to identify fractions

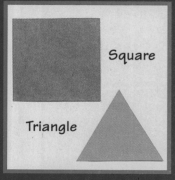

Square

Triangle

- how to identify geometric figures

- congruent
- fraction

- the vocabulary

Try This!

Use what you know about fractions and geometric figures to make congruent squares and triangles.

What You'll Need

plain paper, marker or pen, pencil, scissors

1

Fold a plain sheet of paper as shown. To make a square, cut off any extra paper. Open the paper. Trace the fold line with a marker. Each triangle represents a fraction. Write that fraction in each triangle.

2

Fold the paper in half from corner to corner using the opposite corners than before. Open the paper. Now, fold the paper lengthwise. Open it and fold it in half the other way. Use a pencil to draw a square on the paper as shown.

3

What fraction represents the square? The folds and lines make 16 congruent triangles. What fraction of the triangles is inside the drawn square? Use a pencil to write this in the square.

Are the first fractions you found equal to the last one? Do they look the same?

How would you show $1\frac{3}{4}$ with two squares of paper?

Ready to Go!

Fractions

You can write a fraction to represent part of a region. Five sixths of the circle below is blue.

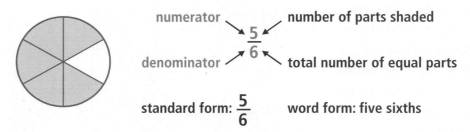

numerator → $\dfrac{5}{6}$ ← number of parts shaded

denominator → ← total number of equal parts

standard form: $\dfrac{5}{6}$ word form: five sixths

You can also use a fraction to represent part of a set. Three fourths of the students in the group below are wearing red shirts.

Activity

Fraction of a Region

1 Roll the two number cubes. Use the numbers you rolled to write a fraction. Use the lesser number, if there is one, for the numerator. Write the word form of the fraction.

2 Use squared paper to represent the fraction you wrote. Outline a shape that has the same number of squares as the number in the denominator. Use the numerator to determine the number of squares to shade with your pencil. For example, for $\frac{1}{2}$, outline a rectangle that contains 2 squares and shade 1.

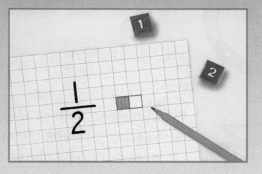

Fraction of a Set

1 Roll the two number cubes. Use the numbers you rolled to write a fraction. Use the lesser number, if there is one, for the numerator. Write the word form of the fraction.

2 Use two different colors of tiles to make a set that represents the fraction you wrote. For example, if you write $\frac{2}{3}$, you can pick 3 tiles: 2 blue and 1 red.

3 Make a drawing of your set.

Show What You Know!

Discuss each question and explain your answer.

1. Critical Thinking In the set at the right, $\frac{2}{3}$ of the blocks are blue. What fraction can you write to represent the part that is red? Explain.

Write the fraction for the shaded part in word form and standard form.

2.
3.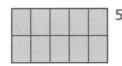
4.
5.

Write the standard form of the fraction.

6. one half   **7.** four ninths   **8.** two thirds   **9.** nine tenths

More Practice Set 9.1, p. 485

Problem Solving

Act It Out

Getting Started

What You'll Need:
▶ cubes

Eighteen fifth graders at Harriet Beecher Stowe Elementary School were surveyed about their activities. Two students sing in the chorus. Half of the remaining students participate in sports. Of the remaining students, one fourth belong to the Crafts Club, and the rest belong to the Science Club. How many of the students belong to the Science Club?

The Science Club

You can Act It Out using a model to solve this problem.

Here's A Way!   **Act It Out using a model.**

1 Understand

- How many students took part in the survey?
- What do you know about the number of students in each activity?
- What do you want to find out?

2 Plan

- Use cubes to represent each student. How many will you need in all?

3 Try It

- Arrange and separate the cubes to model the problem.
- Remove 2 cubes to model the students in chorus.
- Remove half to model those who participate in sports.
- Remove one-fourth of the cubes that are left to model the students in crafts.

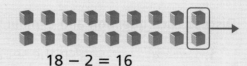

$18 - 2 = 16$

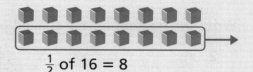

$\frac{1}{2}$ of $16 = 8$

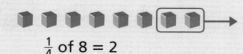

$\frac{1}{4}$ of $8 = 2$

4 Look Back

- There are 6 students in the Science Club.
- How did acting it out with a model help you to solve the problem?

Show What You Know!

Act It Out using a model to solve the problem.

1. There are 24 pieces of fruit in a basket. One third are bananas and one fourth of the rest are apples. Of the remaining pieces of fruit, one third are pears, half are peaches, and the rest are oranges. How many pieces of each kind of fruit are there?

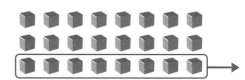

2. **Critical Thinking** How is using a model the same as making a diagram? How is it different?

Work It Out!

Use Act It Out or any strategy to solve the problem.

3. There are 36 plants in the Science Club's vegetable garden. One half are tomatoes, one third are green beans, and one twelfth are radishes. The rest are carrots. How many carrot plants are there?

4. The students want to put posts around their rectangular garden. The garden is 10 ft wide and 20 ft long. The posts will be 5 ft apart, and there will be one post at each corner. What is the least number of posts the students can use? Justify your answer.

5. The 66 students in the Dance Club make a triangular design during their performance. One student forms the top of the triangle. There are 2 students in the next row and 3 in the next row. If this pattern continues, how many rows are there?

6. How many more students will be needed if the triangular design in problem 5 includes 1 more row?

7. The Crafts Club is painting a mural on the gymnasium wall. One-third of the mural will be blue sky. Half of the remaining mural will be grass. One sixth of the mural will be buildings, and the rest will be trees. What fractional part of the mural will be trees?

Share Your Thinking

8. How can acting it out with a model help you to solve problem 7?

9. Is there more than one way to model a problem? Explain.

Equivalent Fractions

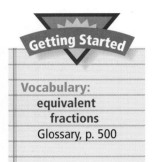

Vocabulary:
equivalent fractions
Glossary, p. 500

Use What You Know

$$\frac{2}{2} = 1$$

Multiplying or dividing a number by a fraction that is equivalent to 1 does not change the value of a number.

Equivalent fractions are different fractions that stand for the same number. You can use folded paper to model equivalent fractions.

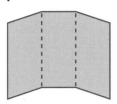 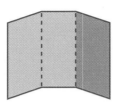 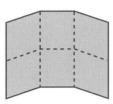 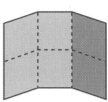

| The paper is folded into thirds. | One third is shaded. | The paper is folded in half to make sixths. | Two sixths are shaded. |

Since the same amount is shaded after folding, the fractions $\frac{1}{3}$ and $\frac{2}{6}$ are equivalent.

You can use different methods to find equivalent fractions without folding paper.

Here's A Way!   **Find equivalent fractions.**

Multiply the numerator and the denominator by the same number. The number cannot be zero.

$$\frac{1}{3} \overset{\times 2}{\underset{\times 2}{=}} \frac{2}{6}$$

You can multiply both the numerator and the denominator by 2.

So, $\frac{1}{3}$ and $\frac{2}{6}$ are equivalent fractions.

Divide the numerator and the denominator by a common factor.

$$\frac{2}{6} \overset{\div 2}{\underset{\div 2}{=}} \frac{1}{3}$$

You can divide both the numerator and the denominator by 2.

So, $\frac{2}{6}$ and $\frac{1}{3}$ are equivalent fractions.

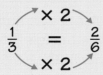 **Talk About It!**   When you multiply to find an equivalent fraction, you can use any number except zero. When you divide to find an equivalent fraction, why do you need to divide by a common factor?

Show What You Know!

What number has the numerator or denominator been multiplied by? Complete to make an equivalent fraction.

1. $\frac{5}{6} = \frac{\blacksquare}{12}$ 2. $\frac{3}{5} = \frac{\blacksquare}{10}$ 3. $\frac{1}{2} = \frac{2}{\blacksquare}$ 4. $\frac{1}{4} = \frac{\blacksquare}{12}$ 5. $\frac{3}{8} = \frac{6}{\blacksquare}$

6. Write another equivalent fraction for each fraction in exercise 5.

What number has the numerator or denominator been divided by? Complete to make an equivalent fraction.

7. $\frac{2}{10} = \frac{\blacksquare}{5}$ 8. $\frac{10}{12} = \frac{\blacksquare}{6}$ 9. $\frac{4}{12} = \frac{1}{\blacksquare}$ 10. $\frac{6}{18} = \frac{\blacksquare}{3}$ 11. $\frac{2}{8} = \frac{1}{\blacksquare}$

Multiply or divide to find an equivalent fraction.

12. $\frac{3}{15}$ 13. $\frac{7}{28}$ 14. $\frac{3}{4}$ 15. $\frac{4}{8}$ 16. $\frac{1}{2}$ 17. $\frac{1}{9}$ 18. $\frac{4}{6}$

19. **Critical Thinking** Explain why $\frac{100}{400}$ is equivalent to $\frac{1}{4}$.

Work It Out!

What number has the numerator or denominator been multiplied by? Complete to make an equivalent fraction.

20. $\frac{1}{2} = \frac{\blacksquare}{10}$ 21. $\frac{3}{6} = \frac{6}{\blacksquare}$ 22. $\frac{4}{5} = \frac{\blacksquare}{10}$ 23. $\frac{3}{5} = \frac{\blacksquare}{15}$ 24. $\frac{5}{12} = \frac{10}{\blacksquare}$ 25. $\frac{1}{3} = \frac{3}{\blacksquare}$

What number has the numerator or denominator been divided by? Complete to make an equivalent fraction.

26. $\frac{15}{15} = \frac{3}{\blacksquare}$ 27. $\frac{14}{16} = \frac{\blacksquare}{8}$ 28. $\frac{12}{15} = \frac{\blacksquare}{5}$ 29. $\frac{15}{25} = \frac{3}{\blacksquare}$ 30. $\frac{10}{15} = \frac{\blacksquare}{3}$ 31. $\frac{21}{24} = \frac{7}{\blacksquare}$

32. **Patterns** Use a pattern to write the next three equivalent fractions. What was the pattern you used?

| $\frac{1}{4}$ | $\frac{2}{8}$ | $\frac{3}{12}$ | ? | ? | ? |

Problem Solving

Use the picture to solve the problem.

38. There are 16 marbles. They are blue, red, large, and small. What fraction of the marbles are:
    a. blue?   b. large?   c. small?   d. not blue?

39. Divide to write an equivalent fraction for each fraction in exercise 38.

More Practice Set 9.3, p. 485

Simplest Form

Started

ry:
st form
y, p. 500

Astronauts Linda Godwin and Rich Clifford performed the first space walk while the space shuttle Atlantis and Mir space station were docked together. They spent 6 out of 24 hours, or $\frac{6}{24}$ of their day, outside the spacecraft.

You can also say they spent $\frac{1}{4}$ of their day walking in space.

Is this the simplest form of the fraction $\frac{6}{24}$?

A fraction is in **simplest form** when the numerator and denominator have no common factor other than one.

Here's A Way! Find the simplest form of $\frac{6}{24}$.

1 Find the factors of the numerator and denominator.

Factors of 6: 1, 2, 3, 6

Factors of 24:
1, 2, 3, 4, 6, 8, 12, 24

2 Find the greatest common factor (GCF) of the numerator and denominator.

The GCF of 6 and 24 is 6.

3 Divide the numerator and denominator by the GCF.

$$\frac{6}{24} \begin{matrix} \div 6 \\ = \\ \div 6 \end{matrix} \frac{1}{4}$$

The simplest form of $\frac{6}{24}$ is $\frac{1}{4}$, since the numerator and denominator have no common factors greater than 1.

Talk About It! What would happen if you divided by a common factor that was not the GCF?

List the factors. Circle the greatest common factor for each pair.

1. 10, 25   **2.** 7, 20   **3.** 9, 12   **4.** 24, 30   **5.** 6, 18   **6.** 27, 36

Write the equivalent fraction that is in simplest form.

7. $\frac{4}{24}$ **8.** $\frac{8}{16}$ **9.** $\frac{8}{64}$ **10.** $\frac{14}{21}$ **11.** $\frac{20}{60}$ **12.** $\frac{9}{12}$ **13.** $\frac{5}{20}$

14. Critical Thinking In which exercises could you use mental math to find the simplest form?

Work It Out!

List the factors. Write the greatest common factor for each pair.

15. 12, 24   **16.** 18, 27   **17.** 5, 10   **18.** 20, 50   **19.** 24, 36   **20.** 15, 18

Write the equivalent fraction in simplest form.

21. $\frac{14}{16}$ **22.** $\frac{10}{12}$ **23.** $\frac{8}{10}$ **24.** $\frac{6}{8}$ **25.** $\frac{20}{24}$ **26.** $\frac{12}{32}$ **27.** $\frac{5}{25}$

28. $\frac{14}{28}$ **29.** $\frac{20}{36}$ **30.** $\frac{10}{40}$ **31.** $\frac{6}{18}$ **32.** $\frac{22}{24}$ **33.** $\frac{7}{21}$ **34.** $\frac{3}{30}$

Problem Solving

35. A mission of space shuttle Columbia in 1994, which carried the first Japanese woman to fly in space, lasted 14 days, 18 hours. In simplest form, what fraction of a day is 18 hours?

36. Astronaut Shannon Lucid set a record for U.S. space flight duration by spending 188 days aboard the Russian space station Mir. Cosmonaut Valery Polyakov spent 439 days aboard Mir. How many days longer is Polyakov's record than Lucid's?

37. Atlantis was scheduled to launch July 31, 1996, to travel to Mir to bring Shannon Lucid home. Atlantis's trip was delayed by the threat of two hurricanes and did not launch until September 16, 1996. How many days behind schedule did the mission begin?

Mixed Review

Write the least common multiple.

38. 12, 3   **39.** 3, 10   **40.** 9, 6   **41.** 8, 5   **42.** 6, 7   **43.** 4, 14

More Practice Set 9.4, p. 486

Estimating Fractions

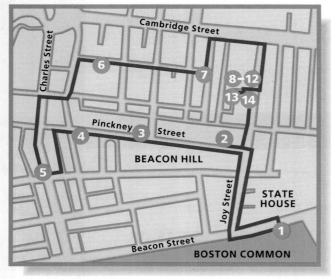

Cambridge Street

Charles Street

6

7

8–12

13 14

Pinckney Street

4 3

2

5

BEACON HILL

Joy Street

STATE
HOUSE

1

Beacon Street

BOSTON COMMON

0   0.1 mi

Scale

The Black Heritage Trail is a walking tour in Boston that includes places important in the history of the African-American community.

The map shows that it is about $\frac{4}{10}$ mi from the first site on the trail to the fourth site, the John J. Smith House. It is about $\frac{8}{10}$ mi from there to the end of the trail. Which part of the trail is about $\frac{1}{2}$ mi and which part is about 1 mi?

You can estimate if a fraction is close to 0, $\frac{1}{2}$, or 1 by comparing the numerator and denominator.

John J. Smith's shop was a destination for enslaved people who had run away.

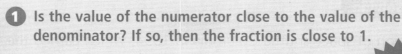

Here's A Way! **Estimate the value of a fraction.**

1 Is the value of the numerator close to the value of the denominator? If so, then the fraction is close to 1.

$\frac{8}{10}$: The numerator 8 is close to the denominator 10, so $\frac{8}{10}$ is close to 1.

$\frac{10}{10} = 1$

2 Is the value of the denominator about twice as great as the value of the numerator? If so, then the fraction is close to $\frac{1}{2}$.

$\frac{4}{10}$: The denominator 10 is about twice as great as the numerator 4, so $\frac{4}{10}$ is close to $\frac{1}{2}$.

Talk About It! Explain how you can use estimation to decide whether $\frac{5}{9}$ is greater than or less than $\frac{11}{13}$.

Other Examples A fraction is close to 0 if the value of the numerator is much less than the value of the denominator.

$\frac{1}{10}$ $\frac{2}{11}$ $\frac{3}{15}$ close to 0

Write whether the fraction is close to 0, $\frac{1}{2}$, or 1.

1. $\frac{1}{10}$ 2. $\frac{4}{6}$ 3. $\frac{3}{7}$ 4. $\frac{7}{8}$ 5. $\frac{3}{20}$ 6. $\frac{2}{15}$ 7. $\frac{13}{12}$ 8. $\frac{56}{100}$

Make the fraction close to $\frac{1}{2}$, but not exactly $\frac{1}{2}$.

9. $\frac{3}{\blacksquare}$ 10. $\frac{\blacksquare}{12}$ 11. $\frac{\blacksquare}{14}$ 12. $\frac{5}{\blacksquare}$ 13. $\frac{12}{\blacksquare}$ 14. $\frac{\blacksquare}{9}$ 15. $\frac{15}{\blacksquare}$ 16. $\frac{\blacksquare}{8}$

17. **Critical Thinking** Discuss how you would make the fraction in exercise 10 close to 1, but not exactly 1. Explain.

Write whether the fraction is close to 0, $\frac{1}{2}$, or 1.

18. $\frac{1}{5}$ 19. $\frac{3}{8}$ 20. $\frac{15}{16}$ 21. $\frac{13}{25}$ 22. $\frac{8}{9}$ 23. $\frac{7}{12}$ 24. $\frac{93}{100}$ 25. $\frac{11}{9}$

Make the fraction close to 0, but not exactly 0.

26. $\frac{2}{\blacksquare}$ 27. $\frac{\blacksquare}{11}$ 28. $\frac{5}{\blacksquare}$ 29. $\frac{\blacksquare}{18}$ 30. $\frac{\blacksquare}{30}$ 31. $\frac{\blacksquare}{15}$ 32. $\frac{3}{\blacksquare}$ 33. $\frac{\blacksquare}{14}$

Make the fraction close to $\frac{1}{2}$, but not exactly $\frac{1}{2}$.

34. $\frac{4}{\blacksquare}$ 35. $\frac{\blacksquare}{13}$ 36. $\frac{8}{\blacksquare}$ 37. $\frac{\blacksquare}{10}$ 38. $\frac{\blacksquare}{21}$ 39. $\frac{6}{\blacksquare}$ 40. $\frac{9}{\blacksquare}$ 41. $\frac{\blacksquare}{7}$

Make the fraction close to 1, but not exactly 1.

42. $\frac{\blacksquare}{9}$ 43. $\frac{\blacksquare}{12}$ 44. $\frac{5}{\blacksquare}$ 45. $\frac{\blacksquare}{80}$ 46. $\frac{64}{\blacksquare}$ 47. $\frac{7}{\blacksquare}$

Problem Solving

48. From the first site on the Black Heritage Trail to the last site is $\frac{12}{10}$ mi. Is the distance more or less than 1 mi? Explain.

49. In 1820, the African-American population of Boston was 1690 people. By 1890, the population had increased to 8125. How much greater was the African-American population in 1890 than in 1820?

50. **Algebraic Reasoning** In the fraction $\frac{n}{6}$, for what values of n will the fraction be closer to 0 than to $\frac{1}{2}$? Closer to 1 than to $\frac{1}{2}$?

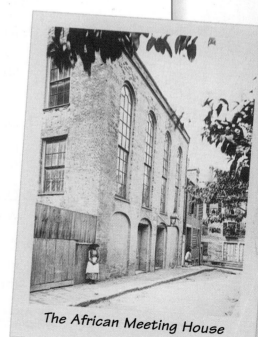

The African Meeting House

More Practice Set 9.5, p. 486

Problem Solving
Is There Enough Information?

Walkathon Pledge Voucher

Name	Dollars per Hour	Additional Pledge
Linda Ruby	$5	

Walkathon Pledge Voucher

Name	Dollars per Hour	Additional Pledge
Ben Hummer	$5	$2 per hour for every ho over 10 hour

A fifth grader took part in a walkathon to raise money for charity. She walked 20 hours from Monday through Friday from 3:00 P.M. to 7:00 P.M. each day. One sponsor pledged $5 for every hour she walked. Another pledged $5 an hour plus an additional $2 for every hour over 10 hours. How much money did the walker raise?

You Decide

- What question do you need to answer?
- What information do you need to solve the problem? What information is not needed?
- What operations will you use to solve the problem?

Work It Out!

Decide what information you need to solve the problem. Then solve.

1. Mrs. Lin and Mr. Diaz each have 24 students in their classes. One-fourth of Mrs. Lin's fifth graders took part in the walkathon, and so did one-third of Mr. Diaz's class. One class raised $20 more than the other. Which class had more walkers in the walkathon?

2. Suppose you walked in a walkathon for $12\frac{1}{2}$ hours. If 3 people pledged $2 for each half-hour you walked, how many half-hours did you walk?

3. One walker raised $150. She walked for 15 of the 20 hours of the walkathon. What fraction of the walkathon did she complete?

4. **Create Your Own** Write a problem that contains extra information. Solve your problem, then trade it with a friend. Find the extra information in each other's problem and solve.

Share Your Thinking

5. How do you decide which information you need and do not need in a problem?

Midchapter Review

for Pages 294–304

for Pages 294–304

Problem Solving

Solve. Show your work. (pages 296, 304)

1. Twenty-eight students sing in the chorus. Half of them are girls. One-fourth of the students play in the band. How many play in the band?

2. A stamp collection has 32 pages of stamps. Half the pages are from foreign countries. One-fourth of the rest have pictures of famous people. The remaining pages have pictures of U.S. monuments. How many pages have U.S. monuments?

Concepts

Find the answers. (pages 294, 298, 300)

3. What does the denominator of a fraction tell you?

4. How can you find an equivalent fraction?

5. When is a fraction in simplest form?

6. When would you estimate a fraction as close to $\frac{1}{2}$?

Skills

Complete to make equivalent fractions. (page 298)

7. $\frac{3}{6} = \frac{\blacksquare}{2}$

8. $\frac{2}{7} = \frac{4}{\blacksquare}$

9. $\frac{10}{12} = \frac{\blacksquare}{6}$

10. $\frac{5}{8} = \frac{10}{\blacksquare}$

11. $\frac{4}{10} = \frac{\blacksquare}{5}$

Write an equivalent fraction that is in simplest form. (page 300)

12. $\frac{2}{6}$

13. $\frac{6}{12}$

14. $\frac{6}{24}$

15. $\frac{6}{9}$

16. $\frac{25}{30}$

Estimate the fraction. Write 0, $\frac{1}{2}$, or 1. (pages 302, 303)

17. $\frac{9}{10}$

18. $\frac{1}{7}$

19. $\frac{8}{15}$

20. $\frac{22}{24}$

21. $\frac{27}{50}$

Math World

Fractions

Around the World

Fractions are often used in measurement. Read

how people around the world have used fractions.

Then play a Native American game.

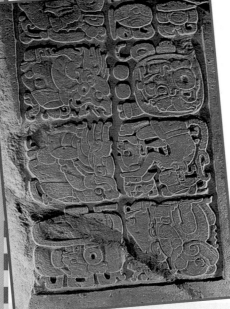

Extra Days and Leap Years

It takes the earth $365\frac{1}{4}$ days, about one year, to go around the sun. We do not have the $\frac{1}{4}$ day on our calendar, so we add them together over four years. Then, they equal one day. This is why every four years we have leap year, a year with 366 days. Ancient people also tried to solve the problem of the extra $\frac{1}{4}$ day. The Maya added five days to their calendars. Roman emperor Julius Caesar tried to solve the problem by making one year 445 days long!

It's Raining, It's Pouring

A light rain is about $\frac{1}{25}$ of an inch of rain each hour. It would take 25 hours of light rain to fill a container 1 in. deep. A heavy rain is about $\frac{3}{5}$ of an inch of rain each hour. In 25 hours, a heavy rain would fill a container 15 inches deep. In Tanzania in east Africa, heavy rains, called monsoon rains, come in the fall and spring. The rain is so heavy that many children have to stay home from school.

306

Try This! Native American Button Game

The Seneca people of New York played a version of this game with elk horn buttons. You and a partner can play with counters.

Throw	Points
Less than $\frac{3}{4}$ of same color	0
$\frac{3}{4}$ of same color	2
$\frac{7}{8}$ of same color	4
$\frac{8}{8}$ of same color	20

1 Use eight counters. Put a small piece of tape on one side of each counter. Decide who will go first.

2 The first player tosses the counters, using the chart to find his or her score.

3 Take turns tossing the counters. Calculate the number of points you get in each toss. Try to be the first to get 40 points.

Meter Reader

A meter was first used in France in 1670. Scientists decided the meter would be $\frac{1}{40,000,000}$ of the distance around the earth. Today, a meter is measured by the speed of light. The distance light travels in $\frac{1}{299,792,458}$ of a second is the length of one meter.

Respond

Make a calendar . . .
that has $365\frac{1}{4}$ days. How will you solve the problem of the $\frac{1}{4}$ day?

Internet:
Houghton Mifflin Education Place
Explore the Math Center at
http://www.eduplace.com

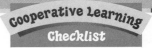
Cooperative Learning
Checklist

☑ Work alone.
☑ Work with a partner.
☑ Work with a group.

Whole Numbers and Mixed Numbers

Use What You Know

A mixed number is made up of a whole number and a fraction, for example, $2\frac{1}{3}$.

Some fractions can be written as whole numbers or mixed numbers. You can use fraction models to help you.

Activity

Exploring Fourths

Table A

Number of Models	Fraction in Fourths
2	$\frac{8}{4}$
3	$\frac{?}{4}$
4	$\frac{?}{4}$
5	$\frac{?}{4}$

❶ Make 5 fraction models for fourths. Use the fourths models to help you complete this activity.

There are 4 fourths, or $\frac{4}{4}$, on one model.

There are 8 fourths, or $\frac{8}{4}$, on two models.

❷ Copy Table A or use your recording sheet.

❸ Describe the pattern in the numerators in Table A.

Exploring Whole Numbers and Fractions

Table B

Fraction Models	Number of Models	Fraction
halves	2	$\frac{4}{2}$
fifths	2	$\frac{?}{5}$
sixths	2	$\frac{?}{6}$
halves	3	$\frac{?}{2}$
fifths	3	$\frac{?}{5}$
sixths	3	$\frac{?}{6}$

❶ Make 3 fraction models each for halves, fifths, and sixths. Discuss and complete these questions with your group.

a. What is the numerator that completes the number sentence $2 = \frac{\blacksquare}{2}$?

Use the models to complete the table. Copy the table or use your recording sheet.

b. How could you complete Table B without using your models?

❷ Write the numerator.

a. $1 = \frac{\blacksquare}{5}$ **b.** $2 = \frac{\blacksquare}{5}$ **c.** $4 = \frac{\blacksquare}{6}$

Exploring Whole and Mixed Numbers

1. The first set of fraction models shows $1\frac{1}{3}$ shaded. Four thirds are shaded. The mixed number $1\frac{1}{3}$ can be written as the fraction $\frac{4}{3}$.

   a. In the second set, how many thirds are shaded?

2. Copy and complete Table C or use the recording sheet.

Table C

Model	Number	Fraction
	1	$\frac{4}{4}$
	$1\frac{1}{4}$	$\frac{?}{4}$
	$1\frac{2}{4}$	$\frac{?}{4}$
	$1\frac{3}{4}$	$\frac{?}{4}$
	2	$\frac{?}{4}$
	3	$\frac{?}{5}$
	$3\frac{1}{5}$	$\frac{?}{5}$
	$3\frac{2}{5}$	$\frac{?}{5}$
	2	$\frac{?}{6}$
	$2\frac{1}{6}$	$\frac{?}{6}$
	$2\frac{2}{6}$	$\frac{?}{6}$

Show What You Know!

Write the mixed number as a fraction. Use models if you need to.

1. $2\frac{2}{10}$ 2. $1\frac{1}{8}$ 3. $2\frac{1}{4}$ 4. $2\frac{3}{6}$ 5. $3\frac{4}{5}$ 6. $4\frac{2}{5}$ 7. $1\frac{5}{6}$ 8. $5\frac{1}{2}$

Complete.

9. $4\frac{3}{\blacksquare} = \frac{23}{5}$ 10. $6\frac{1}{3} = \frac{\blacksquare}{3}$ 11. $\blacksquare\frac{2}{5} = \frac{47}{5}$ 12. $1\frac{\blacksquare}{9} = \frac{13}{9}$ 13. $\blacksquare\frac{4}{\blacksquare} = \frac{19}{5}$

14. **Number Sense** To write a whole number as a fraction with a certain denominator, multiply the whole number by the denominator. Write the product as the numerator. What is the rule for writing mixed numbers as fractions?

15. **Number Sense** When writing a mixed number as a fraction, is the numerator less than or greater than the denominator? Explain.

Writing Fractions

Your class wants to make birdhouses for bluebirds. The birdhouse floor is a square with all sides measuring 4 in. You have 3 boards that are 1 ft long and 4 in. wide. You need to cut them into pieces that are $\frac{1}{3}$ ft long. How many birdhouse floors can you make from the 3 pieces of wood?

If you write the length of each board as thirds, you can find how many floors you can make.

Here's A Way! Write a whole number as a fraction.

1 Write the denominator.

$$3 = \frac{\blacksquare}{3}$$

You need to find thirds, so the denominator is 3.

2 Multiply the whole number by the denominator to get the numerator.

$$3 = \frac{9}{3}$$ $3 \times 3 = 9$

You can write 3 as $\frac{9}{3}$.

You have 9 thirds, so you can make nine birdhouse floors.

Talk About It! Why do you multiply the whole number by the denominator 3 to change the whole number to thirds?

Other Examples To change a *mixed* number to a fraction, write the whole number as a fraction as above and add the fraction part of the mixed number.

$3\frac{1}{2}$

$3 = \frac{6}{2}$ $\frac{6}{2} + \frac{1}{2}$

$\frac{7}{2}$

$4\frac{2}{5}$

$4 = \frac{20}{5}$ $\frac{20}{5} + \frac{2}{5}$

$\frac{22}{5}$

Show What You Know!

Complete each equivalent fraction.

1. $7 = \frac{\blacksquare}{3}$ 2. $2\frac{3}{4} = \frac{\blacksquare}{4}$ 3. $5\frac{7}{9} = \frac{\blacksquare}{9}$ 4. $7 = \frac{\blacksquare}{1}$ 5. $1 = \frac{\blacksquare}{15}$ 6. $1\frac{1}{4} = \frac{\blacksquare}{4}$

Write each mixed number as an equivalent fraction.

7. $2\frac{5}{6}$ 8. $5\frac{3}{4}$ 9. $1\frac{9}{10}$ 10. $7\frac{5}{8}$ 11. $4\frac{4}{5}$ 12. $2\frac{1}{3}$

13. **Critical Thinking** How many equivalent fractions are there for any whole number? Discuss your answer.

Work It Out!

Complete each equivalent fraction.

14. $5 = \frac{\blacksquare}{9}$ 15. $3\frac{2}{3} = \frac{\blacksquare}{3}$ 16. $6\frac{7}{11} = \frac{\blacksquare}{11}$ 17. $5 = \frac{\blacksquare}{11}$ 18. $4 = \frac{\blacksquare}{\blacksquare}$ 19. $4\frac{2}{5} = \frac{\blacksquare}{5}$

Write each whole number as thirds.

20. 7 21. 2 22. 9 23. 10 24. 1 25. 5 26. 11 27. 4

Write each mixed number as an equivalent fraction.

28. $2\frac{1}{2}$ 29. $3\frac{7}{8}$ 30. $12\frac{2}{5}$ 31. $10\frac{5}{9}$ 32. $8\frac{7}{8}$ 33. $4\frac{1}{4}$ 34. $7\frac{4}{7}$ 35. $9\frac{1}{9}$

Problem Solving

36. You are making nest boxes for the great-crested flycatcher. How many floors can you make out of 3 pieces of wood that are 1 ft long and 6 in. wide?

37. **Estimation** You plan to make 24 birdhouses and you have finished making $\frac{5}{12}$ of them. Are you almost finished, halfway finished, or just beginning?

38. A birdhouse for flickers has a hole that is $2\frac{4}{8}$ in. wide. Is this the right size? How can you tell?

39. **Create Your Own** Write a word problem in which you must change $4\frac{3}{4}$ to $\frac{19}{4}$ in order to solve the problem.

Nest Box Dimensions for Various Birds

Species	Floor	Depth	Size of Hole
Chickadee	4 in. × 4 in.	9 in.	$1\frac{1}{8}$ in.
House Wren	4 in. × 4 in.	8 in.	$1-1\frac{1}{4}$ in.
Great-Crested Flycatcher	6 in. × 6 in.	10 in.	$1\frac{3}{4}$ in.
Flicker	7 in. × 7 in.	18 in.	$2\frac{1}{2}$ in.

More Practice Set 9.8, p. 486

311

Writing Mixed Numbers

LESSON 9

Craft paint can be made from ordinary household products. The recipe to the left calls for $\frac{1}{2}$ c of cornstarch. If you want to make 5 batches of paint, you need $\frac{5}{2}$ c of cornstarch. Written as a mixed number, how many cups of cornstarch do you need?

You can use what you know about fractions, mixed numbers, and division to answer this question.

> **Recipe for Craft Paint**
>
> Corn Starch $\frac{1}{2}$ cup
> Cold Water   1 cup
> Unflavored Gelatin $\frac{1}{4}$ oz
> Hot Water   2 cups
> Mild Soap Flakes $\frac{1}{2}$ cup
> Household Dye   1 teaspoon

Here's A Way!   **Write a fraction as a mixed number.**

1 Divide the numerator by the denominator.

$$\frac{5}{2} \implies 2\overline{)5} \implies \begin{array}{r} 2 \\ 2\overline{)5} \\ -4 \\ \hline 1 \end{array}$$

2 Write the remainder as a fraction.

$$2\frac{1}{2} \quad \begin{array}{r} 2 \\ 2\overline{)5} \\ -4 \\ \hline 1 \end{array}$$

remainder
original denominator

So, you need $2\frac{1}{2}$ cups of cornstarch to make 5 batches of paint.

Talk About It!   Can all fractions be written as mixed numbers? Explain. Give examples to support your answer.

Other Examples   Some fractions can be written as whole numbers.

$$\frac{12}{6} \implies \begin{array}{r} 2 \\ 6\overline{)12} \\ -12 \\ \hline 0 \end{array} \implies \text{So, } \frac{12}{6} = 2$$

312   Chapter 9

Show What You Know!

Write each fraction as a whole or mixed number in simplest form.

1. $\frac{7}{4}$ 2. $\frac{15}{5}$ 3. $\frac{11}{9}$ 4. $\frac{18}{6}$ 5. $\frac{36}{8}$ 6. $\frac{26}{12}$ 7. $\frac{17}{3}$ 8. $\frac{21}{10}$

9. **Critical Thinking** In exercise 6, if you write $\frac{26}{12}$ in simplest form first and then divide, what do you notice about your answer?

Work It Out!

Write each fraction as a whole or mixed number in simplest form.

10. $\frac{12}{7}$ 11. $\frac{14}{5}$ 12. $\frac{44}{11}$ 13. $\frac{75}{15}$ 14. $\frac{24}{14}$ 15. $\frac{10}{4}$ 16. $\frac{9}{2}$ 17. $\frac{36}{4}$

18. $\frac{21}{3}$ 19. $\frac{52}{12}$ 20. $\frac{20}{6}$ 21. $\frac{32}{10}$ 22. $\frac{17}{6}$ 23. $\frac{36}{9}$ 24. $\frac{31}{3}$ 25. $\frac{65}{8}$

Problem Solving

Use the recipe on p. 312 to solve the problem.

26. You need $\frac{5}{4}$ oz of unflavored gelatin to make 5 batches of paint. Written as a mixed number, how many ounces is this?

27. **Mental Math** You need $\frac{8}{2}$ c of soap flakes to make 8 batches of paint. Suppose you have a box of soap flakes with 6 c of flakes left. Do you have enough flakes to make 8 batches? Explain.

Mixed Review

Use the prices on the flyer to estimate. Is there enough money to buy each item?

Jar of Paint – $ .79
Paint Brush – $ .49
Paper Pack – $1.79

28. 6 jars of paint with $5   29. 8 brushes with $3   30. 5 paper packs with $10

About how much money will you have left after this purchase?

31. 7 paper packs with $15   32. 1 of each item with $5   33. 3 jars of paint with $3

More Practice Set 9.9, p. 487

Math Journal

How can you tell by looking at a fraction greater than 1 whether it will be a whole number or a mixed number?

Comparing and Ordering

North America

Europe

Asia

Africa

South America

Australia

Antarctica

The land on Earth is divided into seven continents. About $\frac{1}{3}$ of all the land in the world is in Asia. Africa has about $\frac{1}{5}$ of the land. Antarctica makes up about $\frac{1}{10}$ of Earth's land. Which continent has the greatest amount of land?

To compare fractions with different denominators find equivalent fractions with a common denominator.

Here's A Way! **Compare fractions with different denominators.**

1 Find the least common multiple (LCM) of the denominators.

$\frac{1}{3}$ 3: 3, 6, 9, 12, 15, 18, 21, 24, 27, 30

$\frac{1}{5}$ 5: 5, 10, 15, 20, 25, 30

$\frac{1}{10}$ 10: 10, 20, 30

> The LCM of 3, 5, and 10 is 30.

2 Write the equivalent fractions with the least common denominator. Use the LCM.

$$\frac{1}{3} \times \frac{10}{10} = \frac{10}{30} \qquad \frac{1}{5} \times \frac{6}{6} = \frac{6}{30} \qquad \frac{1}{10} \times \frac{3}{3} = \frac{3}{30}$$

3 Compare the numerators and write the fractions in order.

$$3 < 6 < 10, \text{ so } \frac{3}{30} < \frac{6}{30} < \frac{10}{30}, \text{ so } \frac{1}{10} < \frac{1}{5} < \frac{1}{3}$$

Since $\frac{1}{3} > \frac{1}{5} > \frac{1}{10}$, Asia is the largest continent.

Talk About It! When you compare fractions, how can you tell that the answer is reasonable?

Other Examples Compare fractions with the same denominator.

Which is greater: $\frac{1}{4}$ or $\frac{3}{4}$? Look at the numerator.

Since 3 is greater than 1, $\frac{3}{4} > \frac{1}{4}$.

Write the least common denominator for each pair.

1. $\frac{1}{4}$, $\frac{3}{5}$ 2. $\frac{1}{2}$, $\frac{5}{8}$ 3. $\frac{5}{7}$, $\frac{1}{3}$ 4. $10\frac{5}{8}$, $3\frac{1}{12}$ 5. $2\frac{1}{6}$, $3\frac{1}{8}$

6. **Critical Thinking** In exercise 5, if you used the common denominator 24, would you get the same answer as you would get if you used the common denominator 48? Explain.

Compare. Write >, <, or =.

7. $\frac{4}{7}$ ■ $\frac{6}{7}$ 8. $\frac{1}{2}$ ■ $\frac{2}{3}$ 9. $2\frac{1}{5}$ ■ $3\frac{1}{9}$ 10. $7\frac{5}{6}$ ■ $7\frac{4}{7}$ 11. $2\frac{2}{5}$ ■ $2\frac{3}{4}$

Write the numbers in order from least to greatest.

12. $\frac{3}{4}$, $\frac{2}{5}$, $\frac{1}{2}$ 13. $\frac{5}{10}$, $\frac{2}{10}$, $\frac{7}{10}$ 14. $2\frac{4}{5}$, $2\frac{4}{7}$, $3\frac{1}{10}$ 15. $\frac{3}{4}$, $\frac{5}{8}$, $\frac{1}{2}$

Work It Out!

Write the least common denominator for each pair.

16. $\frac{4}{5}$, $\frac{1}{6}$ 17. $\frac{1}{4}$, $\frac{5}{12}$ 18. $\frac{11}{15}$, $\frac{3}{10}$ 19. $4\frac{2}{5}$, $3\frac{1}{10}$ 20. $1\frac{2}{3}$, $3\frac{1}{4}$

Compare. Write >, <, or =. Explain your reasoning.

21. $\frac{5}{11}$ ■ $\frac{1}{11}$ 22. $\frac{3}{5}$ ■ $\frac{2}{3}$ 23. $3\frac{9}{10}$ ■ $3\frac{11}{15}$ 24. $5\frac{4}{5}$ ■ $5\frac{5}{7}$ 25. $6\frac{7}{8}$ ■ $6\frac{5}{9}$

Write the numbers in order from least to greatest.

26. $\frac{7}{10}$, $\frac{3}{5}$, $\frac{8}{15}$ 27. $\frac{2}{3}$, $\frac{3}{4}$, $\frac{5}{8}$ 28. $4\frac{1}{3}$, $4\frac{2}{9}$, $4\frac{7}{12}$

Problem Solving **Using Data**

Use the chart to solve the problem.

29. Write the population of the world regions in order from least to greatest population. (two are equal)

30. Does Asia have a greater fraction of the world's land or of the world's population? (See p. 314)

31. **Create Your Own** Write a problem that can be solved by comparing three or more fractions on the chart.

32. **Estimation** The land area of Antarctica is 5,405,823 sq mi. Estimate the land area of Antarctica to the nearest million square miles.

1996 World Population	
Region	**Fraction of Population**
Africa	$\frac{13}{100}$
North America	$\frac{1}{20}$
Latin America and Caribbean	$\frac{2}{25}$
Asia	$\frac{3}{5}$
Europe	$\frac{13}{100}$
Oceania	$\frac{1}{200}$

More Practice Set 9.10, p. 487

Equivalent Forms

Aquifers are large amounts of water contained in rock and gravel under the earth. This water provides about $\frac{60}{100}$ of the water used for drinking and irrigation in the United States. How would you write $\frac{60}{100}$ as a decimal?

$$\frac{60}{100} = 60 \text{ hundredths or } 0.60$$

It is easy to write a fraction as a decimal when the fraction has a denominator of 10, 100, or 1000. Look at the examples in the table.

To write a fraction such as $\frac{2}{5}$ as a decimal, you first write it as an equivalent fraction with a denominator of 10, 100, or 1000.

Number	Fraction	Decimal
5 tenths	$\frac{5}{10}$	0.5
7 hundredths	$\frac{7}{100}$	0.07
135 thousandths	$\frac{135}{1000}$	0.135

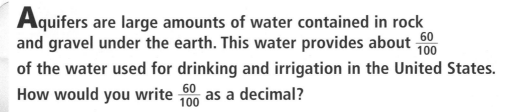

limestone

well

dense stone

Here's A Way! Write $\frac{2}{5}$ as a decimal.

1 Multiply to find an equivalent fraction with a denominator of 10, 100, or 1000.

$$\frac{2}{5} \overset{\times 2}{\underset{\times 2}{=}} \frac{4}{10}$$

2 Write the equivalent fraction as a decimal.

$$\frac{4}{10} = 0.4$$

So, $\frac{2}{5} = \frac{4}{10}$ or 0.4

Talk About It! Suppose you write $\frac{40}{100}$ as the equivalent fraction for $\frac{2}{5}$. Will the decimal equivalent change? Will its original value change? Explain.

Write each fraction as a decimal.

1. $\frac{45}{100}$ 2. $\frac{1}{4}$ 3. $\frac{4}{100}$ 4. $\frac{7}{20}$ 5. $\frac{1}{2}$ 6. $\frac{1}{5}$ 7. $\frac{3}{500}$ 8. $\frac{65}{100}$

9. $\frac{9}{25}$ 10. $\frac{1}{20}$ 11. $\frac{3}{1000}$ 12. $\frac{1}{10}$ 13. $\frac{6}{50}$ 14. $\frac{10}{250}$ 15. $\frac{15}{25}$ 16. $\frac{999}{1000}$

17. **Critical Thinking** Write $\frac{3}{10}$, $\frac{3}{100}$, and $\frac{3}{1000}$ as decimals. What do you notice?

Work It Out!

Write each fraction as a decimal.

18. $\frac{9}{1000}$ 19. $\frac{3}{4}$ 20. $\frac{1}{200}$ 21. $\frac{23}{1000}$ 22. $\frac{4}{5}$ 23. $\frac{11}{500}$ 24. $\frac{20}{50}$ 25. $\frac{7}{10}$

26. $\frac{5}{10}$ 27. $\frac{1}{100}$ 28. $\frac{2}{25}$ 29. $\frac{3}{20}$ 30. $\frac{7}{25}$ 31. $\frac{250}{1000}$ 32. $\frac{50}{250}$ 33. $\frac{12}{20}$

34. $\frac{3}{5}$ 35. $\frac{3}{50}$ 36. $\frac{1}{50}$ 37. $\frac{1}{500}$ 38. $\frac{9}{100}$ 39. $\frac{9}{10}$ 40. $\frac{15}{200}$ 41. $\frac{16}{25}$

For each fraction pair, write an equivalent decimal from the box.

42. $\frac{1}{50}$, $\frac{2}{100}$ 43. $\frac{1}{4}$, $\frac{4}{16}$ 44. $\frac{2}{4}$, $\frac{1}{2}$ 45. $\frac{55}{100}$, $\frac{11}{20}$

0.25	0.02	0.4
0.55		0.5

Problem Solving Using Data

Use the chart to solve the problem. Use mental math when you can.

46. Write as a decimal the fraction of the total area of the United States that is made up of rivers and lakes.

47. Do rivers and lakes in Colombia take up more or less than $\frac{85}{1000}$ of its total area? How can you tell?

48. About $\frac{7}{10}$ of the earth's surface is covered with water. Only $\frac{1}{100}$ of this is fresh water. How can you write these two fractions as decimals?

49. The total area of India's rivers and lakes is 314,400 square kilometers. This is 108,390 square kilometers greater than that of the United States. What is the total area of rivers and lakes in the United States?

Country	Fraction of Area Made Up of Rivers and Lakes
Canada	$\frac{19}{250}$
United States	$\frac{11}{500}$
Colombia	$\frac{11}{125}$
Tanzania	$\frac{1}{16}$

More Practice Set 9.11, p. 487

12 Fractions and Decimals

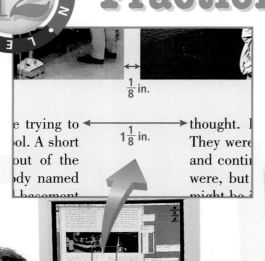

$\frac{1}{8}$ in.

e trying to ⟷ thought.
ol. A short $1\frac{1}{8}$ in. They were
out of the and conti
dy named were, but
basement might be

Working on a computer screen, a newspaper designer arranges photographs and articles to look as they will on the newspaper page.

Suppose a newspaper designer wants to leave $\frac{1}{8}$ in. of space between two pictures and $1\frac{1}{8}$ in. between two columns of text. The computer only reads measurements in decimals. How could the measurements be written so the computer can read them?

Here's A Way! Find an equivalent decimal for $\frac{1}{8}$ and $1\frac{1}{8}$.

Write a fraction as a decimal. Divide the numerator by the denominator.

$$\frac{1}{8} = 8)\overline{1.00}$$

$$
\begin{array}{r}
0.125 \\
8)\overline{1.00} \\
-8 \\
\hline
20 \\
-16 \\
\hline
40 \\
-40 \\
\hline
0
\end{array}
$$

So, $\frac{1}{8} = 0.125$

Write a mixed number as a decimal. Divide the numerator by the denominator and add the whole number.

$1\frac{1}{8}$

$1 + 0.125$

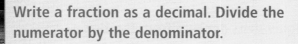

So, $1\frac{1}{8} = 1.125$

1.125

Talk About It! Explain two different ways to find an equivalent decimal for $2\frac{3}{5}$.

Other Example To write a decimal as a mixed number, decide if the decimal represents tenths, hundredths, or thousandths. Write the equivalent mixed number. Simplify if you can.

$3.5 = 3$ and 5 tenths or $3\frac{5}{10}$ or $3\frac{1}{2}$ So, $3.5 = 3\frac{1}{2}$

Write each number as a decimal.

1. $\frac{17}{20}$ 2. $2\frac{5}{8}$ 3. $1\frac{4}{5}$ 4. $\frac{1}{2}$ 5. $\frac{9}{25}$ 6. $\frac{7}{100}$ 7. $3\frac{1}{4}$ 8. $\frac{7}{8}$

Write each decimal as a fraction or mixed number in simplest form.

9. 0.9   10. 0.45   11. 0.625   12. 2.02   13. 1.65   14. 4.1   15. 0.250

16. **Critical Thinking** Name three other fractions that have the same equivalent decimal as $\frac{1}{2}$.

Work It Out!

Write each number as a decimal.

17. $\frac{8}{40}$ 18. $\frac{47}{94}$ 19. $2\frac{77}{100}$ 20. $5\frac{3}{8}$ 21. $3\frac{18}{24}$ 22. $\frac{3}{4}$ 23. $\frac{11}{22}$ 24. $4\frac{2}{5}$

Write each decimal as a fraction or mixed number in simplest form.

25. 0.050   26. 8.6   27. 3.25   28. 0.375   29. 0.36   30. 7.003   31. 0.55

32. **Patterns** Copy and complete the chart. Write each decimal to the thousandths place. What pattern do you see?

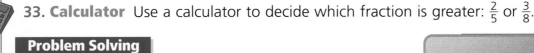

Fraction	$\frac{1}{8}$	$\frac{2}{8}$	$\frac{3}{8}$	$\frac{4}{8}$	$\frac{5}{8}$	$\frac{6}{8}$	$\frac{7}{8}$
Decimal	0.125	0.250	?	?	?	?	?

33. **Calculator** Use a calculator to decide which fraction is greater: $\frac{2}{5}$ or $\frac{3}{8}$.

Problem Solving

34. You are designing a newsletter on a computer. You want the type to indent around a picture. The indent is $\frac{3}{4}$ in. and $1\frac{1}{2}$ in. How can you type these dimensions into the computer in decimal form?

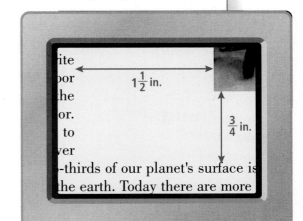

35. A certain issue of a newspaper has 16 pages in Section A, 10 pages in Section B, 16 pages in Section C, and 10 pages in Section D. How many pages long is the newspaper?

More Practice Set 9.12, p. 488

Math Journal

Name a situation in which you would prefer to use fractions and a situation in which you would prefer to use decimals. Explain.

LESSON 13

Problem Solving
Using Strategies

You can read more about kangaroos in the pages of *Zoobooks*.

Kangaroos graze like deer, hop like rabbits, and can go without water for long periods of time like camels. They range in size from a 1 lb musky rat kangaroo to a grey kangaroo that can weigh up to 200 lb.

Problem Solving Process
✓ Understand
✓ Plan
✓ Try It
✓ Look Back

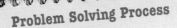

Choose a Strategy You Have Learned
✓ Make a Table
✓ Act It Out
✓ Guess and Check
✓ Look for a Pattern
✓ Work Backward
✓ Make a List
✓ Work a Simpler Problem
✓ Draw a Picture
   Write an Equation

After it is born, a baby tree kangaroo spends about 3 months more in its mother's pouch than most other baby kangaroos. Suppose a grey kangaroo is born in a zoo. It lives several months in its mother's pouch. As soon as the baby grey kangaroo leaves, a tree kangaroo is born and spends several months in its mother's pouch. The babies were in the pouches for a total of $1\frac{1}{4}$ years. How many months did each baby stay in its mother's pouch?

• How long were the baby kangaroos in pouches? How much longer was the tree kangaroo in its mother's pouch?

• What do you want to find out?

• How many months is $1\frac{1}{4}$ years?

• Explain a strategy you can use to solve the problem. Then solve it.

Use any strategy to solve the problem. Show your work.

1. Suppose a small zoo has 30 birds in its bird exhibit. Four of the birds are green parrots, $\frac{1}{10}$ of them are red parrots. Half are cockatiels and the rest are toucans. How many more toucans than red parrots does the bird exhibit have?

2. Some large kangaroos live in groups called mobs. Suppose one mob begins with 2 kangaroos and on the next day increases to 4 members. On the third day, the mob has 8 members. If this pattern continues, how many kangaroos will be in the mob on the fifth day?

Day	1	2	3	4	5
Number of Kangaroos	2	4	8	16	?

3. Suppose a survey of zoos around the world showed that 126 kangaroos were born last year. If there were 12 more males than females, how many females were born?

4. You want to spend 6 hours observing the animals at the zoo. You decide to spend half the time watching the jungle animals and $\frac{1}{3}$ of the remaining time looking at water animals. You want to divide the rest of your time equally watching the marsupials and the birds. How long will you watch the marsupials?

5. How many inches taller is a 7 ft grey kangaroo than a 14 in. musky rat kangaroo?

6. About 2 million years ago, giant kangaroos that stood about 9 or 10 ft tall lived in Australia. They became extinct about 40,000 years ago. For how many years did this type of kangaroo exist?

7. There are 3 red and 3 grey kangaroos in a zoo. The zookeeper wants to put 1 red and 1 grey kangaroo together in a separate area. How many different ways can the kangaroos be paired?

8. How can you be sure that you found all possible ways of pairing the kangaroos in problem 7?

Chapter 9 Test

for Pages 292–321

Test-Taking Tips
If you have difficulty with a word problem, try drawing a picture or solving a simpler problem first.

Problem Solving

Solve using a strategy you have learned. Show your work. (page 268)

1. There are 38 marchers in a parade. The first marcher and every fourth one after that is wearing a red band on his or her hat. The second marcher and every fourth one after that is wearing blue. Everyone else is wearing yellow. How many marchers are wearing yellow?

2. Some fifth graders were surveyed about their favorite subject. One-twelfth said history was their favorite. One-fourth said they liked English best. One-half liked math best. The rest had no favorite. If 24 students were asked the question, how many had no favorite?

Concepts

Write the fraction that tells what part is shaded. (page 294)

3.
4.
5.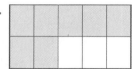
6.

Tell whether each fraction is close to 0, $\frac{1}{2}$, or 1. (page 302)

7. $\frac{1}{20}$

8. $\frac{12}{13}$

9. $\frac{5}{8}$

10. $\frac{2}{25}$

Explain how to multiply or divide to find an equivalent fraction. (page 298)

11. $\frac{3}{5}$

12. $\frac{12}{18}$

13. $\frac{1}{6}$

14. $\frac{3}{9}$

Which group includes non-equivalent fractions? Write a, b, c, or d. (page 298)

15. a. $\frac{7}{8}$ $\frac{14}{16}$ $\frac{35}{40}$
   b. $\frac{18}{27}$ $\frac{6}{9}$ $\frac{30}{45}$
   c. $\frac{9}{21}$ $\frac{3}{7}$ $\frac{18}{49}$
   d. $\frac{6}{8}$ $\frac{3}{4}$ $\frac{54}{72}$

16. a. $\frac{7}{21}$ $\frac{21}{63}$ $\frac{20}{60}$
   b. $\frac{12}{20}$ $\frac{3}{5}$ $\frac{15}{35}$
   c. $\frac{8}{9}$ $\frac{32}{36}$ $\frac{16}{18}$
   d. $\frac{4}{22}$ $\frac{2}{11}$ $\frac{20}{110}$

Find the simplest form of the fraction. (page 300)

17. $\frac{20}{24}$

18. $\frac{5}{13}$

Write a fraction for each mixed number. (page 308)

19. $3\frac{1}{6}$

20. $1\frac{7}{8}$

Complete to make an equivalent fraction. (page 310)

21. $6 = \frac{\blacksquare}{2}$

22. $3 = \frac{\blacksquare}{7}$

Write each fraction as a whole or mixed number in simplest form. (page 312)

23. $\frac{26}{4}$

24. $\frac{40}{10}$

Write the numbers in order from least to greatest. (page 314)

25. $3\frac{1}{2}$ $3\frac{2}{5}$ $3\frac{3}{8}$

26. $\frac{4}{5}$ $\frac{1}{2}$ $\frac{3}{4}$

Write each fraction as a decimal. Write each decimal as a fraction or mixed number in simplest form. (pages 316, 318)

27. $\frac{6}{25}$

28. $\frac{62}{1000}$

29. $\frac{5}{8}$

30. 1.55

31. 0.525

32. 0.070

 Performance Task

(page 320)

Fifty fifth-grade students at Chavez Elementary held a book fair. Each student participated in one event. Use the graph to find out what fraction of the students participated in each event, and explain your strategy. Find the simplest form of each fraction.

Keep in Mind . . .

Your work will be evaluated on the following:

☑ Correct denominator

☑ Fractions for each event

☑ Fractions matched to data

☑ Fractions simplified

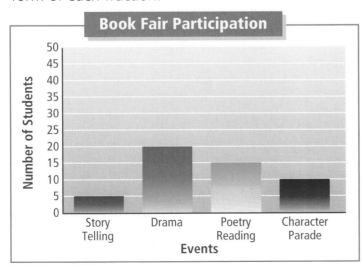

Book Fair Participation

Cumulative Review

Circle Graphs (Chapter 4)
Analyze data in the circle graph.

Here's A Way!

Use the fractions to analyze the information in a circle graph.

Favorite Sports

Total: 20 students, $\frac{2}{5}$, or 8, of the students chose football as their favorite.

Use the circle graph to answer the following questions.

1. Which sport was chosen by the most students?

2. How does the fraction of students who chose baseball compare with the fraction who chose Other?

3. What fraction of the students chose basketball? How many students is this?

4. Which two sports were chosen by the same number of students?

5. What other type of graph could have shown the information?

6. What kind of data does a circle graph show best?

Least Common Multiple (Chapter 2)
Find the least common multiple of 5 and 6.

Here's A Way!

List the multiples of each number.

Multiples of 5:

   5, 10, 15, 20, 25, (30), 35

Multiples of 6:

   6, 12, 18, 24, (30), 36, 42

Circle the least number that is in both lists.

30 is the least common multiple of 5 and 6.

Find the least common multiple for each set of numbers.

7. 2 and 5

8. 5 and 8

9. 3, 5, and 9

10. 4, 5, and 8

11. 5, 7, and 10

12. 5, 7, 8, and 10

13. Is the least common multiple of two numbers ever equal to the lesser of the two numbers? Explain.

14. How do you know when the least common multiple will be less than the product of the numbers?

Dividing Decimals (Chapter 7)

Divide 17.3 by 100.

> **Here's A Way!**
>
> Count the number of zeros in the multiple of 10.
>
> **100 has 2 zeros.**
>
> Move the decimal point two places to the left.
>
> $17.3 \div 100 = 0.173$

Use mental math to divide.

15. $27 \div 10$

16. $94.2 \div 100$

17. $702 \div 100$

18. $5721 \div 1000$

19. $3000 \div 1000$

20. $56.9 \div 10$

21. If you move the decimal point of a number 3 places to the left, what number have you divided by?

Fractions (Chapter 9)

Write $5\frac{3}{4}$ as a fraction.

> **Here's A Way!**
>
> Write the whole number as a fraction, using the same denominator as in the fraction part.
>
> Multiply the whole number by the denominator to get the numerator:
>
> $4 \times 5 = 20; \ 5 = \frac{20}{4}$
>
> Add the two fractions:
>
> $5\frac{3}{4} = \frac{20}{4} + \frac{3}{4} = \frac{23}{4}$

Write each number as an equivalent fraction with the denominator of 6.

22. 2

23. 9

24. 5

Write each mixed number as an equivalent fraction.

25. $7\frac{1}{3}$

26. $2\frac{5}{8}$

27. $6\frac{1}{4}$

28. When writing a mixed number as a fraction, why do you need to multiply the whole number by the denominator of the fraction?

Problem Solving

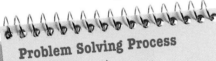

Problem Solving Process
- ✓ Understand
- ✓ Plan
- ✓ Try It
- ✓ Look Back

Choose a Strategy You Have Learned
- ✓ Make a Table
- ✓ Act It Out
- ✓ Guess and Check
- ✓ Look for a Pattern
- ✓ Work Backward
- ✓ Make a List
- ✓ Work a Simpler Problem
- ✓ Draw a Picture
-    Write an Equation

Choose one of the strategies you know to solve these problems. Show your work.

29. For 4 weeks a student kept a record of the time she spent exercising: 145 minutes, 180 minutes, 85 minutes, 170 minutes. What was her average weekly exercise time?

30. At one school, lunches cost $1.25 for students and $2.00 for adults. How many students and adults can buy lunches for a total cost of exactly $9.00?

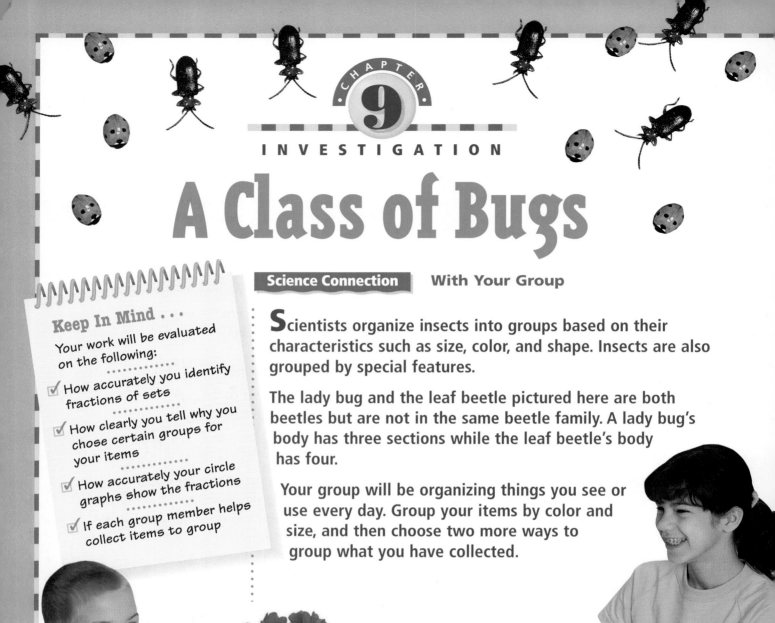

A Class of Bugs

Science Connection   **With Your Group**

Scientists organize insects into groups based on their characteristics such as size, color, and shape. Insects are also grouped by special features.

The lady bug and the leaf beetle pictured here are both beetles but are not in the same beetle family. A lady bug's body has three sections while the leaf beetle's body has four.

Your group will be organizing things you see or use every day. Group your items by color and size, and then choose two more ways to group what you have collected.

1 Plan It

- Each group member should bring 5 or 6 things to class to put into groups.
- Your group will need exactly 24 items.

Size

$\frac{3}{24}$ under 2 in

$\frac{5}{24}$ over 10 in

$\frac{8}{24}$ 2 in–5 in

$\frac{8}{24}$ 5 in–10 in

Color $\frac{4}{24}$

2 Put It Together

- Working as a group, place your items together. Make a list of all the ways your items can be grouped.
- Group by color and size. Then, choose two other ways to group your items. Make a table like the one on this page to show the four groups you will use.
- Have each member take turns dividing the items in each group. Have another person record the data on the table.
- For each group, write fractions that describe how the items are divided.

Groups
color
size
furry
from nature
man made

item	watch	baseball card	house plant
size	$7\frac{1}{4}$ in long	4 in long	13 in tall
color	brown and blue, white face	white on the edges, blue cap, mostly brown, green and white	green with yellow flowers, green pot

3 Wrap It Up

- Use the fractions you have written to make a circle graph for each group you have created. Color and label the sections on the graph.
- Write a paragraph telling why your group chose these categories for your items.

4 Discuss Your Results

- Did you meet the objectives listed in Keep In Mind?
- Share your results with other groups. Find one more way to classify the items from other groups.

Internet

> Visit the **Math Center** at **Houghton Mifflin Education Place.**
http://www.eduplace.com

Addition and Subtraction of Fractions

Math Power

Use What You Know

$$\frac{2}{5} + \frac{1}{5}$$

- how to show fraction sums

$$\frac{1}{6} = \frac{1}{6}$$
$$\frac{2}{3} = \frac{4}{6}$$

- how to find common denominators

- how to measure in inches

Try This!

The Inca people of South America played an instrument called a panpipe. Use what you know about fractions and measuring to make one for yourself. As you measure each new piece, set it to one side.

What You'll Need

craft stick or cardboard

Measure and cut a piece of straw that is $3\frac{1}{4}$ inches long. Measure and cut another piece that is $4\frac{1}{4}$ inches longer than the first piece. Cut another piece that is 2 inches shorter than the second piece.

2

Measure and cut a piece of straw that is $2\frac{1}{4}$ inches long. Cut another piece that is 1 inch shorter. Measure and cut a piece that is $4\frac{3}{8}$ inches long. Cut another piece that is $2\frac{1}{4}$ inches longer.

3

Put the straws in order from longest to shortest. Glue them to a craft stick or small piece of cardboard. Blow across the top of the straws to make musical sounds!

How is the ruler like a fraction bar?

Without using the ruler, could you have added $4\frac{3}{8}$ inches and $2\frac{1}{4}$ inches? Why or why not?

Ready to Go!

Fractions with Like Denominators

You can add and subtract fractions with like denominators. Using the short word form of a fraction can help you.

fraction: $\frac{7}{8}$ short word form: 7 eighths

Cooperative Learning Checklist

☑ Work alone.
☑ Work with a partner.
☑ Work with a group.

Activity

Adding Fractions

Use the circle on the recording sheet that is divided into 12 equal parts, or make your own.

1 Write a fraction that represents the whole circle: $\frac{}{}$.

Then, write the fraction in short word form: _____ _____.

2 Shade 5 parts of the circle blue and 3 parts green.

a. Write a fraction for each shaded part: $\frac{}{}$ blue and $\frac{}{}$ green

b. Write each fraction in short word form:
_____ _____ and _____ _____.

3 Write an addition sentence using the fractions you just wrote. Simplify your answer.

a. short word form: _____ _____ + _____ _____ = _____ _____.

b. fractions: $\frac{}{} + \frac{}{} = \frac{}{}$

Subtracting Fractions

Use the circle that is divided into 9 parts, or make your own.

1 Write a fraction that represents the whole circle: $\frac{}{}$. Then, write the fraction in short word form: _____ _____

2 Shade 6 parts of the circle red.

a. Write a fraction for the part that is red: $\frac{}{}$

b. Write the short word form for the part that is red:
_____ _____.

3 Write a subtraction sentence that represents the part of the circle that is not red. Write the sentence using short word form, then, using fractions.

Exploring Properties

Use a circle that is divided into 6 parts.

1 Color 3 parts red, 2 parts green, and 1 part blue. Write an addition sentence about this circle.

    a. short word form: _____ _____ + _____ _____ + _____ _____ = _____ _____.

    b. fractions: $\frac{\blacksquare}{\blacksquare} + \frac{\blacksquare}{\blacksquare} + \frac{\blacksquare}{\blacksquare} = \frac{\blacksquare}{\blacksquare}$

2 Use the commutative property for addition to write the addition sentence a different way. Simplify your answer.

    a. $\frac{\blacksquare}{\blacksquare} + \frac{\blacksquare}{\blacksquare} + \frac{\blacksquare}{\blacksquare} = \frac{\blacksquare}{\blacksquare}$

3 Write an addition sentence to illustrate the associative property for addition.

    a. $\left(\frac{\blacksquare}{\blacksquare} + \frac{\blacksquare}{\blacksquare}\right) + \frac{\blacksquare}{\blacksquare} = \frac{\blacksquare}{\blacksquare} + \left(\frac{\blacksquare}{\blacksquare} + \frac{\blacksquare}{\blacksquare}\right)$

commutative

Use What You Know

The addition properties for whole numbers also apply to fractions.

Zero Property
$$\frac{2}{5} + 0 = \frac{2}{5}$$

Commutative Property
$$\frac{2}{7} + \frac{3}{7} = \frac{3}{7} + \frac{2}{7}$$

Associative Property
$$\left(\frac{1}{8} + \frac{4}{8}\right) + \frac{4}{8} =$$
$$\frac{1}{8} + \left(\frac{4}{8} + \frac{4}{8}\right)$$

Show What You Know!

Write the answer in simplest form.

1. 1 fifth + 2 fifths   2. 6 tenths + 3 tenths   3. $\frac{7}{12} + \frac{5}{12}$ 4. $\frac{3}{8} + \frac{1}{8}$

Complete.

5. $\left(\frac{2}{6} + \frac{3}{6}\right) + \frac{5}{6} = \frac{2}{6} + \left(\blacksquare + \frac{5}{6}\right)$ 6. $\frac{4}{13} + \blacksquare = \frac{4}{13}$ 7. $\left(\frac{4}{5} - \frac{2}{5}\right) + \frac{1}{5} = \blacksquare$

Write the answer in simplest form.

8. $\frac{5}{6} - \frac{4}{6}$ 9. $\frac{8}{10} - \frac{6}{10}$ 10. $\frac{10}{12} - \frac{3}{12}$ 11. $\frac{7}{9} - \frac{4}{9}$ 12. $\frac{3}{8} + \frac{3}{8}$

Write >, <, or =.

13. $\frac{3}{6} + \frac{2}{6} \,\blacksquare\, \frac{2}{6} + \frac{2}{6}$ 14. $\frac{4}{5} - \frac{3}{5} \,\blacksquare\, \frac{3}{5} + \frac{1}{5}$

15. $\frac{3}{8} + \frac{4}{8} \,\blacksquare\, \frac{4}{8} + \frac{3}{8}$ 16. $\frac{2}{9} + \frac{3}{9} \,\blacksquare\, \frac{4}{9} + \frac{1}{9}$

17. A pizza is cut into 8 equal slices. You eat 3 slices for lunch and 2 more for a snack. What portion of the pizza do you eat?

18. **Critical Thinking** Explain the associative property of addition in your own words.

More Practice Set 10.1, p. 488

Estimation: Fractions

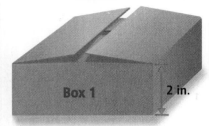

Box 1

2 in.

$\frac{3}{8}$ in.

Mystery

$\frac{15}{16}$ in.

Mystery

Box 2

$\frac{9}{10}$ in.

$\frac{5}{8}$ in.

Brain Teasers

$\frac{3}{4}$ in.

You want to mail the mystery books in box 1. Is the box deep enough to hold both of them? You want to mail the book of brainteasers in box 2. Will there be enough space left to include a notepad that is $\frac{3}{4}$ in. thick?

You can use estimation to answer the questions.

Here's A Way! **Estimate sums and differences.**

Addition Estimate $\frac{15}{16}$ in. $+ \frac{3}{8}$ in.

1 Decide whether each fraction is closer to 0, $\frac{1}{2}$, or 1.

$\frac{15}{16}$ is close to **1**

$\frac{3}{8}$ is close to $\frac{1}{2}$

2 Estimate the sum.

$$1 + \frac{1}{2} = 1\frac{1}{2}$$

Together, the mystery books are about $1\frac{1}{2}$ in. thick. You can use box 1 for both books.

Subtraction Estimate $\frac{9}{10}$ in. $- \frac{5}{8}$ in.

1 Decide whether each fraction is close to 0, $\frac{1}{2}$, or 1.

$\frac{9}{10}$ is close to **1**

$\frac{5}{8}$ is close to $\frac{1}{2}$

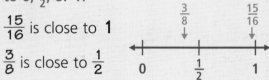

2 Estimate the difference.

$$1 - \frac{1}{2} = \frac{1}{2}$$

Think: $1 = \frac{2}{2}$

Then: $\frac{2}{2} - \frac{1}{2} = \frac{1}{2}$

There is about $\frac{1}{2}$ in. space left in box 2. Since $\frac{1}{2} < \frac{3}{4}$, you cannot include the notepad.

Talk About It! Is the estimated sum, $1\frac{1}{2}$ in., greater or less than the actual sum? Explain.

Decide whether the fraction is close to 0, $\frac{1}{2}$, or 1.

1. $\frac{8}{9}$ 2. $\frac{2}{12}$ 3. $\frac{6}{13}$ 4. $\frac{9}{20}$ 5. $\frac{3}{20}$ 6. $\frac{8}{10}$ 7. $\frac{43}{100}$

Estimate the answer.

8. $\frac{4}{5} + \frac{1}{10}$ 9. $\frac{7}{8} + \frac{8}{9}$ 10. $\frac{4}{7} - \frac{6}{11}$ 11. $\frac{2}{20} + \frac{8}{15}$ 12. $\frac{2}{7} + \frac{1}{12}$

13. $\frac{12}{13} - \frac{9}{10}$ 14. $\frac{6}{7} - \frac{1}{25}$ 15. $\frac{19}{22} + \frac{5}{9}$ 16. $\frac{14}{16} - \frac{6}{10}$ 17. $\frac{1}{9} + \frac{13}{15}$

18. **Critical Thinking** Explain how you got your estimate for exercise 14.

Work It Out!

Decide whether the fraction is close to 0, $\frac{1}{2}$, or 1.

19. $\frac{6}{11}$ 20. $\frac{1}{25}$ 21. $\frac{10}{12}$ 22. $\frac{24}{26}$ 23. $\frac{7}{15}$ 24. $\frac{5}{100}$ 25. $\frac{9}{20}$ 26. $\frac{2}{13}$

Estimate the answer.

27. $\frac{1}{12} + \frac{9}{11}$ 28. $\frac{7}{8} - \frac{2}{25}$ 29. $\frac{2}{11} + \frac{1}{12}$ 30. $\frac{5}{9} - \frac{8}{17}$

31. $\frac{5}{6} - \frac{7}{15}$ 32. $\frac{10}{21} + \frac{2}{20}$ 33. $\frac{3}{5} + \frac{1}{10}$ 34. $\frac{9}{19} - \frac{1}{8}$

35. $\frac{3}{6} + \frac{14}{15}$ 36. $\frac{9}{10} - \frac{6}{7}$ 37. $\frac{8}{10} + \frac{12}{14}$ 38. $\frac{5}{11} - \frac{4}{50}$

Use estimation. Write >, <, or =.

39. $\frac{5}{6} + \frac{4}{5} \blacksquare \frac{5}{8} + \frac{4}{9}$ 40. $\frac{3}{5} - \frac{1}{2} \blacksquare \frac{7}{8} - \frac{1}{4}$

41. $\frac{5}{6} - \frac{5}{6} \blacksquare \frac{3}{4} - \frac{3}{4}$ 42. $\frac{3}{7} + \frac{3}{8} \blacksquare \frac{4}{7} + \frac{5}{9}$

Problem Solving

Use the table to solve the problem.

43. You are using a mailing box that is $1\frac{1}{2}$ in. in depth. Can you send all four packages? Explain.

44. Which 3 packages fit in a mailer 1 in. deep?

45. **Number Sense** When is 0 a reasonable estimate for an addition problem?

Depths of Packages	
Package	Depth
A	$\frac{1}{8}$ in.
B	$\frac{14}{16}$ in.
C	$\frac{1}{16}$ in.
D	$\frac{7}{16}$ in.

More Practice Set 10.2, p. 488

Fractions with Unlike Denominators

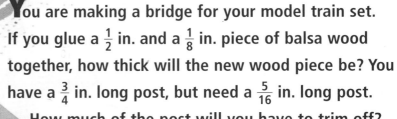

You are making a bridge for your model train set. If you glue a $\frac{1}{2}$ in. and a $\frac{1}{8}$ in. piece of balsa wood together, how thick will the new wood piece be? You have a $\frac{3}{4}$ in. long post, but need a $\frac{5}{16}$ in. long post. How much of the post will you have to trim off? You need to work with fractions.

Here's A Way! Add and subtract fractions.

Addition Find $\frac{1}{2}$ in. $+$ $\frac{1}{8}$ in. — Find equivalent fractions with the same denominators.

1 Find the least common denominator (LCD).

$$\frac{1}{2} = \frac{\blacksquare}{8}$$

$$\frac{1}{8} = \frac{1}{8}$$

2 Write equivalent fractions with the LCD.

$$\frac{1}{2} \overset{\times 4}{\underset{\times 4}{=}} \frac{4}{8}$$

$$\frac{1}{8} = \frac{1}{8}$$

3 Add. Simplify if you can.

$$\frac{4}{8} + \frac{1}{8} = \frac{5}{8}$$

So, $\frac{1}{2} + \frac{1}{8} = \frac{5}{8}$

You will have a piece of wood that is $\frac{5}{8}$ in. thick.

Subtraction Find $\frac{3}{4}$ in. $-$ $\frac{5}{16}$ in.

1 Find the LCD.

$$\frac{3}{4} = \frac{\blacksquare}{16}$$

$$\frac{5}{16} = \frac{5}{16}$$

2 Write equivalent fractions.

$$\frac{3}{4} \overset{\times 4}{\underset{\times 4}{=}} \frac{12}{16}$$

$$\frac{5}{16} = \frac{5}{16}$$

3 Subtract. Simplify.

$$\frac{12}{16} - \frac{5}{16} = \frac{7}{16}$$

So, $\frac{3}{4} - \frac{5}{16} = \frac{7}{16}$

You will have to trim $\frac{7}{16}$ in. of wood off the post.

Talk About It! Why do you use the LCM as the least common denominator?

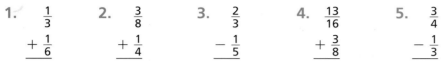
Use What You Know

$\frac{2}{2} = 1, \frac{3}{3} = 1, \frac{4}{4} = 1$

Multiplying or dividing the numerator and denominator of a fraction by the same number does not change the value of the fraction. It is the same as multiplying or dividing by 1.

Write the answer in simplest form.

1. $\frac{1}{3}$
    $+ \frac{1}{6}$

2. $\frac{3}{8}$
    $+ \frac{1}{4}$

3. $\frac{2}{3}$
    $- \frac{1}{5}$

4. $\frac{13}{16}$
    $+ \frac{3}{8}$

5. $\frac{3}{4}$
    $- \frac{1}{3}$

6. $\frac{1}{2} - \frac{1}{3}$ 7. $\frac{3}{4} - \frac{1}{8}$ 8. $\frac{5}{16} + \frac{1}{2}$ 9. $\frac{3}{10} + \frac{3}{20}$ 10. $\frac{2}{3} - \frac{3}{12}$

11. **Critical Thinking** Why do you need to write equivalent fractions with the same denominator in order to add or subtract?

Work It Out!

Write the answer in simplest form.

12. $\frac{1}{2}$
     $+ \frac{1}{6}$

13. $\frac{7}{8}$
     $- \frac{3}{4}$

14. $\frac{15}{16}$
     $- \frac{1}{2}$

15. $\frac{1}{6}$
     $+ \frac{3}{10}$

16. $\frac{2}{8}$
     $+ \frac{3}{5}$

17. $\frac{2}{3}$
     $- \frac{1}{9}$

18. $\frac{3}{4} + \frac{4}{5}$ 19. $\frac{7}{12} - \frac{1}{4}$ 20. $\frac{8}{9} - \frac{2}{3}$ 21. $\frac{3}{10} - \frac{1}{5}$ 22. $\frac{11}{12} + \frac{5}{6}$

Number Sense Choose the letter of the example with the greater sum.

23. a. $\frac{1}{2} + \frac{1}{8}$ b. $\frac{1}{2} + \frac{1}{4}$ 24. a. $\frac{2}{3} + \frac{1}{6}$ b. $\frac{2}{3} + \frac{1}{4}$

Problem Solving

25. Draw a model to show $\frac{1}{3} + \frac{1}{4}$. Record the number sentence and sum.

26. A bus travels $\frac{1}{3}$ of the way and then stops. It then travels $\frac{2}{9}$ of the way before stopping again. How much of the trip is left?

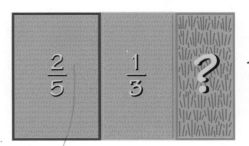

27. You mow $\frac{2}{5}$ of the lawn before taking a break. Afterwards, you complete $\frac{1}{3}$ more. How much of the lawn do you have to finish?

28. **Calculator** Remember that fractions can be expressed as decimals. How can you use a calculator to find $\frac{1}{5} + \frac{7}{10}$? How can you express the answer as a fraction?

More Practice Set 10.3, p. 489

Problem Solving
Is the Answer Reasonable?

A chef in a restaurant prepared two orders of lasagna. Each order contained $\frac{1}{12}$ of the pan of lasagna. The chef told the restaurant manager that $\frac{1}{24}$ of the lasagna had been served.
Is the chef's statement reasonable?

You Decide

- How can you find the total amount served?
- How do you add fractions with like denominators?
- How much lasagna was served in two orders?
- How does this amount compare with the chef's statement?

Work It Out!

Decide if the last sentence in each story is reasonable. Explain.

1. Four friends are planning a bake sale. Ned and Gina will each bake $\frac{1}{3}$ of the muffins. Jerome will bake $\frac{1}{4}$ of the muffins. Kyla wants to know how much of the set of muffins she will bake. To find out, she adds $\frac{1}{3} + \frac{1}{3} + \frac{1}{4}$ and then subtracts the sum from 1.

2. Three sisters share some grapes. Inez eats $\frac{1}{2}$ of the grapes, Carla eats $\frac{1}{2}$ of them, and Nella eats $\frac{1}{2}$.

3. Mika and T.J. are sharing a sandwich. Mika says "I'll take the middle half."

Share Your Thinking

4. How can you check to make sure that answers are reasonable?

Midchapter Review

for Pages 328-336

for Pages 328-336

Problem Solving

Solve. Show your work. (pages 330–335, 336)

1. Amy memorizes $\frac{1}{5}$ of the U.S. state capitals one week. The next week she memorizes $\frac{4}{10}$ more. What fraction of the capitals does she still have to learn?

2. Casey memorizes $\frac{4}{5}$ of the capitals, but then he forgets $\frac{3}{10}$ of them. Does he remember more than half of the capitals?

Use data from the table.

3. What fraction of U.S. state names begin with a consonant?

4. Jed says that fewer than half of U.S. state names have 5 or more letters. Is he correct?

State names that	
• begin with a vowel	$\frac{6}{25}$
• have two words	$\frac{1}{5}$
• have more than 10 letters	$\frac{1}{5}$
• have fewer than 5 letters	$\frac{3}{50}$

Concepts

Is the best estimate about 0, about $\frac{1}{2}$, or about 1? Explain. (page 332)

5. $\frac{2}{9} + \frac{9}{11}$

6. $\frac{7}{8} - \frac{7}{15}$

Skills

Add or subtract. Write the answer in simplest form. (pages 330, 334)

7. $\frac{3}{4} + \frac{1}{4}$

8. $\frac{7}{9} - \frac{4}{9}$

9. $\frac{7}{8} - \frac{1}{4}$

10. $\frac{2}{6} + \frac{1}{3}$

Match each expression with the correct sum. (pages 330, 334)

11. $\frac{1}{4} + \frac{1}{4}$

12. $\frac{3}{4} + \frac{1}{8}$

13. $\frac{5}{8} + \frac{1}{8}$

a. $\frac{7}{8}$

b. $\frac{6}{8}$

c. $\frac{1}{2}$

Math World

People around the world have used creative ways to show addition and subtraction of fractions. Try using fractions to create art.

Adding to Divide

The Rhind papyrus uses loaves of bread to explain addition of fractions. Ahmes, an Egyptian scribe, tells how to divide one loaf, two loaves, and four loaves of bread equally among 10 people. He does not show how to divide three loaves because it is the same as dividing one loaf and two loaves. One loaf would be divided into 10 equal pieces. Each person would get $\frac{1}{10}$. Two loaves would each be divided into five pieces. Each person would get $\frac{1}{5}$. To find how much each person would get when dividing three loaves, just add $\frac{1}{10}$ and $\frac{1}{5}$.

Natural Fractals

A fractal is a pattern that endlessly repeats itself. These patterns are often found in nature. Many snowflakes have patterns that are fractals. This fern, found in Costa Rica, is an example of a fractal. The leaves continually repeat the same pattern. Can you find other fractals in nature?

This is a tree fern which grows in the rain forest of Costa Rica

Try This! Cantor's Dust

Fractals can be complicated, like the one pictured here, or very simple, like Cantor Dust. Cantor Dust, discovered by Georg Cantor, a German mathematician, was one of the earliest known fractal patterns. The pattern is made by subtracting $\frac{1}{3}$ of each line. Follow these steps to make this classic fractal pattern known as Cantor Dust.

1 On a piece of grid paper, shade 27 squares along the bottom row.

2 Moving up, skip a row. Shade the first 9 squares of the next row. Then, shade the last 9 squares of that same row. You have subtracted the middle $\frac{1}{3}$ of the line, making two new lines.

3 Above the line on the left, skip another row and subtract the middle $\frac{1}{3}$ of the line below. Shade the first $\frac{1}{3}$ and the last $\frac{1}{3}$ only. Repeat this step above the line on the right.

4 Skip another row and subtract the middle $\frac{1}{3}$ from the line below. Once again, shade the first $\frac{1}{3}$ and the last $\frac{1}{3}$ of the line.

5 Continue subtracting the middle $\frac{1}{3}$ from each new line until you have 5 rows of lines. You have created Cantor Dust.

Respond

Find how many ways . . .

you can divide five loaves of bread among ten people. Draw pictures to show different ways.

Internet:
Houghton Mifflin Education Place
Explore the Math Center at
http://www.eduplace.com

Mixed Numbers with Like Denominators

Hillside Ballet

Monday

Class: 8:15 – 9:30 $(1\frac{1}{4}$ h$)$

Rehearsal: 10:45 – 12:00
and 1:00 – 5:00 $(5\frac{1}{4}$ h$)$

Tuesday

Rehearsal: 10:00 – 12:00
and 1:00 – 5:45 $(6\frac{3}{4}$ h$)$

Professional dancers rehearse and attend class daily. The notebook shows a dancer's schedule. How many hours will she train on Monday? How much longer will she rehearse on Tuesday than on Monday?

You can add and subtract mixed numbers to answer these questions.

Here's A Way!   Add and subtract mixed numbers.

Addition Find $1\frac{1}{4}$ h $+ 5\frac{1}{4}$ h.

1 If the denominators are the same, add the numerators.

$$\begin{array}{r} 1\frac{1}{4} \\ + 5\frac{1}{4} \\ \hline \frac{2}{4} \end{array}$$

2 Add the whole numbers. Simplify if you can.

$$\begin{array}{r} 1\frac{1}{4} \\ + 5\frac{1}{4} \\ \hline 6\frac{2}{4} = 6\frac{1}{2} \end{array}$$

The dancer will train $6\frac{1}{2}$ h on Monday.

Subtraction Find $6\frac{3}{4}$ h $- 5\frac{1}{4}$ h.

1 Check that the denominators are the same. Subtract the numerators.

$$\begin{array}{r} 6\frac{3}{4} \\ - 5\frac{1}{4} \\ \hline \frac{2}{4} \end{array}$$

2 Subtract the whole numbers. Simplify if you can.

$$\begin{array}{r} 6\frac{3}{4} \\ - 5\frac{1}{4} \\ \hline 1\frac{2}{4} = 1\frac{1}{2} \end{array}$$

So, the dancer will rehearse $1\frac{1}{2}$ h more on Tuesday than on Monday.

Talk About It! How can you use estimation to check that your answers are reasonable?

Write the answer in simplest form.

1. $4\frac{1}{4}$
   $+\ 3\frac{1}{4}$

2. $7\frac{3}{8}$
   $-\ 2\frac{1}{8}$

3. $1\frac{1}{12}$
   $+\ 1\frac{3}{12}$

4. $6\frac{1}{5}$
   $+\ 2\frac{3}{5}$

5. $9\frac{7}{10}$
   $-\ 6\frac{7}{10}$

6. $3\frac{3}{4} + 8$

7. $4\frac{2}{5} - 2\frac{1}{5}$

8. $10\frac{11}{20} - 5\frac{7}{20}$

9. $9\frac{3}{4} - 9\frac{1}{4}$

10. **Critical Thinking** Why do some sums and differences of mixed numbers need simplifying?

Write the answer in simplest form.

11. $2\frac{1}{6}$
    $+\ 2\frac{2}{6}$

12. $5\frac{11}{12}$
    $-\ 4\frac{1}{12}$

13. $3\frac{5}{8}$
    $-\ 2\frac{1}{8}$

14. $12\frac{13}{16}$
    $-\ 1\frac{13}{16}$

15. $7\frac{3}{10}$
    $+\ 62\frac{3}{10}$

Mental Math

16. $2\frac{3}{4} + 5$

17. $10\frac{4}{5} - 8$

18. $2\frac{1}{7} + 2\frac{1}{7}$

19. $25\frac{1}{2} - 6$

Problem Solving Using Data

Use the chart to solve the problem.

20. How much time does Jon spend rehearsing on the weekend?

21. How much longer does Jon rehearse on Sunday than on Monday?

Jon's Rehearsal Schedule

Day	Mon.	Tues.	Wed.	Thur.	Fri.	Sat.	Sun.
Number of Hours	$1\frac{1}{4}$	$\frac{3}{4}$	$\frac{1}{4}$	—	$1\frac{1}{4}$	2	$1\frac{3}{4}$

22. How long does Jon rehearse on Tuesday and Wednesday altogether?

23. **Number Sense** Jon rehearsed an extra $\frac{1}{4}$ h. He started at 3:00 P.M. and ended at 3:30 P.M. What day of the week was it?

Mixed Review Write the answer. Use mental math.

24. $3.8 \div 10$

25. 0.53×10

26. 0.15×100

27. $4.27 \div 100$

More Practice Set 10.5, p. 489

LESSON 6

Estimation: Mixed Numbers

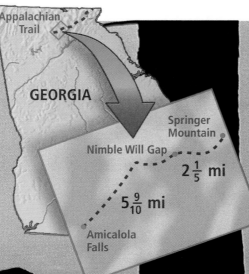

Appalachian Trail

GEORGIA

Springer Mountain

Nimble Will Gap

$2\frac{1}{5}$ mi

$5\frac{9}{10}$ mi

Amicalola Falls

The Appalachian National Scenic Trail is the nation's longest marked footpath. This map shows a section of the trail in Georgia. About how far is it from Amicalola Falls State Park to Springer Mountain?

You can use a different method to estimate with mixed numbers.

Here's A Way! Estimate.

Addition Estimate $5\frac{9}{10}$ mi + $2\frac{1}{5}$ mi.

| Close to 1 | Close to 0 |

❶ Look at the fraction. Decide if it is close to 0, $\frac{1}{2}$, or 1.

$5\frac{9}{10}$ → $5 + 1$ or 6

$2\frac{1}{5}$ → 2

❷ Estimate the sum. $6 + 2 = 8$

It is about 8 mi from the park to Springer Mountain.

Subtraction Estimate $4\frac{5}{8} - 1\frac{1}{6}$.

| Close to $\frac{1}{2}$ | Close to 0 |

❶ Look at the fraction. Decide if it is close to 0, $\frac{1}{2}$, or 1.

$4\frac{5}{8}$ → $4\frac{1}{2}$

$1\frac{1}{16}$ → 1

❷ Estimate the difference. $4\frac{1}{2} - 1 = 3\frac{1}{2}$

So, $4\frac{5}{8} - 1\frac{1}{6}$ is about $3\frac{1}{2}$.

Talk About It! How can you tell when an estimate is greater or less than an actual answer?

Write the number from the box closest to each number below.

$5\frac{3}{5}$		$6\frac{1}{10}$		$8\frac{9}{10}$
	$7\frac{7}{8}$		$8\frac{5}{12}$	

1. 8   2. 9   3. $8\frac{1}{2}$ 4. $5\frac{1}{2}$ 5. 6

Estimate.

6. $6\frac{1}{10} + 2\frac{5}{6}$ 7. $3\frac{5}{9} - \frac{1}{7}$ 8. $2\frac{7}{9} + 2\frac{9}{10}$ 9. $8\frac{1}{6} - 7\frac{7}{15}$

10. **Critical Thinking** A student estimates that the sum of three fractions is 0. What can you say about the numerators and denominators of the fractions?

Work It Out!

Estimate.

11. $2\frac{4}{7} + 3\frac{2}{9}$ 12. $4\frac{7}{8} - 1\frac{3}{10}$ 13. $1\frac{5}{9} + \frac{11}{20}$ 14. $6\frac{12}{14} - 5\frac{2}{13}$

15. $4\frac{1}{16} - 3\frac{14}{15}$ 16. $2\frac{1}{10} + 9\frac{6}{7}$ 17. $4\frac{5}{6} - 3\frac{7}{13}$ 18. $2\frac{1}{6} + 3\frac{1}{5} + 4\frac{1}{7}$

19. $8\frac{7}{15} - 4\frac{1}{9}$ 20. $7\frac{9}{11} - 1\frac{2}{10}$

21. $1\frac{2}{7} + 5\frac{4}{5} + 3\frac{3}{6}$ 22. $5\frac{1}{6} + \frac{13}{25}$

Problem Solving   Using Data

Use the chart to estimate the answer.

23. About how far is it from Cooper Gap to Stover Creek?

24. About how far is it from Stover Creek to Gooch Gap?

25. Which two consecutive locations on the chart are farthest apart?

The Appalachian Trail (GA to NC)

Location	Miles from Springer Mountain
Springer Mountain	0
Stover Creek	$3\frac{3}{5}$
Long Creek Falls	5
Logging Road	$5\frac{4}{5}$
Hightower Gap	$8\frac{1}{10}$
Cooper Gap	$11\frac{3}{5}$
Gooch Gap	$16\frac{1}{10}$

More Practice Set 10.6, p. 490

Math Journal

Why should you think about fractional parts of mixed numbers when you estimate?

Adding Mixed Numbers

Fruit Smoothie

1¼ c yogurt
1½ c milk
¼ c honey
1 sliced banana
2/3 c strawberries
½ c ice

Mix yogurt and milk together. Add remaining ingredients and blend until smooth.

If you begin making a fruit smoothie by mixing the yogurt and milk in a blender, how many cups of mixture will be in your blender?

You can use what you know about fractions and addition to find the total amount of the two ingredients.

Here's A Way! Find $1\frac{1}{4}$ c + $1\frac{1}{2}$ c.

1 Estimate the sum. Decide if the fraction is close to 0, $\frac{1}{2}$, or 1.

So the sum is about $2\frac{1}{2}$ c.

$$1\frac{1}{4} + 1\frac{1}{2} \qquad 1 + 1\frac{1}{2} = 2\frac{1}{2}$$

close to 0

2 Find the least common denominator. Write equivalent fractions.

$$1\frac{1}{4} = 1\frac{1}{4}$$
$$+ 1\frac{1}{2} = 1\frac{2}{4}$$

The LCM of 4 and 2 is 4. So, 4 is the LCD.

3 Add the fractions. Add the whole numbers. Simplify if you can.

$$1\frac{1}{4}$$
$$+ 1\frac{2}{4}$$
$$\overline{2\frac{3}{4}}$$

simplest form

Your blender will have $2\frac{3}{4}$ c in it. The estimate shows that the answer is reasonable.

Talk About It! Why do you add fractions first, then whole numbers?

Other Examples Notice that you need a common denominator.

a.
$$2\frac{2}{3} = 2\frac{8}{12}$$
$$+ 3\frac{1}{4} = 3\frac{3}{12}$$
$$\overline{5\frac{11}{12}}$$

b.
$$7\frac{5}{6} = 7\frac{20}{24}$$
$$+ \frac{1}{8} = \frac{3}{24}$$
$$\overline{7\frac{23}{24}}$$

Write the mixed number in simplest form.

1. $8\frac{11}{10}$　　　2. $1\frac{9}{6}$　　　3. $4\frac{7}{4}$　　　4. $2\frac{12}{10}$　　　5. $3\frac{14}{8}$

Write the sum in simplest form.

6. $1\frac{1}{4}$
$+ 2\frac{1}{8}$

7. $6\frac{2}{5}$
$+ \frac{3}{10}$

8. $4\frac{1}{6}$
$+ 2\frac{1}{4}$

9. $4\frac{3}{4}$
$+ \frac{3}{4}$

10. $2\frac{1}{3}$
$+ 7\frac{5}{8}$

11. **Critical Thinking** How do you know that $3\frac{8}{5}$ is not in simplest form?

Work It Out!

Write the sum in simplest form.

12. $2\frac{3}{5} + 1\frac{1}{15}$　　　13. $\frac{13}{20} + 3\frac{3}{10}$　　　14. $1\frac{5}{9} + \frac{3}{4}$　　　15. $3\frac{1}{2} + 2\frac{2}{3}$

16. $5\frac{1}{4}$
$+ 5\frac{3}{8}$

17. $4\frac{4}{5}$
$+ 2\frac{3}{20}$

18. $\frac{3}{16}$
$+ 1\frac{7}{8}$

19. $5\frac{1}{24}$
$+ 3\frac{1}{3}$

20. $3\frac{3}{12}$
$+ 2\frac{1}{6}$

Mental Math Add.

21. $5 + 4\frac{7}{25}$　　　22. $4\frac{4}{5} + 8$　　　23. $2\frac{3}{8} + 2\frac{1}{4}$　　　24. $2\frac{2}{5} + \frac{1}{10}$

Problem Solving　Using Data

Use the recipe to solve the problem.

25. Will the ingredients for the apple salad fit in a 2-cup bowl? Explain.

26. Will the pineapple and the celery fit in a 1-cup bowl? Explain.

27. If you double the recipe, how many cups of apples and pineapple will you need?

28. **Algebraic Reasoning** Suppose you want to make apple salad for a school picnic. Let n equal the number of batches you will make. Write an expression that tells how many cups of apples you will need to prepare.

Apple Salad

$1\frac{1}{2}$ c apples, cut into chunks

$\frac{2}{3}$ c canned pineapple

$\frac{1}{3}$ c chopped celery

2 tbsp raisins

3 tbsp plain yogurt

3 tbsp mayonnaise

1 tbsp pineapple juice

$\frac{1}{8}$ tsp cinnamon

tbsp = tablespoon, tsp = teaspoon

More Practice Set 10.7, p. 490

LESSON 8

Subtracting Mixed Numbers

Artist Patricia Malarcher creates unusual wall hangings using metallic fabric called mylar.

Suppose that the artist needs $5\frac{1}{2}$ yd of mylar for a new wall hanging and already has $3\frac{1}{5}$ yd. How many more yards does she need?

You need to find $5\frac{1}{2}$ yd $- 3\frac{1}{5}$ yd.

Patricia Malarcher at work

Here's A Way! Find $5\frac{1}{2}$ yd $- 3\frac{1}{5}$ yd.

1 Estimate the difference.

$$5\frac{1}{2} - 3\frac{1}{5} \longrightarrow 5\frac{1}{2} - 3 = 2\frac{1}{2}$$

close to 0   estimated difference

---

2 Find the least common denominator. Write equivalent fractions.

$$5\frac{1}{2} = 5\frac{5}{10}$$
$$-3\frac{1}{5} = 3\frac{2}{10}$$

The LCM of 2 and 5 is 10. So, 10 is the LCD.

3 Subtract the fractions. Subtract the whole numbers. Simplify if you can.

$$\begin{array}{r} 5\frac{5}{10} \\ -3\frac{2}{10} \\ \hline 2\frac{3}{10} \end{array}$$

simplest form

The artist needs $2\frac{3}{10}$ more yards of mylar. The answer is close to the estimate of $2\frac{1}{2}$ yd, so it is reasonable.

Talk About It! How can you check the answer?

Other Examples
Why were these denominators selected?

a.
$$\begin{array}{r} 7\frac{5}{6} = 7\frac{5}{6} \\ -4\frac{1}{3} = 4\frac{2}{6} \\ \hline 3\frac{3}{6} = 3\frac{1}{2} \end{array}$$

b.
$$\begin{array}{r} 5\frac{8}{14} = 5\frac{8}{14} \\ -\frac{1}{2} = \frac{7}{14} \\ \hline 5\frac{1}{14} \end{array}$$

Write the difference in simplest form.

1. $3\frac{7}{8} = 3\frac{14}{16}$
    $-1\frac{1}{16} = 1\frac{1}{16}$

2. $6\frac{7}{10} = 6\frac{21}{30}$
    $-2\frac{1}{6} = 2\frac{5}{30}$

3. $4\frac{2}{3}$
    $-3\frac{3}{7}$

4. $8\frac{1}{4}$
    $-3\frac{1}{12}$

5. $5\frac{6}{9}$
    $-2\frac{2}{3}$

6. $19\frac{1}{2}$
    $-\frac{3}{7}$

7. $5\frac{3}{4}$
    $-1\frac{1}{8}$

8. **Critical Thinking** Describe the way you found the least common denominator in exercise 6. How is it different from the way you found the LCD in exercise 7?

Work It Out!

Write the difference in simplest form.

9. $4\frac{7}{9}$
    $-1\frac{1}{3}$

10. $6\frac{11}{12}$
    $-5\frac{1}{2}$

11. $9\frac{7}{8}$
    $-2\frac{3}{16}$

12. $12\frac{3}{5}$
    $-7\frac{4}{15}$

13. $7\frac{3}{4}$
    $-7\frac{1}{8}$

14. $7\frac{2}{3}$
    $-4\frac{2}{7}$

15. $6\frac{1}{4}$
    $-\frac{1}{16}$

16. $23\frac{3}{10}$
    $-1\frac{1}{6}$

17. $8\frac{1}{3}$
    $-7\frac{1}{8}$

18. $6\frac{8}{9}$
    $-5\frac{2}{3}$

Number Sense Choose the letter with the greater difference.

19. a. $1\frac{1}{2} - 1\frac{1}{4}$ b. $1\frac{1}{2} - 1\frac{1}{8}$

20. a. $4\frac{1}{4} - 2\frac{3}{4}$ b. $4\frac{3}{4} - 2\frac{3}{4}$

Patterns Write the next three numbers. Describe the pattern.

21. $1\frac{1}{2}$, 3, $4\frac{1}{2}$, 6, $7\frac{1}{2}$, ■, ■, ■

22. $\frac{1}{2}$, $1\frac{5}{8}$, $2\frac{3}{4}$, $3\frac{7}{8}$, 5, ■, ■, ■

Problem Solving

23. A ceramist uses $2\frac{5}{16}$ lb of clay to make a bowl and $1\frac{1}{8}$ lb of clay to make a vase. How much heavier is the bowl than the vase?

24. A weaver needs $42\frac{3}{4}$ yd of wool yarn to make a placemat. He plans to use $18\frac{1}{8}$ yd of beige wool. The rest will be green. How much green wool will he use?

More Practice Set 10.8, p. 490

LESSON 9

Renaming for Subtraction

Horses are measured in a unit called a *hand* which is equal to 4 in. You can also compare the size of two horses using customary units such as feet.

How much taller is the Clydesdale than the miniature horse?

You can use what you know about subtracting fractions to find the difference.

$6\frac{1}{3}$ ft

$2\frac{1}{2}$ ft

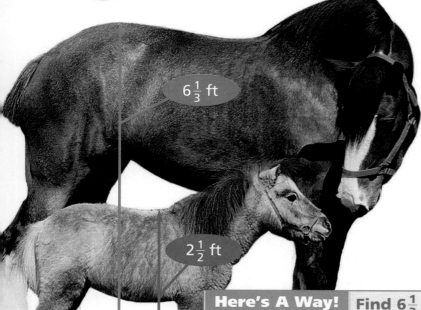

Here's A Way! Find $6\frac{1}{3}$ ft $- 2\frac{1}{2}$ ft.

1 Look at the denominators. If they are different, write equivalent fractions using the LCD.

$$6\frac{1}{3} = 6\frac{2}{6}$$
$$- 2\frac{1}{2} = 2\frac{3}{6}$$

2 Since $\frac{2}{6} < \frac{3}{6}$, you need to rename.

$$6\frac{2}{6}$$
$$- 2\frac{3}{6}$$

Think: $6 = 5 + \frac{6}{6}$

Then: $5\frac{6}{6} + \frac{2}{6} = 5\frac{8}{6}$

3 Subtract the fractions. Subtract the whole numbers. Simplify if you can.

$$5\frac{8}{6}$$
$$- 2\frac{3}{6}$$
$$3\frac{5}{6} \quad \text{simplest form}$$

The Clydesdale is $3\frac{5}{6}$ ft taller than the miniature horse.

Talk About It! When subtracting mixed numbers, sometimes you need to rename them. Explain.

Other Examples The whole number is renamed.

$$5 = 4\frac{3}{3}$$
$$- 2\frac{1}{3} = - 2\frac{1}{3}$$
$$2\frac{2}{3}$$

Use What You Know

Any fraction is equal to 1 if the numerator and denominator are the same.

You can rename any whole number as a mixed number.

$4 = 3 + \frac{4}{4}$

$5 = 4 + \frac{6}{6}$

$9 = 8 + \frac{3}{3}$

Write the difference in simplest form.

1. $4\frac{1}{3}$
   $-\,2\frac{2}{3}$

2. $9\frac{2}{7}$
   $-\,5\frac{5}{7}$

3. $3\frac{1}{6}$
   $-\,1\frac{1}{3}$

4. 6
   $-\,1\frac{3}{8}$

5. 6
   $-\,3\frac{3}{4}$

6. **Critical Thinking** How did you rename 6 in exercise 4? in exercise 5? Why did you rename 6 differently to solve each problem?

Work It Out!

Write the difference in simplest form.

7. $2\frac{1}{4}$
   $-\,\frac{3}{4}$

8. $8\frac{1}{6}$
   $-\,2\frac{5}{6}$

9. 7
   $-\,5\frac{2}{7}$

10. $6\frac{3}{8}$
    $-\,2\frac{3}{4}$

11. $4\frac{1}{6}$
    $-\,3\frac{1}{3}$

12. $6\frac{1}{5} - 3\frac{4}{5}$

13. $9 - \frac{7}{8}$

14. $10\frac{1}{4} - 5\frac{1}{2}$

15. $7\frac{1}{8} - 6\frac{1}{4}$

16. $5\frac{2}{3} - 3\frac{3}{4}$

17. $12\frac{1}{3} - 9\frac{5}{6}$

18. $8\frac{4}{9} - 7\frac{2}{3}$

19. $2\frac{1}{5} - \frac{7}{10}$

20. $3\frac{1}{6} - 1\frac{3}{4}$

21. $4 - 3\frac{1}{8}$

22. $8\frac{1}{3} - 2\frac{5}{9}$

23. $25\frac{5}{12} - 3\frac{2}{3}$

Problem Solving Using Data

Use data in the chart to find the answer.

24. How much taller is the Arabian horse than the Mustang?

25. How much taller is the quarter horse than the Przewalski's (Pehr zheh VAHL skeez) horse?

26. Which two horses are about $\frac{1}{2}$ ft apart in height?

Height of Horses

Breed of Horses	Height
Arabian	$4\frac{5}{6}$ ft
Mustang	$4\frac{2}{3}$ ft
Przewalski's horse	$4\frac{1}{3}$ ft
American quarter horse	5 ft

More Practice Set 10.9, p. 491

Math Journal

Compare subtracting mixed numbers with renaming to subtracting whole numbers with renaming. How are they alike? How are they different? Give examples to justify your answers.

Problem Solving
Make a Table

Suppose you plan a bicycle trip. You decide to ride half the distance on the first day. On each new day, you travel half the remaining distance. How much of the trip will be left after you have traveled this way for 5 days?

Here's A Way! Use Make a Table to solve the problem.

1 Understand

- What question do you need to answer?
- What fraction shows the distance traveled on the first day?
- What fraction is half of that distance? (Use fraction models or drawings to help.) Do you see a pattern?

2 Plan

- Make a table to organize the information to solve the problem.
- What label will you use for each column?
- How will you begin to complete the table?

3 Try It

- How can you add fractions in the chart with unlike denominators?
- How can you use information from the chart to answer the question?

Day	Distance Each Day	Total Distance
1	$\frac{1}{2}$	$\frac{1}{2}$
2	$\frac{1}{4}$	$\frac{1}{2} + \frac{1}{4} = \frac{2}{4} + \frac{1}{4} = \frac{3}{4}$
3	$\frac{1}{8}$	$\frac{3}{4} + \frac{1}{8} = \frac{6}{8} + \frac{1}{8} = \frac{7}{8}$
4	$\frac{1}{16}$	$\frac{7}{8} + \frac{1}{16} = \frac{14}{16} + \frac{1}{16} = \frac{15}{16}$
5	$\frac{1}{32}$	$\frac{15}{16} + \frac{1}{32} = \frac{30}{32} + \frac{1}{32} = ?$

4 Look Back

- After five days of traveling, $\frac{1}{32}$ of the trip is left.
- How did the table help you solve the problem?

Make a Table to solve the problem.

1. In May, you save $10. Each month, you increase the amount that you save by $8. How much will you have saved by the end of the year?

2. **Critical Thinking** How did the table help you in problem 1?

Month	Amount Saved that Month	Total Amount Saved
May	$10	$10
June	$10 + 8	$28
July	?	?
August	?	?

Use Make a Table or any strategy to solve the problem.

3. An airline had a contest offering 2000 mi of free air travel. The airline reported that 358,000 people entered the contest and there were 5 winners. Write a fraction that shows what part of the total contestants were winners.

4. Another contest offers two prizes. Which would you choose, Prize A or Prize B? Why?

5. A bus travels $1\frac{1}{2}$ mi before making the first stop. It travels $2\frac{1}{4}$ mi before making the second stop and 3 mi before making the third stop. If the pattern continues and the fifth stop is the end of the route, how long is the entire route?

6. Three friends are taking an 876-mile train trip. They travel $\frac{1}{3}$ of the way and stop. Then, they travel $\frac{1}{4}$ of the way and stop again. What part of the trip is left? How many miles are left?

Prize A
1 million dollars on day 1
$\frac{1}{2}$ million on day 2
$\frac{1}{4}$ million on day 3
and so on for 1 week.

Prize B
$1000 dollars on day 1
Twice as much on day 2
Twice as much again on day 3
and so on for 1 week.

7. How does making a table help you to solve problems?

Write each fraction as a decimal.
Write each decimal as a fraction or mixed number.

8. $\frac{3}{8}$ 9. $\frac{2}{5}$ 10. $\frac{1}{4}$ 11. $\frac{3}{12}$ 12. $\frac{7}{10}$

13. 0.1   14. 0.33   15. 0.107   16. 5.02   17. 8.7

351

Problem Solving
Using Strategies

You can read more about bears in the pages of *Ranger Rick*.

Ranger Rick

Well, egg-scuse me! Can't a baby crocodile hatch in private?

There are more black bears in the world than any other kind of bear. And all of them are hungry. In fact, bears will eat almost anything.

Problem Solving Process

✓ Understand
✓ Plan
✓ Try It
✓ Look Back

Choose a Strategy You Have Learned

✓ Make a Table
✓ Act It Out
✓ Guess and Check
✓ Look for a Pattern
✓ Work Backward
✓ Make a List
✓ Work a Simpler Problem
✓ Draw a Picture
    Write an Equation

Imagine that you're watching a black bear munching caterpillars. In the first $\frac{1}{2}$ hour, it eats 100 of them. Each $\frac{1}{2}$ hour after that, it eats 100 more than the previous $\frac{1}{2}$ hour. You get tired of watching after it has gobbled 3600 caterpillars. How long were you watching this hungry bear?

- What is the question you have to answer?
- How many caterpillars were eaten in the first $\frac{1}{2}$ hour?
- How does the number of caterpillars eaten increase?
- Explain the strategy or strategies that can help you to solve this problem. Then solve it.

Work It Out!

Use any strategy to solve the problem. Show your work.

1. An adult black bear standing on its hind legs can be about 11 ft tall. The combined heights of 2 cubs is 11 ft. One of the cubs is 6 in. taller than the other. How tall are the 2 cubs?

2. Estimate that the 25,000 caterpillars the bear ate were each about 1 in. long. If you lined them up end-to-end, about how long would the line be? Would it be more or less than $\frac{1}{2}$ mi? (Hint: 1 mi = 5280 ft.)

3. Twelve fifth-graders can weigh as much as 1 full grown black bear. If a bear weighs 840 lb, what is the average weight of the 12 fifth-grade students? How many more pounds does the black bear weigh than the average fifth-grader?

4. Black bears can run 30 miles per hour. At this rate, how far can a bear run in $\frac{1}{5}$ hour?

5. Not all black bears are black! They can be many different colors. In one park, $\frac{1}{4}$ of the black bears are light brown, and $\frac{1}{3}$ are dark brown. The rest are black. What fraction of the bears are black?

6. Scientists observe bears to study their eating habits. Suppose a scientist observes a bear every day for a week. She watches the bear $1\frac{1}{2}$ h the first day, 3 h the second, and $4\frac{1}{2}$ h the third day. If the pattern continues, how long will the scientist spend watching the bear on the last day?

7. A black bear has sharp claws that can be $2\frac{1}{2}$ in. long. Bears have 5 claws on each foot. How many claws are there in a group of 25 bears?

8. Black bears are usually born in litters of 2 or 3 cubs. Suppose that there are 15 cubs in one park. Every mother bear in the park had 2 or 3 cubs. How many mother bears might there be?

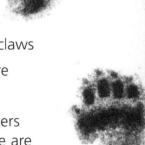

Share Your Thinking

9. Compare the strategy you used to solve problem 8 with a classmate's strategy. Explain the steps in your solution.

Chapter 10 Test

for Pages 328–353

Test-Taking Tips

Estimate to check your answers. Benchmarks such as $\frac{1}{4} = 0.25$ can help you.

Problem Solving

Solve. Show your work. (pages 336, 344, 346, 350, 352)

1. A student practiced the long jump. Her first jump was $4\frac{1}{8}$ feet long. Each of her next jumps was $\frac{1}{4}$ foot longer than the jump before it. How long was her fourth jump?

2. Another student practiced the shot put. His first throw was $8\frac{1}{2}$ feet. Each of his next throws was $1\frac{1}{8}$ feet longer than the throw before it. How far did he throw on his fifth try?

Find the answer. Use the chart about Carl Lewis for problems 3 and 4. (page 346)

3. How much farther did Carl Lewis jump in 1988 than in 1992?

4. How much farther did Carl Lewis jump in 1984 than in 1996?

5. In the 1996 summer Olympics, Randy Barnes won a gold medal in the shot put. His throw was 70 ft, $11\frac{1}{4}$ in. How far from 71 ft was his throw?

Lewis's Long Jump Gold Medals	
Year	**Distance**
1984	28 feet, $\frac{1}{4}$ inch
1988	28 feet, $7\frac{1}{4}$ inches
1992	28 feet, $5\frac{1}{2}$ inches
1996	27 feet, $10\frac{3}{4}$ inches

Concepts

Use number sense to choose the equivalent expression. Write a, b, c, or d. (page 334)

6. $\frac{1}{2} + \frac{3}{4}$ a. $\frac{1}{2} + \frac{4}{3}$ b. $\frac{2}{4} + \frac{3}{4}$ c. $\frac{1}{2} + \frac{3}{2}$ d. $\frac{2}{4} + \frac{6}{4}$

7. $\frac{7}{10} - \frac{1}{3}$ a. $\frac{7}{10} - \frac{2}{3}$ b. $\frac{7}{20} - \frac{2}{20}$ c. $\frac{21}{30} - \frac{10}{30}$ d. $\frac{10}{7} - \frac{3}{1}$

Tell how you would rename to subtract. Do not subtract. (page 346)

8. $5\frac{1}{4} - 3\frac{3}{4}$ 9. $3\frac{1}{6} - 1\frac{1}{2}$ 10. $9\frac{1}{5} - 4\frac{1}{4}$

354

Add. Show your work. (pages 330, 334, 340, 344)

11. $\begin{array}{r} 4\frac{1}{4} \\ +\ 3\frac{1}{4} \\ \hline \end{array}$

12. $\begin{array}{r} \frac{5}{8} \\ +\ \frac{1}{4} \\ \hline \end{array}$

13. $\begin{array}{r} 4\frac{1}{5} \\ +\ 1\frac{4}{5} \\ \hline \end{array}$

14. $\begin{array}{r} 12 \\ +\ 8\frac{5}{21} \\ \hline \end{array}$

15. $\begin{array}{r} 1\frac{1}{8} \\ +\ 2\frac{1}{5} \\ \hline \end{array}$

16. $\begin{array}{r} \frac{5}{6} \\ +\ \frac{3}{4} \\ \hline \end{array}$

Subtract. Show your work. (pages 330, 334, 346, 348)

17. $\frac{7}{8} - \frac{3}{8}$

18. $3\frac{2}{5} - \frac{3}{10}$

19. $5\frac{7}{9} - 5\frac{2}{3}$

20. $4\frac{1}{6} - 3\frac{11}{12}$

Write the letter of the correct difference. (page 308)

21. $\frac{3}{4} - \frac{1}{5}$ a. $\frac{11}{20}$

22. $4\frac{1}{5} - 3\frac{3}{4}$ b. $\frac{1}{20}$

23. $2\frac{2}{5} - 2\frac{1}{4}$ c. $\frac{19}{20}$

24. $1\frac{4}{5} - 1\frac{3}{4}$ d. $\frac{3}{20}$

25. $5\frac{1}{5} - 4\frac{1}{4}$ e. $\frac{9}{20}$

 Performance Task

(pages 336, 350, 352)

Imagine that four classes in your school are planning a day of electrical explorations. Each student will need 2 batteries, 6 connecting wires, 8 alligator clips, and 3 switches. Create a table giving the number of each item that will be needed.

- Label the columns with the names of four teachers and the number of students in each of their classes.

- Add a row for each item and record the number of that item each class will need.

- For each item, calculate the total number needed.

Keep in Mind . . .

Your work will be evaluated on the following:

☑ Clearly labeled table

☑ Number of students per class

☑ Correct data in table

☑ Correct totals per item

Cumulative Review

Multiplying Money (Chapter 6)
Find $1.49 × 6.3.

Here's A Way!

Multiply. To place the decimal point in the product, add the decimal places in both factors.

$1.49   2 decimal places
  6.3   1 decimal place

$1.49 × 6.3 = $9.387
Round to the nearest cent: $9.39

Write the product. Round dollar amounts to the nearest cent.

1. $9.90
  ×   0.6

2. $18.41
  ×   2

3. $7.07
  ×   1.8

4. $53.81
  ×   5.9

5. $2.83 × 0.4

6. $28.15 × 12

7. $25.43 × 6

8. $3.42 × 176.3

9. Which decimal place do you round to when you round to the nearest cent?

Estimating Money Quotients (Chapter 7)
Estimate $5.89 ÷ 3.

Here's A Way!

Replace dollars with cents:
  $5.89 = 589 cents
Replace cents with compatible numbers. Use mental math to divide.
  600 ÷ 3 = 200
The cost is about $2.00.

Write the letter of the most reasonable estimate.

10. $7.93 ÷ 5   a. $.10   b. $1.00   c. $10.00

11. $57.83 ÷ 9   a. $.06   b. $.60   c. $6.00

12. $.91 ÷ 7   a. $.01   b. $.10   c. $1.00

13. Is the actual quotient in the example greater than or less than $2.00? Explain.

Ordered Pairs (Chapter 8)
Use the grid at right to find the location of point A.

Here's A Way!

Read across from zero to find the first number in line with point A (1). Then read up from that number to find the second number (2).
  Location of point A is (1, 2).

Write the ordered pair for each point.

14. B   15. C

16. D   17. E

18. F   19. G

20. Explain how to plot the point (4, 5).

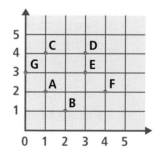

Fractions in Simplest Form (Chapter 9)

Find the simplest form of $\frac{6}{9}$.

Here's A Way!

Divide the numerator and denominator by their greatest common factor (GCF), which is 3.

$$\frac{6 \div 3}{9 \div 3} = \frac{2}{3}$$

Write the equivalent fraction in simplest form.

21. $\frac{6}{12}$ 22. $\frac{10}{15}$ 23. $\frac{22}{24}$

24. $\frac{25}{50}$ 25. $\frac{28}{35}$ 26. $\frac{9}{36}$

27. When a fraction is in simplest form, what factors do the numerator and the denominator have in common?

Add and Subtract Mixed Numbers

(Chapter 10)

Add $2\frac{1}{3}$ and $3\frac{2}{5}$.

Here's A Way!

Find the least common denominator. The least common multiple of 3 and 5 is 15. So, 15 is the least common denominator.
Write equivalent fractions.

$$\frac{1}{3} = \frac{1 \times 5}{3 \times 5} = \frac{5}{15} \qquad \frac{2}{5} = \frac{2 \times 3}{5 \times 3} = \frac{6}{15}$$

Add the fractions. Then add the whole numbers. Simplify.

$$2\frac{5}{15} + 3\frac{6}{15} = 5\frac{11}{15}$$

Write the sum or difference in simplest form.

28. $\quad 8\frac{3}{10}$
    $+ \quad 2\frac{2}{5}$

29. $\quad 3\frac{7}{10}$
    $- \quad 1\frac{1}{4}$

30. $\quad 4\frac{5}{8}$
    $- \quad 3\frac{1}{6}$

31. $\quad \frac{1}{3}$
    $+ \quad \frac{3}{8}$

32. $5\frac{1}{3} + \frac{3}{4}$

33. $9\frac{1}{2} - 7\frac{1}{6}$

34. $\frac{9}{10} - \frac{3}{5}$

35. $10\frac{4}{9} + 4\frac{1}{3}$

36. Suppose you add two fractions using a common denominator that is not the least common denominator. How will that affect your answer?

Problem Solving

Problem Solving Process

✓ Understand
✓ Plan
✓ Try It
✓ Look Back

Choose a Strategy You Have Learned

✓ Make a Table
✓ Act It Out
✓ Guess and Check
✓ Look for a Pattern
✓ Work Backward
✓ Make a List
✓ Work a Simpler Problem
✓ Draw a Picture
  Write an Equation

Choose one of the strategies you know to solve these problems. Show your work.

37. Four friends are to line up in order from tallest to shortest. Friend A is 2 inches shorter than friend B. Friend B is not as tall as friend C but is 3 inches taller than friend D. How should they line up?

38. A beach towel is on sale for $7 less than the original price. The sale price of the beach towel is $4 more than the sale price of a bath towel, which is $13.99. What was the original price of the beach towel?

Fields of Fruit

Science Connection   **With Your Group**

Keep In Mind . . .

Your work will be evaluated on the following:

☑ How you use your knowledge of fractions to divide the land

☑ How clearly your maps show the failed attempts

☑ How accurately your map divides the land

☑ How well your group solved the problem of overlapping land

Did you know Navel oranges and nectarines are mutants? A fruit is mutant when its original form has been changed to produce a new kind of fruit. Many fruit producers have orchards where scientists work to improve the fruit grown there.

Your group will design an orchard where you will grow four kinds of fruit trees. You will need to decide how to divide the land between the four kinds of trees. You must use as much of the land as possible.

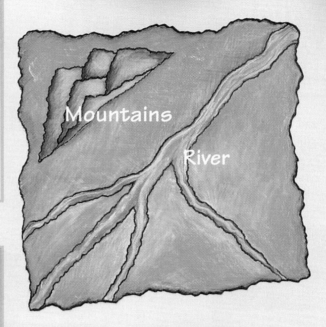

Plan It

1

- Have each group member trace the map to the right using $\frac{1}{4}$" squared grid paper. Include the mountains and river.
- Each square on the map equals one acre. Estimate the number of acres that can be planted. Subtract the number of acres covered by mountains from the total acres on the map.

Mountains

River

Put It Together

2

- Each group member will choose a fruit tree from the list. Find how many acres your 500 trees will need.
- Using a pencil, mark on your map where you want to locate your orchard.
- Compare the sections each group member has chosen. If the land you chose overlaps another person's land, work together to find a solution.

Acres Needed

Fruit Trees	100 trees need
Apricot	$6\frac{2}{5}$ acres
Peach	$2\frac{3}{4}$ acres
Pear	$1\frac{3}{4}$ acres
Plum	$\frac{2}{3}$ acres

Discuss Your Results

4

- Did you meet the objectives listed in Keep In Mind?
- How did other groups solve the problem of dividing the land?

Wrap It Up

3

- Use the grid maps to show each attempt at dividing the land.
- When you have found a solution, fill in one map using a different color for each group member's section.

Internet

> Visit the **Math Center** at Houghton Mifflin Education Place. http://www.eduplace.com

Math Power

Use What You Know

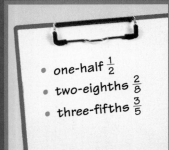

- one-half $\frac{1}{2}$
- two-eighths $\frac{2}{8}$
- three-fifths $\frac{3}{5}$

• how to write fractions in words

four groups of two jacks is eight jacks

• how to write math sentences in words

$\frac{3}{4}$

• how to show fractions

Multiplication and Division of Fractions

Try This!

Multiplying fractions can be as easy as pie! Use what you know about multiplying whole numbers to multiply fractions.

What You'll Need

paper, pencil, markers

1

Draw a picture that shows five groups of four pies. Write a multiplication sentence in words to tell how many pies are shown. Now, use one group of four pies to show multiplication of fractions.

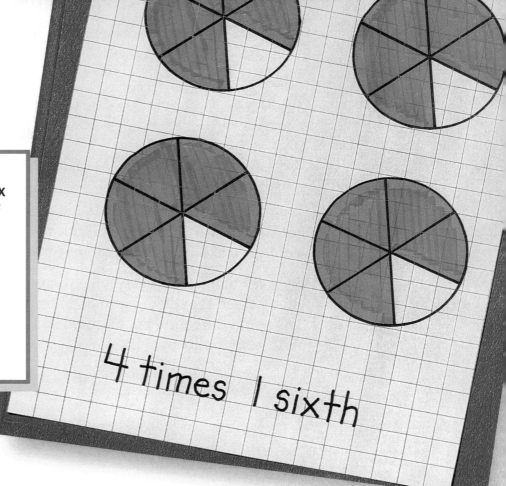

Show four pies cut into six equal pieces. Color five of the pieces in each pie to show that they have not been eaten. Write a multiplication sentence in words to show how many sixths altogether have been eaten.

4 times 1 sixth

Repeat step 2 but use five pies cut into four equal pieces. Shade three of the pieces in each pie.

How are the sentences you wrote similar? How are they different?

How would you write the mathematical sentences using numbers?

Ready to Go!

Fraction Factors

Getting Started

What You'll Need:
► crayons
► paper
► pencil
► fraction strips
► scissors

Use What You Know

You can write *6* as a fraction: $\frac{6}{1}$.

You can use fraction strips to show $1\frac{2}{3}$.

Suppose a friend asks you to make Strawberry Soup. The recipe calls for $\frac{1}{4}$c of strawberries for 1 serving, but you want to make 6 servings. You need to find $6 \times \frac{1}{4}$.

In this situation, you can solve the problem by using fraction models and repeated addition. Since you can represent the problem with repeated addition, you can also represent it with a multiplication sentence.

Whole Number		Fraction	Repeated Addition	Multiplication Sentence
6	×	$\frac{1}{4}$	$\frac{1}{4} + \frac{1}{4} + \frac{1}{4} + \frac{1}{4} + \frac{1}{4} + \frac{1}{4}$	$\frac{6}{1} \times \frac{1}{4} = \frac{6}{4}$

Activity

Use Fraction Strips

❶ Copy and complete the chart as shown below.

	Whole Number		Fraction	Repeated Addition Sentence	Multiplication Sentence
1.	4	×	$\frac{1}{2}$	?	?
2.	5	×	$\frac{3}{8}$	?	?
3.	3	×	$\frac{2}{3}$	?	?
4.	2	×	$\frac{3}{4}$	?	?

❷ Use fraction strips to find the product. Find and cut out the correct fraction strip.

$\frac{1}{2}$

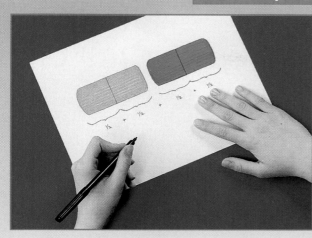

1. Shade the strip to show the fraction. For example, shade $\frac{1}{2}$.

2. Continue shading fractions. For example, to show $4 \times \frac{1}{2}$, you need to shade 4 groups of $\frac{1}{2}$.

3. Write a repeated addition sentence below the strips to represent the models.

4. Find the sum. Simplify if necessary.

5. Fill in the correct column in your chart.

Use Multiplication

To multiply a fraction by a whole number, for example $7 \times \frac{1}{4}$, you need to:

1. Write both factors as a fraction. $\frac{\blacksquare}{1}$, $\frac{1}{\blacksquare}$

2. Write a multiplication sentence. Fill in the correct column in the chart. $\frac{\blacksquare}{1} \times \frac{1}{\blacksquare} = \frac{\blacksquare}{\blacksquare}$

3. Then, multiply the numerators. Multiply the denominators. Simplify. What is the product? How does the product compare with the sum you wrote? How is multiplying fractions similar to adding the same fractions repeatedly? How is it different?

Show What You Know!

Discuss each question and explain your answer.

1. **Critical Thinking** Write a rule for multiplying fractions by whole numbers.

2. **Critical Thinking** When multiplying fractions by whole numbers, how does writing the whole number as a fraction help you?

3. **Number Sense** Which product is greater than 1: $\frac{1}{3} \times 5$ or $\frac{1}{8} \times 5$?

Find each product. Use fraction strips and repeated addition if you need to.

4. $3 \times \frac{1}{3}$ 5. $6 \times \frac{1}{3}$ 6. $6 \times \frac{4}{5}$ 7. $4 \times \frac{2}{3}$ 8. 6×6

9. $2 \times \frac{4}{1}$ 10. $8 \times \frac{1}{4}$ 11. $5 \times \frac{5}{6}$ 12. $5 \times \frac{1}{2}$ 13. $4 \times \frac{3}{8}$

14. **Estimate** Is the product of $3 \times \frac{1}{2}$ greater or less than 1? Explain.

15. **Critical Thinking** Does it matter whether you multiply the denominators first or numerators first?

Multiplying with Fractions

$\frac{2}{3}$ of 4 meters

The Marabou stork has a 4-m wingspan, the largest wingspan of any bird. The black vulture's wingspan is about $\frac{2}{3}$ of that length. What is the black vulture's wingspan?

4 meters

You can multiply to find the answer.

Here's A Way! Find $\frac{2}{3} \times 4$.

1 Write the whole number as a fraction.

$$4 \longrightarrow \frac{4}{1}$$

$$\frac{2}{3} \times 4 = \frac{2}{3} \times \frac{4}{1}$$

2 Multiply the numerators. Multiply the denominators.

$$\frac{2}{3} \times \frac{4}{1} = \frac{8}{3}$$

3 Simplify if you can.

$$\frac{8}{3} = 2\frac{2}{3}$$

The black vulture's wingspan is $2\frac{2}{3}$ meters.

Talk About It! When you multiply a whole number by a fraction less than 1, is the product greater than or less than the whole number? Explain.

Write the product in simplest form.

1. $\frac{2}{3} \times 6$
2. $\frac{1}{6} \times 12$
3. $\frac{1}{2} \times 16$
4. $\frac{6}{5} \times 15$
5. $9 \times \frac{1}{2}$

6. $\frac{2}{5} \times 15$
7. $5 \times \frac{3}{8}$
8. $6 \times \frac{4}{3}$
9. $8 \times \frac{5}{4}$
10. $16 \times \frac{9}{7}$

11. **Critical Thinking** Look at exercises 8–10. What do you notice when you multiply a whole number by a fraction greater than 1?

Work It Out!

Write the product in simplest form.

12. $\frac{1}{4} \times 12$
13. $\frac{1}{2} \times 20$
14. $21 \times \frac{1}{3}$
15. $29 \times \frac{1}{8}$
16. $\frac{2}{5} \times 25$

17. $30 \times \frac{5}{6}$
18. $\frac{4}{9} \times 18$
19. $14 \times \frac{3}{7}$
20. $16 \times \frac{4}{5}$
21. $\frac{17}{10} \times 20$

Problem Solving

22. The pterodactyl, an extinct flying reptile, had a wingspan of 50 ft. The California condor's wingspan is about $\frac{1}{6}$ of that. What is the wingspan of the California condor?

23. The California condor has a body length of about 4 ft. About how many times the body length is the wingspan?

24. The osprey's body length is $\frac{1}{3}$ the length of its 6 ft wingspan. How long is its body?

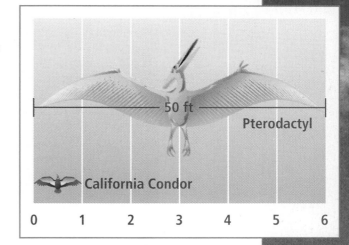

50 ft
Pterodactyl
California Condor
0 1 2 3 4 5 6

Number Sense A number is a **perfect number** if it is $\frac{1}{2}$ of the sum of its factors. For example, the number 6 is a perfect number.

Factors of 6: 1, 2, 3, 6 ➡ $1 + 2 + 3 + 6 = 12$ $\frac{1}{2}$ of 12 is 6.

What perfect number is between 20 and 30?

Mixed Review
Use front-end estimation or rounding to estimate.

25. 5×68
26. 6×327
27. 333×32
28. 12×67

More Practice Set 11.2, p. 491

Estimation: Finding a Fraction of a Number

Use What You Know

Compatible numbers are numbers that are easy to work with using mental math.

$237 \div 62 \Rightarrow 240 \div 60$

$240 \div 60 = 4$

So $237 \div 62$ is about 4.

Suppose your fifth-grade class is putting on a play. You need to reserve about $\frac{1}{4}$ of the rows of seats for family and friends of the actors. If there are 24 rows of seats in the auditorium, about how many rows should you reserve?

You can find $\frac{1}{4}$ of 24 using mental math.

$\frac{1}{4} \times 24$ $\frac{1}{4} \times \frac{24}{1}$ $\frac{24}{4}$ or 6

Sometimes you may only need an estimated product.

About how much is $\frac{1}{4}$ of 35?

$24 \div 4$

Here's A Way! Estimate $\frac{1}{4} \times 35$.

1 Look for compatible numbers.

$\frac{1}{4} \times 35$

$\frac{1}{4} \times 36$

Choose a number close to 35 that is evenly divided by 4.

2 Estimate the product.

$\frac{1}{4} \times 36 = 9$

So $\frac{1}{4} \times 35$ is about 9.

Talk About It! When estimating the product of a fraction and a whole number, how can you tell if your estimate is high?

Other Examples Notice that the denominator of the fraction divides the compatible whole number evenly

a. Estimate $\frac{1}{4}$ of $26.99.

Think: $\frac{1}{4}$ of $24.00 is $6.00 or $\frac{1}{4}$ of $28.00 is $7.00. Both 6 and 7 are reasonable estimates.

b. Estimate $\frac{1}{5}$ of 28.

Think: $\frac{1}{5}$ of 25 is 5 or $\frac{1}{5}$ of 30 is 6. Both 5 and 6 are reasonable estimates.

Use mental math.

1. $\frac{1}{4}$ of 40   2. $\frac{1}{5}$ of 35   3. $\frac{1}{6}$ of 36   4. $\frac{1}{6}$ of 30   5. $\frac{1}{7}$ of $490   6. $\frac{1}{8}$ of $480

Estimate.

7. $\frac{1}{8}$ of 19   8. $\frac{1}{7}$ of $495   9. $\frac{1}{3}$ of 126   10. $\frac{1}{9}$ of 68   11. $\frac{1}{2}$ of 689   12. $\frac{1}{7}$ of $211

13. **Critical Thinking** Explain how you arrived at your estimate for exercise 12. What is another reasonable estimate for exercise 12?

Work It Out!

Use mental math to solve.

14. $\frac{1}{5}$ of 25   15. $\frac{1}{2}$ of 18   16. $\frac{1}{7}$ of 42   17. $\frac{1}{3}$ of 300

18. $\frac{1}{9}$ of 810   19. $\frac{1}{8}$ of 640   20. $\frac{1}{4}$ of 4000   21. $\frac{1}{3}$ of 1500

Estimate.

22. $\frac{1}{6}$ of 63   23. $\frac{1}{5}$ of 33   24. $\frac{1}{7}$ of 62   25. $\frac{1}{4}$ of 910

26. $\frac{1}{2}$ of 766   27. $\frac{1}{6}$ of 468   28. $\frac{1}{8}$ of $5869   29. $\frac{1}{9}$ of 3122

Problem Solving   Using Data

30. Ms. Ruby's class sold almost $\frac{1}{2}$ of the tickets sold by grade 5. About how many tickets did they sell?

31. Each ticket sold for $3. What is the value of tickets sold?

32. One student sold $\frac{1}{5}$ of all the tickets sold by grade 2. How many tickets did she sell?

33. Each grade will receive $\frac{1}{2}$ of the money raised by their ticket sales. About how much money will grade 5 receive?

Number of Tickets Sold	
Grade Level	Tickets Sold
2	50
3	93
4	84
5	177

More Practice Set 11.3, p. 491

Math Journal

Explain how using compatible numbers can help you estimate a fraction of a number.

Problem Solving
Guess and Check

LESSON 4

The Hernandez family is on vacation at the Grand Canyon in Arizona. The children take pictures with the family camera. Margarita uses $\frac{1}{3}$ of the pictures on the roll of film. Paul takes one picture. The twins use $\frac{2}{3}$ of the pictures that are left. After everyone has taken pictures, there are 5 pictures left. How many pictures were on the original roll?

Here's A Way! Use Guess and Check to solve the problem.

1 Understand

- You need to know how many pictures are on the original roll of film.

2 Plan

- Guess how many pictures could have been on the roll of film.
- Check to see if your guess works. If your guess does not work, use the results to help you make a better guess.

Guess 1: Margarita used $\frac{1}{3}$ of
36 = 12; 36 − 12 = 24 left.
36   Paul took 1 photo; 24 − 1 = 23
left. So twins used $\frac{2}{3}$ of 23,
but $\frac{2}{3}$ of 23 is not a whole
number, so 36 was a wrong
guess.

Guess 2: Margarita used $\frac{1}{3}$ of
24 = 8; 24 − 8 = 16 left. Paul
24   took 1 photo; 16 − 1 = 15 left.
So twins used $\frac{2}{3}$ of 15 which
is 10. 15 − 10 = 5 photos left.
24 is the correct guess.

3 Try It

- Try 36 as a first guess.
- The answer must be a whole number.
- Will your next guess be higher or lower?

4 Look Back

- How can checking each guess help you solve the problem?
- There were 24 pictures on the original roll.

Show What You Know!

Use Guess and Check to solve the problem.

1. A tour group hiked part of the Bright Angel trail at the Grand Canyon. A sack lunch was provided. Half of the sack lunches had ham and cheese sandwiches. Three of the lunches had tuna sandwiches. A fourth of the remaining lunches had egg salad sandwiches. The 9 remaining lunches had peanut butter and jelly sandwiches. How many sack lunches were there in all?

2. **Critical Thinking** Explain how you chose your first guess to solve problem 1.

Work It Out!

Use Guess and Check or any strategy to solve the problem.

3. Harriet wants to buy a souvenir outfit at the Bright Angel Lodge gift shop. She wants to get a hat, a T-shirt, and a pair of shorts. The hat she wants comes in red or white. The T-shirts come in white, red, blue, or striped. The shorts come in white, red, or blue. How many different outfits does she have to choose from?

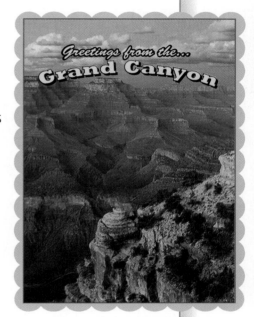

4. Mariana bought postcards of the Grand Canyon to send her friends. Some postcards were on sale for 20¢ each. The other postcards cost 30¢ each. Mariana spent $2.30 on postcards. How many postcards did she buy at the sale price? How many at the regular price? Find at least 3 different possibilities.

5. On her vacation, Mrs. Martinez kept a record of the difference in the gasoline price at each place she stopped. Before she left, she filled up at home and paid $1.43 per gallon. What was the cost of gasoline at the sixth stop on her vacation?

6. After buying souvenirs, Francisco had 12 coins worth $1.50 left in his pocket. The coins were quarters, dimes, and nickels. How many coins of each type did he have?

7. A box of 24 Grand Canyon slides cost $50.00. Will each slide cost more or less than $2.00? Explain.

Change in Gasoline Prices	
Stop Number	**Price Difference in Cents**
1	up 6
2	down 9
3	up 5
4	up 11
5	down 2
6	down 3

Share Your Thinking

8. In problem 6, how can Guess and Check help you solve the problem?

Fractions and Multiplication

Getting Started

What You'll Need:
- ▶ paper
- ▶ 2 markers, red and blue
- ▶ recording sheet (TR)

Use What You Know

You can use an array to represent a multiplication problem in which a fraction is multiplied by another fraction.

4

3

Suppose you use $\frac{2}{3}$ of $\frac{3}{4}$ of a jar of paint on a project. How much of the whole jar will you use? You need to find $\frac{2}{3}$ of $\frac{3}{4}$.

Drawing an array can help you solve this exercise.

Activity

Working with Arrays

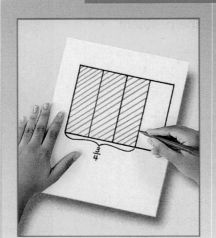

Before you begin, decide if the result of this multiplication will be greater or less than 1. Since $\frac{3}{4}$ jar is already less than 1, the product will also be less than 1.

1 Outline a rectangle as shown.

2 Divide the rectangle into 4 equal parts using vertical lines. With your red marker, shade 3 fourths to represent $\frac{3}{4}$.

Show the Second Factor

1 Now draw horizontal lines to divide the rectangle into 3 equal parts. Shade 2 thirds blue to represent $\frac{2}{3}$.

a. When you divided the rectangle into thirds, into how many smaller parts was the whole rectangle divided?

Explore the Product

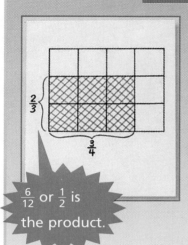

$\frac{2}{3}$

$\frac{3}{4}$

$\frac{6}{12}$ or $\frac{1}{2}$ is the product.

1 What fraction can you write to represent the part that is both red and blue? (There are 4 columns and 3 rows, or 4×3 parts in the whole box. This is the new denominator of the product. There are 3 columns and 2 rows, or 3×2 parts in the product. This is the new numerator of the product.)

2 What number sentence can you write to show $\frac{2}{3}$ of $\frac{3}{4}$?

3 Look at the numerators of the two fractions you multiplied. What do you notice about the numerator of the answer?

4 Look at the denominators of the two fractions you multiplied. What do you notice about the denominator of the answer?

Show What You Know!

Copy and complete the model to find the answer.

1. $\frac{1}{3} \times \frac{1}{2}$

2. $\frac{4}{5} \times \frac{3}{4}$

3. **Critical Thinking** When you multiply two fractions that are less than 1, what will be true of the product? Explain.

4. Copy and complete the chart below.

Fraction	Multiplication Problem	Product
$\frac{1}{2}$ of $\frac{3}{4}$	$\frac{1}{2} \times \frac{3}{4}$	?
$\frac{1}{2}$ of $\frac{2}{3}$	$\frac{1}{2} \times \frac{2}{3}$	?
$\frac{1}{3}$ of $\frac{1}{4}$	$\frac{1}{3} \times \frac{1}{4}$	?
$\frac{3}{4}$ of $\frac{2}{5}$	$\frac{3}{4} \times \frac{2}{5}$	?
$\frac{1}{2}$ of $\frac{4}{5}$	$\frac{1}{2} \times \frac{4}{5}$	?

5. **Patterns** Look at the last line of the chart in exercise 4. Given your answer for $\frac{1}{2}$ of $\frac{4}{5}$, what do you predict as your answer for $\frac{1}{2} \times \frac{8}{5}$? $\frac{1}{2} \times \frac{12}{5}$?

Mixed Review   **Finding Simplest Form**

Add or subtract.

6. $2\frac{1}{4} + \frac{3}{4}$

7. $3\frac{5}{8} - \frac{3}{8}$

8. $\frac{4}{9} + \frac{1}{2}$

9. $6 - 2\frac{3}{10}$

10. $3\frac{1}{6} + 7\frac{1}{3}$

Multiplying Fractions

Suppose your gym class lasts $\frac{3}{4}$ of an hour. On Thursdays, you play basketball for $\frac{2}{3}$ of that time. How long will you play basketball?

Multiply $\frac{2}{3}$ by $\frac{3}{4}$ to find the answer.

As you saw in the last lesson, the model shows the product.

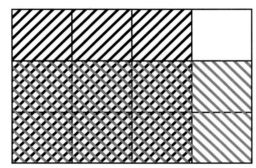

First shade $\frac{3}{4}$ of the rectangle.

Then shade $\frac{2}{3}$ of the rectangle.

The rectangle is divided into 12 parts, and 6 parts are shaded twice.

You can also multiply.

| **Here's A Way!** | Find $\frac{2}{3} \times \frac{3}{4}$. |

1 Multiply the numerators.

$$\frac{2}{3} \times \frac{3}{4} = \frac{2 \times 3}{\blacksquare}$$

2 Multiply the denominators.

$$\frac{2}{3} \times \frac{3}{4} = \frac{2 \times 3}{3 \times 4}$$

3 Simplify the product if possible.

$$\frac{2 \times 3}{3 \times 4} = \frac{6}{12} = \frac{1}{2}$$

So, you will play basketball for $\frac{1}{2}$ of an hour.

Talk About It! Explain why the denominator in the product is 2.

Show What You Know!

Write the product in simplest form. Use a model if you need help.

1. $\frac{1}{5} \times \frac{1}{2}$
2. $\frac{3}{4} \times \frac{2}{3}$
3. $\frac{2}{3} \times \frac{1}{4}$
4. $\frac{5}{8} \times \frac{1}{2}$
5. $\frac{1}{3} \times \frac{5}{6}$

6. $\frac{1}{4} \times \frac{2}{7}$
7. $5 \times \frac{3}{4}$
8. $\frac{4}{9} \times \frac{1}{3}$
9. $3 \times \frac{2}{3}$
10. $4 \times \frac{1}{12}$

11. **Critical Thinking** How could you have used mental math to solve exercises 9 and 10?

Work It Out!

Write the product in simplest form. Use a model if you need help.

12. $\frac{2}{5} \times \frac{1}{3}$
13. $\frac{1}{2} \times \frac{1}{6}$
14. $\frac{3}{4} \times \frac{1}{3}$
15. $\frac{3}{10} \times \frac{1}{2}$
16. $\frac{3}{7} \times \frac{4}{5}$
17. $\frac{1}{6} \times \frac{1}{7}$

18. $\frac{7}{9} \times 3$
19. $12 \times \frac{1}{8}$
20. $\frac{5}{7} \times \frac{1}{2}$
21. $\frac{2}{3} \times \frac{1}{4}$
22. $\frac{3}{5} \times \frac{2}{7}$

Calculator Use a calculator to multiply fractions.

To multiply fractions using a Math Explorer, find the [/] and [Simp] keys. To multiply $\frac{4}{5} \times \frac{3}{4}$, type [4] [/] [5] [X] [3] [/] [4] [=]. The calculator shows 12/20 with a message that tells you to simplify. Type [Simp] [=]. Now the calculator shows 6/10. Simplify again to get 3/5. Use Math Explorer to work exercises 23–30.

23. $15 \times \frac{1}{6}$
24. $\frac{9}{10} \times \frac{3}{8}$
25. $\frac{2}{5} \times \frac{1}{4}$
26. $\frac{1}{3} \times \frac{5}{8}$

27. $\frac{1}{3} \times \frac{1}{6}$
28. $5 \times \frac{2}{5}$
29. $\frac{3}{10} \times 20$
30. $\frac{5}{6} \times \frac{1}{5}$

Problem Solving Using Data

Use the Class Schedule for problems 31–36.

31. Which class period is the longest?

32. A film on bees lasted $\frac{1}{2}$ of Period 4. How long was it?

33. How many minutes a day are spent in class?

34. Marty says he missed $\frac{1}{4}$ of Period 1. How late was he?

35. The Nature Club spent $\frac{1}{2}$ of its $\frac{3}{4}$-hour meeting on a nature walk. What fraction of an hour was spent on the nature walk?

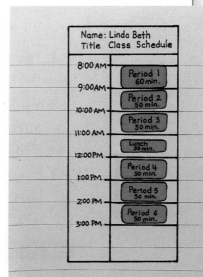

Name: Linda Beth
Title Class Schedule

8:00 AM — Period 1 60 min.
9:00 AM — Period 2 50 min.
10:00 AM — Period 3 50 min.
11:00 AM — Lunch 30 min.
12:00 PM — Period 4 50 min.
1:00 PM — Period 5 50 min.
2:00 PM — Period 6 50 min.
3:00 PM

More Practice Set 11.6, p. 492

Problem Solving
Choose a Computation Method

You saw ballet tights on sale for $3.89 a pair. What is the greatest number of pairs of tights you can buy with $20?

You Decide

- Do you need to use exact numbers to find the answer?

- How can estimating help to solve this problem? Explain.

- Decide whether you will estimate or find the exact answer. Explain your decision.

Work It Out!

Decide to estimate or find the exact answer. Solve and explain.

1. You want to order workout clothes from a catalog. You have a $50 budget. Can you order a sweatshirt for $18.99, two T-shirts for $8.50 each, and a pair of sweatpants for $21.50?

2. You buy a pair of leggings for $6.99 and a pair of socks for $2.59. How much change should you receive from a $10 bill?

3. Your intermediate dance class wears matching shorts and shirts for a recital. The outfits cost $28.95 each. How many outfits can be purchased for $180?

4. You purchase 18 hats for the chorus to wear during a concert. The hats cost $2.15 each. You receive a bill for $45.18. Is this bill correct?

Share Your Thinking

5. Choose one of the problems you solved using estimation. Solve it by finding the exact answer. Was your exact answer very different from your estimated answer? Explain.

Midchapter Review

for Pages 362–374

for Pages 362–374

Problem Solving

Solve. Show your work. (pages 368, 374)

1. For a dinner of fewer than 30 people, places are set with paper napkins for children and cloth napkins for adults. There are $\frac{3}{4}$ as many places with cloth napkins as places with paper napkins. How many people could be at this dinner? How many are adults, and how many are children? Give two possible answers.

2. Would you estimate or compute the answer? Suppose you need 25 hours of reading time to win a prize. If you read $\frac{2}{3}$ of an hour a day, 5 days a week for 4 weeks, will you have enough hours?

Concepts

Find the answers. (pages 362, 364, 372)

3. If you multiply a whole number by a fraction less than 1, could the product be greater than the whole number? Explain.

4. Which product is greater than 1: $5 \times \frac{1}{7}$ or $7 \times \frac{1}{5}$? Explain.

5. Explain how to estimate $\frac{1}{6}$ of 278.

6. Explain how to find the product of two fractions.

Skills

Write the product in simplest form. (pages 362, 364, 370, 372)

7. $2 \times \frac{1}{3}$

8. $5 \times \frac{1}{2}$

9. $6 \times \frac{2}{5}$

10. $12 \times \frac{1}{6}$

11. $48 \times \frac{3}{8}$

12. $\frac{1}{10} \times \frac{2}{3}$

13. $\frac{3}{8} \times \frac{1}{4}$

14. $\frac{5}{6} \times \frac{1}{2}$

15. $\frac{3}{5} \times \frac{7}{9}$

16. $\frac{5}{7} \times \frac{7}{8}$

Estimate. (page 366)

17. $\frac{1}{3}$ of 57

18. $\frac{1}{4}$ of 409

19. $\frac{1}{5}$ of 313

20. $\frac{1}{9}$ of 751

21. $\frac{1}{7}$ of $2985

Math World

Fractions have been used for many years and are still important today. Read about how fractions are used, then play a game with fractions.

Dividing By the Book

This page comes from Philippi Calandri's *Arithmetice*, a book that was published in Italy about 500 years ago. Near the bottom of the page is the exercise $\frac{2}{5} \div \frac{7}{9}$. To find the answer, Calandri multiplied $\frac{2}{5}$ by the reciprocal of $\frac{7}{9}$, or $\frac{9}{7}$. This method is still being used today. You will learn about it in the next lesson.

Speaking of Fractions

Fractions are often used to describe populations. For example, about a third of the population of Argentina lives in the capital city, Buenos Aires. If the total population in 1996 was about 34,700,000, how would you find the number of people living in the capital?

Try This!

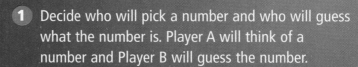

EGYPTIAN GUESSING GAME

STEP 1: Multiply the number you chose by $\frac{1}{3}$.

STEP 2: Add the new number to the number you started with.

STEP 3: Multiply the number you got in step 2 by $\frac{1}{3}$.

STEP 4: Subtract the number you got in step 3 from the number you got in step 2.

STEP 5: Tell your partner the number you got in step 4.

Egyptians may have played this guessing game about 3600 years ago. The game is explained in an ancient scroll found in Egypt. Try playing with a partner.

1 Decide who will pick a number and who will guess what the number is. Player A will think of a number and Player B will guess the number.

2 Player A chooses a number that can be divided by 9. The number must be between 10 and 100. Then, follow the five steps to the left. If you need to, use paper and pencil to do the math.

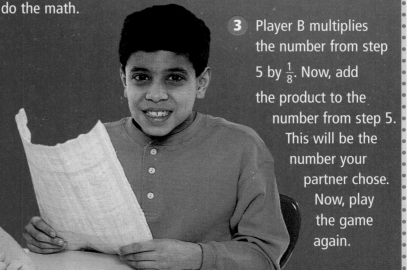

3 Player B multiplies the number from step 5 by $\frac{1}{8}$. Now, add the product to the number from step 5. This will be the number your partner chose. Now, play the game again.

Textbook case

In math textbooks, fractions are almost always written with the numerator above the fraction bar and the denominator below. Fractions can also be written with a slash instead of a bar. It is believed that this type of fraction was first used in Latin America in the 1700s.

Respond

With a partner . . .
find the population of your school. What fraction of the total population is your class?

Internet:
Houghton Mifflin Education Place
Explore the Math Center at
http://www.eduplace.com

377

Fractions and Division

Getting Started

What You'll Need:
▶ paper
▶ pencil

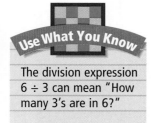

Use What You Know

The division expression $6 \div 3$ can mean "How many 3's are in 6?"

Number lines can help you divide with fractions. Dividing with fractions is similar to dividing with whole numbers. For example, the division expression $1 \div \frac{1}{4}$ can mean "How many $\frac{1}{4}$ parts are in 1?"

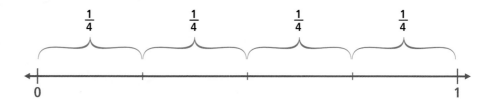

The number line shows that there are 4 fourths in 1.

So, $1 \div \frac{1}{4} = 4$.

Is the quotient greater or less than the dividend? Did this happen when you divided with whole numbers?

Activity

Use a Number Line

1. Use number lines to complete the charts. Begin with Chart A.

2. Look at the division sentences in Chart A. What fraction is the divisor in each sentence? Do you think the quotient of $6 \div \frac{1}{2}$ is greater or less than 6?

3. Which number line will you use to find the quotient of $2 \div \frac{1}{2}$. How many halves are in 2?

4. Use your number line to complete the chart.

5. Use a number line on page 379 to complete Chart B.

How Many Halves in:	Division Sentence	How Many Thirds in:	Division Sentence
1	$1 \div \frac{1}{2} = 2$	1	$1 \div \frac{1}{3} = 3$
2	$2 \div \frac{1}{2} =$	2	$2 \div \frac{1}{3} =$
3	$3 \div \frac{1}{2} =$	3	$? \div ? =$
4	$? \div ? =$	4	$? \div ? =$
5	$? \div ? =$	5	$? \div ? =$

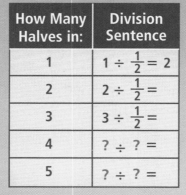

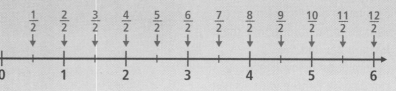

Find the Pattern

6 What pattern do you see in the quotients in the chart?

7 Use the pattern to predict the quotient of $6 \div \frac{1}{2}$ and $6 \div \frac{1}{3}$.

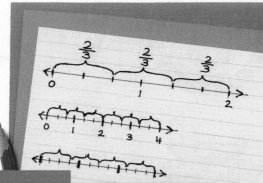

Divide with Greater Fractions

8 Now use a number line to find $2 \div \frac{2}{3}$. How many two thirds are there in 2?

9 Why is the quotient of $2 \div \frac{1}{3}$ greater than the quotient of $2 \div \frac{2}{3}$?

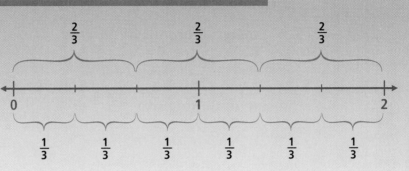

Show What You Know!

Solve. Use the number lines to help you.

1. $3 \div \frac{3}{8}$

2. $1 \div \frac{1}{3}$

3. How many four eighths in 8?

4. $6 \div \frac{3}{4}$

5. $3 \div \frac{1}{8}$

6. How many three fourths in 3?

7. **Critical Thinking** Write a rule for finding the quotient of a whole number and a fraction whose numerator is 1.

Use number lines or a pattern to find the quotient.

8. $4 \div \frac{1}{3} = \blacksquare$

9. $6 \div \frac{1}{3} = \blacksquare$

10. $4 \div \frac{2}{3} = \blacksquare$

11. $6 \div \frac{2}{3} = \blacksquare$

12. $3 \div \frac{1}{4} = \blacksquare$

13. $5 \div \frac{1}{8} = \blacksquare$

14. $3 \div \frac{3}{4} = \blacksquare$

15. $5 \div \frac{5}{8} = \blacksquare$

16. **Number Sense** Look at exercises 8–15. Is there another way to find the quotients? Explain.

More Practice Set 11.8, p. 492

379

Reciprocals

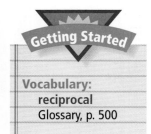

Sometimes a math problem can be solved using a pattern. Patterns can be found in fractions that have a product of 1.

For example, find $6 \times \frac{1}{6}$.

$6 \times \frac{1}{6}$ means 6 groups of $\frac{1}{6}$.

$\frac{1}{6} + \frac{1}{6} + \frac{1}{6} + \frac{1}{6} + \frac{1}{6} + \frac{1}{6} = 1$

The sum of 6 groups of $\frac{1}{6}$ is $\frac{6}{6}$ or 1. Then, $\frac{6}{1} \times \frac{1}{6} = 1$.

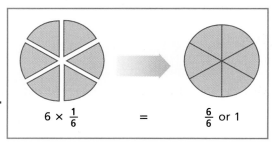

$6 \times \frac{1}{6}$ $=$ $\frac{6}{6}$ or 1

So, 6 and $\frac{1}{6}$ are reciprocals. Two numbers that have a product of 1 are **reciprocals** of each other.

Here's another way to find the reciprocal.

Here's A Way! Find the reciprocal of 6.

1 Write the whole number or mixed number as a fraction.

6 or $\frac{6}{1}$

2 Find a number that when multiplied by $\frac{6}{1}$ will have a product of 1.

Think: $\frac{6}{1} \times \blacksquare = 1$.

3 Check by multiplying.

$\frac{6}{1} \times \frac{1}{6} = 1$

So, $\frac{1}{6}$ is the reciprocal of **6**.

Talk About It! What do you notice about two numbers whose product equals 1?

Other Examples Write the number as a fraction and find its reciprocal.

a. $1\frac{1}{2}$ or $\frac{3}{2}$

$\frac{2}{3}$ is a reciprocal of $\frac{3}{2}$

$\frac{3}{2} \times \frac{2}{3} = \frac{6}{6}$ or 1

b. $2\frac{3}{5}$ or $\frac{13}{5}$

$\frac{5}{13}$ is a reciprocal of $\frac{13}{5}$

$\frac{13}{5} \times \frac{5}{13} = \frac{65}{65}$ or 1

c. $\frac{3}{5}$

$\frac{5}{3}$ is a reciprocal of $\frac{3}{5}$

$\frac{3}{5} \times \frac{5}{3} = \frac{15}{15}$ or 1

Look at the fractions in the box at the right to answer the questions below.

1. Write the reciprocal of each fraction that is greater than 1. Are the reciprocals greater than or less than 1?

2. Write the reciprocal of each fraction that is less than 1. Are the reciprocals greater than or less than 1?

$$\frac{10}{9} \qquad \frac{7}{2}$$
$$\frac{3}{5} \qquad \frac{1}{2}$$

3. **Critical Thinking** Is the reciprocal of a mixed number greater than or less than 1? Explain.

Work It Out!

Write the number as a fraction. Find its reciprocal.

4. 9
5. $2\frac{1}{2}$
6. 8
7. $1\frac{5}{8}$
8. $2\frac{1}{8}$
9. $4\frac{1}{7}$
10. $3\frac{4}{5}$
11. 10

12. $5\frac{1}{6}$
13. $12\frac{1}{2}$
14. $4\frac{1}{3}$
15. $9\frac{1}{2}$
16. $3\frac{1}{4}$
17. $9\frac{1}{7}$
18. $8\frac{1}{6}$
19. 11

Look at the fractions in the box at the right to answer the question.

20. Which numbers have reciprocals less than 1? Greater than 1?

21. Which number has the reciprocal closest to 0?

22. Which number has the reciprocal closest to 1?

23. Which number has a whole number as its reciprocal?

$$\frac{11}{9} \qquad \frac{1}{3}$$
$$\frac{6}{8} \qquad 7$$

Problem Solving

24. If 7 friends split a carton of milk, and 1 person drinks twice as much as everyone else, what fraction of the milk does each person drink?

25. Suppose you and 3 friends each ate $\frac{3}{8}$ of a pizza. How much pizza was eaten in all?

Mixed Review   Compare. Write >, <, or =.

26. $3\frac{1}{5}$ ● $\frac{13}{5}$
27. $7\frac{2}{3}$ ● $\frac{23}{3}$
28. $1\frac{5}{6}$ ● $1\frac{11}{16}$
29. $2\frac{9}{10}$ ● $2\frac{9}{11}$

More Practice Set 11.9, p. 492

Math Journal

What are two ways to check if two numbers are reciprocals?

Dividing by Fractions

A potter has a 7-lb container of clay. If it takes $\frac{7}{8}$ lb to make one mug, how many mugs can she make from the clay? As you saw in the last lesson, a number line can help you find the quotient.

Use a number line to represent 7 lb of clay.

Mark off $\frac{7}{8}$ to represent the clay needed for each mug.

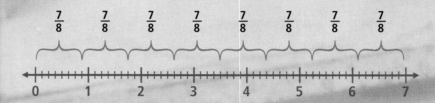

So, there are 8 groups of $\frac{7}{8}$ in 7. This is written $7 \div \frac{7}{8} = 8$.

With 7 lb of clay, a potter can make 8 mugs. You can also use reciprocals and multiplication to solve.

Here's A Way! Find $7 \div \frac{7}{8}$.

1 Find the reciprocal of the divisor.

$$7 \div \frac{7}{8}$$

reciprocal: $\frac{8}{7}$

2 Write a multiplication sentence using the reciprocal.

$$7 \times \frac{8}{7}$$

3 Multiply. Simplify if necessary.

$$7 \times \frac{8}{7} = \frac{7}{1} \times \frac{8}{7}$$
$$= \frac{56}{7} \text{ or } 8$$

Multiplying by a reciprocal of a fraction gives the same result as dividing by the fraction.

So, the potter can make 8 mugs with 7 lb of clay.

Talk About It! When you divide by fractions less than 1, why is the quotient greater than the dividend?

Other Examples

$$3 \div \frac{3}{5} = 3 \times \frac{5}{3}$$
$$= \frac{3}{1} \times \frac{5}{3} = \frac{15}{3} = 5$$

$$2 \div \frac{4}{6} = \frac{2}{1} \times \frac{6}{4}$$
$$= \frac{12}{4} = 3$$

Complete.

1. $8 \div \frac{2}{3} = \frac{8}{1} \times \frac{\blacksquare}{\blacksquare}$

2. $6 \div \frac{3}{4} = \frac{6}{1} \times \frac{\blacksquare}{\blacksquare}$

3. $1 \div \frac{\blacksquare}{\blacksquare} = 1 \times \frac{9}{1} = \blacksquare$

4. $6 \div \frac{2}{8}$

5. $7 \div \frac{2}{4}$

6. $8 \div \frac{1}{6}$

7. $3 \div \frac{1}{6}$

8. $2 \div \frac{1}{8}$

9. $4 \div \frac{1}{8}$

10. **Critical Thinking** When solving a division sentence, explain why you should use the reciprocal of the *second* number.

Work It Out!

Complete.

11. $3 \div \frac{1}{6} = 3 \times \frac{\blacksquare}{\blacksquare}$

12. $4 \div \frac{1}{5} = 4 \times \frac{\blacksquare}{\blacksquare} = \blacksquare$

13. $2 \div \frac{\blacksquare}{\blacksquare} = 2 \times \frac{8}{2} = \blacksquare$

14. **Mental Math** If $8 \div \frac{2}{5} = 20$, use mental math to find $80 \div \frac{2}{5}$.

15. $5 \div \frac{3}{8}$

16. $6 \div \frac{3}{4}$

17. $8 \div \frac{1}{3}$

18. $3 \div \frac{1}{4}$

19. $2 \div \frac{1}{4}$

20. $4 \div \frac{1}{4}$

21. $5 \div \frac{4}{8}$

22. $6 \div \frac{3}{8}$

23. $7 \div \frac{1}{4}$

24. $2 \div \frac{2}{3}$

25. $4 \div \frac{2}{3}$

26. $8 \div \frac{2}{3}$

27. **Patterns** What patterns do you notice in exercises 24–26 and their answers?

28. **Algebraic Reasoning** When dividing 5 by $\frac{2}{3}$, Sue multiplied 5 by the reciprocal of $\frac{2}{3}$. Jo multiplied $\frac{2}{3}$ by the reciprocal of 5. Who was right?

Problem Solving

Use the chart to solve.

29. How many teacups can be made from 21 lb of clay?

30. If you made two sugar bowls from 3 lb of clay, would you have enough left over to make a small vase?

31. About how much clay would you need to make three mugs, two teacups, a small vase, and four sugar bowls?

Pottery Pieces	
Item	amount of clay
mug	$\frac{7}{8}$ lb
tea cup	$\frac{3}{5}$ lb
small vase	$\frac{2}{3}$ lb
sugar bowl	$\frac{3}{4}$ lb

Mixed Review

Write the quotient.

32. $56\overline{)729}$

33. $73 \div 14$

34. $25\overline{)\$475}$

35. $210 \div 21$

36. $70\overline{)588}$

Problem Solving
Using Strategies

You can read more about sea otters in the pages of *Zoobooks.*

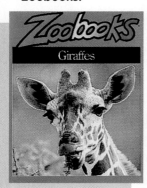

Zoobooks
Giraffes

Hunted almost to the point of extinction, sea otters have made an amazing comeback. They eat, sleep, give birth, and feed their young in the northern parts of the Pacific Ocean.

Problem Solving Process
✓ Understand
✓ Plan
✓ Try It
✓ Look Back

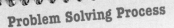

Choose a Strategy You Have Learned
✓ Make a Table
✓ Act It Out
✓ Guess and Check
✓ Look for a Pattern
✓ Work Backward
✓ Make a List
✓ Work a Simpler Problem
✓ Draw a Picture
   Write an Equation

Sea otters dive to an average depth of 35 feet, but some are known to dive to depths of almost 300 feet. Imagine that an otter makes a dive of 35 feet on the first dive and then resurfaces. On the second dive, the otter dives 10 feet deeper and resurfaces. On each of the next five dives, the otter continues to dive 10 feet deeper than the previous dive, before resurfacing. How many feet will the otter have traveled during these 7 dives?

- What is the question you have to answer?
- How deep did the otter dive on the first dive?
- How deep is the otter's second dive?
- How much does the depth of the dive increase each time?
- How far does the otter travel each time it dives and resurfaces? Explain.
- Explain a strategy that can help you to solve the problem.

Work It Out!

Use any strategy to solve the problem. Show your work.

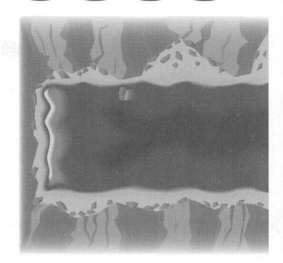

1. Suppose a sea otter lived off the coast of Russia in a rocky cove shaped like a rectangle. This region has a perimeter of 102 miles. If the width is $\frac{1}{2}$ the length, what is the width? What is the length?

2. Each day, a sea otter eats an amount of food that is about one fourth of its weight. An average sea otter weighs about as much as an average fifth-grader. Here are the weights of 4 typical fifth-graders: 73 lb, 77 lb, 85 lb, and 69 lb. Based on the average weight of these fifth-graders, about how much food does the sea otter eat each day?

3. A full-grown male sea otter can weigh as much as 92 lb. A full-grown female sea otter weighs about $\frac{3}{4}$ the weight of a full-grown male. About how much does a full-grown female weigh?

4. Sea otters have approximately 1 million hairs per square inch. German shepherds have approximately $\frac{1}{25}$ as much hair per square inch as sea otters. The average human has about $\frac{1}{40}$ as much hair per square inch as a German shepherd. About how many hairs per square inch does the average human have?

5. The total length of a sea otter (head to tail) is only about $\frac{1}{3}$ the length of a sea lion. If a sea otter is 45 inches long, about how long is a grown sea lion?

6. The full-grown male sea lion is about 20 times heavier than a full-grown male sea otter. About how heavy do sea lions become?

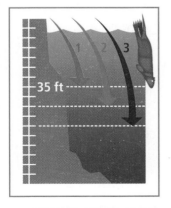

7. Male sea otters have a body length, not including their tail, that is about $\frac{4}{5}$ of their total length. Suppose a male sea otter is 45 inches long from the tip of his head to the tip of his tail. About how long is the sea otter's body?

8. The Weddell seal can dive 8 times the maximum depth that the sea otter can dive. About how deep can the Weddell seal dive? (Refer to page 384 to help you.)

Share Your Thinking

9. Compare the strategy you used for problem 5 with a classmate's.

Chapter 11 Test

for Pages 362–385

Test-Taking Tips
When multiplying with fractions, it is a good idea to estimate the product to make sure your answer is reasonable.

Problem Solving

Solve using Guess and Check or another strategy. Show your work. (page 368)

1. A florist prepared a bouquet of fewer than 20 flowers. The bouquet was $\frac{1}{4}$ mums. There were 4 more daisies than mums. Of the remaining flowers, there were an equal number of tulips and roses. How many flowers were in the bouquet?

2. Suppose you bought 4 software items for $77. The strategy game cost $\frac{3}{4}$ the price of the science title. The math title cost $\frac{4}{3}$ the price of the action game. The action game cost $15. Find the price of each.

Choose whether you will estimate or compute the exact answer. Answer the questions using the chart. (page 374)

3. If you have $5, can you buy the ingredients to make peanut butter and jelly sandwiches?

4. If you buy 2 loaves of bread, a bag of apples, and 1 gallon of milk, how much change should you receive from $20?

Cost of Grocery Items

Grocery Items	Cost
bag of apples	$1.99
loaf of bread	$1.59
$\frac{1}{2}$ gallon of cider	$2.89
1 lb of peanut butter	$2.29
jar of grape jelly	$1.29
1 gallon of milk	$4.29

Concepts

Find the answer. (pages 372, 378, 380, 382)

5. Explain how to find the reciprocal of a whole number.

6. Using the reciprocal of the fraction below, write a division sentence that would have the same answer as $8 \times \frac{3}{4}$.

7. Do you agree or disagree with the statement? Give examples to support your answer.
   a. The reciprocal of a number is always less than the number.
   b. When you multiply two fractions that are both less than 1, the product will be less than 1.

Which choice gives the product in its simplest form? Write a, b, c, or d.
(pages 362, 364, 370, 372)

8. $10 \times \frac{1}{3}$ a. $\frac{10}{3}$ b. $3\frac{1}{3}$ c. 30   d. $\frac{3}{10}$

9. $3 \times \frac{1}{9}$ a. $\frac{9}{3}$ b. $\frac{3}{9}$ c. 3   d. $\frac{1}{3}$

Write the product in simplest form. (pages 362, 364, 370, 372)

10. $6 \times \frac{4}{7}$ 11. $7 \times \frac{5}{6}$ 12. $5 \times \frac{3}{10}$ 13. $\frac{2}{3} \times 15$ 14. $36 \times \frac{4}{5}$

Write each number as a fraction. Then find its reciprocal. (page 380)

15. 5 16. $4\frac{1}{2}$ 17. $6\frac{5}{8}$

Use a reciprocal to find the answer. (page 382)

18. $4 \div \frac{1}{2}$ 19. $3 \div \frac{1}{3}$ 20. $8 \div \frac{2}{5}$ 21. $6 \div \frac{1}{4}$

 Performance Task

(pages 362, 364, 378, 380, 382)

Suppose you have been hired to design two fruit-and-nut baskets. The contents of the regular basket must weigh no less than 5 lb, but no more than $5\frac{3}{8}$ lb. The contents of the deluxe basket must weigh no less than 9 lb but no more than $9\frac{1}{2}$ lb. Use the table to plan the baskets.

Use at least 5 different items in the regular basket and 7 in the deluxe. Show your work.

Orange	$\frac{5}{8}$ lb
Tangerine	$\frac{3}{16}$ lb
Pear	$\frac{1}{3}$ lb
Kiwi Fruit	$\frac{1}{8}$ lb
Almond Packages	$\frac{1}{4}$ lb
Cashew Packages	$\frac{1}{8}$ lb
Mixed Nut Packages	$\frac{3}{4}$ lb

Keep In Mind . . .

Your work will be evaluated on the following:

☑ Two designs for baskets

☑ Correct ranges for weights

☑ Correct total weights

☑ Numbers of Items used

Cumulative Review

Congruency (Chapter 8)

Are △ABC and △DEF congruent?

Here's A Way!

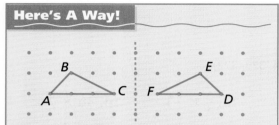

Figures are congruent if they have the same size and shape.

△ABC is congruent to △DEF if you can slide, flip, or turn △ABC so that it exactly matches △DEF.

△DEF is a flip of △ABC, so the triangles are congruent.

Use the figures to answer questions 1–6.

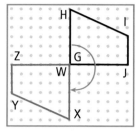

1. Is figure *GHIJ* congruent to figure *WXYZ*? Explain.

Copy and complete each statement.

2. ∠*IHG* ≅ ■   3. $\overline{ZW}$ ≅ ■

4. ∠*HGJ* ≅ ■   5. $\overline{HI}$ ≅ ■

6. How could you use 2 flips to show that figure *GHIJ* is congruent to figure *WXYZ*?

Fractions and Decimals (Chapter 9)

Find an equivalent decimal for $\frac{3}{5}$.

Here's A Way!

Divide the numerator by the denominator.

$$5\overline{)3.0}$$
$$\underline{30}$$
$$0$$

$\frac{3}{5} = 0.6$

Write each number as a decimal.

7. $\frac{1}{4}$ 8. $2\frac{1}{2}$

9. $\frac{5}{8}$ 10. $\frac{23}{25}$

11. $4\frac{9}{100}$ 12. $3\frac{9}{12}$

13. Explain how to write 0.6 as a fraction in simplest form.

Multiply Fractions (Chapter 11)

Find $\frac{5}{8} \times \frac{2}{3}$.

Here's A Way!

Multiply the numerators, then the denominators.

$$\frac{5}{8} \times \frac{2}{3} = \frac{5 \times 2}{8 \times 3} = \frac{10}{24}$$

Simplify if possible: $\frac{10}{24} = \frac{5}{12}$

Write the product in simplest form.

14. $\frac{1}{8} \times \frac{3}{5}$ 15. $\frac{1}{3} \times \frac{3}{4}$

16. $2 \times \frac{1}{6}$ 17. $\frac{3}{7} \times \frac{1}{2}$

18. $\frac{2}{9} \times \frac{3}{10}$ 19. $6 \times \frac{3}{4}$

20. How could you have used mental math in exercise 15?

Renaming Mixed Numbers (Chapter 10)

Find $4\frac{1}{5} - 2\frac{1}{2}$.

Here's A Way!

The denominators are different, so write equivalent fractions using the least common denominator (LCD).

$$4\frac{1}{5} - 2\frac{1}{2} \quad \blacktriangleright \quad 4\frac{2}{10} - 2\frac{5}{10}$$

Since $\frac{2}{10} < \frac{5}{10}$, rename $4\frac{2}{10}$ as $3\frac{12}{10}$.

Subtract. Simplify if possible.

$$4\frac{2}{10} - 2\frac{5}{10} = 3\frac{12}{10} - 2\frac{5}{10} = 1\frac{7}{10}$$

Write the sum or difference in simplest form.

21. $\begin{array}{r} 5\frac{1}{6} \\ -\ 2\frac{5}{6} \\ \hline \end{array}$

22. $\begin{array}{r} 7\frac{2}{5} \\ -\ 3\frac{4}{5} \\ \hline \end{array}$

23. $\begin{array}{r} 9 \\ -\ 1\frac{3}{4} \\ \hline \end{array}$

24. $\begin{array}{r} 2\frac{1}{10} \\ -\ 1\frac{7}{10} \\ \hline \end{array}$

25. $\begin{array}{r} 7\frac{3}{4} \\ +\ 2\frac{1}{3} \\ \hline \end{array}$

26. $\begin{array}{r} 6\frac{1}{2} \\ +\ 3\frac{4}{5} \\ \hline \end{array}$

27. When is it necessary to rename?

Problem Solving

Problem Solving Process

✓ Understand
✓ Plan
✓ Try It
✓ Look Back

Choose a Strategy You Have Learned

✓ Make a Table
✓ Act It Out
✓ Guess and Check
✓ Look for a Pattern
✓ Work Backward
✓ Make a List
✓ Work a Simpler Problem
✓ Draw a Picture
   Write an Equation

Choose one of the strategies you know to solve these problems. Show your work.

28. Twenty-five students bought a beverage to go with their lunch. Seven students bought lowfat milk. One third of the remaining students bought chocolate milk. Of the remaining students, $\frac{1}{4}$ had apple juice and the rest bought fruit punch. How many students bought fruit punch?

29. Mrs. Gomez drives 3.5 miles to a daycare center to drop off her daughter. She then drives 16.75 miles to work. She returns home by the reverse route. Later she drives 1.2 miles to a store. How many miles does she drive in all by the time she returns home from the store?

Traveling Food

History Connection   **With Your Group**

Did you know that the Irish potato was not originally from Ireland? Potatoes were first grown in South America and brought to Spain in 1570 by Spanish explorers. From there they traveled through Europe. Tomatoes and cocoa beans were also first grown in Central and South America. They are now grown all over the world.

Your group will plan the refreshments for a Parent-Teacher Night. Use the recipe on the next page and recipes from home that have been handed down through your family.

1

Plan It

- Decide on a theme based on the type of foods you will make or the region they came from.

- Each group member will bring one favorite recipe from home. Use the recipes to plan a menu.

2

Put It Together

- The recipe on this page is for polvorones, or Mexican wedding cookies. How many cookies does the recipe make? Estimate how many you will need for your parents and teachers. Then, find how much you will need of each ingredient.

- Make a chart that shows each ingredient and the amount needed.

- Next, use the recipes you brought from home. Calculate how much you will need of each ingredient and add this to your chart.

3

Wrap It Up

- Make a shopping list of all the ingredients on your chart. If an ingredient is listed more than once, combine the amounts needed.

- Use your theme to make and decorate a menu for Parent-Teacher Night.

Polvorones

Number of servings: 20 dozen cookies

- 11 1/4 cups of all-purpose flour, sifted
- 4 1/2 cups confectioners sugar
- 3 1/3 cups finely chopped pecans
- 5 teaspoons vanilla extract
- 3 3/4 cups butter or margarine, soft
- 1/4 cup ice water, as needed
- confectioners sugar for sprinkling
- Heat oven to 350°F

1. Put flour, confectioners sugar, and nuts in large bowl and mix well.
2. Mix in vanilla and butter or margarine until mixture forms a soft ball. Add a little water if mixture is too dry.
3. Pinch off an amount about the size of a ping-pong ball and roll into a ball. Place on cookie sheet about one inch apart.
4. Bake about 12 minutes or until set and golden. When done, remove from cookie sheet and sprinkle with confectioners sugar.

4

Discuss Your Results

- Did you meet the objectives listed in Keep In Mind?

- What other items would you need for the Parent-Teacher Night? How would you decide how much you need?

Internet

> Visit the **Math Center** at Houghton Mifflin Education Place.
http://www.eduplace.com

Math Power

Use What You Know

- how to tally data

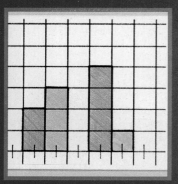

- how to make a double bar graph

- how to make predictions

Ratio, Percent, and Probability

Try This!

The two pictures on the next page are identical except for the color. Some will see the candle, and others will see the two people. Use the pictures to predict what people will see first.

What You'll Need

paper, pencil, grid paper

①

Cover the second picture with a piece of paper. Ask five family members or friends what they see in the first picture. Take the first answer they give. Keep a tally of their answers, but do not let them see the tally.

First Picture

Candle | People

|| | |||

Second Picture

Candle | People

|||

First Picture

Second Picture

2

Now, cover the first picture and ask five more people what they see in the second picture. Keep another tally of their answers. On a double-bar graph, show how many saw the candle compared to how many saw the people in each picture.

3

Write a paragraph predicting in which picture people will most likely see the candle first. Repeat steps 1 and 2. Was your prediction correct?

How does the bar graph help you predict what could happen next?

Compare how many people saw the candle in each picture.

Ready to Go!

LESSON 1

Exploring Ratio

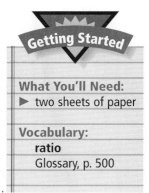

Getting Started

What You'll Need:
▶ two sheets of paper

Vocabulary:
ratio
Glossary, p. 500

A ratio compares two quantities. Suppose there are five pieces of chalk and only two erasers in your classroom. The ratio of chalk to erasers is 5 to 2. The ratio of erasers to chalk is 2 to 5.

Where's the Ratio?

Activity

• Form two teams.

• On a sheet of paper, each team makes a table like the one below. Number from 1 to 10 on each table.

Comparing Objects	Ratio
1. Chalk to Erasers	5 to 2
2.	

How To Play!

1 Identify objects in your classroom that you want to compare using ratios. Find 10 groups of objects to compare.

2 Fill in the ratios in the table.

3 Copy the ratios, but not the list of objects, onto another sheet of paper. Exchange papers with the other team.

4 Try to find the objects that each of the other team's ratios represent. As you identify each one, write it down. Could some ratios be used for more than one pair of objects? If so, which ratios?

Show What You Know!

1. **Critical Thinking** In writing a ratio, when could you write either object first so that they are equal, for example, $\frac{\text{pencils}}{\text{markers}} = \frac{\text{markers}}{\text{pencils}}$?

2. **Critical Thinking** For each ratio you find, can you tell the total number of objects? Explain.

3. Your teacher has assigned you 15 math problems and 7 social studies questions for homework. Write a ratio that compares:
   a. the number of math problems to social studies questions
   b. the number of social studies questions to math questions
   c. the number of math problems to all problems

Ratios

There are over 100,000 different kinds of glass! The most common glass, soda-lime glass, has about 6 parts silica (sand), 1 part calcium carbonate (lime), and 3 parts sodium carbonate (soda).

You can use ratios to compare the quantities of ingredients in soda-lime glass.

Sea glass is glass that has been worn smooth by the sea and the sand.

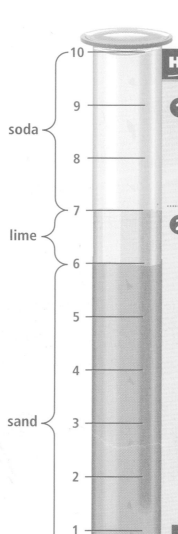

Here's A Way! **Compare quantities using ratios.**

1 **Understand the ratio.**

- In soda-lime glass there are 6 parts sand + 1 part lime + 3 parts soda or 10 parts in all.
- 6 of the 10 parts are sand, 1 of the 10 is lime, and 3 of the 10 are soda.

2 **Write the ratio and interpret the answer.**

A ratio can be written in three ways.

Glass Ingredients

Relationship	As a word ratio	With symbols	As a fraction
sand to total	6 to 10	6:10	$\frac{6}{10}$
lime to total	1 to 10	1:10	$\frac{1}{10}$
soda to total	3 to 10	3:10	$\frac{3}{10}$

Order is important. You know that $\frac{6}{10}$ is not the same fraction as $\frac{10}{6}$. In the same way, the ratio 6 to 10 is not the same as 10 to 6.

Talk About It! Does the ratio of sand to soda tell you the total number of parts of glass? Why or why not?

1. **Critical Thinking** How are ratios in fraction form like fractions? How are they different?

Use the picture below to write the ratios.

2. red bottles to blue bottles?

3. green bottles to all bottles?

4. blue bottles to green bottles?

5. What does the ratio of 4:6 refer to?

6. Does the ratio of 12 to 4 refer to the ratio of blue bottles to all bottles? Explain.

Work It Out!

Write each ratio three different ways.

7. **a.** red to green marbles   **b.** green to yellow marbles   **c.** red to yellow marbles
   d. yellow marbles to all marbles   **e.** red marbles to all other marbles   **f.** blue and green marbles to red and yellow marbles

Problem Solving   Using Data

Crown glass is used to make windows. It is made of the same substances as soda-lime glass but in the different ratios shown.

8. Suppose 100 pounds of Crown glass is to be made. How many pounds will be needed of these ingredients:
   a. sand?   **b.** lime?   **c.** soda?

Crown Glass Ratios

Relationship	As a word ratio	With a symbol	As a fraction
sand to total	72 to 100	72:100	$\frac{72}{100}$
lime to total	15 to 100	15:100	$\frac{15}{100}$
soda to total	13 to 100	13:100	$\frac{13}{100}$

9. A glass maker is making 100 lb of Crown glass. He orders 15 lb of lime and tells you that he needs about six times as much sand as lime. Is this correct? Explain your answer.

10. Are sand, soda, and lime the only substances used in making Crown glass? How can you tell using the ratios?

More Practice Set 12.2, p. 493

LESSON 3

Understanding Equal Ratios

You are mixing fruit punch for your class picnic. For each qt of punch, the recipe calls for 2 tbsp of drink mix and 3 tbsp of sugar for each qt of water. Use this recipe to write ratios.

Fruit Punch

2 tbsps   drink mix
3 tbsps   sugar

for each
1 qt water

Simple Ratios

1 Use the counters to help you find these ratios.

a. What is the ratio of the number of tablespoons of drink mix to the number of tablespoons of sugar for 1 qt? How can you represent this ratio with counters?

2 Suppose you want 2 qt of fruit punch. Use counters to show the number of tablespoons of mix and sugar you would need.

b. Will the 2-qt mixture and the 1-qt mixture taste the same? Explain.

Ratio Patterns

1 Complete the table below. You may want to use counters to help you.

a. What pattern do you see in the table? Are the ratios equal? Explain.

Quarts of punch	1	2	3	4	5	6
Tbsp of punch mix	2	4	?	?	?	?
Tbsp of sugar	3	6	?	?	?	?

Equal Ratios

1. Use equivalent fractions to help you understand **equal ratios**.

   a. You know that to find equivalent fractions you multiply or divide the numerator and denominator by the same number. You find equal ratios the same way. Is the ratio $\frac{2}{3}$ equal to the ratios $\frac{4}{6}$, $\frac{6}{9}$, $\frac{8}{12}$, $\frac{10}{15}$, and $\frac{12}{18}$?

   b. Write two more ratios that are equal to $\frac{2}{3}$.

   c. If you used the two ratios you wrote to make fruit punch, how many quarts of water would you need for each?

Comparing Ratios

1. Use what you have learned about equal ratios to answer the questions.

   a. What is the ratio of concentrate to water for Orange Delight?

   b. Which two of the drinks will have the same amount of orange flavor?

   c. Which drink will have the strongest orange flavor?

Orange Delight	Orange Sunshine	Orange Supreme	Orange Fresh
2 cups concentrate	4 cups concentrate	4 cups concentrate	3 cups concentrate
4 cups water	3 cups water	8 cups water	5 cups water

Show What You Know!

Use ratios to solve.

1. Write the letter of each ratio that is equal to $\frac{4}{5}$.

   a. $\frac{9}{10}$ b. $\frac{8}{10}$ c. $\frac{4}{10}$ d. $\frac{12}{15}$ e. $\frac{16}{20}$

2. Write two equal ratios for each.

   a. $\frac{1}{3}$ b. $\frac{2}{5}$ c. $\frac{3}{10}$ d. $\frac{5}{16}$ e. $\frac{6}{5}$

3. **Critical Thinking** A bowl of fruit punch contains 3 c of pineapple juice and 2 c of cranberry juice.

   a. What do you need to make 4 bowls of punch?   b. What is the ratio of juices for 1 bowl?   c. For 4 bowls?

4. Suppose that at your school picnic each student will drink $\frac{1}{2}$ cup of juice. If you use the Orange Fresh recipe, how much concentrate and water is needed for 160 students? Explain.

Equal Ratios

The length of Lincoln's face in the Lincoln Memorial is 42 inches. Most people's faces have about a 2 to 3 ratio of width to length. What is the width of Lincoln's face in the Lincoln Memorial?

Here's A Way! Find equal ratios.

1 Use the ratio 2:3 to write equal ratios → $\dfrac{\text{Width}}{\text{Length}} = \dfrac{2}{3} = \dfrac{\blacksquare}{42}$

2 Find the missing number of the ratio by writing an equivalent fraction. → $\dfrac{2}{3} = \dfrac{2 \times 14}{3 \times 14} = \dfrac{28}{42}$

The width of Lincoln's face in the Lincoln Memorial is about 28 inches.

Talk About It! Why were both 2 and 3 multiplied by 14?

Other Example Sometimes you divide to find the missing number.

$\dfrac{28}{84} = \dfrac{4}{\blacksquare}$ You can use the fact that $4 \times 7 = 28$ or $28 \div 7 = 4$.

$\dfrac{28}{84} = \dfrac{28 \div 7}{84 \div 7} = \dfrac{4}{12}$ So, the missing number is 12.

1. **Critical Thinking** For most people, the ratio of head length to body length is about 1:7. The length of the Lincoln statue's head is 42 inches. How would you use the ratio to tell how tall Lincoln's statue would be if it were standing? Write the height the Lincoln statue would be if it were standing.

Decide if the ratios are equal. Write *yes* or *no*.

2. 5 to 3 and 10 to 8

3. 4 to 1 and 12 to 3

4. 2:5 and 4:10

5. 2:3 and 6:9

6. $\frac{6}{3}$ and $\frac{16}{13}$

7. $\frac{3}{4}$ and $\frac{30}{40}$

Write the missing number.

8. 2 to 1 is the same as 12 to ■

9. 3 to 5 is equal to ■ to 10

10. $\frac{3}{5} = \frac{■}{20}$

11. $\frac{18}{6} = \frac{■}{1}$

12. $\frac{10}{50} = \frac{2}{■}$

13. $\frac{5}{4} = \frac{15}{■}$

Work It Out!

Write the letter of the equal ratio.

14. 1:4   a. 4:1   b. 2:8   c. 8:4   d. 3:6

15. $\frac{1}{7}$ a. $\frac{7}{14}$ b. $\frac{7}{1}$ c. $\frac{8}{56}$ d. $\frac{7}{28}$

16. 3 to 2   a. $\frac{4}{6}$ b. 7:6   c. $\frac{3}{4}$ d. $\frac{15}{10}$

17. **Number Sense** Explain why 1:4 is not equal to 4:1. Draw pictures to support your answer.

Write the missing number.

18. 3 to 1 is the same as 15 to ■

19. 16 to 8 is equal to ■ to 2

20. $\frac{3}{9} = \frac{1}{■}$

21. $\frac{36}{45} = \frac{4}{■}$

22. $\frac{■}{6} = \frac{4}{24}$

23. $\frac{4}{7} = \frac{■}{21}$

24. $\frac{■}{9} = \frac{1}{3}$

25. $\frac{10}{16} = \frac{5}{■}$

26. $\frac{1}{■} = \frac{5}{5}$

27. $\frac{9}{12} = \frac{■}{36}$

Problem Solving

28. A set of 6 Lincoln Memorial glasses is $9.50. If you buy them one at a time, they cost $2.00 each. How much do you save by buying a set rather than buying one at a time?

29. The souvenir shop sells pencils in packs of 5 for $2.25. A shop close to the monument sells the same pencils in packs of 3 for $1.65. Which store has the better buy?

More Practice Set 12.4, p. 493

Problem Solving
Write an Equation

Suppose you are making a video about your school. After taping 10 seconds about the cafeteria, you find that you have used 15 ft of tape. If you spend 60 seconds on your math class, how many feet of tape will you use?

Here's A Way! Write a Word Equation to solve the problem.

1 Understand

- You need to find the number of feet of tape used to film math class.

2 Plan

- Write a Word Equation about equal ratios to solve this problem.

3 Try It

- Write a word equation using the information you have.

$$\frac{\text{amount of tape for cafeteria}}{\text{amount of time for cafeteria}} = \frac{\text{amount of tape for math class}}{\text{amount of time for math class}}$$

- Replace each part of the word equation with the numbers you know, and then find the amount of tape that will make the ratios equal.

$$\frac{15}{10} = \frac{\text{Amount of tape for math class}}{60} \quad \times 6$$

So, the amount of tape needed for math class is 15 × 6 or 90 feet of tape.

4 Look Back

- Why is 90 ft of tape a reasonable solution?
- How did writing a word equation help you to solve the problem?

Show What You Know!

Use Write a Word Equation to solve the problem.

1. Suppose you want to film reading class for three times as long as math class. How many feet of tape will you need for reading class?

2. **Critical Thinking** You have 50 ft of tape left. Will you be able to film your favorite teacher for 30 seconds?

3. To buy more film, you can get 3 tapes for $23.46 or 4 tapes for $28.00. Which is the better deal? How much will you save on each tape?

Work It Out!

Use Write a Word Equation or any strategy to solve the problem.

4. You want to film recess. The ratio of recess film time to reading film time will be equal to the ratio of cafeteria film time to math film time. How long will you film recess?

   $$\frac{\text{filming time for recess}}{\text{filming time for reading}} = \frac{\blacksquare}{\blacksquare}$$

5. Many cameras run at a rate of 24 frames each second. At this speed, how many frames are used for a 20-second scene?

Choose the number sentence that represents the problem.

6. A scene you have shot at 24 frames each second has used 840 frames of film. How long is the scene?

   a. 840 × 24   **b.** 840 ÷ 24   **c.** 840 + 24 + 24

7. If you taped four English classes for 50 s, 32 s, 44 s, and 36 s, what was the mean length of time for filming the classes?

   a. 50 + 32 + 44 + 36   **b.** (50 + 32 + 44 + 36) ÷ 4

   c. (50 − 32) + (44 − 36)

Share Your Thinking

8. How does writing a word equation help you to know where to place numbers in a problem?

Exploring Percent

Percent is a ratio that compares a number to 100. Percent means "per hundred." Fractions and decimals can help you understand percents.

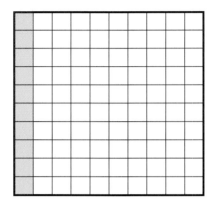

10 out of 100 is $\frac{10}{100}$
or 10 percent.

You write: 10%.

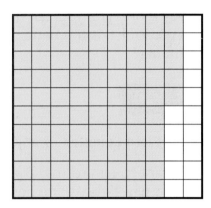

85 out of 100 is $\frac{85}{100}$
or 85 percent.

You write: 85%.

Activity

Ratios as Percent

Use percent to write ratios of 100.

1 Write each ratio as a percent, using the percent symbol, %.

   a. $\frac{50}{100}$ b. $\frac{30}{100}$ c. $\frac{5}{100}$ d. $\frac{73}{100}$ e. $\frac{0}{100}$

Hundredths Grid and Percent

Use a hundredths grid.

1 Shade $\frac{1}{2}$ of your grid. Label it Grid A. How many squares are shaded? How many squares are in the whole grid?

2 Write the ratio of shaded squares to total squares as a fraction.

   a. What percent of the grid is shaded?

   b. How do the areas of the shaded and unshaded parts compare?

Comparing Percents

Use other hundredths grids.

1 On one grid, shade a square area 5 squares by 5 squares. Label it Grid B. Write a ratio of shaded squares to total squares.

　a. What percent of your grid is shaded?

　b. Compare the shaded areas on both of your grids. How do they compare?

2 Shade $\frac{3}{4}$ of a third grid. Label it Grid C. Write the ratio of shaded squares to total squares. What percent of this grid is shaded?

　a. How do the shaded areas on the third grid compare with your first two grids?

Work It Out!

Use ratios and percents to solve.

1. Show the ratio by shading a hundredths grid. Then write the percent.

　a. $\frac{15}{100}$　　　　　　b. $\frac{42}{100}$　　　　　　c. $\frac{60}{100}$

2. **Critical Thinking** What do you think the *-cent* in *percent* means? Can you use percents to write all ratios shown on a hundredths grid?

3. Label the grids from exercise 1 *D*, *E*, and *F*, then complete the chart.

	Number of Shaded Squares	Total Number of Squares	Ratio of Shaded Squares to Total Squares	Percent Shaded
Grid A	50	?	?	50%
Grid B	?	100	?	?
Grid C	?	?	$\frac{75}{100}$	?
Grid D	15	?	?	?
Grid E	?	100	?	42%
Grid F	?	?	$\frac{60}{100}$	?

4. How would you show 100% on a hundredths grid?

5. What percent of each circle is shaded orange?

　a. 　　　b. 　　　c.

Estimation: Percent

Fruit sellers display the most popular fruits to attract customers. This vendor gives more area to strawberries than to other fruits because she thinks strawberries are the best sellers. About what percent of her space is used for strawberries?

Here's A Way! Estimate percents.

Imagine $\frac{1}{2}$ and $\frac{1}{4}$ of the space.

Estimate the percent using $\frac{1}{2}$ and $\frac{1}{4}$ as guidelines.

- The strawberries cover slightly more than $\frac{1}{4}$ or 25% of the stand.

- The strawberries cover between 25% and 50% of the space, but much closer to 25%. A good estimate is about 30%.

Talk About It! Why is 30% a more reasonable estimate than 40%?

Other Examples Use the picture to help you to estimate the percents covered by other fruit.

- About 20% of the fruit is apples.
- About 10% of the fruit is grapes.

You can also imagine it divided this way.

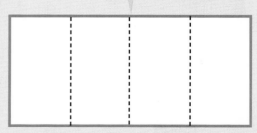

1. **Critical Thinking** How does thinking about the fractions $\frac{1}{4}$, $\frac{1}{2}$, and $\frac{3}{4}$ help you estimate percents?

2. Use the fruit tart. Estimate the percent of the tart that is covered by:
   a. raspberries
   b. blueberries
   c. kiwis
   d. bananas

Work It Out!

Write the letter of the most reasonable estimate for the percent shaded blue.

3.

   a. 25%
   b. 50%
   c. 70%

4.

   a. 50%
   b. 70%
   c. 95%

5.

   a. 40%
   b. 50%
   c. 60%

6.

   a. 100%
   b. 95%
   c. 75%

Estimate what percent of each fruit or vegetable has been cut off.

7.

8.

9.

Mixed Review

Write the answer in simplest form.

10. $\frac{1}{2} \times \frac{1}{3}$

11. $\frac{2}{5} \div \frac{1}{2}$

12. $\frac{3}{4} \times \frac{2}{3}$

13. $\frac{4}{5} \div \frac{2}{3}$

14. $\frac{3}{4} \times \frac{5}{6}$

15. $\frac{4}{5} \div \frac{1}{10}$

16. $\frac{9}{10} \times \frac{1}{3}$

17. $\frac{3}{8} \div \frac{1}{2}$

More Practice Set 12.7,

8 Equivalent Forms

Nearly 99 out of 100 homes in the United States have televisions.

About 60% of U.S. homes have cable television.

Almost 0.7 of all homes in the United States have two televisions.

You are writing a report on television in the United States. You have found the data shown here in an almanac: How can you understand these numbers in terms of ratios, fractions, and percents?

Here's A Way! Use equivalent forms to represent numbers.

1 You can change a ratio into a fraction with 100 in the denominator. Then, write the fraction as a percent.

$$99 \text{ out of } 100 = \frac{99}{100} = 99\%$$

So, 99% of homes in the United States have television sets.

2 You can write a percent as a decimal. Then, write the decimal as a fraction and a ratio.

$$60\% = 0.60 = \frac{60}{100} \implies \frac{60}{100} \overset{\div 20}{\underset{\div 20}{=}} \frac{3}{5}$$

Simplify when you can.

So, 3 out of 5 homes in the United States have cable television.

3 You can change a decimal with tenths to a decimal with hundredths. Then, write a fraction and a percent.

$$0.7 = 0.70 = \frac{70}{100} = 70\%$$

So, about 70% of homes in the United States have 2 television sets.

Talk About It! Can percents, fractions, and decimals all express the same information? Explain.

Write each percent as a fraction in simplest form.

1. 10%   2. 1%   3. 5%   4. 50%   5. 14%   6. 8%

Write an equivalent fraction with hundreths, then write each fraction as a percent.

7. $\frac{5}{20}$ 8. $\frac{1}{5}$ 9. $\frac{1}{25}$ 10. $\frac{3}{4}$ 11. $\frac{3}{5}$ 12. $\frac{3}{10}$

Write each decimal as a percent.

13. 0.35   14. 0.80   15. 0.15   16. 0.66   17. 0.04   18. 0.09

19. How would 75% look in a calculator display window? Explain.

Number Sense Compare using >, <, or =.

20. 45% ● 0.45   21. 0.3 ● 3%   22. 0.6 ● 60%   23. 0.1 ● 100%

Work It Out!

Write each percent as a decimal and as a fraction in simplest form.

24. 60%   25. 4%   26. 23%   27. 70%   28. 20%   29. 48%

Write each decimal or fraction as a percent.

30. $\frac{13}{25}$ 31. 0.31   32. $\frac{6}{20}$ 33. $\frac{3}{10}$ 34. 0.02   35. $\frac{2}{5}$

Copy and complete the table. Write the fraction in simplest form.

	Fraction	Percent	Decimal
36.	$\frac{4}{5}$	?	0.8
37.	?	15%	?
38.	?	?	0.09
39.	?	70%	?

More Practice Set 12.8 p. 494

Finding Percent

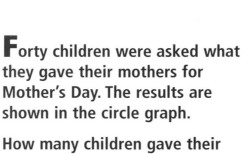

Forty children were asked what they gave their mothers for Mother's Day. The results are shown in the circle graph.

How many children gave their mothers flowers?

Mother's Day Gifts

Homemade Card 25%
Candy 20%
Other 5%
Flowers 50%

Here's A Way!　　　　**Find 50% of 40.**

1 Look at the circle graph. You can see the relationships below.

$$50\% = 0.50 = \frac{50}{100} \quad \overset{\div\, 50}{\underset{\div\, 50}{\circlearrowright}} \quad \frac{1}{2}$$

Use the fact that 50% is equal to $\frac{1}{2}$ to solve the problem.

2 To find 50% of 40, rewrite the problem as $\frac{1}{2}$ of 40 and solve mentally.

$$\frac{1}{2} \text{ of } 40 = 20$$

So, 20 out of 40 children gave flowers.

Talk About It!　How did knowing that 50% is equivalent to $\frac{1}{2}$ help you solve the problem?

Other Example How many children gave homemade cards to their mothers?

Find 25% in the circle graph. Write 25% as a fraction. Then solve.

$$25\% = \frac{25}{100} = \frac{1}{4}$$

$$\frac{1}{4} \text{ of } 40 = 10$$

So, 10 out of 40 children gave homemade cards.

1. **Critical Thinking** How does knowing 50% and 25% of a number help you find 75% of the number?

Write the answer. Use mental math.

2. 50% of 30

3. 50% of 120

4. 25% of 120

5. 75% of 120

6. 50% of 220

7. 25% of 300

8. 50% of 140

9. 25% of 80

10. 25% of 240

Work It Out!

11. 50% of 70

12. 25% of 16

13. 50% of 48

14. 75% of 20

15. 50% of 110

16. 25% of 180

17. 75% of 160

18. 50% of 250

19. 25% of 8

20. 50% of 302

21. 75% of 600

22. 25% of 1000

Problem Solving   **Using Data**

Twenty family members came to a July 4 picnic. The circle graph shows what each brought with them.

23. How many people brought main courses?

24. How many people brought desserts?

25. Altogether, how many people brought drinks and paper goods?

What Everyone Brought

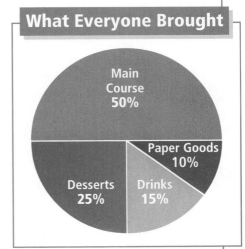

Mixed Review

Write the answer in simplest form.

26. $\frac{1}{2} - \frac{1}{3}$

27. $\frac{1}{2} + \frac{2}{5}$

28. $\frac{3}{4} - \frac{2}{3}$

29. $\frac{2}{3} + \frac{4}{5}$

30. $\frac{5}{6} - \frac{3}{4}$

31. $\frac{4}{5} + \frac{1}{10}$

32. $\frac{9}{10} - \frac{1}{3}$

33. $\frac{3}{8} + \frac{1}{2}$

More Practice Set 12.9, p. 495

Math Journal

In your own words, explain how you would find 25% of a number.

Percent of a Number

Sometimes the most important household chores are the ones kids enjoy least. A survey of 500 students found that some chores are less popular than others. How many of the 500 students chose vacuuming as their least favorite chore?

Least Liked Chores

Chore	Percentage of students who dislike it
Washing dishes	30%
Cleaning room	27%
Taking out garbage	15%
Making beds	10%
Yard work	7%
Laundry	6%
Vacuuming	5%

Here's A Way! Find 5% of 500.

1 Write the percent as a fraction.

$$5\% = \frac{5}{100}$$

2 Multiply the number by the fraction.

$$\frac{5}{100} \times 500 = \frac{5}{100} \times \frac{500}{1} = \frac{2500}{100} = 25$$

So, 25 students chose vacuuming as their least favorite chore.

Talk About It! How did changing the percent to a fraction help you find the answer?

Other Example If you have a calculator, it is often easier to change a percent to a decimal and multiply.

What is 38% of 265?

38% of 265

38% = 0.38

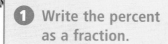

$0.38 \times 265 = 100.7$

You may want to use the calculator for this step.

1. **Critical Thinking** Since 10% of 500 is 50, what is a quick way to find 20% of 500? 30% of 500?

Write the percent of the number. Use mental math when you can.

2. 40% of 900
3. 50% of 20
4. 30% of 50
5. 75% of 120

6. 1% of 100
7. 20% of 300
8. 5% of 528
9. 25% of 44

10. **Critical Thinking** When is it easier to find the percent of a number using decimals instead of percents? Using fractions instead of percents?

Work It Out!

Write the percent of the number. Use mental math when you can.

11. 10% of 120
12. 20% of 70
13. 25% of 24
14. 4% of 404

15. 30% of 10
16. 80% of 50
17. 50% of 200
18. 42% of 150

19. 1% of 200
20. 25% of 8
21. 60% of 600
22. 90% of 1000

23. 100% of 659
24. 10% of 250
25. 20% of 250
26. 75% of 10

Problem Solving

Use the chart on page 412 for exercises 27–29.

27. How many of the 500 students chose either yard work or laundry as their least favorite chore?

28. Suppose that boys and girls answered the survey questions the same way. If 40% of the students were boys, about how many boys said making beds was their least favorite chore?

29. Suppose 12,500 students were surveyed. How many of them would say they liked washing dishes least?

Mixed Review

Write the answer in simplest form.

30. $1\frac{1}{2} + \frac{2}{3}$
31. $3 - \frac{5}{6}$
32. $\frac{7}{8} + 1\frac{1}{4}$

33. $5 - 2\frac{2}{5}$
34. $3\frac{2}{5} - \frac{14}{5}$
35. $\frac{5}{6} - \frac{2}{3}$

More Practice Set 12.10, p. 495

Problem Solving
Choose a Computation Method

Suppose you plan to practice 20 hours each week to prepare for your piano recital. Your piano teacher recommends the schedule shown. How many total hours will you spend on each activity?

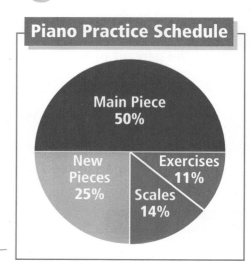

Piano Practice Schedule

- Main Piece 50%
- New Pieces 25%
- Exercises 11%
- Scales 14%

You Decide

- Which percents are easy to express as fractions?
- How many total hours will you use?
- Decide which computation method you will use for each percent. Explain your decision.

Work It Out!

Solve. Write whether you used mental math or paper and pencil.

1. 50% of 16
2. 40% of 35
3. 9% of 100
4. 25% of 40
5. 85% of 20
6. 37% of 100
7. 50% of 50
8. 30% of 180
9. 25% of 80
10. 50% of 7
11. 10% of 30
12. 25% of 14

13. Suppose that there are only two weeks left until the recital. How much time will you spend on
   a. your main piece?
   b. scales?
   c. hand exercises?
   d. new pieces?

 14. **Create Your Own** Write two word problems about your piano practice schedule:
   a. one that you would solve by using mental math.
   b. one that you would solve by using paper and pencil.

Share Your Thinking

15. Is it easier to use mental math or paper and pencil to compute 50% of 12? Explain why.

More Practice Set 12.11, p. 496

Midchapter Review
for Pages 392–414

Problem Solving

Solve. Show your work. (pages 402, 414)

1. Michelle is walking in a 6-mile walk-a-thon. She begins at 9:50 A.M. and passes the 1 mile mark at 10:10 A.M. If she continues at the same pace, at what time will she finish?

2. Of the 120 fifth graders who were asked, 60 percent said that they were interested in going on a trip to the natural history museum. How many fifth graders are interested in the trip?

Concepts

Find the answer. (pages 398, 400, 404, 406, 408)

3. Boys and girls are in the ratio of 4 to 5 in class 5-109. There are 12 boys in the class. How can you find the number of girls?

4. There are 25 students in class 5-201. Somebody tells you that 45 percent are boys. How can you tell that this is impossible?

5. How can you write 0.37 as a percent?

6. 75 percent of the students in class 5-107 ride to school. How can you write the fraction who ride in lowest terms?

Skills

Write the missing number. (pages 400, 408)

7. $\frac{3}{4} = \frac{9}{\blacksquare}$ 8. $\frac{1}{6} = \frac{\blacksquare}{18}$ 9. $\frac{10}{15} = \frac{2}{\blacksquare}$ 10. $\frac{9}{21} = \frac{3}{\blacksquare}$

Write each decimal as a percent. (page 408)

11. 0.24   12. 0.07   13. 0.98   14. 0.13

Write the answer. Use mental math when you can. (pages 410, 412, 414)

15. 20% of 120   16. 10% of 90   17. 47% of 200   18. 60% of 190

Math World

Many graphs, city plans, and games require the use of ratio and percent. Read about how land was divided by percents. Then play a game using ratios.

Polar Percents

No one *owns* Antarctica. In 1961, twelve countries signed a treaty to remove any claim they had to Antarctica so that the entire territory could be used for peaceful, scientific purposes only. The Antarctic Treaty has now been signed by forty nations and is a model of international cooperation. This map shows how Antarctica was divided before the treaty went into effect. Find the region on the map claimed by three nations—Great Britain, Argentina, and Chile. This region is 6% of the total area.

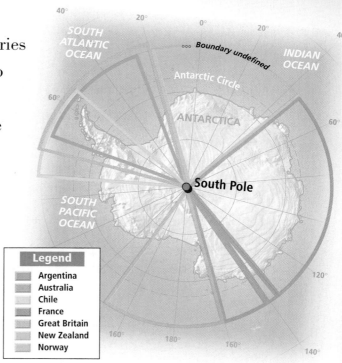

Legend
- Argentina
- Australia
- Chile
- France
- Great Britain
- New Zealand
- Norway

A Plan for Nippur

The city of Nippur (nee PAWR) was located in what is now Iraq. This plan of the city is about 3500 years old. Scientists who uncovered the city carefully measured the walls and discovered that the city plan was drawn using a ratio.

Try This!

The African Game of Abia

Abia is a traditional game played by people in Cameroon in West Africa. The game uses ratios to keep score. Here is one version of the game for four players.

Materials:
paper cup, 7 counters, coins, paper, pencil

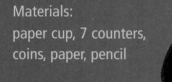

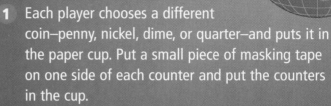

1. Each player chooses a different coin—penny, nickel, dime, or quarter—and puts it in the paper cup. Put a small piece of masking tape on one side of each counter and put the counters in the cup.

2. One player shakes the cup to mix the coins and counters and then pours them out. Listed below are the ratios for keeping score.

3. Use the chart to determine the score. For example, if two counters are taped and two of the coins are heads, the two players who used those coins win the toss. If you have a ratio that is not on the chart no one wins the toss.

4. Use tallies to keep track of how many tosses each player wins. Play ends when one player has won five tosses.

Ratios

Taped Counters	Heads up	
2	2	Two Win
3	2	Two Win
2	4	All Win
3	4	All Win
7	1	One Wins
7	2	Two Win
7	4	All Lose

Roman Numerals

Roman numerals are actually letters. Numbers less than 100 are made by combining four Roman symbols: I which equals 1, V which equals 5, X which equals 10, and L which equals 50. While addition and subtraction are possible using Roman numerals, multiplication and division can not be done. Could you divide 96 by 3 using Roman numerals?

Respond

With a partner . . .

create a game like Abia that uses ratio for scoring.

Internet:
Houghton Mifflin Education Place
Explore the Math Center at
http://www.eduplace.com

417

LESSON 12

Exploring Probability

You can use what you know about ratios to help you predict the number of red and blue centimeter cubes in the mystery bag.

Activity

Copy the tables below. You will each need one copy.

Getting Started

What You'll Need:
▶ 3 red centimeter cubes
▶ 3 blue centimeter cubes
▶ paper bag

Table A

Color	Trial 1		Trial 2		Trials 1 + 2
	Tallies	Total	Tallies	Total	Total
Red	?	?	?	?	?
Blue	?	?	?	?	?

Prediction of the Number of Cubes of Each Color

Color	After Trial 1	After Trial 2	Actual Number
Red	?	?	?
Blue	?	?	?

1

One person secretly puts 3 cubes in the bag, either 2 red and 1 blue, or 1 red and 2 blue.

• Without looking into the bag, pick 1 cube.

• Put a tally mark in the row for that color under Trial 1 in Table A.

• Return the cube to the bag.

• Mix the cubes in the bag.

• Repeat this procedure until you have picked 15 times.

Count the tally marks and write the total number for each color in the Trial 1 Total column.

- After Trial 1 write a prediction of the number of red cubes and the number of blue cubes in Table B in the section.
- Explain how you made your prediction to your partner.

- Carry out Trial 2 by repeating the first two activities.
- Write your tallies, totals, and predictions in your charts.

Compare your two predictions.

- Did your prediction change from the first trial to the second?
- Open the bag and look inside. Compare your predictions with the actual number of cubes.
- Tell your partner whether you think your prediction was a good one and give your reasons.

Repeat this activity, but switch roles. The partner who hid the cubes should now pick cubes from the bag and try to guess its contents.

Show What You Know!

Critical Thinking Suppose the following tallies were collected in several experiments similar to the one you just completed. What numbers of red and blue cubes could have been in the bag? Complete the chart with your estimates.

Total Number of Cubes in the Bag	What was picked	What do you think was in the bag
1. 6	5 red, 31 blue	?
2. 10	11 red, 39 blue	?
3. 10	45 red, 5 blue	?
4. 8	15 red, 17 blue	?

Share Your Thinking

5. Would you be more likely to believe the results of an experiment done 1000 times than one done 100 times? Explain.

6. Television commercials sometimes tell you that 4 out of 5 doctors recommend a product. Do they ever tell you how many doctors they asked? Why is that information important?

Probability and Ratio

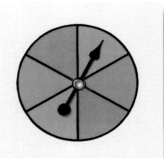

Are you more likely to see a wild alligator in Florida than in Indiana? Is it more likely to snow in January in Vermont than in Georgia? You often hear people talk about the chance of something happening. **Probability** is a measure of chance.

If you could spin the spinner at the left, what is the probability of the arrow landing on green?

Vocabulary:
   outcome
   probability
   Glossary, p. 500

Here's A Way! | **Find the probability of spinning green.**

1 Find all the possible **outcomes** of spinning the spinner. An outcome is a possible result of an experiment.

Since there are 6 sections in all, there are 6 possible outcomes when you spin this spinner.

2 Find the number of outcomes that give the result you want.

There are 2 green sections.

3 Check to see whether all sections have the same chance of coming up on each spin.

Each section is the same size, so each has the same chance of coming up.

4 Write the probability as a ratio of the outcomes you want, to the total number of outcomes.

The ratio of green sections to total sections is 2 to 6. On each spin, you have a 2 to 6, or 2:6, or $\frac{2}{6}$ chance of landing on green.

Talk About It! Which form of the ratio is most helpful in understanding the results of this probability experiment? Explain.

Other Example Shari, Kim, Bill, Raul and Pete are playing a game. If one of these student's names is drawn from the hat, the probability it will be a girl's name is $\frac{2}{5}$.

Write each probability in the form of a ratio and fraction.

Suppose you shuffled cards with the names of the states labeled below and placed them facedown on a table.

1. What is the probability of choosing a state name that begins with the letter K?

2. What is the chance of choosing a state in the Northeast?

3. What is the probability of choosing a state with the letter O in its abbreviation?

4. **Critical Thinking** Is there a greater chance of choosing a state that is east or west of Texas? Explain.

5. What is the probability of choosing a state that is east of the Mississippi River?

Look at the six children in the photo to answer the questions below. Write each probability in the form of a ratio and fraction.

6. What is the probability of choosing a child with a red shirt?

7. What is the chance of choosing a girl with dark hair?

8. What is the probability of choosing a girl wearing red?

9. What is the chance that if you choose a student, your choice will be either a boy or girl?

10. What is the chance of choosing an adult?

More Practice Set 12.13, p. 496

LESSON 14

Problem Solving
Using Strategies

Zillions conducted a survey about the sports kids think are best. They asked boys and girls which sports they thought were the most fun.

There were 600 student responses to the survey. Waterskiing, snowboarding, and ice hockey earned some of the highest scores, but those sports did not make the top-10 list because only one out of every three students had tried them. Of the students who responded, how many had tried waterskiing, snowboarding, or ice hockey?

You can read more about the best sports in *Zillions*

Problem Solving Process
✓ Understand
✓ Plan
✓ Try It
✓ Look Back

Choose a Strategy You Have Learned
✓ Make a Table
✓ Act It Out
✓ Guess and Check
✓ Look for a Pattern
✓ Work Backward
✓ Make a List
✓ Work a Simpler Problem
✓ Draw a Picture
✓ Write an Equation

- What is the question you have to answer?
- What is the ratio of students who had tried the sports to the total number of students?
- In the equation below, what operation is being used to answer the question?

$$\frac{1}{3} = \frac{\blacksquare}{600}$$

- Explain a strategy that you can use to solve the problem.

Work It Out!

Use any strategy to solve the problem. Show your work.

1. Both boys and girls ranked downhill skiing as the most fun sport. Suppose 5 out of 12 kids surveyed were boys. Half of them said downhill skiing was their most fun sport. How many boys chose other sports as their most fun sport?

2. Girls ranked swimming as their second most fun sport. Suppose 5 out of 12 kids surveyed were boys. If one out of five girls chose swimming as their most fun sport, how many chose swimming?

3. A scale balances with a football on one side, and a softball and two hockey pucks on the other side. A football and a hockey puck will balance a softball and baseball. A softball will balance a baseball and hockey puck. How many hockey pucks will balance a football?

4. A football field is 300 feet long with an additional 30-foot long area at each end. A hockey rink is 200 feet long. What is the difference in total length between a football field and a hockey rink?

5. In a football game, the ratio of points for a touchdown and extra point to a field goal is 7 to 3. Suppose a team scored 2 field goals and had a total of 27 points. How many touchdowns and extra points did they have during the game?

6. In the after-school center at the Jefferson School, there are baseball, soccer, and basketball leagues. A total of 142 students participate. Each baseball team has 9 players, each soccer team 11, and each basketball team 5. How many teams in each sport can there be?

7. The Jefferson School Center bought 240 pieces of sports equipment. If 50% of it was for baseball, 30% was for basketball, and 20% was for soccer, how many pieces were bought for each sport?

Share Your Thinking

8. How does understanding the relationship between ratio and percent help you to solve problems?

LESSON 15

Problem Solving
Choose a Computation Method

Choose a Computation Method

Ask Yourself:

Do I need an exact answer or an estimate?

Should I use a model, paper and pencil, mental math, or a calculator?

What operation should I use?

Superman the Escape, a roller coaster in California, is 415 feet high and was designed for speeds up to 100 miles per hour.

Suppose you want to buy a book of 3 tickets for $13.99. If you pay with a $20 bill, how much change will you receive?

You Decide

- Can I quickly compute the answer mentally or is the calculation too difficult?

- Decide whether you would use mental math or a calculator. Explain your decision.

Work It Out!

Solve each problem. Write whether you used mental math or a calculator.

1. $80 + 120 + 30$
2. $12.2 + 6.205$
3. 10×530
4. $12 \times \frac{1}{2}$
5. $\frac{3}{4} \times \frac{1}{5}$
6. $6000 \div 8$
7. 25.1×7.8
8. $240 \div 6$
9. 50% of 12
10. $\frac{3}{9} + \frac{2}{9}$
11. 32×56
12. 25% of 40
13. 0.8×30
14. 90% of 80
15. $\frac{1}{5} \times 20$
16. $100 \div \frac{1}{2}$

Problem Solving

17. The ticket booth sells ride tickets individually for $5.15 each. Is it less expensive to buy a book of three tickets for $13.99 or to buy three individually? Explain.

18. Suppose you worked at the ticket booth. In one hour you sold a total of 46 tickets. Some are books of 3, some are single tickets. If you sold 10 more single tickets than sets of 3 tickets, how many single tickets did you sell? How many sets of tickets did you sell?

19. A ride lasts 2 min 30 s and it takes 3 min 30 s on average to unload and reload passengers. How many rides can there be in 1 hour?

20. If the staff could reduce the time it takes to unload and reload customers by one minute, how many more rides could they offer in a 12-hr day?

21. The highest point on one roller coaster is 325 ft above the ground. If the greatest difference between the highest and lowest points on the ride is 265 ft, how close to the ground does the ride come?

22. Suppose a roller coaster has 15 seats that are filled in the following order: 1, 5, 9, 13, 2, 6, ... Which is the last filled seat?

23. **Create Your Own** Write a word problem of your own that would be easier to solve:
    a. using mental math
    b. using a calculator

Share Your Thinking

24. How do you know when to use mental math?

More Practice Set 12.15, p. 496

Chapter 12 Test

for Pages 392–425

Test-Taking Tips
First, read over the test. If you need to ask a question, ask it before you begin writing answers.

Problem Solving

Use the data below to solve. Show your work. (pages 402, 412, 422)

Two candidates, Steven and Cheryl, ran for student council president. A total of 450 students voted. Cheryl got 62 percent of the votes. All the other votes went to Steven.

1. How many students voted for Cheryl?

2. What percent of the vote did Steven receive?

3. How many students voted for Steven?

4. By how many votes did Cheryl win the election?

Use the recipe to solve problems 5–6.
(pages 394, 396, 398, 400)

5. In order to make 45 cookies, how much flour will you need?

6. If you want to make only half the number of cookies in the recipe, how much butter will you need?

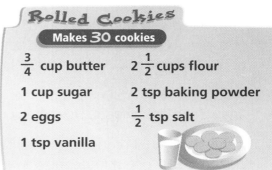

Rolled Cookies

Makes 30 cookies

$\frac{3}{4}$ cup butter $2\frac{1}{2}$ cups flour

1 cup sugar   2 tsp baking powder

2 eggs $\frac{1}{2}$ tsp salt

1 tsp vanilla

Concepts

Use the spinner to answer questions 7–9. (pages 418, 420)

7. What is the probability of landing on a country in North America?

8. What is the probability of landing on a country in South America?

9. What is the probability of landing on a country in Asia?

Find the answer. (pages 406, 410)

10. The stadium in which the Toronto Blue Jays baseball team plays has seats for 60,000 people. When the stadium is 75 percent full, are there more than or fewer than 40,000 people in the seats? Explain your answer.

Decide if the ratios are equal. Write yes or no. (pages 398, 400)

11. 6 to 4 and 10 to 8   **12.** 1 to 5 and 3 to 15   **13.** $\frac{7}{3}$ and $\frac{21}{9}$

14. 2:3 and 24:16   **15.** 8 to 7 and 24:21   **16.** 2:3 and 6:9

Which decimal and fraction are equivalent to the percent? Write a, b, c, or d.
(page 408)

17. 70%   a. 7.0, $\frac{1}{70}$ b. 0.70, $\frac{7}{100}$ c. 0.070, $\frac{70}{100}$ d. 0.70, $\frac{7}{10}$

18. 44%   a. 0.044, $\frac{44}{100}$ b. 4.4, $\frac{1}{44}$ c. 0.44, $\frac{11}{25}$ d. 1.44, $\frac{22}{50}$

19. 20%   a. 0.20, $\frac{1}{5}$ b. 0.020, $\frac{10}{50}$ c. 2.0, $1\frac{1}{5}$ d. 0.020, $\frac{1}{5}$

Write each percent as a decimal and as a fraction in simplest form. (page 408)

20. 35%   **21.** 73%   **22.** 60%

The cube is numbered 1–6. Find the probability of these events. (page 420)

23. rolling an even number

24. rolling a multiple of 3

25. rolling a number greater than 7

Performance Task

(pages 410, 412, 414)

Use the supermarket flyer and the discount coupons to plan a shopping trip. You have $20.00. How close can you come to spending all of it?

Show your calculations. Make a shopping list including prices and totals.

Keep In Mind . . .

Your work will be evaluated on the following:

✓ Variety of items in list

✓ Numbers and prices of items

✓ Percent discount calculated

✓ $ 20 to spend

PAY ONLY **80%** FOR ALL OTHER PRODUCTS

PAY ONLY **75%** FOR ANY CANNED PRODUCT

Vegetable Soup **$.90** per can

Pretzels **$1.50** per bag

Ravioli **$1.20** per can

Frozen Yogurt **$2.00** per pint

Milk **$.80** per quart

Spring Water **$1.00** per gallon

Cranberry Juice **$1.80** per bottle

Deli Sandwich **$2.50** each

Cumulative Review

Perimeter (Chapter 5)
Find the perimeter of the pentagon.

Here's A Way!

Find the length
of each side:

4 m

3 m

2.5

2.5

4 m

4 m, 3 m, 4 m, 2.5 m, and 2.5 m
Find the sum of the sides: **16 m**

Find the perimeter.

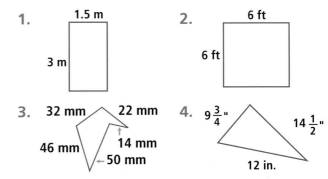

1. 1.5 m / 3 m

2. 6 ft / 6 ft

3. 32 mm / 22 mm / 46 mm / 14 mm / 50 mm

4. $9\frac{3}{4}$" / $14\frac{1}{2}$" / 12 in.

5. Why is $4 \cdot s$ an expression for the perimeter of a square if the length of a side is s?

Equivalent Metric Measures (Chapter 7)
Write 3.7 centimeters as millimeters.

Here's A Way!

Multiply to write a larger unit as a
smaller one.
1 cm = 10 mm, so multiply by 10.
3.7 cm × 10 = 37 mm
To write a *smaller* unit as a *larger*
one, divide.

Write the missing number.

6. 8010 m = ■ km

7. 9.5 cm = ■ mm

8. 17.2 m = ■ cm

9. 25 cm = ■ m

10. 592 mm = ■ m

11. 0.7 m = ■ cm

12. If you write 350 meters as kilometers, will the number of kilometers be greater or less than 350? Explain.

Similar Figures (Chapter 8)
Draw a figure similar to figure ABCD.

Here's A Way!

Find each ordered pair.
A (1, 3), *B* (2, 1),
C (5, 3), *D* (3, 6)
Multiply each
number by 2.
A (2, 6), *B* (4, 2),
C (10, 6), *D* (6, 12)
Plot the new vertices on a grid.

Draw the figure on grid paper. Then answer the questions.

13. Draw a figure with vertices *E* (1, 1), *F* (3, 4), *G* (6, 4), and *H* (4, 1).

14. What type of quadrilateral is figure *EFGH*?

15. Find the coordinates for a figure similar to *EFGH*. Call the figure *E'*, *F'*, *G'*, *H'*. Multiply each number by 2.

   a. *E'* = ■

   b. *F'* = ■

   c. *G'* = ■

   d. *H'* = ■

16. How could you make a similar figure larger than the second figure?

428

Add and Subtract Mixed Numbers

(Chapter 10)

Find $5\frac{1}{12} - 3\frac{5}{12}$.

Here's A Way!

The denominators are the same.

Rename: $5\frac{1}{12} = 4\frac{13}{12}$

Subtract the numerators, then the whole numbers, and then simplify:

$4\frac{13}{12} - 3\frac{5}{12} = 1\frac{8}{12} = 1\frac{2}{3}$

Write the answer in simplest form.

17. $\begin{array}{r} 7\frac{4}{5} \\ -\ 2\frac{1}{5} \end{array}$
18. $\begin{array}{r} 8\frac{1}{6} \\ +\ 2\frac{1}{6} \end{array}$
19. $\begin{array}{r} \frac{7}{9} \\ +\ \frac{1}{9} \end{array}$

20. $9\frac{5}{11} - 5\frac{7}{11}$
21. $\frac{13}{15} - \frac{4}{15}$
22. $9\frac{3}{10} + 9\frac{3}{10}$

23. Why is it important to check that the denominators are the same before adding or subtracting fractions?

Dividing by Fractions (Chapter 11)

Find $8 \div \frac{2}{5}$.

Here's A Way!

Find the reciprocal of the divisor.

Rewrite as a multiplication sentence using the reciprocal.

$8 \times \frac{5}{2}$

Multiply. Simplify if possible.

$8 \times \frac{5}{2} = \frac{40}{2} = 20$

Use the reciprocal of the fraction and multiply to solve the division problem.

24. $4 \div \frac{5}{6}$
25. $7 \div \frac{3}{8}$
26. $8 \div \frac{1}{2}$

27. $3 \div \frac{3}{4}$
28. $9 \div \frac{3}{5}$
29. $6 \div \frac{2}{3}$

30. When you divide a whole number by a fraction, is the quotient greater or less than the dividend? Explain.

Problem Solving

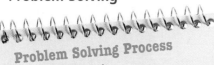

Problem Solving Process
✓ Understand
✓ Plan
✓ Try It
✓ Look Back

Choose a Strategy You Have Learned
✓ Make a Table
✓ Act It Out
✓ Guess and Check
✓ Look for a Pattern
✓ Work Backward
✓ Make a List
✓ Work a Simpler Problem
✓ Draw a Picture
✓ Write an Equation

Choose one of the strategies you know to solve these problems. Show your work.

31. A store has all its employees wear polo shirts with the store logo on them. Employees have a choice of red, blue, or yellow for the shirt, and the logo can be embroidered in either black or white thread. How many different combinations of polo shirts and logos are possible?

32. Suppose you buy books at the school book fair that cost $2.95, $1.95, and $6.95. Would you have enough money left from $15.00 to buy your lunch for $1.25? Explain your thinking.

Brain Activity

Science Connection   **With Your Group**

When you look at something, your eyes see it upside down and reversed. The brain changes the image so it looks as it should. Each eye sends a slightly different message to the back of the brain and the brain interprets the message so you understand what you are seeing.

Since each eye sees things a little differently, if you cover one eye what you see will change position. Your group will record what happens when you use only one eye and then both eyes.

1
Plan It

- Cut out three yellow circles that are 5 cm, 15 cm, and 25 cm in diameter. Cut out two blue circles that are 10 cm and 20 cm in diameter. Glue them together so they make a target.

- Make five small clay balls.

2
Put It Together

- Place the target flat on a table. Have one person stand about four feet from the target and cover one eye.

- Have another person hold a clay ball over the target. The first person tells the ball-holder to move the ball so it will drop in the middle of the target.

- Record where the ball lands on the target. Have each person do this five times for each eye and then for both eyes.

- Combine your data to complete the group data chart shown on the page.

3
Wrap It Up!

- Make a circle graph that shows what percent of your group hit the 5 cm circle using the left eye, right eye, and both eyes.

- Write a paper explaining your results. Predict the probability of getting the same results with another group of students.

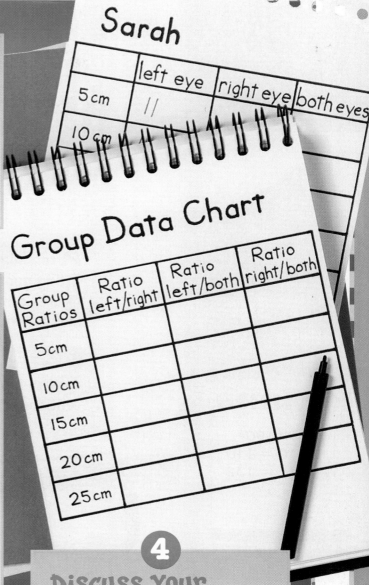

Sarah

	left eye	right eye	both eyes
5 cm	II		
10 cm			

Group Data Chart

Group Ratios	Ratio left/right	Ratio left/both	Ratio right/both
5 cm			
10 cm			
15 cm			
20 cm			
25 cm			

4
Discuss Your Results

- Did you complete the items listed in Keep In Mind?

- How is this experiment helpful in understanding how vision works?

Internet

> Visit the **Math Center** at **Houghton Mifflin Education Place.** http://www.eduplace.com

Use What You Know

- how to make patterns

$10 \times 9 = 90$
$11 \times 10 = 110$
$12 \times 11 = 132$

- how to multiply two-digit numbers

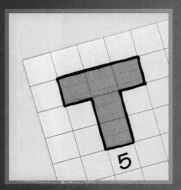

5

- how to count centimeter squares

Area and Volume

Try This!

A tessellation is a pattern formed by fitting geometric figures together. The figures cannot overlap or leave gaps. Try making your own tesselation.

What You'll Need

construction or colored paper, scissors, tape, centimeter squared paper

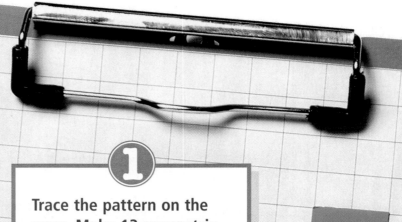

1

Trace the pattern on the page. Make 13 geometric figures using colored paper. Cut the following:

six yellow figures
three red figures
two blue figures
two green figures

To make your tesselation, place the geometric figures together so they form a pattern. Do not overlap the figures or leave gaps. Tape the figures together.

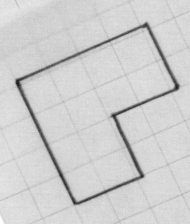

How much area does your pattern cover? Lay the tracing paper with the pattern on the grid paper. How many squares does the pattern cover? Your tesselation uses 13 figures. How many total centimeter squares does it cover?

How did you find how many centimeter squares your tesselation covers?

If you arranged the figures differently, would they cover a different number of squares?

Ready to Go!

Area of a Rectangle

What You'll Need:
▶ centimeter square tiles
▶ centimeter ruler
▶ centimeter square grid paper

Vocabulary:
area
Glossary, p. 500

Cooperative Learning Checklist

☑ Work alone.
☑ Work with a partner.
☑ Work with a group.

The number of square units needed to cover a surface is its **area**. Some units used to measure area are:

Customary Units and Metric Units
Square inches (in²)
Square feet (ft²)
Square yards (yd²)
Square centimeters (cm²)
Square meters (m²)

Activity

• **Use square tiles to find areas.**

1

• Use square tiles to construct the rectangle being made in the photo here. How many rows and columns of tiles do you need?

• Count the number of square tiles to find the area. How is this number related to the length and width of the rectangle?

You can also find the area of a rectangle by using the following formula:

Area of a rectangle = length × width
$A = l \times w$

a. What numbers would you use to find the area of the rectangle?

• Draw and label three other rectangles with an area of 40 in² and with whole number lengths and widths.

• Copy the square shown here onto grid paper. Are the length and width related?

• All four sides of a square are the same length, so you can represent the length of each with the variable s. Use the letter s to write a formula for the area of squares.

a. Use the formula to find the area of this square.

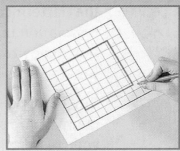

1. **Critical Thinking** How is the area of a figure different from its perimeter?

Find the area of each rectangle. Remember to use square units.

2. length = 7 in.
   width = 6 in.

3. length = 3 cm
   width = 4.5 cm

4. side = 5 yd

5. length = 12 ft
   width = 10 ft

6. side = 8.1 m

7. length = 9.4 cm
   width = 3.6 cm

8.
   ——— 4 cm ———

9. — $\frac{3}{4}$ in. —
   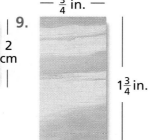
   2 cm
   $1\frac{3}{4}$ in.

10.
    1 in.
    ——— 1 in. ———

11. side = 1.2 mm

12. length = 22.5 m
    width = 20.2 m

13. length = 35 mi
    width = 23 mi

14. length = 200 cm
    width = 30 cm

15. side = 40 cm

16. length = 0.4 in.
    width = 0.9 in.

17. **Critical Thinking** How can you find the number of square inches in one square foot?

18. **Number Sense** Which is a greater area, 2000 in.^{2} or 25 ft^2? How much greater? Support your answer.

Problem Solving

19. A 5-in. by 7-in. picture is put in a 8-in. by 11-in. frame. Will the picture take up more than half the area inside the frame?

20. The area of a square puzzle is 144 in.^{2} Will it fit on a square table with an area of 1 ft^2?

21. **Critical Thinking** Write two word problems, one to find the area of a square, and the other to find the area of a rectangle.

More Practice Set 13.1, p. 497

Math Journal

Why is area always written in square units?

Estimation: Area

What You'll Need:
▶ quarter-inch squared paper

If you have ever searched for wildlife, you know how difficult it is to see animals. Often, the only evidence of animals is their tracks. People interested in nature learn about tracks as one way of knowing about wildlife. The track shown is made by a gray squirrel.

When you want to identify animal tracks, it is important to know both the track's shape and size. You can estimate the area of the track by using a grid.

Here's A Way! **Estimate the area.**

1 Count the number of whole squares in each track.

- There are 9 whole squares in the track.

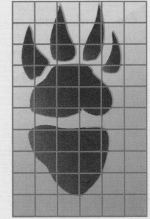

2 Put together parts of other squares.

- Begin with the largest pieces and then combine smaller remaining pieces.
- The partial squares have a sum of about 7 squares.

3 Add all the squares.

- Altogether, the area of the track is about 9 + 7 or 16 square units.

Talk About It!

How did you decide which partial squares would add to approximately 1 square unit?

Show What You Know!

Estimate the area of each track. Give your answer in square units.

1.

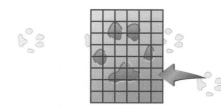

bobcat

2.

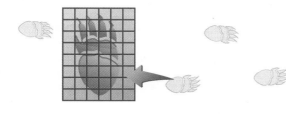

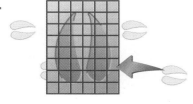

porcupine

3. **Critical Thinking** Explain why there can be more than one reasonable estimate for exercises 1–2.

Work It Out!

Estimate the area of each animal track to the nearest square unit.

4.

deer

5.

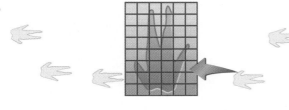

badger

6. The track left by a beaver is similar to that of a badger, but may be up to twice as long. Draw a track that might have been left by a beaver. Then estimate its area.

7. **Critical Thinking** Suppose you used squared grid paper that had squares four times as large for exercise 6. What would have been the effect on the estimate of the area?

More Practice Set 13.2, p. 497

437

Problem Solving
Draw a Picture

If you are building a swimming pool, and your initial is L, you might want to build it in the shape of the letter L. Suppose your pool measures 50 ft along the left side of the L and 40 ft across the bottom. Each part of the L is 20 ft wide. The pool needs to be covered with a tarp for winter. What is the area of the tarp that you must buy?

Here's A Way! | Use Draw a Picture to solve the problem.

1 Understand

- How can you use what you know about the areas of rectangles to help you find the area of the tarp?
- How can you use the formula $A = l \times w$? How can you find l and w?

2 Plan

- Draw a picture to help you see what the pool looks like.
- Write the dimensions on the picture.
- Look for rectangles.

3 Try It

- Divide the L-shape into two rectangles.
- Notice you have the dimensions of rectangles A and B.
- Find the area of each rectangle.
- Add the two areas to find the total.

4 Look Back

- The tarp must be 1400 ft².
- How did drawing a picture help you to solve the problem?

Show What You Know!

Use Draw a Picture to solve the problem.

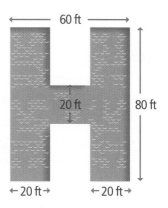

60 ft
20 ft
80 ft
20 ft
20 ft

1. Harry Hiller has a swimming pool in the shape of the letter H. It is 80 feet along the left side. The total width of the pool is 60 feet. Each part of the H-pool is 20 feet wide. What is the area of the pool?

2. **Critical Thinking** Tarp comes in square or rectangular shapes. Harry wants to cover the whole pool with only one piece of tarp. How can he do this? How big should the tarp be?

Work It Out!

Use Draw a Picture or any strategy to solve the problem.

3. Suppose you put a sidewalk completely around the L-shaped swimming pool on page 438. The sidewalk is 5 feet wide. What is the area of the sidewalk?

4. Carrie started swimming on Monday and will swim every fifth day after that. Sandra began on Tuesday and will swim every third day. On which day of the week will Carrie and Sandra first swim together?

5. Jason paid $1.50 for a bus ride to the swimming pool. He paid with 10 coins. If none of the coins was a dime, what coins did he use?

6. An H-shaped pool has two lines of symmetry. Name three other capital letters that have at least one line of symmetry. Draw pictures of the letters.

7. Amber and Barry swim laps at different pools. Amber swims 20 laps in a 50-meter pool. Her swim takes 30 minutes. Barry swims 40 laps in a 30-meter pool. His swim takes 40 minutes. Who is the faster swimmer? How did you decide?

8. It takes you 30 minutes to swim 25 laps. If your speed did not change, how many laps would you swim in 45 minutes?

Share Your Thinking

9. Compare the strategies you used for problems 3–8 with a classmate's. For which problems did you use the same strategy?

10. When is drawing a diagram helpful in solving a problem?

Area of a Triangle

Did you know that the area of a rectangle is related to the area of a triangle? Find out how in these activities.

Activity

Rectangles and Right Triangles

The area of a right triangle is related to the area of a rectangle.

A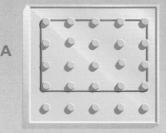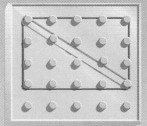

1 Use rubber bands to make rectangle A on your geoboard. What is the area of rectangle A?

2 Make a diagonal as shown. How many congruent triangles are made from the rectangle?

a. What fraction of the area of the rectangle is the area of each triangle?

b. What is the area of each triangle?

3 Make two other rectangles on your geoboard. Follow the same steps as for rectangle A to divide them into triangles. Find the area of the triangles.

Rectangles and Other Triangles

1 Draw a 4 x 6 rectangle on dot paper. At 2 units from each left corner draw a segment that divides the rectangle into a smaller rectangle and square. Draw the diagonals of these figures as shown, to form several triangles.

2 Color the triangles as shown. What is the area of the blue triangle? the red triangle? the sum of the triangles?

Make each triangle on your geoboard or copy it onto geoboard dot paper. Write the area of each triangle.

1.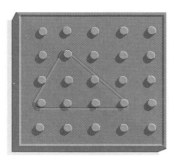

2.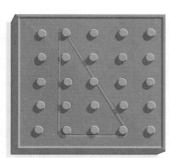

3.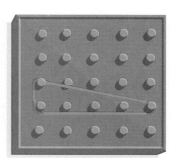

4.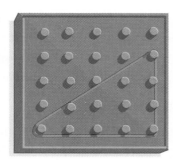

5.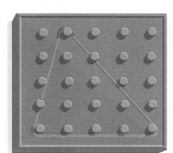

6.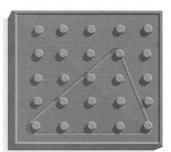

7. **Critical Thinking** If one of the sides of the triangle is parallel to the edge of a geoboard, how can you use rectangles to find the area of that triangle?

Problem Solving

8. A kite can be made from triangles of material. Suppose you have a rectangular piece of material that is 5 ft². What is the area of the largest right-triangle kite that you can make from that material?

9. Colorful rhombus-shaped kites can be made from triangles as well. If two similar right triangles, each with an area of 1 ft², are used to make a rhombus-shaped kite with an area of 2 ft², what other name can you call that rhombus?

10. If it takes four similar right triangles, each with an area of 1.5 ft², to make a kite with an area of 6 ft², what shape is the kite?

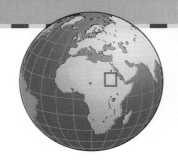

Problem Solving
Logical Reasoning

Gebel Barkal (JEH bel BAR kal), located on the Nile River, was once a major center of ancient Nubia in Africa. It is now an archaeological site.

Archaeologists can use grids to divide up a site before excavating. Suppose four archaeologists want to search Gebel Barkal for artifacts. They need to divide the area equally, but certain parts of the site cannot be searched. How can you shade the grid to show where each archaeologist will search?

You Decide

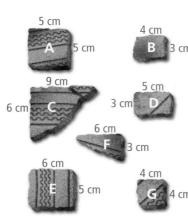

Logical Reasoning

Ask Yourself:

Can I eliminate any possibilities?

Can I sort the information?

- Do you need to find the total area of the site? Explain your answer.
- Will your plan be exactly the same as the plans of other students in your class? Is there more than one possible plan?

Work It Out!

Does the problem have more than one answer? Solve and explain.

1. One archaeologist wants to return to camp for supplies. On the map, his location is at point A and the camp is at point C. What is the shortest route he can take?

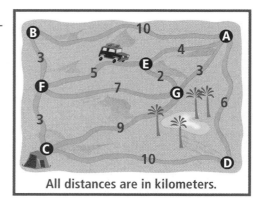

All distances are in kilometers.

2. The remains of a wall are to be examined for clues to the past. The wall is 40 feet long and 6 feet high. If the four archaeologists share the work equally, how could they divide up the wall?

3. Suppose these seven pieces of pottery were found at the site. They will be packed in two boxes so that each box contains pieces with the same total area. List the pieces that should be in each box.

Share Your Thinking

4. In a real situation, why might you want to find other solutions to a problem after having found one solution?

Midchapter Review

for Pages 432–442

Solve. Show your work. (pages 434, 438, 442)

1. A tennis court is 78 feet long. When 4 players use the court, they use all 36 feet of its width. Two players use 9 feet less of the width. What is the area of the tennis court for 2 players?

2. You have space in your backyard to lay out a rectangular play area using 100 feet of rope. Describe two different areas that use all the rope.

3. What shape rectangle would give you the greatest play area?

Concepts

Find the answers. (pages 434, 440)

4. Explain how you would find the number of square feet in one square yard.

5. How many square inches are there in one square foot?

6. Draw a diagram to show how you can use a rectangle to find the area of any right triangle.

7. How could you use a rectangle to find the area of the geoboard triangle?

Skills

Find the area of each rectangle in square units. (page 434)

8.

5 in.

16 in.

9.

7 ft

7 ft

10.

3 cm

7 cm

11. length = 60 in.
    width = 12 in.

12. length = 24.5 ft
    width = 14 ft

13. side = 15 mi

Math World

People in other countries have used many different ways to measure area and volume. Read about them and practice one from China.

As Big As . . .

Have you ever tried to estimate the size of a large area by comparing it to a football field? People all over the world use playing fields to compare area. In other countries, soccer and rugby are much more popular than American football. People in Brazil may not know exactly how big an American football field is, but they are familiar with a soccer field since soccer is very popular there. Which do you think is larger, a soccer field or a football field?

Area and Volume in Babylon

We know a great deal about the mathematics of the Babylonians because a large number of the clay tablets on which they wrote have survived. Experts who have studied these tablets know that the Babylonians found the area of a rectangle the same way we do today—by multiplying the length by the width. The tablets also show that we use the same method to find the volume of a rectangular prism. Even though the tablets are 4000 years old, the way we find area and volume has not changed.

Try This!

ANCIENT CHINESE UNIT OF AREA

In the past, many cultures had a unit called the pace. A pace was equal to the length of one step. An early unit of area in China called the *bu* (boo) was equal to one pace times one pace. A field with an area of 240 bu was a *mu* (moo). Follow these steps to measure areas in bu.

1 Measure an area 3 paces long and 4 paces wide. What is the area of this rectangle in bu?

2 Measure an area 5 paces long and 3 paces wide. What is the area of this rectangle in bu?

3 Measure in paces the length and width of a room. Write a mathematical sentence to show the area of the room in bu.

4 If the area of one mu is 240 bu and one side is 15 paces, what is the adjacent side? Write a mathematical sentence to find the answer. Step off an area that would be one mu.

Pyramid Packing

To find the volume of a pyramid, Chou Shu-Hsüeh, a Chinese mathematician, would pack the pyramid with small spheres. The spheres were used as units of measurement. He found the volume by counting how many spheres were needed to fill the pyramid.

Respond

With a partner . . .
find the area of your classroom. How many classrooms could fit in one football field?

 Internet:
Houghton Mifflin Education Place
Explore the Math Center at
http://www.eduplace.com

Solids

The World Trade Center in New York City is a rectangular prism.

There are solids all around us. Solids are three-dimensional figures that have length, width, and height. In this lesson, you will explore identifying solids.

Activity

Solids

1 Look at the solids shown below.

| A triangular pyramid | B pentagonal prism | C sphere | D cylinder | E cone |

a. Which solid has 1 flat surface? Which has two flat surfaces?
b. Which has more than two flat surfaces?

Pyramids and Prisms

1 Look at the two kinds of solids shown below. They are pyramids and prisms. You can identify them by their faces, edges, and vertices.

Hexagonal Pyramid   Hexagonal Prism

  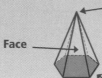 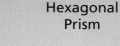 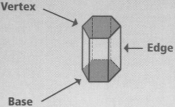

Vertex

Face

Edge

Base

2 Look at the shape that forms the base of a pyramid. What do you notice about the number of sides compared to the number of faces?

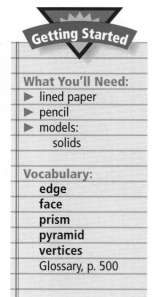

Getting Started

What You'll Need:
- lined paper
- pencil
- models:
  solids

Vocabulary:
edge
face
prism
pyramid
vertices
Glossary, p. 500

Cooperative Learning
Checklist

☑ Work alone.
☑ Work with a partner.
☑ Work with a group.

Complete the Chart

1. Copy and complete the chart. Identify the characteristics of the remaining figures. If you need to, copy each figure onto a separate piece of paper.

2. Count the faces, vertices, edges, and bases of the figure. Write the number of each in the chart.

Solid	Bases	Other Faces	Edges	Vertices
a. Triangular Prism	?	?	?	?
b. Hexagonal Prism	?	?	?	?
c. Triangular Pyramid	?	?	?	?
d. Pentagonal Pyramid	?	?	?	?

Show What You Know!

Copy and complete the chart.

1. **Critical Thinking** Name the polygon that is the base of each solid in the above exercises. The bases of each polygon are shaded.

Solid	Bases	Other Faces	Edges	Vertices
1. Square Prism	?	?	?	?
2. Square Pyramid	?	?	?	?
3. Cone	?	?	?	?

Name the figure from its description.

2. It has 4 faces. All are triangles.

3. It has 2 flat surfaces, and contains no polygons.

4. It has 7 faces. All but 2 are rectangles.

5. It has 1 flat face, but contains no polygons.

6. **Critical Thinking** A silo is used for storing grain. It is usually shaped like a cylinder. When seen from a long distance, what figure do you think a silo appears to be?

More Practice Set 13.6, p. 498

LESSON 7

Surface Area and Solids

Cooperative Learning Checklist

☐ Work alone.
☑ Work with a partner.
☐ Work with a group.

What You'll Need:
▶ centimeter linking cubes
▶ recording sheet

Vocabulary:
surface area
Glossary, p. 500

In this lesson, you will learn to measure the **surface area** of a solid. The large solid shown is formed by putting together eight centimeter linking cubes.

Each of these small cubes has 6 faces. Each face is called a unit square. When the small cubes are combined to make a large solid, not all of the unit squares can be seen. When you find the sum of the unit squares that can be seen, you are finding the surface area.

Making a model can help you find the surface area of a solid.

Activity

Exploring Solids

1. Use 8 centimeter linking cubes to make a solid like the one shown above.

2. Copy the chart below and enter the data as you answer each question.
   a. How many unit squares do you see on the top of the solid?

3. Turn the solid over. How many unit squares are visible on the bottom?
   a. How many unit squares do you see on each of the other 4 sides?
   b. Find the sum of unit squares on the top, bottom, and all sides of the solid you made. What is the surface area of the solid?

	Top	Side 1	Side 2	Side 3	Side 4	Bottom
Square Units	4	4	?	?	?	?

Finding Greatest and Least Surface Area

Using the same number of cubes, build solids with different surface areas.

1 Use 8 cubes to build each solid shown below. Then find each surface area.

a. What is the least surface area you found for an 8-cube solid? The greatest surface area?

Build Your Own Solids

1 Build your own solids.

2 Make a solid figure using 12 cubes. What is the surface area?

3 Experiment with the 12 cubes to make solids with the least and the greatest surface area. What was the greatest surface area you found? The least?

4 Record your results on a copy of Chart A.

Chart A

	Surface Area	Sketch of Solid
Least	?	?
Greatest	?	?

Show What You Know!

Discuss and answer each question.

1. **Critical Thinking** Does changing the shape of a solid affect its surface area? Explain.

2. **Critical Thinking** What shape results in the least surface area? What shape has the greatest surface area?

3. Use 10 cubes. Make solids with the least and greatest surface area. Sketch your solids.

4. Predict which of the solids on the right, each made with 16 cubes, will have the least surface area. Predict which will have the greatest surface area. Test your prediction.

Volume of a Rectangular Prism

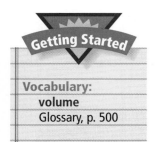

Getting Started

Vocabulary:
volume
Glossary, p. 500

Volume is the amount of space inside a solid. Volume is measured in units such as cubic centimeters (cm³) and cubic inches (in.³). To measure the volume of a solid, imagine the solid as an empty container that can be filled with cubes.

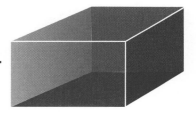

To find the volume of a rectangular prism, think about layers of cubes. 1 cm

1 cm
1 cm

Here's A Way! **Find the volume of a rectangular prism.**

1 Find the number of cubes in one layer. Count the cubes or multiply the length of the layer by its width.

$8 \times 5 = 40$

2 Multiply the number of cubes in the first layer by the number of layers.

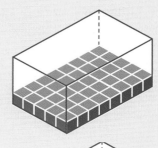

Volume = length × width × height

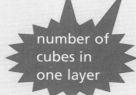

number of cubes in one layer

number of layers

Volume = 8 cm × 5 cm × 4 cm or 160 cm³.

So, the volume of the rectangular prism is 160 cm³.

Talk About It! Why do we use cubic units to measure volume?

Other Examples The length of all sides of the cube are the same. So, the volume of the cube is: 5 ft × 5 ft × 5 ft, or 125 ft³.

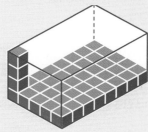

5 ft

5 ft

5 ft

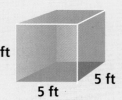

Show What You Know!

Find the volume. Write your answer in cubic units.

1.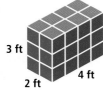

3 ft
4 ft
2 ft

2.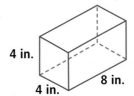

4 in.
4 in.
8 in.

3.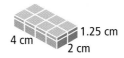

4 cm
1.25 cm
2 cm

4. Find the volume of a box that is 6 in. long, 3 in. wide, and 10 in. high.

5. Critical Thinking Describe one way that you might be able to check your answers to exercises 1–4.

Work It Out!

Find the volume. Write your answer in cubic units.

6.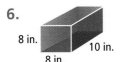

8 in.
10 in.
8 in.

7.

6 mm
2.75 mm
4 mm

8.

10 m
10 m
10 m

Write the missing measurement.

	Length	Width	Height	Volume
9.	4 ft	4 ft	4 ft	?
10.	8 m	?	5 m	120 m³
11.	5 mm	7 mm	?	350 mm³

Problem Solving

12. Estimation You can use a benchmark to estimate volume. Use 1 cubic in. to estimate the volume of the boxes. What is the estimated volume of box A? box B?

Box A   Box B   Benchmark

1 cubic in.

13. Storage space in a basement is 15 ft long, 4 ft wide, and 2 ft high. How many boxes that measure 3 ft long, 2 ft wide, and 1 ft high can fill in the space?

14. Critical Thinking Which do you think has a greater volume, the cylinder or the prism? Explain.

15. Critical Thinking A box has a volume of 48 cm³. What could its height, length, and width be? Is there more than one answer? Explain.

3 in.
6 in.
6 in.
3 in.
3 in.

More Practice Set 13.8, p. 498

Cooperative Learning
Checklist

☐ Work alone.
☑ Work with a partner.
☐ Work with a group.

Volume of Irregular Solids

Many real-life solids are not simple rectangular prisms. By using what you know about finding the volume of rectangular prisms, you can find the volume of certain solids with different shapes.

Activity

Exploring Rectangular Prisms

Each rectangular prism shown at the left is made from 20 centimeter cubes.

1 Use 16 centimeter cubes. Build three different rectangular prisms. They can be similar to the ones built with 20 cubes, or they can be different.

2 Complete Table A on your recording sheet or on your own paper.
  a. What do you notice about the volume of each prism?
  b. What would be the volume of a solid made from 15 centimeter cubes?

Table A

	Length	Width	Height	Volume
Prism 1	?	?	?	?
Prism 2	?	?	?	?
Prism 3	?	?	?	?

Combining Rectangular Prisms

1 Examine how the volumes of some solids are related to the volumes of rectangular prisms.
  a. Each small cube is 1 cm^3. What is the volume of prism A? Prism B?

2 You can combine prisms A and B to make solid C. How would you find the volume of solid C? What is the volume?

3 Use centimeter cubes to make prisms A and B. Combine them to form a solid that has a different shape from solid C. What is the volume of the new solid?

Show What You Know!

Build the prisms shown in each row of Table B. Then, combine prisms A and B to make a solid C. Sketch solid C. Copy and complete the table.

Table B

1.

Prism A	Prism B	Solid C
Volume: 8 units	Volume: 5 units	? Volume: 13 units

2.

Prism A	Prism B	Solid C
Volume: 8 units	Volume: 9 units	? Volume: 17 units

3. **Number Sense** Why is the volume of solid C in exercise 2 greater than in exercise 1?

4. Use centimeter cubes to make solid D shown. Separate the solid into two prisms.
   a. What is the volume of each prism?
   b. What is the volume of solid D?

D

Find each volume. The small cubes are each 1 cm³. You may wish to build each solid using centimeter cubes.

5.

6.

7. **Critical Thinking** What do you know about the volume of all solids built using 50 centimeter cubes?

8. **Critical Thinking** How can you use what you know about the volume of a rectangular prism to find the volume of another solid?

Mixed Review

Write the answer.

9. $38.66 + 52.87$ 10. $62.36 - 47.27$ 11. $420.79 + 219$ 12. $203 - 98.91$

13. 2.125×4 14. $18.81 \div 9$ 15. 4.51×0.6 16. $0.16 \div 4$

Problem Solving

Using Strategies

LESSON 10

You can read about chocolate in the pages of *National Geographic World*.

An average person in the United States consumes over eleven pounds of chocolate in a year. It takes about 400 cacao beans to make one pound of chocolate. Cacao beans are shipped in huge sacks from African and South American countries to plants in the United States.

Problem Solving Process
✓ Understand
✓ Plan
✓ Try It
✓ Look Back

Choose a Strategy You Have Learned
✓ Make a Table
✓ Act It Out
✓ Guess and Check
✓ Look for a Pattern
✓ Work Backward
✓ Make a List
✓ Work a Simpler Problem
✓ Draw a Picture
✓ Write an Equation

Suppose sacks of cacao beans are stored flat on the floor in a room like the one shown below. The length of the floor on each of the three longest sides is 30 ft. All other floor lengths are 10 ft. How many square feet of floor space are there in the storeroom?

- What question do you have to answer?
- How can drawing a picture help you to solve the problem?
- What lengths will you use to label each side on your picture?
- How can you find the area of each rectangular part?
- How can you find the area of the storeroom?

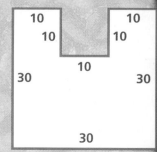

Work It Out!

Use any strategy to solve the problem. Show your work.

1. A cacao bean storeroom in the shape of a rectangle has an area of 680 square ft. If the width of the room is 23 ft less than the length, what are the room's dimensions?

2. If it takes about 400 cacao beans to make 1 lb of chocolate, how many beans are needed to make $12\frac{1}{2}$ lb?

3. Chocolate provides energy. An adult can get enough food energy from 35 chocolate chips to walk 1 mi. Suppose you wanted to walk around Earth, a distance of about 25,000 mi. Suppose you planned to get all your energy from chocolate chips. About how many chips would you have to eat? Explain why this may not be the best way to get your food energy.

4. Chocolate has lots of fat. A 1-oz piece of chocolate may have 6 g of fat. Each gram of fat provides your body with 9 calories. How many calories from fat will you get from a 4-oz chocolate bar?

5. You are told to eat only 35 g of fat a day. If you have 23 g of fat already, can you have a 4-oz candy bar? Explain.

6. Suppose a 50-lb bag of cacao beans has dimensions 2 ft by 4 ft by 1 ft. A 50-cubic ft space is available for storage. Can 6 of the bags be stored in the space? Explain.

7. The fifth, tenth, twentieth, and fortieth visitors to a chocolate plant each receive a gift from the owners of the factory. If the pattern continues, will the sixtieth visitor receive a gift? If not, which visitor will receive the next gift?

8. Cacao beans grow in pods on trees. Pods hold different numbers of beans, from 20 up to 50. Suppose a worker opens the first pod and finds 20 beans. If each pod opened after that contains 5 more beans than the previous pod, how many beans will have been collected after the sixth pod is opened?

9. A sample of 100 pods were opened. 30% had more than 40 beans. 70% contained less than 40 beans, but more than 20. If 45 pods had between 31 and 40 beans, how many pods have 30 or fewer?

Chapter 13 Test

for Pages 432–455

Test-Taking Tips
After you build a model, reread the problem to be sure the model matches the description.

Problem Solving

Solve. Show your work. (pages 438, 454)

1. Martina designed her vegetable garden using these plans.

   • The garden will be in two rectangles, the smaller of which is square.
   • One side of the square runs along the short side of the rectangle.
   • She needs 18 feet of fence for the other three sides of the square.
   • She needs 62 feet of fence for the entire garden.

   Show two possible plans for the garden. What will be the total area?

2. Route 66 crosses much of the United States from Chicago to Los Angeles. Among the cities you pass as you drive west from Chicago are Albuquerque, St. Louis, Oklahoma City, and Tulsa. Albuquerque is closest to Los Angeles. Oklahoma City is between Tulsa and Albuquerque. The first city you pass is St. Louis. In what order do you pass these cities driving from Chicago to Los Angeles?

3. The driving distance between Chicago and St. Louis is 313 miles. From St. Louis to Los Angeles is another 1864 miles. From Los Angeles to Albuquerque is 814 miles. What is the driving distance between St. Louis and Albuquerque?

Concepts

You want to describe a solid to your partner so that she can tell whether it is a prism or a pyramid. (page 446)

4. What can you say about the number of bases to help her decide?

5. What can you say about the faces to help her decide?

You have 12 centimeter cubes with which to construct a figure.
(pages 448, 450, 452)

6. Describe how you would construct a figure to have the greatest possible surface area.

7. If you use all 12 cubes, what will be the volume of the figure?

Choose the correct area for the figure. Write a, b, c, or d. (pages 434, 440)

8. a rectangle *ABCD* in which side *AB* is 7 cm and side *BC* is 5 cm
   a. 12 cm²   b. 35 cm²   c. 24 cm²   d. 49 cm²

9. a right triangle in which the height is 8 cm and the base is 6 cm
   a. 24 cm²   b. 48 cm²   c. 20 cm²   d. 48 cm²

Find the surface area of each figure. Each small square is 1 cm². (page 448)

10.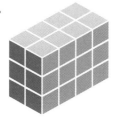

11.

12.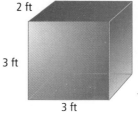
2 ft
3 ft
3 ft

Find the volume. Give your answer in cubic units. (page 450)

13.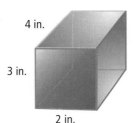
4 in.
3 in.
2 in.

14.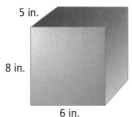
5 in.
8 in.
6 in.

15.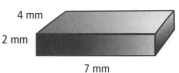
4 mm
2 mm
7 mm

16. Find the volume of a cube if the surface area of each face is 4 cm².

📁 Performance Task

(pages 446, 448, 450, 452)

Use blocks or interlocking cubes to build two different rectangular prisms that have the same volume.

- Be sure the prisms have different dimensions.

- Show how you calculate the volume of each prism.

- Explain how two solids can have different dimensions but the same volume.

Keep In Mind . . .
Your work will be evaluated on the following:

☑ Different dimensions

☑ Same volume

☑ Correct calculations

☑ Clear explanation

Cumulative Review

Estimate Products (Chapter 6)

Estimate 5 × $5.27.

Here's A Way!

Round down to find a low estimate.
5 × $5 = $25
Round up to find a high estimate.
5 × $6 = $30
The actual product will be between the two estimates.

Write the missing number.

1. 8 × $3.84 Estimate: between $24 and ■

2. 4 × 3.6 Estimate: between ■ and 16

3. 9 × $1.15 Estimate: between ■ and ■

4. 6 × 7.35 Estimate: between ■ and ■

5. Could you buy 5 pairs of socks with $15 if each pair costs $2.59? Explain.

Order Fractions (Chapter 9)

Write the numbers in order from least to greatest. $\frac{5}{8}$ $\frac{1}{4}$ $\frac{1}{2}$

Here's A Way!

Find the least common denominator. Write equivalent fractions.

$\frac{5}{8} = \frac{5}{8}$ $\frac{1}{4} = \frac{2}{8}$ $\frac{1}{2} = \frac{4}{8}$

Compare numerators to order.

$\frac{2}{8} < \frac{4}{8} < \frac{5}{8}$ so $\frac{1}{4} < \frac{1}{2} < \frac{5}{8}$

Order the numbers from least to greatest.

6. $\frac{1}{2}$ $\frac{2}{5}$ $\frac{7}{10}$

7. $\frac{11}{12}$ $\frac{7}{12}$ $\frac{5}{12}$

8. $\frac{7}{8}$ $\frac{5}{6}$ $\frac{1}{6}$

9. $2\frac{1}{4}$ $3\frac{11}{12}$ $1\frac{5}{6}$

10. $5\frac{2}{3}$ $5\frac{2}{9}$ $6\frac{1}{6}$

11. $\frac{1}{5}$ $\frac{3}{10}$ $\frac{7}{20}$

12. Compare $\frac{7}{20}$ and $\frac{7}{15}$. How could you find the answer without finding the least common denominator?

Multiply Fractions (Chapter 11)

Find $\frac{2}{3} × 10$.

Here's A Way!

Rename the whole number. $\frac{2}{3} × \frac{10}{1}$

Multiply numerators and denominators. $\frac{2}{3} × \frac{10}{1} = \frac{20}{3}$

Simplify. $\frac{20}{3} = 6\frac{2}{3}$

Write the products in simplest form.

13. $6 × \frac{1}{9}$

14. $\frac{2}{7} × 15$

15. $\frac{3}{4} × 36$

16. $50 × \frac{1}{6}$

17. $30 × \frac{3}{5}$

18. $\frac{3}{7} × 14$

19. Without multiplying, tell which product is greater: $\frac{1}{5} × 27$ or $\frac{1}{6} × 27$. Why?

Equal Ratios (Chapter 12)

Find the missing number: $\frac{5}{6} = \frac{\blacksquare}{30}$

Find the missing number in the ratio by writing an equivalent fraction.
Think: $30 \div 6 = 5$, so multiply by 5.

$$\frac{5}{6} = \frac{5 \times 5}{6 \times 5} = \frac{25}{30}$$

Write the missing number of the equal ratios.

20. 4 to 5 is the same as 40 to $\blacksquare$

21. 18 to 3 is equal to $\blacksquare$ to 1

22. $\frac{5}{20} = \frac{1}{\blacksquare}$

23. $\frac{8}{16} = \frac{\blacksquare}{2}$

24. $\frac{2}{\blacksquare} = \frac{4}{10}$

25. $\frac{\blacksquare}{14} = \frac{8}{28}$

26. Explain how you found the equal ratio in exercise 22.

Area (Chapter 13)

Find the area of the rectangle.

8 cm

14 cm

Write the formula for finding the area of a rectangle.
$A = l \times w$
Substitute the length and the width:
$A = 14 \text{ cm} \cdot 8 \text{ cm}$
Multiply: $A = 112 \text{ cm}^2$

Write the area of each rectangle. Remember to use square units in your answer.

27. length = 7 in.   width = 3 in.

28. length = 2.1 m   width = 5 m

29. length = 10 ft   width = 15 ft

30. length = 9.4 km   width = 3.6 km

31. Which would have the greater area, a square that measures 12 in. on a side or a rectangle that measures 10 in. by 14 in.? Explain.

Problem Solving

Problem Solving Process
- ✓ Understand
- ✓ Plan
- ✓ Try It
- ✓ Look Back

Choose a Strategy You Have Learned
- ✓ Make a Table
- ✓ Act It Out
- ✓ Guess and Check
- ✓ Look for a Pattern
- ✓ Work Backward
- ✓ Make a List
- ✓ Work a Simpler Problem
- ✓ Draw a Picture
- ✓ Write an Equation

Choose one of the strategies you know to solve these problems. Show your work.

32. Suppose you want to put in a brick walkway and patio. The walkway is to be 2 ft wide and 20 ft long. The patio area is to be 8 ft². What is the total area that will be covered in brick?

33. A bulletin board is 6 ft by 9 ft. Could you cover the bulletin board with 60 sheets of 10 in. by 12 in. construction paper? Explain.

Packaging Inventions

Consumer Connection | With Your Group

The tea bag is possibly one of the world's most creative packaging ideas. It was invented in 1904 by Thomas Sullivan, a New York businessman. He put samples of tea in small silk bags and sent them to customers. His customers found the tea bags easy to use and less expensive than loose tea.

Your group will create a way to package items of an unusual shape. Decide what package design you will use for your product. The design must fit the package pattern on the next page. Work together to complete the project.

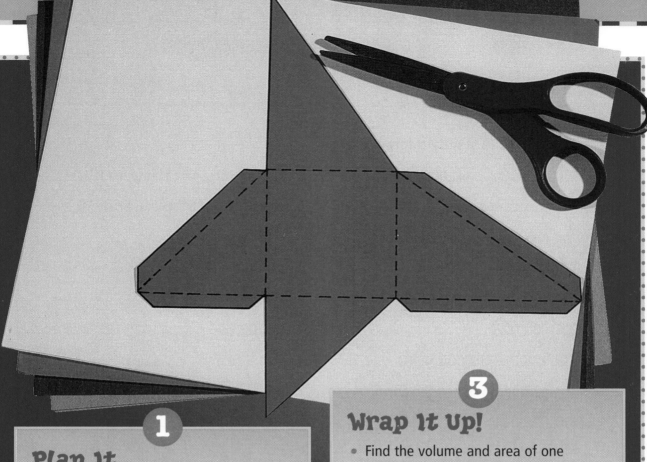

1

Plan It

- Trace the package pattern above on a piece of tracing paper. Lay the tracing paper on a piece of poster board.

- Trace the lines, pressing down hard so the outline of the pattern can be seen. Cut out the pattern.

2

Put It Together

- Use the pattern to make 30 square pyramids. Draw your design on the patterns before cutting them out.

- Fold the pyramids on the dotted lines. Tape the sides together.

- The pyramids will be sold in packages of three. Find a way to put together three pyramids for shipping.

3

Wrap It Up!

- Find the volume and area of one package of three. Find the size of the container you will need to ship ten packages without space left over. Make the container out of poster board.

- Write a paragraph explaining why your packaging idea is a good one.

4

Discuss Your Results

- Did you complete the items listed in Keep In Mind?

- How would you present your packaging idea to a company selling the product?

Internet

> Visit the **Math Center** at **Houghton Mifflin Education Place.** http://www.eduplace.com

461

More Practice

Set 1.2   Use with pages 4–5.

Write the number in standard form.

1. 700,000,000 + 60,000 + 400 + 5   2. 392 billion, 474 thousand, 103

3. 508 thousand, 22   4. 81 million, 666 thousand, 10

Write the number in short word form.

5. 9,000,240   6. 14, 001

7. 200,000 + 60,000 + 4000 + 300 + 50

8. 606,700,028   9. 20,003,800

10. 1,000,000 + 10,000 + 10

Write the number in expanded form.

11. 500,672,000

12. 3,034,090

13. 207,508,119

14. 9,073,824,035

15. 85,000

16. 4,001,000,763

Set 1.3   Use with pages 6–7.

Add or subtract. Use mental math.

1. 30 + 70   2. 2000 + 200   3. 610 + 100   4. 500 − 100

5. 2600 − 300   6. 860 − 400   7. 9000 − 2000   8. 600 + 290

9. 340 + 30   10. 500 + 900   11. 740 + 50   12. 1400 − 500

Set 1.5   Use with pages 10–11.

Write your estimate. Remember to adjust.

1. 3125 + 791 + 1239   2. $72.15 + $31.27 + $14.32

3. $1.90 + $1.70 + $1.30   4. 429 + 37 + 985

Estimate. Write < or >.

5. 135 + 792 ● 900

6. $71.63 + $7.992 ● $80.00

7. 9987 + 4250 ● 15,000

8. 625 + 713 + 8372 ● 2100

9. $12.97 + $7.042 ● $19.00

10. 7282 + 2822 ● 7500

Set 1.6   Use with pages 12–13. ●●●●●●●●●●●●●●●●●●●●●●●●●●●●●●●●●●●●●●

Write the letter of the closer estimate.

1.	872	2.	$79.81	3.	52,157	4.	8823
	− 365		− 3.05		− 7,385		− 5317

a. 500   a. $75   a. 50,000   a. 3500
b. 550   b. $80   b. 45,000   b. 3000

Estimate. Which two numbers in the box below have a difference of:

5. about 8000?

6. about 200?

7. about 850?

8. about 3900?

9217		1123
	274	
913		4812

Which number is a reasonable estimate? Write a or b.

9. 8591 − 384
   a. 8200
   b. 5000

10. $72.29 − $3.31
   a. $40.00
   b. $70.00

Set 1.7   Use with pages 14–15. ●●●●●●●●●●●●●●●●●●●●●●●●●●●●●●●●●●●●●●

Write the answer.

1.	2067	2.	500,005	3.	4603	4.	23, 061	5.	21,117
	+ 1876		− 497,206		− 2815		− 2,909		+ 2,227

6.	3004	7.	$12.70	8.	6103	9.	47,192	10.	808,615
	+ 1299		− 3.59		− 47		+ 31,050		+ 103,276

11. 46 lb 5 oz + 13 lb 4 oz

12. 18 min 14 s + 14 min 18 s

13. $72.48 + $50.03 + $10.61

14. 6715 + 283 + 14,409

Set 1.9   Use with pages 18.

Write the sum. Use mental math.

1. 13 + 18
2. 67 + 19
3. 32 + 37
4. 11 + 65
5. 28 + 52
6. $36 + $12
7. $41 + $16
8. 24 + 25
9. 72 + 21
10. 87 + 12
11. 18 ft + 52 ft
12. 16 yd + 66 yd
13. 47 + 47
14. 31 cm + 66 cm
15. 22 + 33
16. $13 + $29

Set 1.12   Use with pages 26–27.

Write the value of the underlined digit.

1. 7.0<u>3</u>5
2. 4.81<u>5</u>
3. 6.<u>2</u>02
4. 1.89<u>1</u>
5. 21.<u>1</u>2
6. 3.70<u>2</u>
7. <u>5</u>.991
8. 7.3<u>6</u>2

Write the word form of each decimal.

9. 505.55
10. 2.801
11. 3.6
12. 0.035

Write an equivalent decimal.

13. 7.01
14. 3.50
15. 6.020
16. 54.88
17. 5.600
18. 4.9
19. 101.01
20. 1.7

Set 1.13   Use with pages 28–29.

Compare. Write >, <, or =.

1. 379 ● 401
2. 6.02 ● 6.20
3. 5.05 ● 5.050
4. 8279 ● 8218
5. 0.81 ● 0.809
6. 7.530 ● 7.53
7. 0.406 ● 0.460
8. 0.37 ● 0.37

Order the numbers from least to greatest.

9. 6.06, 6.60, 0.660, 0.606
10. 0.520, 0.502, 0.25, 0.200
11. 470, 469, 407, 469.001
12. 9.82, 2.99, 9.88, 8.92
13. 0.9, 0.851, 0.87, 0.859
14. 3200, 3020, 3002.9, 900

Use with pages 30–31. •

Round each number to the greatest place.

1. 3.81   2. 72.63   3. 1.47   4. 24.09   5. 1.609

6. 43   7. 375   8. 252   9. 1099   10. 6742

Round each number to the nearest hundred.

11. 415   12. 149   13. 152   14. 6511   15. 1448

16. 9185   17. 7777   18. 4601   19. 2138   20. 23,380

Use with pages 34–35. •

Write the sum.

1.   0.902   2.   1787.35   3. $28.75   4.   9.206   5.   3.751
   + 0.408   +   65.31   +   3.55   + 0.88   + 1.647

6. 7.42 mg + 10.071 mg + 58.609 mg

7. $2008.42 + $0.97 + $5113.26

8. $412 + $623.50

9. 70.5 cm + 56.2 cm + 30.8 cm

Use with pages 36–37. •

Write the difference.

1.   6.711   2.   3450.00   3.   96.2 cm   4. $502.15
   − 6.007   − 983.76   − 70.5 cm   − 102.45

5.   24.18   6.   0.509   7.   48.000   8.   15.111
   − 8.10   − 0.059   − 0.692   − 2.747

9.   0.37   10.   3.4 m   11.   1536.014   12.   0.090
   − 0.06   − 1.6 m   − 827.900   − 0.009

13. 0.8 − 0.463   14. 270.01 − 53.5   15. 6.9 − 4.217

16. 27.095 − 0.095   17. $400 − $89.99   18. 303.01 − 300.03

Use with pages 38–39. •••

Write the difference. Use mental math.

1. 70 − 19   2. 60 − 39   3. 8 − 4.9   4. $1.00 − $0.89

5. 300 − 99   6. $12.00 − $1.99   7. 87 − 79   8. 977 − 299

9. 700 ft − 399 ft   10. 7 − 3.8   11. 614 − 499   12. 81 − 29

13. $2.17 − $1.99   14. 7928 − 999   15. 14 − 2.9   16. $50.00 − $29.99

Use with pages 48–49. •••

Write the value of each expression.

1. What is $r + 4$ if $r = 3$; if $r = 77$?   2. What is $d + 40$ if $d = 10$; if $d = 15$?

3. What is $m − 2$ if $m = 8$; if $m = 12$?   4. What is $y − 0$ if $y = 10$; if $y = 23$?

5. What is $b + \frac{1}{4}$ if $b = 1$; if $b = 13$ 6. What is $30 − c$ if $c = 15$; if $c = 20$?

Use with pages 50–51. •••

Copy and complete each table.

1. To write years as months, multiply the number of years (y) by 12.

Years (y)	Number of Months ($12 \cdot y$)
3	3 · 12 or ▓
7	▓ or ▓
0	▓ or ▓

2. To write pounds as ounces, multiply the number of pounds (p) by 16.

Pounds (p)	Number of Ounces ($16 \cdot p$)
2	2 · 16 or ▓
4	▓ or ▓
6	▓ or ▓

3. To write hours as minutes, multiply the number of hours (*h*) by 60.

Hours (*h*)	Number of Minutes (60 · *h*)
1	1 · 60 or ▦
5	▦ or ▦
3	▦ or ▦

4. To write yards as feet, multiply the number of yards (*y*) by 3.

Yards (*y*)	Number of Feet (3 · *y*)
13	13 · 3 or ▦
19	▦ or ▦
0	▦ or ▦

Set 2.3 Use with pages 52–53. •

Write the first two common multiples.

1. 3, 12

2. 3, 6

3. 5, 10

4. 7, 4

5. 6, 20

6. 6, 15

7. 2, 6, 21

8. 3, 5, 6

Write the least common multiple.

9. 3, 9

10. 4, 5

11. 2, 12

12. 6, 8

13. 8, 10

14. 2, 17

15. 4, 5, 6

16. 7, 9

17. 12, 18

18. 2, 4, 12

19. 3, 8, 16

20. 10, 15, 40

Set 2.4 Use with pages 54–55. •

Write the product. Use mental math.

1. 4×700

2. 300×6

3. 50×80

4. 30×30

5. 20×900

6. 600×90

7. $6 \times 2 \times 5$

8. $5 \times 3 \times 8$

9. $4 \times 5 \times 7$

Solve. Use mental math.

10. $5 \cdot f = 45$

11. $k \times 7 = 21$

12. $v \cdot 6 = 60$

13. $x \cdot 9 = 81$

14. $p \times 9 = 63$

15. $c \times 9 = 54$

16. $l \times 4 = 36$

17. $10 \times s = 70$

Set 2.5 Use with pages 56–57.

Write your estimate.

1. 22 × 27
2. 8 × 27
3. 88 × 3
4. 26 × 16
5. 909 × 4
6. 615 × 6
7. 274 × 5
8. 7 × 263

Set 2.7 Use with pages 62–63.

1. $1.46
   × 4
2. 97 in.
   × 8
3. 823
   × 5
4. 61 km
   × 2
5. 46
   × 6

6. 7 × 321 mL
7. 9 × 45
8. 3 × 39
9. 6 × 125
10. 97 × 5
11. $8.12 × 3
12. 64 × 9
13. 444 × 4

Complete.

14. 384 × 7 = (300 × ■) + (84 × ■)
15. 3 × 609 = (■ × 600) + (■ × 9)
16. 2 × 1083 = (2 × ■) + (■ × 83)
17. 412 × 6 = (400 × ■) + (12 × ■)

Set 2.8 Use with pages 64–65.

Complete. Write >, <, or =.

1. 40 · 5 ● 70 × 2
2. 70 × 7 ● 5 × 8
3. 4 × 60 ● 90 × 3
4. 12 × 5 ● 30 × 2
5. 4 × 60 ● 50 × 5
6. 50 × 10 ● 100 × 5

Write the product.

7. 38
   × 62
8. $4.04
   × 13
9. 27 m
   × 47
10. 28
   × 15
11. 73
   × 82

12. 276
   × 85
13. 79
   × 79
14. 653
   × 48
15. 807
   × 74
16. 119
   × 36

17. 17 × 384
18. $9.50 × 61
19. 19 × 80
20. 80 × 19

Use with pages 68–69. •••

Write the product.

1. 503	2. 716	3. 423	4. 609	5. 250 m
× 824	× 950	× 324	× 871	× 100

6. $2.97	7. 805	8. 737	9. 516	10. 467
× 455	× 369	× 104	× 927	× 432

11. 214 × 108   12. 367 × 525

13. 707 × 941   14. 824 × 673

Use with pages 72–73. •••

Write the product. Use mental math.

1. 3 × 99   2. 5 × 99   3. 9 × 99   4. 8 × $0.99

5. 4 × 199   6. 4 × $1.99   7. 2 × 39   8. 3 × 39

9. 4 × $0.39   10. 2 × $0.19   11. 4 × $0.19   12. 4 × 29

Use with pages 82–83. •••

Copy and complete each chart.

1. To write the number of millimeters as centimeters, divide the number of millimeters (t) by 10.

Millimeters (t)	Number of Centimeters ($\frac{t}{10}$)
10	$\frac{10}{10}$, or ▦
20	▦, or ▦
40	▦, or ▦

2. To write the number of cups as pints, divide the number of cups (b) by 2.

Cups (b)	Number of Pints ($\frac{b}{2}$)
4	$\frac{4}{2}$, or ▦
12	▦, or ▦
20	▦, or ▦

Use with pages 84–85.

Choose the compatible numbers. Write a, b, or c.

1. 352 ÷ 6
   a. 350 ÷ 6
   b. 360 ÷ 6
   c. 340 ÷ 6

2. 7)2713
   a. 7)2800
   b. 7)2700
   c. 7)3000

3. 8)727
   a. 8)720
   b. 8)730
   c. 8)740

4. 1543 ÷ 8
   a. 1500 ÷ 8
   b. 1550 ÷ 8
   c. 1600 ÷ 8

Write your estimate.

5. 4)175   6. 7)370   7. 3)162   8. 9)251

9. 1723 ÷ 2   10. 8614 ÷ 9   11. 17,912 ÷ 5   12. 47,534 ÷ 8

Set 3.3 **Use with pages 86–87.**

Write the answer.

1. 4)57   2. 5)57   3. 7)298   4. 3)374   5. 2)44

6. 4)187   7. 9)735   8. 6)52   9. 4)35   10. 8)256

11. 7)301   12. 3)994   13. 50)565   14. 9)382   15. 7)86

16. 688 ÷ 8   17. 69 ÷ 4   18. 57 ÷ 2

19. 434 ÷ 7   20. 87 ÷ 3   21. 608 ÷ 7

Set 3.4 **Use with pages 88–89.**

Write the answer.

1. 4)83   2. 5)530   3. 2)181   4. 3)610

5. 3)122   6. 8)7920   7. 6)5943   8. 7)3605

9. 5)2005   10. 3)4829   11. 9)46,302   12. 4)20,206

13. 9160 ÷ 4   14. 45,031 ÷ 6   15. 27,090 ÷ 7

16. $\frac{95}{3}$ 17. $\frac{98}{4}$ 18. $\frac{130}{5}$

Use with pages 96–97. •

Write the quotient.

1. $30\overline{)90}$ 2. $40\overline{)800}$ 3. $20\overline{)8000}$ 4. $60\overline{)4200}$

5. $3\overline{)21,000}$ 6. $400\overline{)1600}$ 7. $80\overline{)4000}$ 8. $9\overline{)540}$

9. $900 \div 30$ 10. $6300 \div 700$ 11. $12,000 \div 20$ 12. $1000 \div 50$

Set 3.8   Use with pages 98–99. •

Choose the reasonable estimate. Write a, b, or c.

1. $9\overline{)43,791}$
   a. 50   b. 500   c. 5000

2. $47\overline{)3279}$
   a. 7   b. 70   c. 700

3. $\$7328 \div 81$
   a. $90   b. $900   c. $9000

4. $2931 \div 7$
   a. 4   b. 40   c. 400

Write your estimate.

5. $7\overline{)457}$ 6. $2\overline{)739}$ 7. $69\overline{)3219}$ 8. $37\overline{)1632}$

9. $222 \div 61$ 10. $979 \div 40$ 11. $7415 \div 89$ 12. $33,125 \div 78$

Set 3.9   Use with pages 100–101. •

Write the answer.

1. $27\overline{)77}$ 2. $36\overline{)82}$ 3. $12\overline{)39}$ 4. $21\overline{)57}$

5. $18\overline{)99}$ 6. $13\overline{)259}$ 7. $34\overline{)714}$ 8. $77\overline{)982}$

9. $91 \div 11$ 10. $364 \div 28$ 11. $910 \div 35$ 12. $637 \div 9$

13. $129 \div 12$ 14. $512 \div 16$ 15. $423 \div 17$ 16. $976 \div 8$

Use with pages 102–103. •

Write the quotient.

1. 30)816   2. 15)467   3. 49)1000   4. 62)9052

5. 29)794   6. 56)8288   7. 90)277   8. 38)2651

9. 81)6006   10. 3)1352   11. 27)6918   12. 5)3497

13. 69)5427   14. 9)40,400   15. 86)3612   16. 93)92,535

17. 902 ÷ 22   18. 602 ÷ 74   19. 5183 ÷ 68

20. 1220 ÷ 59   21. 4212 ÷ 36   22. 38,612 ÷ 17

Use with pages 104–105. •

Write the answer.

1. 7 + 12 − 2   2. 18 − 9 + 7   3. 12 ÷ 4 × 6

4. 11 + 4 × 2   5. 6 + 10 ÷ 5   6. 15 − 4 ÷ 2 × 3

7. 27 − (16 + 3)   8. 13 + (7 − 6)   9. (5 + 7) ÷ 6

10. (7 × 9) ÷ 9   11. 1 + (3 × 4) + 1   12. 27 ÷ (3 × 3) − 3

Use with pages 108–109. •

Write the factors of each number.

1. 8   2. 50   3. 27   4. 16

5. 9   6. 24   7. 34   8. 35

9. 49   10. 42   11. 56   12. 17

Write the greatest common factor for each set of numbers.

13. 8, 50   14. 8, 16   15. 9, 24   16. 17, 34

17. 35, 49   18. 50, 56   19. 42, 24   20. 42, 56

Complete the factoring.

1.

2.

3.

4.
54
/ \
6 x ⬜
/ | | \
⬜ x ⬜ x ⬜ x ⬜

Write the prime factorization. Use a factor tree.

5. 15   6. 8   7. 32   8. 21

9. 64   10. 42   11. 36   12. 60

13. 56   14. 30   15. 80   16. 28

Solve each problem.

1. $13 \times 5 \times 4$ 2. $30 \times 4 \div 2$ 3. $306 \div 18$ 4. $1085 \div 31$

5. $200 \div 40$ 6. 376×9357 7. $5185 \div 305$ 8. $185 + 17 \times 4$

9. School children organized a giant poster display of the Milky Way. They bought star stickers that came 12 stars to a sheet. How many stars did they get from 75 sheets?

10. The poster project started with 273 children. The project was completed by 310 children. How many children were added to the project?

Write the mean and range, and the mode if possible for each. You may use a calculator.

1. Ages: 28 yr, 35 yr, 33 yr, 37 yr, 38 yr, 33 yr

2. January temperatures (°F): 8°, 10°, 8°, 1°, 2°, 8°, 12°

3. Number of points scored, 12, 17, 10, 1, 20, 13, 25

4. August temperatures (°F): 96°, 98°, 96°, 96°, 99°, 91°

5. Number of students: 23, 25, 25, 25, 27

6. Number of pages read: 101, 51, 44, 39, 103, 111, 59, 44

7. Basketball player heights: 71 in., 71 in., 78 in., 76 in., 79 in.

8. Number of miles driven: 6 mi, 5 mi, 27 mi, 18 mi, 34 mi, 91 mi, 1 mi

Use with pages 128–129. •••••••••••••••••••••••••••••••

Order the numbers from least to greatest. Write the median, mean, and range.

1. Number of people: 106, 114, 149, 125, 101

2. Temperatures across region (°F): 47°, 44°, 43°, 47°, 44°

3. Pet weights: 3 lb, 25 lb, 15 lb, 16 lb, 3 lb, 29 lb, 14 lb

4. Jacket prices: $63, $50, $49, $71, $57, $55, $32, $90, $73

Set 4.5 **Use with pages 134–135.** •••••••••••••••••••••••••••••••

Write the answer. Use estimation.

1. About how many puppets were sold in 1990? 1992?

2. In which years were more than 300 puppets sold?

3. In which year were about 475 puppets sold?

4. About how many more puppets were sold in 1993 than in 1990?

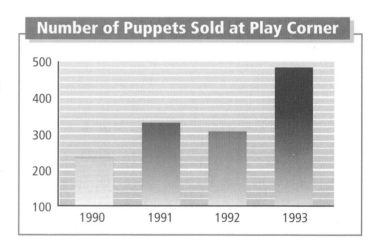

Number of Puppets Sold at Play Corner

Set 4.6 **Use with pages 136–137.** •••••••••••••••••••••••••••••••

1. Use squared paper. Make a line graph that shows the population changes in Jeffersonville.

Population of Jeffersonville

Year	1987	1988	1989	1990	1991	1992
Population	1200	1400	1500	1700	1700	2100

Use your line graph to answer each question.

2. Between which two years did the population change the most?

3. What do you think will happen to the population of Jeffersonville over the next few years?

Use one of the graphs to answer each question.

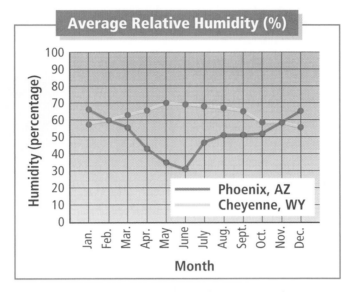

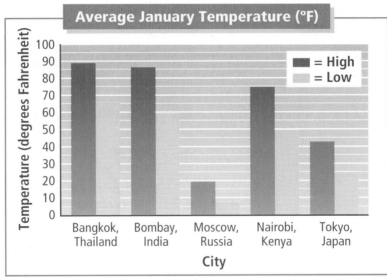

1. Which city has the highest average humidity in December? In April?

2. In which month did Cheyenne and Phoenix have the greatest difference in humidity?

3. In which 2 months did the two cities have about the same amount of humidity?

4. Which city has the highest average temperature in January? The lowest?

5. Which city has the smallest range between high and low temperature in January?

6. Which two cities have about the same high and low temperatures?

Use the graph to answer each question.

1. How many students prefer either water, soda, or milk?

2. What fraction of the students prefer juice?

3. Do more than half of the students prefer either milk or water?

4. What fraction represents the number of students who prefer milk or "other"?

Favorite Drinks

Other 3 | Water 2 | Juice 5 | Milk 7 | Soda 3

Estimate the length of each leaf to the nearest inch and then measure.

1.

2.

Estimate the length of each object to the nearest $\frac{1}{2}$ inch and then measure.

3.

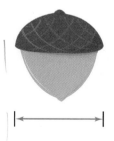

4.

Measure each object to the nearest $\frac{1}{4}$ inch and then to the nearest $\frac{1}{8}$ inch.

5.

6.

7.

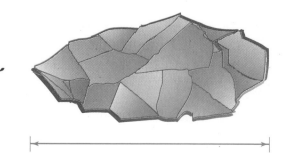

Write the perimeter.

1.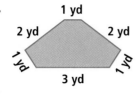
   1 yd
   2 yd   2 yd
   1 yd   1 yd
   3 yd

2.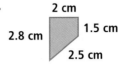
   1 in.
   4 in.   4 in.
   1 in.

3.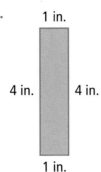
   2 cm
   1.5 cm
   2.8 cm
   2.5 cm

4. Rectangular pool:
   length = 25 m
   width = 10 m

5. Square wrestling mat:
   side = 34 ft

6. Rectangle:
   length = 15 ft
   width = 11 ft

7. Square:
   side = 12.5 cm

8. Rectangle:
   length = 16.3 m
   width = 4.7 m

9. Square:
   side = 5.25 m

10. Triangular garden:
    Each side = 9 ft

11. Triangle:
    sides = 4.7 cm, 8 cm, 9.3 cm

Write how much time will pass.

1. from 1:15 P.M. to 4:20 P.M.

2. from 7:45 A.M. to 10:12 A.M.

3. from 11:00 A.M. to 4:30 P.M.

4. from 8:10 P.M. to 2:45 A.M.

5. from 10:53 P.M. to 1:05 A.M.

6. from 9:14 A.M. to 2:35 P.M.

7. from 3:30 P.M. to 11:20 P.M.

8. from 9:15 P.M. to 12:47 A.M.

9. 25 h 9 min
    + 11 h 7 min

10. 10 h 17 min
    + 6 h 12 min

11. 47 min 25 s
    − 16 min 19 s

12. 17 h 8 min
    + 7 h 5 min

13. 30 min 45 s
    − 18 min 31 s

14. 16 min 23 s
    + 16 min 25 s

Use with pages 180–181. ●●●●●●●●●●●●●●●●●●●●●●●●●●●●●●●●●

Copy and complete. What time is it in the other three cities?

Washington, D.C.	St. Louis	Denver	Portland
3:30 P.M.	2:30 P.M.	1:30 P.M.	12:30 P.M.
12:45 A.M.	?	?	?
?	?	4:10 P.M.	?
?	1:00 P.M.	?	?
?	?	?	4:18 P.M.

Use with pages 184–185. ●●●●●●●●●●●●●●●●●●●●●●●●●●●●●●●●●

Write the letter of the more reasonable temperature.

1. a heated swimming pool.
   a. 25°C   b. 25°F

2. an office
   a. 68°F   b. 20°F

3. an ice cube
   a. 32°C   b. 32°F

4. a mug of hot cocoa
   a. 50°C   b. 15°C

5. a cup of warm cider
   a. 50°C   b. 15°C

6. a snowball
   a. 0°C   b. 50°F

Use with pages 200–201. ●●●●●●●●●●●●●●●●●●●●●●●●●●●●●●●●●

Write the missing number.

1. 4 × $6.25 Estimate: between $24 and $▓

2. 6 × $3.89 Estimate: between $▓ and $24

3. 3 × $9.15 Estimate: between $▓ and $▓

4. 2 × 7.6 Estimate: between ▓ and ▓

5. 5 × 8.2 Estimate: between ▓ and ▓

6. 3 × 4.72 Estimate: between ▓ and ▓

Write the product.

1. 11.3 $\times$ 5	2. 46.1 $\times$ 2	3. 2.9 $\times$ 6	4. 76.5 $\times$ 3
5. 3.8 $\times$ 3	6. 25.6 $\times$ 8	7. 55.5 $\times$ 9	8. 61.2 $\times$ 5
9. 89.4 $\times$ 7	10. 7.3 $\times$ 3	11. 48.6 $\times$ 4	12. 37.9 $\times$ 2
13. 22.6 $\times$ 5	14. 54.1 $\times$ 6	15. 9.1 $\times$ 7	16. 1.2 $\times$ 8

17. 6.5×2 18. 4.8×3 19. 31.3×9

20. 31.7×8 21. 94.2×6 22. 53.5×4

23. 8.4×5 24. 72.6×2 25. 28.1×7

Write the product.

1. 3.06 $\times$ 4	2. 0.05 $\times$ 9	3. 1.03 $\times$ 5	4. 2.07 $\times$ 1
5. 0.002 $\times$ 7	6. 1.08 $\times$ 0	7. 6 $\times$ 0.08	8. 3.02 $\times$ 5
9. 8.09 $\times$ 6	10. 0.046 $\times$ 2	11. 7.004 $\times$ 9	12. 0.05 $\times$ 4

13. 5.03×4 14. 0.09×7 15. 12.08×5 16. 4.06×3

17. 0.027×5 18. 3.01×9 19. 0.05×8 20. 1.07×2

Solve each problem. Write whether you estimated or computed the exact answer.

1. A greeting card costs $1.39. Is $5.00 enough to buy 4 of them?

2. Sally reads 2 books a week. How many will she read in one year? (Hint: There are 52 weeks in a year.)

3. It takes 4 hours for Craig to drive from his house to Long Lake. If he drives an average of 47 miles per hour, how far is it to Long Lake?

4. What is the greatest number of 59¢ erasers that you can buy for $5.00?

Write the product. Round dollar amounts to the nearest cent.

1. 5.7 × 2.3	2. 4.8 × 9.6	3. 25 × 1.2	4. $6.82 × 3.4
5. 8.1 × 10	6. 3.7 × 0.04	7. 29.3 × 6.5	8. 0.7 × 1000
9. 3.51 × 8	10. $6.42 × 1.3	11. 5.09 × 0.7	12. $4.28 × 6.3
13. 0.94 × 4.2	14. 8.77 × 6	15. $0.15 × 2.9	16. 746.9 × 4.5

17. $0.35 × 7.5   18. 0.8 × 0.1   19. 2.9 × 41.5   20. $1.75 × 8

21. $0.75 × 3.6   22. 2.48 × 0.2   23. $33.30 × 100   24. 6.08 × 7

Equivalent Measures of Length

1 centimeter (cm) = 10 millimeters (mm)
1 meter (m) = 1000 millimeters (mm)
1 meter (m) = 100 centimeters (cm)
1 kilometer (km) = 1000 meters (m)

Use the table. Write the letter of the equivalent measure.

1. 81 km a. 810,000 m b. 81,000 m c. 0.081 m

2. 50.301 m a. 50,301 cm b. 503.01 cm c. 5030.1 cm

3. 426 mm a. 0.0426 m b. 4260 m c. 0.426 m

4. 0.38 cm a. 0.0038 mm b. 3800 mm c. 3.8 mm

Complete.

5. 1000 m = 1 ▦

6. 37 cm = ▦ mm

7. 56,022 m = ▦ cm

8. 9.88 km = ▦ m

9. 1.497 cm = ▦ mm

10. 15 mm = ▦ m

Complete. Write >, <, or =.

11. 5730 mm ● 573 m

12. 741 cm ● 7.41 m

13. 0.7 cm ● 6.2 mm

14. 128 km ● 12,000 m

15. 924 mm ● 0.000924 km

16. 0.65 cm ● 0.65 mm

Write the letter of the reasonable estimate. Write a, b, or c.

1. $4.37 ÷ 6
   a. $0.07 b. $0.70 c. $7.00

2. $0.68 ÷ 3
   a. $0.02 b. $0.20 c. $2.00

3. $9.15 ÷ 4
   a. $0.02 b. $0.20 c. $2.00

4. $0.59 ÷ 2
   a. $0.03 b. $0.30 c. $3.00

5. $8.56 ÷ 3
   a. $0.03 b. $0.30 c. $3.00

6. $4.63 ÷ 9
   a. $0.05 b. $0.50 c. $5.00

7. $52.98 ÷ 6
   a. $0.09 b. $0.90 c. $9.00

8. $324.05 ÷ 5
   a. $0.60 b. $6.00 c. $60.00

Write the quotient.

1. 4)36.04   2. 5)$2.80   3. 7)7.49

4. 2)$105.10   5. 6)28.812   6. 9)0.333

7. 4)82.4   8. 8)1.64   9. 8)15.2

10. 3)42.27   11. 5)28.535   12. 4)69.632

13. 9.06 ÷ 3   14. 2.702 ÷ 2   15. $5.88 ÷ 6

16. 66.69 ÷ 9   17. 0.36 ÷ 8   18. 0.735 ÷ 5

Write the quotient.

1. 6)3   2. 4)11   3. 8)$46   4. 5)92   5. 2)79

6. 5)$2   7. 4)38   8. 4)5   9. 6)15   10. 5)3

11. 2)13   12. 5)97   13. 4)29   14. 5)27   15. 6)$87

16. 4)66   17. 8)$38   18. 8)29   19. 5)9   20. 4)86

21. 36 ÷ 8   22. 75 ÷ 6   23. $11 ÷ 2

24. 4 ÷ 5   25. 9 ÷ 4   26. 63 ÷ 8

27. $81 ÷ 6   28. 42 ÷ 5   29. 27 ÷ 6

For the slide shown, copy and complete each statement.

1. △SZI ≅ ▓   2. $\overline{ZI}$ ≅ ▓

3. ∠ZSI ≅ ▓   4. $\overline{PR}$ ≅ ▓

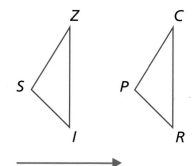

For the flip shown, copy and complete each statement.

5. △DLA ≅ ▢

6. $\overline{LA}$ ≅ ▢

7. $\overline{DL}$ ≅ ▢

8. ▢ ≅ ∠ JYP

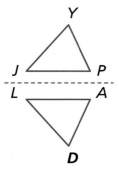

9. On dot paper, draw any triangle *DHY* and its flip image, triangle *JML*, so that $\overline{DY}$ ≅ $\overline{JL}$, $\overline{YH}$ ≅ $\overline{LM}$, and ∠ *HYD* ≅ ∠ *MLJ*.

10. On dot paper, draw any triangle *BFG* and its slide image, triangle *KNQ*, so that $\overline{BF}$ ≅ $\overline{KN}$, $\overline{BG}$ ≅ $\overline{KQ}$, and ∠ *BGF* ≅ ∠ *KQN*.

Set 8.3   **Use with pages 262–263.** •

Draw angles with the following measures. Tell what kind of angle each is. Write acute, obtuse, or right.

1. 120°	2. 45°	3. 160°	4. 60°	5. 75°	6. 105°
7. 15°	8. 140°	9. 170°	10. 100°	11. 90°	12. 70°

Set 8.4   **Use with pages 264–265.** •

Copy each figure onto dot paper. Draw the half-turn image for each figure using the turn center given.

1.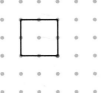

2.

3.

**Copy each figure onto dot paper.
Draw the three-quarter turn image for each using the turn center given.**

4.

5.

6.

Write the ordered pair for the vertex.

1. *K*   2. *B*

3. *P*   4. *R*

5. *L*   6. *D*

Write the vertex for the ordered pair.

7. (6,2)   8. (8,5)

9. (5,5)   10. (8,3)

11. (7,5)   12. (6,6)

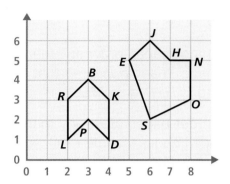

Copy the figure and its grid onto squared paper. Write the ordered pair for each vertex. Multiply the ordered pair of each vertex by 2. Then draw the similar figure.

13.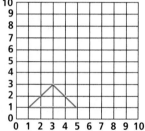

14.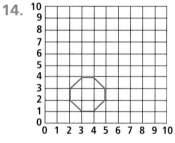

Copy the figure and its grid onto squared paper. Write the ordered pair for each vertex. Divide the ordered pair of each vertex by 2. Then draw the similar figure.

15.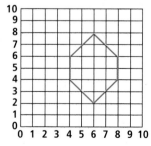

16.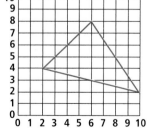

Write the word form and standard form of the fraction that tells what part is shaded.

1.

2.

3.

4.

Write the standard form of each fraction.

5. seven ninths

6. twelve fifteenths

7. one half

8. seven sevenths

9. fourteen sixteenths

10. three fourths

11. six twelfths

12. three twentieths

1. $\frac{6}{12} = \frac{\blacksquare}{4}$

2. $\frac{1}{3} = \frac{\blacksquare}{30}$

3. $\frac{7}{42} = \frac{\blacksquare}{6}$

4. $\frac{5}{5} = \frac{\blacksquare}{15}$

5. $\frac{2}{5} = \frac{8}{\blacksquare}$

6. $\frac{12}{36} = \frac{1}{\blacksquare}$

7. $\frac{16}{20} = \frac{\blacksquare}{5}$

Write an equivalent fraction.

9. $\frac{1}{4}$

10. $\frac{2}{5}$

11. $\frac{3}{8}$

12. $\frac{12}{48}$

13. $\frac{6}{9}$

14. $\frac{32}{36}$

15. $\frac{7}{8}$

16. $\frac{4}{2}$

17. $\frac{5}{50}$

18. $\frac{15}{20}$

19. $\frac{12}{32}$

20. $\frac{1}{2}$

21. $\frac{3}{5}$

22. $\frac{7}{21}$

23. $\frac{20}{25}$

Use with pages 300–301. ••

List the factors for each number. Underline the greatest common factor.

1. 6, 8   2. 25, 35

3. 12, 42   4. 54, 63

5. 10, 100   6. 30, 50

7. 16, 24   8. 7, 21

Write an equivalent fraction that is in simplest form.

9. $\frac{12}{48}$ 10. $\frac{15}{25}$ 11. $\frac{6}{18}$ 12. $\frac{20}{30}$ 13. $\frac{16}{30}$

14. $\frac{24}{30}$ 15. $\frac{3}{30}$ 16. $\frac{36}{40}$ 17. $\frac{9}{12}$ 18. $\frac{12}{24}$

19. $\frac{10}{15}$ 20. $\frac{7}{21}$ 21. $\frac{7}{35}$ 22. $\frac{20}{24}$ 23. $\frac{10}{110}$

Set 9.5   **Use with pages 302–303.** ••

Write whether each fraction is close to 0, $\frac{1}{2}$, or 1.

1. $\frac{1}{10}$ 2. $\frac{7}{12}$ 3. $\frac{13}{12}$ 4. $\frac{21}{100}$ 5. $\frac{6}{25}$

6. $\frac{5}{6}$ 7. $\frac{2}{5}$ 8. $\frac{4}{3}$ 9. $\frac{7}{10}$ 10. $\frac{3}{20}$

11. $\frac{7}{5}$ 12. $\frac{19}{24}$ 13. $\frac{79}{100}$ 14. $\frac{15}{24}$ 15. $\frac{1}{5}$

16. $\frac{6}{13}$ 17. $\frac{28}{31}$ 18. $\frac{2}{19}$ 19. $\frac{63}{70}$ 20. $\frac{26}{50}$

Set 9.8   **Use with pages 310–311.** ••

Write each mixed number as an equivalent fraction.

1. $1\frac{2}{5}$ 2. $6\frac{3}{5}$ 3. $8\frac{1}{2}$ 4. $5\frac{2}{3}$ 5. $3\frac{5}{16}$

6. $4\frac{2}{3}$ 7. $3\frac{1}{8}$ 8. $2\frac{13}{20}$ 9. $6\frac{3}{10}$ 10. $4\frac{1}{4}$

11. $3\frac{3}{8}$ 12. $3\frac{5}{6}$ 13. $5\frac{1}{5}$ 14. $2\frac{1}{12}$ 15. $3\frac{3}{10}$

16. $2\frac{3}{8}$ 17. $6\frac{4}{5}$ 18. $7\frac{2}{3}$ 19. $3\frac{2}{3}$ 20. $3\frac{1}{12}$

Write each fraction as a mixed number or as a whole number in simplest form.

1. $\frac{60}{20}$ 2. $\frac{27}{8}$ 3. $\frac{25}{5}$ 4. $\frac{19}{4}$ 5. $\frac{21}{3}$

6. $\frac{13}{5}$ 7. $\frac{10}{3}$ 8. $\frac{26}{12}$ 9. $\frac{54}{10}$ 10. $\frac{34}{6}$

11. $\frac{52}{2}$ 12. $\frac{48}{6}$ 13. $\frac{16}{12}$ 14. $\frac{7}{4}$ 15. $\frac{55}{25}$

16. $\frac{32}{8}$ 17. $\frac{16}{10}$ 18. $\frac{7}{3}$ 19. $\frac{14}{3}$ 20. $\frac{29}{8}$

Compare. Write >, <, or =.

1. $\frac{1}{4} \bullet \frac{3}{12}$ 2. $\frac{5}{8} \bullet \frac{2}{3}$ 3. $1\frac{1}{10} \bullet 2\frac{7}{8}$ 4. $5\frac{8}{12} \bullet 1\frac{3}{6}$

5. $4\frac{6}{12} \bullet 4\frac{2}{4}$ 6. $\frac{4}{5} \bullet \frac{5}{8}$ 7. $3\frac{3}{10} \bullet 3\frac{1}{4}$ 8. $\frac{7}{12} \bullet \frac{4}{5}$

Write the numbers in order from least to greatest.

9. $\frac{3}{4}, \frac{1}{2}, \frac{1}{3}$ 10. $\frac{3}{10}, \frac{1}{5}, \frac{1}{7}$ 11. $\frac{2}{5}, \frac{1}{6}, \frac{3}{4}$ 12. $\frac{2}{3}, \frac{3}{4}, \frac{1}{3}$

13. $\frac{1}{2}; 1\frac{3}{10}; 1\frac{2}{5}$ 14. $\frac{1}{2}, \frac{5}{8}, \frac{7}{12}$ 15. $1\frac{3}{4}; 1\frac{7}{10}; 1\frac{4}{5}$ 16. $2\frac{1}{4}; 1\frac{5}{12}; 1\frac{1}{6}$

Write each fraction as a decimal.

1. $\frac{2}{10}$ 2. $\frac{3}{100}$ 3. $\frac{1}{1000}$ 4. $\frac{72}{100}$ 5. $\frac{4}{5}$ 6. $\frac{1}{25}$ 7. $\frac{7}{50}$ 8. $\frac{7}{20}$

For each fraction pair, write an equivalent decimal from the box.

9. $\frac{4}{10}, \frac{2}{5}$ 10. $\frac{4}{16}, \frac{1}{4}$

11. $\frac{1}{100}, \frac{6}{600}$ 12. $\frac{4}{5}, \frac{12}{15}$

0.4	0.01	0.8
	0.1	0.25

Write each number as a decimal.

1. $\frac{7}{8}$ 2. $\frac{1}{4}$ 3. $1\frac{3}{5}$ 4. $3\frac{9}{10}$ 5. $5\frac{63}{100}$ 6. $2\frac{6}{12}$

7. $\frac{4}{10}$ 8. $\frac{4}{16}$ 9. $6\frac{1}{2}$ 10. $3\frac{2}{5}$ 11. $1\frac{1}{100}$ 12. $7\frac{2}{25}$

Write the decimal as a fraction or mixed number in simplest form.

13. 0.83   14. 0.8   15. 2.625   16. 0.45

17. 4.03   18. 0.86   19. 5.875   20. 7.012

Write the answer in simplest form.

1. $\frac{3}{10} + \frac{7}{10}$ 2. $\frac{5}{12} - \frac{1}{12}$ 3. $\frac{5}{8} + \frac{1}{8}$ 4. $\frac{1}{8} + \frac{5}{8}$ 5. $\frac{7}{8} - \frac{3}{8}$

6. $\frac{6}{10} - \frac{2}{10}$ 7. $\frac{8}{20} - \frac{7}{20}$ 8. $\frac{5}{6} + \frac{5}{6}$ 9. $\frac{5}{12} - \frac{3}{12}$ 10. $\frac{1}{5} + \frac{2}{5}$

11. $\frac{13}{16} - \frac{1}{16}$ 12. $\frac{3}{6} - \frac{1}{6}$ 13. $\frac{8}{15} + \frac{14}{15}$ 14. $0 + \frac{1}{4}$ 15. $\frac{8}{9} - \frac{5}{9}$

16. $\frac{21}{24} + \frac{3}{24}$ 17. $\frac{3}{24} + \frac{21}{24}$ 18. $\frac{9}{10} - \frac{3}{10}$ 19. $\frac{1}{5} + \frac{1}{5}$

Estimate the fraction as close to 0, $\frac{1}{2}$, or 1.

1. $\frac{1}{5}$ 2. $\frac{15}{18}$ 3. $\frac{2}{13}$ 4. $\frac{5}{11}$ 5. $\frac{2}{5}$

6. $\frac{4}{9}$ 7. $\frac{9}{17}$ 8. $\frac{5}{4}$ 9. $\frac{17}{367}$ 10. $\frac{201}{416}$

Estimate the answer.

11. $\frac{5}{8} + \frac{3}{7}$ 12. $\frac{1}{4} + \frac{4}{5}$ 13. $\frac{7}{9} - \frac{3}{4}$ 14. $\frac{4}{9} + \frac{2}{19}$

15. $\frac{11}{8} - \frac{4}{3}$ 16. $\frac{1}{21} - \frac{1}{29}$ 17. $\frac{11}{11} + \frac{3}{7}$ 18. $\frac{3}{4} - \frac{2}{9}$

19. $\frac{9}{10} + \frac{11}{12}$ 20. $\frac{6}{7} + \frac{5}{9}$ 21. $\frac{6}{11} - \frac{1}{15}$ 22. $\frac{12}{13} - \frac{1}{12}$

Set 10.3   Use with pages 334–335. •

Write the answer in simplest form.

1. $\frac{1}{2}$ 2. $\frac{3}{4}$ 3. $\frac{7}{12}$ 4. $\frac{9}{10}$ 5. $\frac{1}{2}$
$+ \frac{2}{3}$ $- \frac{1}{3}$ $- \frac{1}{2}$ $- \frac{2}{5}$ $+ \frac{1}{4}$

6. $\frac{5}{8}$ 7. $\frac{2}{3}$ 8. $\frac{3}{4}$ 9. $\frac{11}{12}$ 10. $\frac{1}{8}$
$- \frac{1}{4}$ $+ \frac{5}{18}$ $+ \frac{3}{8}$ $- \frac{1}{3}$ $- \frac{1}{8}$

11. $\frac{4}{5} - \frac{1}{6}$ 12. $\frac{7}{8} - \frac{7}{10}$ 13. $\frac{1}{3} + \frac{5}{6}$ 14. $\frac{3}{4} + \frac{1}{10}$

15. $\frac{1}{4} + \frac{3}{5}$ 16. $\frac{2}{3} - \frac{3}{8}$ 17. $\frac{5}{6} - \frac{3}{4}$ 18. $\frac{5}{8} + \frac{7}{12}$

Set 10.5   Use with pages 340–341. •

Write the answer in simplest form.

1. 5 2. $3\frac{4}{5}$ 3. $6\frac{2}{3}$ 4. $7\frac{5}{2}$ 5. $9\frac{3}{4}$
$+ 1\frac{3}{8}$ $- 3\frac{2}{5}$ $- 3\frac{1}{3}$ $+ \frac{7}{2}$ $+ 8$

6. $17\frac{2}{3}$ 7. $4\frac{3}{12}$ 8. $38\frac{5}{6}$ 9. $10\frac{1}{4}$ 10. $4\frac{9}{10}$
$- 8\frac{1}{3}$ $+ 3\frac{7}{12}$ $- 30\frac{1}{6}$ $+ 5$ $- 3\frac{7}{10}$

11. $4\frac{21}{24} - 4\frac{7}{24}$ 12. $8\frac{2}{3} - 6$ 13. $3\frac{1}{10} + 6\frac{9}{10}$ 14. $1\frac{7}{8} - \frac{3}{8}$

15. $8\frac{2}{7} + 1\frac{5}{7}$ 16. $5\frac{3}{4} - 2\frac{1}{4}$ 17. $4\frac{5}{16} + 3\frac{3}{16}$ 18. $1\frac{5}{12} + 7\frac{3}{12}$

Write your estimate.

1. $1\frac{1}{3} + 2\frac{4}{7}$ 2. $4\frac{7}{8} + 3\frac{2}{15}$ 3. $7\frac{1}{16} + 6\frac{2}{33}$ 4. $5\frac{4}{7} - 3\frac{1}{2}$

5. $8\frac{1}{20} - 7\frac{19}{21}$ 6. $\frac{1}{4} + 2\frac{5}{8} + \frac{1}{9}$ 7. $6\frac{22}{23} + \frac{1}{17}$ 8. $4\frac{5}{9} - \frac{4}{7}$

9. Estimate to find the two mistakes Rita made. Write the letter of each incorrect answer.

Rita

a. $2\frac{1}{2} + 6\frac{4}{9} = 8\frac{5}{11}$ b. $4\frac{1}{2} + 3\frac{3}{8} = 7\frac{7}{8}$

c. $5\frac{9}{10} - 3\frac{2}{5} = 2\frac{1}{2}$ d. $\frac{9}{11} - \frac{4}{5} = \frac{5}{6}$

Write the sum in simplest form.

1. $4\frac{5}{8}$ 2. $1\frac{2}{3}$ 3. $3\frac{1}{3}$ 4. $8\frac{7}{12}$ 5. $4\frac{3}{4}$
$+\ 5\frac{1}{3}$ $+\ 7\frac{1}{4}$ $+\ 2\frac{1}{6}$ $+\ 1$ $+\ \frac{1}{2}$

6. $3\frac{7}{12}$ 7. $4\frac{3}{4}$ 8. $11\frac{7}{10}$ 9. $1\frac{4}{5}$ 10. $2\frac{1}{2}$
$+\ \frac{1}{6}$ $+\ 4\frac{5}{8}$ $+\ 6\frac{1}{4}$ $+\ 1\frac{1}{8}$ $+\ 5\frac{11}{12}$

11. $4\frac{1}{5} + 10$ 12. $7\frac{3}{4} + 1\frac{2}{5}$ 13. $5\frac{1}{2} + 4\frac{3}{10}$ 14. $\frac{3}{4} + 2\frac{2}{3}$

Solve. Write each answer in simplest form.

1. $7\frac{3}{5}$ 2. $6\frac{9}{10}$ 3. $5\frac{2}{5}$ 4. $1\frac{3}{4}$ 5. $3\frac{1}{2}$
$-\ 4\frac{3}{10}$ $-\ 2\frac{1}{4}$ $-\ \frac{1}{10}$ $-\ 1\frac{3}{8}$ $-\ 2\frac{1}{6}$

6. $5\frac{5}{8}$ 7. $3\frac{7}{8}$ 8. $9\frac{4}{5}$ 9. $3\frac{5}{6}$ 10. $8\frac{7}{8}$
$-\ 1\frac{1}{3}$ $-\ 1\frac{2}{5}$ $-\ \frac{7}{12}$ $-\ 2\frac{1}{3}$ $-\ 1\frac{2}{3}$

11. $8\frac{3}{5} - 2$ 12. $14\frac{1}{8} - \frac{1}{8}$ 13. $9\frac{5}{12} - 3\frac{1}{4}$ 14. $5\frac{3}{4} - 3\frac{7}{12}$

Write the difference in simplest form.

1. 9
   $- 1\frac{5}{8}$

2. $2\frac{3}{4}$
   $- 1\frac{7}{8}$

3. $8\frac{1}{12}$
   $- 3\frac{1}{10}$

4. $6\frac{2}{5}$
   $- 2\frac{1}{10}$

5. $1\frac{1}{2}$
   $- \frac{1}{4}$

6. 5
   $- \frac{4}{5}$

7. $6\frac{2}{5}$
   $- 3\frac{3}{4}$

8. 4
   $- 3\frac{3}{5}$

9. $7\frac{1}{4}$
   $- 6\frac{5}{6}$

10. $8\frac{3}{10}$
    $- 5\frac{3}{5}$

11. $6 - 2\frac{16}{100}$

12. $12\frac{1}{2} - 7\frac{11}{12}$

13. $3\frac{2}{3} - 1\frac{9}{10}$

14. $7\frac{2}{5} - 5\frac{7}{8}$

Write the product in simplest form.

1. $\frac{1}{4}$ of 14

2. $\frac{1}{3}$ of 8

3. $\frac{2}{5}$ of 10

4. $\frac{1}{12}$ of 24

5. $\frac{5}{8}$ of 8

6. $\frac{2}{3} \times 3$

7. $5 \times \frac{1}{4}$

8. $\frac{4}{5} \times 9$

9. $\frac{1}{3} \times 6$

10. $7 \times \frac{3}{4}$

11. $6 \times \frac{1}{12}$

12. $\frac{1}{2} \times 5$

13. $\frac{3}{5} \times 10$

14. $8 \times \frac{3}{4}$

15. $\frac{1}{10} \times 4$

Use mental math to solve.

1. $\frac{1}{3}$ of $1500

2. $\frac{1}{2}$ of 40

3. $\frac{1}{5}$ of $200

4. $\frac{1}{6}$ of 30

5. $\frac{1}{4}$ of 28

6. $\frac{1}{3}$ of $120

7. $\frac{1}{8}$ of 6400

8. $\frac{1}{8}$ of 160

9. $\frac{1}{2}$ of 240

10. $\frac{1}{5}$ of 450

11. $\frac{1}{4}$ of $80

12. $\frac{1}{3}$ of 240

Estimate.

13. $\frac{1}{4}$ of 230

14. $\frac{1}{8}$ of 50

15. $\frac{1}{5}$ of $42

16. $\frac{1}{3}$ of 84

17. $\frac{1}{3}$ of 130

18. $\frac{1}{5}$ of 1741

19. $\frac{1}{2}$ of $935

20. $\frac{1}{8}$ of 10

21. $\frac{1}{4}$ of 2108

22. $\frac{1}{3}$ of 789

23. $\frac{1}{2}$ of $5

24. $\frac{1}{8}$ of 111

Write the product in simplest form.

1. $\frac{1}{4} \times 16$ 2. $\frac{2}{3} \times 9$ 3. $12 \times \frac{3}{4}$ 4. $\frac{5}{6} \times \frac{2}{5}$ 5. $\frac{2}{3} \times \frac{1}{5}$

6. $\frac{1}{2} \times \frac{3}{4}$ 7. $\frac{5}{6} \times \frac{3}{10}$ 8. $\frac{4}{5} \times 15$ 9. $\frac{1}{2} \times \frac{1}{5}$ 10. $8 \times \frac{1}{5}$

11. $\frac{3}{4} \times \frac{2}{3}$ 12. $\frac{2}{3} \times \frac{1}{6}$ 13. $\frac{3}{10} \times \frac{4}{5}$ 14. $\frac{1}{6} \times \frac{3}{4}$ 15. $\frac{1}{4} \times \frac{3}{5}$

16. $\frac{2}{3} \times \frac{1}{5}$ 17. $\frac{2}{3} \times \frac{3}{5}$ 18. $\frac{3}{5} \times \frac{2}{3}$ 19. $\frac{4}{5} \times \frac{1}{3}$ 20. $\frac{1}{5} \times 3$

Use the number line to write each quotient.

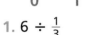   

1. $6 \div \frac{1}{3}$ 2. $6 \div \frac{2}{3}$

3. $5 \div \frac{1}{8}$ 4. $5 \div \frac{5}{8}$

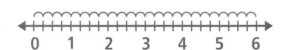   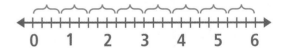

5. $6 \div \frac{1}{4}$ 6. $6 \div \frac{3}{4}$

Write the reciprocal of the number.

1. $\frac{3}{8}$ 2. $\frac{1}{5}$ 3. $\frac{2}{3}$ 4. 7   5. 8

6. 50   7. $\frac{5}{2}$ 8. $1\frac{1}{2}$ 9. $2\frac{3}{4}$ 10. $4\frac{1}{5}$

11. 10   12. $\frac{9}{3}$ 13. $6\frac{1}{3}$ 14. $3\frac{2}{10}$ 15. $5\frac{3}{5}$

Write each ratio three different ways.

1. marbles to jacks

2. daisies to tulips

3. baseballs to footballs

Write each ratio in fraction form.

4. 8 divers to 32 swim-team members

5. 30 crayons to 3 boxes

6. 53 girls to 50 boys

7. 16 poems out of 48 stories

8. 9 chickens to 63 farm animals

Write each ratio using the word *to*.

9. $\frac{3}{20}$

10. $\frac{18}{5}$

11. $\frac{7}{12}$

12. $\frac{9}{4}$

Decide if the ratios are equal. Write yes or no.

1. 2 to 1 and 1 to 2

2. 2:3 to 3:4

3. 5:2 to 10:4

4. 5:2 and 15 to 6

5. $\frac{1}{6}$ and $\frac{4}{24}$

6. $\frac{3}{8}$ and $\frac{6}{24}$

7. 10 to 1 and 5 to 1

8. 7:9 and 35:45

9. 4 to 5 and 12 to 15

Write the missing number.

10. 4 to 1 is the same as 12 to ■.

11. 3 to 6 is the same as ■ to 2.

12. $\frac{2}{5} = \frac{■}{15}$

13. $\frac{18}{■} = \frac{9}{2}$

14. $\frac{10}{8} = \frac{■}{4}$

15. $\frac{■}{6} = \frac{6}{18}$

16. $\frac{3}{9} = \frac{■}{3}$

17. $\frac{7}{5} = \frac{14}{■}$

18. $\frac{21}{24} = \frac{■}{8}$

19. $\frac{■}{4} = \frac{12}{16}$

20. $\frac{2}{7} = \frac{■}{49}$

21. $\frac{9}{15} = \frac{3}{■}$

22. $\frac{4}{5} = \frac{32}{■}$

23. $\frac{8}{56} = \frac{■}{7}$

24. $\frac{■}{9} = \frac{40}{90}$

25. $\frac{24}{20} = \frac{■}{10}$

26. $\frac{18}{81} = \frac{2}{■}$

27. $\frac{4}{1} = \frac{■}{18}$

28. $\frac{16}{12} = \frac{■}{6}$

29. $\frac{36}{48} = \frac{■}{8}$

30. $\frac{2}{7} = \frac{12}{■}$

31. $\frac{5}{15} = \frac{1}{■}$

Write the letter of the most reasonable estimate for the percent shaded.

1.	2.	3.	4.
a. 25%	a. 50%	a. 10%	a. 0%
b. 50%	b. 70%	b. 40%	b. 50%
c. 70%	c. 90%	c. 90%	c. 100%

Estimate what percent of each flag is green.

5.	6.	7.
Ireland	Bangladesh	United Arab Emirates

Estimate what percent of each flag is red.

8. Ireland   9. Bangladesh   10. United Arab Emirates

Write each percent as a fraction in simplest form.

1. 15%	2. 35%	3. 25%	4. 10%	5. 8%
6. 16%	7. 55%	8. 40%	9. 34%	10. 2%
11. 75%	12. 9%	13. 12%	14. 5%	15. 45%
16. 4%	17. 64%	18. 37%	19. 18%	20. 89%

21. Write each percent in exercises 1–10 as a decimal.

Write each decimal as a percent.

22. 0.45   23. 0.5   24. 0.17   25. 0.21   26. 0.6

27. 0.9   28. 0.12   29. 0.8   30. 0.49   31. 0.05

32. 0.99   33. 0.02   34. 0.06   35. 0.7   36. 0.01

Write each fraction as a percent.

37. $\frac{7}{10}$ 38. $\frac{3}{5}$ 39. $\frac{1}{4}$ 40. $\frac{4}{25}$ 41. $\frac{9}{10}$

42. $\frac{4}{5}$ 43. $\frac{12}{25}$ 44. $\frac{2}{5}$ 45. $\frac{1}{10}$ 46. $\frac{8}{25}$

47. $\frac{9}{50}$ 48. $\frac{9}{20}$ 49. $\frac{3}{50}$ 50. $\frac{1}{20}$ 51. $\frac{24}{25}$

Set 12.9   Use with pages 410–411.

Write the answer. Use mental math.

1. 50% of 12   2. 25% of 8   3. 25% of 36

4. 50% of 30   5. 50% of 50   6. 25% of 60

7. 50% of 120   8. 25% of 140   9. 25% of 200

10. 25% of 280   11. 50% of 280   12. 50% of 300

13. How can finding the answer to exercise 2 help you find 75% of 8?

Set 12.10   Use with pages 412–413.

Find the percent of the number. Use mental math when you can.

1. 20% of 60   2. 15% of 60   3. 6% of 60   4. 50% of 120

5. 4% of 200   6. 30% of 57   7. 25% of 120   8. 10% of 54

9. 65% of 200   10. 75% of 100   11. 80% of 300   12. 5% of 90

13. 50% of 90   14. 20% of 80   15. 25% of 400   16. 14% of 42

17. 10% of 38   18. 2% of 200   19. 25% of 800   20. 85% of 60

Set 12.11   Use with page 414. ••

Solve each problem. Write whether you used mental math or paper and pencil.

1. 25% of 4   2. 30% of 60   3. 7% of 50

4. 45% of 20   5. 64% of 25   6. 63% of 100

7. 15% of 80   8. 50% of 92   9. 50% of 93

10. 38% of 25   11. 22% of 150   12. 43% of 200

Set 12.13   Use with pages 420–421. •••••••••••••••••••••••••••••••••••••

Write each probability in the form of a ratio.

1. What is the probability of spinning the number 5?

2. What is the probability of spinning a number less than 3?

3. What is the probability of spinning the number 10?

4. What is the chance of spinning an odd number?

5. What is the chance of spinning a number less than 7?

Set 12.15   Use with pages 424–425. •••••••••••••••••••••••••••••••••••••

Solve each problem. Write whether you used a calculator or mental math.

1. 93 + 124   2. 31.2 − 19.7   3. $25.01 + $17.01

4. 72 × 100   5. 53 × 38   6. 280 ÷ 4

7. 13.9 × 27.1   8. 3588 ÷ 46   9. 450 ÷ 18

10. $\frac{1}{8} + \frac{7}{8}$ 11. $\frac{2}{3} \times \frac{7}{9}$ 12. 37% of 200

Write the area of each rectangle. Remember to use square units in your answer.

1. 3 ft

12 ft

2. 8 ft

3 ft

3. 6 m

9 m

4. 9.4 cm

9.4 cm

5. 7 in
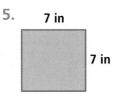
7 in

6. 4.5 m

15 m

7. length = 18.75 m
width = 3 m

8. length = 27 mi
width = 13 mi

9. length = 10 ft
width = 4 ft

10. length = 8.25 cm
width = 2 cm

11. side = 6.4 in.

12. side = 12 ft

Estimate the area. Give your answer in square units.

1.
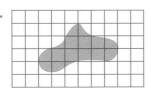

2.
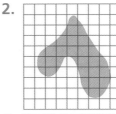

3.
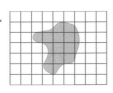

4.
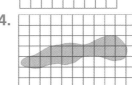

Name the polygon that is the base.

1.
Triangular Pyramid

2.
Cube

3.
Square Pyramid

4.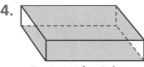
Rectangular Prism

5.
Triangular
Prism

6.
Pentagonal
Pyramid

Write the missing measurement.

	Length	Width	Height	Volume
1.	3 m	4 m	?	60 m³
2.	15 in.	?	3 in.	450 in.³
3.	8 ft	6 ft	12 ft	?
4.	9 mm	20 mm	?	1260 mm³
5.	?	2 m	18 m	144 m³
6.	30 ft	7 ft	4 ft	?

Write the volume. Give your answer in cubic units.

7.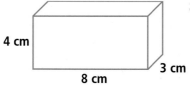

8.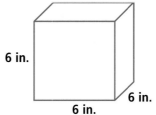

9.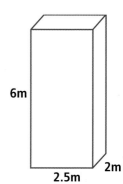

Table of Measures

The charts on this page identify common measures. Check the glossary and index for more information on specific terms.

Customary Measures

Length

1 foot (ft) = 12 inches (in.)
1 yard (yd) = 3 feet
1 yard = 36 inches
1 mile (mi) = 5280 feet
1 mile = 1760 yards

Liquid

1 cup (c) = 8 fluid ounces (fl oz)
1 pint (pt) = 2 cups
1 quart (qt) = 2 pints
1 gallon (gal) = 4 quarts

Weight

1 pound (lb) = 16 ounces (oz)
1 ton (T) = 2000 pounds

Metric Measures

Length

1 centimeter (cm) = 10 millimeters (mm)
1 decimeter (dm) = 10 centimeters
1 meter (m) = 10 decimeters
1 meter = 100 centimeters
1 meter = 1000 millimeters
1 kilometer (km) = 1000 meters

Liquid

1 liter (L) = 1000 milliliters (mL)
1 milliliter = 1 cubic centimeter (cm^3)

Mass

1 gram (g) = 1000 milligrams (mg)
1 kilogram (kg) = 1000 grams

Time

Time

1 minute (min) = 60 seconds (s)
1 hour (h) = 60 minutes
1 day (d) = 24 hours
1 week (wk) = 7 days
1 year (yr) = 12 months (mo)
1 year = 52 weeks

Glossary

acute angle An angle that measures less than 90°.

addend A number added to another in an addition problem. Example: ⑤ + ⑨ = 14

angle A figure formed by two rays that have a common endpoint.

area The number of units needed to cover a surface.

associative property of addition Changing the grouping of addends does not change the sum.
Example: 3.6 + (1.7 + 8.3) = 13.6
(3.6 + 1.7) + 8.3 = 13.6

associative property of multiplication Changing the grouping of factors does not change the product
Example: (1 × 2) × 5 = 10
1 × (2 × 5) = 10

bar graph A graph that uses bars to show data.

Books Read by Students

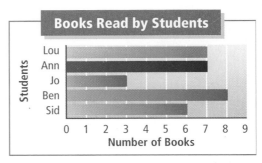

Number of Books

base (of a figure) A special face of a solid. The bases in the two examples are shaded.

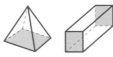

base (of an exponent) The number that is the repeated factor.
Example: 2 × 2 × 2 = ②³

capacity The maximum amount that a container can hold.

Celsius (°C) The metric temperature scale in which 0°C is the freezing point of water and 100°C is the boiling point of water.

circle A closed plane curve with every point the same distance from the center.

circle graph A graph that uses a circle to show all the parts of the whole.

Al's Budget

circumference The distance around the circle.

common factor A number that is a factor of two or more numbers.
Example: common factors of 18 and 24: 1, 2, 3, 6

common multiple A number that is a multiple of two or more numbers.
Example: common multiples of 2 and 3: 6, 12, 18, 24, 30, 36

commutative property of addition Changing the order of addends does not change the sum.
Example:　　2.4 + 5.9 = 8.3
　　　　　　5.9 + 2.4 = 8.3

commutative property of multiplication Changing the order of factors does not change the product.
Example:　　3 × 5 = 15
　　　　　　5 × 3 = 15

compatible numbers Numbers that are easy to work with mentally, and are used in place of actual numbers to get an estimate, usually in division
Example:
237 ÷ 62 240 ÷ 60
Estimate: 4

composite number A number that has more than two factors.
Example: 15 is a composite number because its factors are 1, 3, 5, and 15.

computer program A set of commands that tells a computer what to do.

congruent (segments or angles) (≅) Equal in measure.

congruent figures Figures that have exactly the same size and shape.

cube A solid having six square faces the same size.

customary system The measurement system that uses foot, quart, pound, and degree Fahrenheit.

cylinder A solid that has two parallel congruent circular bases and one curved surface.

·············· **D** ··············

data Facts and figures from which conclusions can be drawn.

decimal A number with one or more digits to the right of a decimal point.
Examples: 1.4　2.03　0.569

decimal point A symbol used to separate ones and tenths in decimals or dollars and cents in money amounts.
Examples: 3.2　$1.50

decimal points

degree (angles) A unit for measuring angles.

degree (temperature) A unit for measuring temperature.

denominator The number written below the bar in a fraction.

Example: $\frac{1}{4}$ denominator

diagonal A line segment that joins two vertices of a polygon, but is not a side of the polygon.

diameter The distance across a circle through the center.

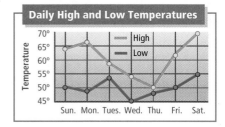

Diameter = 3 cm

difference The answer in a subtraction problem.
Example: 12 − 5 = 7

difference

digit Any one of the symbols 0, 1, 2, 3, 4, 5, 6, 7, 8, or 9 used to write numbers.

distributive property of multiplication The product of a number and the sum of two numbers is equal to the sum of the two products.
Example:
3 × (2 + 4) = (3 × 2) + (3 × 4)

dividend The number that is divided in a division problem.
Example: 36 ÷ 9 = 4

dividend

divisible Capable of being divided into equal parts without a remainder.

divisor The number by which the dividend is divided in a division problem.
Example: 36 ÷ 9 = 4

divisor

double-bar graph A bar graph that allows you to compare two sets of data.

double line graph A line graph that allows you to compare two sets of data over time.

Daily High and Low Temperatures

edge The line segment where two faces of a solid meet.

← edge

elapsed time The amount of time that passes between the start and end of a given period.

endpoint The point at the end of a line segment.

endpoints

equal ratios Ratios that show the same relationship or comparison.
Example: 2 to 3, 4 to 6, and 6 to 9 are equal ratios.

equilateral triangle A triangle that has three congruent sides and three congruent angles.

equivalent Having the same value.

equivalent decimals Decimals that have the same value.
Example: 0.6, 0.60, 0.600 are equivalent decimals.

equivalent fractions Fractions that have the same value.
Example: $\frac{8}{12} = \frac{4}{6} = \frac{2}{3}$

equivalent measures
Measures that name the same value.
Example: 1 meter, 100 centimeters, and 1000 millimeters are equivalent measures.

estimate A number close to an exact value. An estimate tells *about* how much.

evaluate Find the value of an expression.
Example:
Evaluate $x + 3$ when $x = 2$.
    $x + 3 = 2 + 3 = 5$

even number A whole number ending in 0, 2, 4, 6, or 8.
Examples: 56 92

event A set of one or more outcomes of an experiment.

expanded form A number written as the sum of the values of the digits. Example: The number 2469 can be written as $2000 + 400 + 60 + 9$.

experimental probability The probability of an event based on the results of an experiment.

exponent A number that shows how many times a factor is repeated.
Example: $3 \times 3 \times 3 \times 3 = 3^{4}$

expression A combination of numbers and symbols that represents a mathematical quantity.
Examples: $7 + 3$, $4 \cdot n$

face A flat surface of a solid.

factors (multiplication) The numbers used in a multiplication problem.
Example: $\boxed{2} \times \boxed{9} = 18$

factors (division) Numbers that divide another number with no remainder.
Examples: 2 and 3 are factors of 6
$6 \div \boxed{3} = 2$ $6 \div \boxed{2} = 3$

Fahrenheit (°F) The customary temperature scale in which 32°F is the freezing point of water and 212°F is the boiling point of water.

flip A motion in which every point of a figure moves over a line to create a mirror image.

flip image The position of a figure after a flip.

Flip Image

fraction A number that names part of a whole or part of a set. A fraction is written with a numerator and denominator.
Examples: $\frac{1}{4}$, $1\frac{1}{2}$

front-end estimation Estimate made by looking at the digits with the greatest place value to find about how much.

$$\begin{array}{rcl} 468 & \Rightarrow & 400 \\ +\ 328 & \Rightarrow & 300 \\ \hline & & 700 \end{array}$$

graph A picture that shows data by using bars, lines, symbols, fractions of a circle.

greatest common factor The largest factor of two or more numbers.
Example: greatest common factor of 12, 18, and 30: 6

grouping property of addition See associative property of addition.

grouping property of multiplication See associative property of multiplication.

half turn A turn that causes a figure to face in the opposite direction. A 180° turn.

half-turn symmetry If a figure matches itself after a half turn about its center point, then the figure has half-turn symmetry.

hexagon A polygon with six sides.

horizontal axis A horizontal reference line on a grid.

intersect To cross or meet.

intersecting lines Lines that cross or meet.

intersecting planes Planes that intersect to form a line.

irregular polygon A polygon with sides and angles that are not congruent.

isosceles triangle A triangle that has at least two congruent sides.

least common denominator (LCD) The smallest common denominator for a set of fractions.
Example: LCD of $\frac{1}{2}$, $\frac{1}{3}$, $\frac{1}{4}$: 12

least common multiple (LCM) The smallest common multiple of a set of numbers.
Example: least common multiple of 2 and 3: 6

line A collection of points along a straight path that goes on forever.

line graph A graph that displays data by using connected line segments.

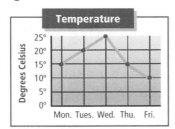

line of symmetry A line along which you could fold a figure so that both halves match.

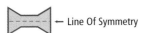 ← Line Of Symmetry

line plot A diagram showing the frequency of data on a number line.

line segment Part of a line consisting of two endpoints and all the points in between.

A •————————• Z

line symmetry A figure has line symmetry when it can be folded along a line so that the two halves match exactly.

mass The amount of matter in an object.

mean The average of a set of numbers, found by adding the numbers in the set and dividing by the number of addends.

median The middle number in a set when the numbers are ordered from least to greatest.

mental math Finding an exact answer to a math problem without using paper and pencil.

metric system The measurement system that uses meter, liter, gram and degree Celsius.

mixed number A number that has a whole number part and a fraction part.
Example: $2\frac{1}{6}$

mode The number that occurs most often in a set of data.

multiple A product of two whole numbers.
Example: $4 \times 2 = 8$ The number 8 is a multiple of 4 and 2.

multiplication property of one If any number is multiplied by one, the product is the same as that number.
Example: 4 × 1 = 4 51 × 1 = 51

multiplication property of zero If any number is multiplied by zero, the product is zero.
Example: 7 × 0 = 0 0 × 238 = 0

negative numbers Numbers less than zero; numbers that show a loss or decrease.
Example: ⁻32

net A flat pattern that folds into a solid.

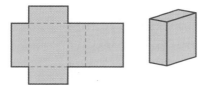

numerator The number written above the bar in a fraction.
Example: $\frac{1}{4}$ numerator

obtuse angle An angle that measures more than 90° and less than 180°.

odd number A whole number ending in 1, 3, 5, 7, or 9.
Examples: 67, 99

ordered pair A pair of numbers that gives the coordinates of a point on a graph.

order of operations Rules for finding the value of an expression.

order property of addition See commutative property of addition.

order property of multiplication See commutative property of multiplication.

outcome A possible result of an experiment.

parallel Planes or lines in the same plane that do not intersect.

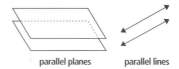

parallel planes   parallel lines

parallelogram A quadrilateral with two pairs of parallel sides.

pentagon A polygon with five sides.

percent A ratio based on 100.

perfect number A number that is $\frac{1}{2}$ the sum of its factors.
Example: the factors of 6 are 1, 2, 3, and 6.
1 + 2 + 3 + 6 = 12
Since 6 is half of 12, 6 is a perfect number.

perimeter The distance around a figure.

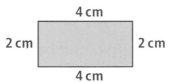

4 cm + 2 cm + 4 cm + 2 cm = 12 cm

perpendicular lines Two lines or line segments that intersect at right angles.

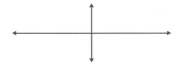

Pi (π) The number (≈3.14) that represents the ratio of the circumference of a circle to the length of its diameter.

pictograph A graph that uses pictures or symbols to show data. The key identifies the number of data items represented by each symbol.

place value The value of a digit based on its position in a number. Example: In 7949, the 7 is in the thousands place and stands for 7000.

plane A flat surface that goes on forever in all directions.

plane region part of a plane

point An exact place or position in space, represented by a dot.

polygon A closed figure formed by line segments joined only at their endpoints.

positive numbers Numbers

greater than zero; numbers that show a gain or increase. Example: ⁺15

prediction A guess about something that will happen based on known facts.

prime factorization The expression of a number as the product of prime factors. Example: the prime factorization of 56 is 7 × 2 × 2 × 2.

prime number A number greater than 1 that has exactly two factors, itself and 1. Example: 2, 3, 7, 11, and 17 are prime numbers.

prism A three-dimensional figure that has two congruent parallel bases joined by faces that are parallelograms.

probability The likelihood that something will happen; a measure of chance.

product The answer in a multiplication problem. Example: 5 × 3 = 15

pyramid A solid that has a polygon for a base and whose other faces are triangles that share a common vertex.

507

quadrilateral A polygon with four sides.

quarter turn A 90° turn about a turn center.

quotient The answer in a division problem.
Example: 36 ÷ 9 = 4

quotient

radius (radii) The distance from the center of a circle to any point on the circle.

1.3 cm

radius = 1.3 cm

range The difference between the greatest number and least number in a group.

rate A comparison of two quantities with different units of measure.

ratio A comparison of two quantities with the same units of measure.
Examples: 62 to 100, 62 : 100,
$$\frac{62}{100}$$

ray A part of a line that has one endpoint. This is ray $\overrightarrow{CD}$.

C   D

reciprocals Two numbers whose product is 1. The reciprocal of a fraction is formed by interchanging the numerator and denominator.

The reciprocal of $\frac{2}{3}$ is $\frac{3}{2}$.

$$\frac{2}{3} \times \frac{3}{2} = \frac{6}{6} = 1$$

rectangle A quadrilateral having four right angles.

rectangular prism A prism with rectangular bases.

regular polygon A polygon with congruent sides and congruent angles.

rhombus A quadrilateral with four congruent sides.

right angle An angle measuring 90°.

90°

right triangle A triangle with a 90° angle.

90°

scalene triangle A triangle that has no congruent sides or congruent angles.

side of a polygon One of the line segments that make up the polygon.

similar figures (≈) Figures that have the same shape, but need not have the same size.

simplest form A fraction whose numerator and denominator have no common factor other than 1.

Example: $\frac{2}{3}$ is the simplest form of $\frac{8}{12}$.

slide A motion in which every point of a figure moves the same distance and in the same direction.

slide image A figure after it has moved to a different location as the result of a slide.

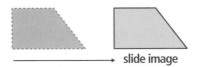

slide image

sphere A solid figure that has the shape of a ball.

square A figure with four right angles and four equal sides.

standard A measurement that is agreed upon generally.

standard form The usual, or common, way of writing a number using digits.
Example: The standard form of twenty-seven is 27.

stem-and-leaf plot A way to organize data by place value. The plot below shows this data: 20, 29, 31, 42, 45, 48

Stem-and-leaf plot	
2	0, 9
3	1
4	2, 5, 8

sum The answer in an addition problem.
Example: 5 + 4 = 9

surface area The sum of the areas of all faces or surfaces of a solid.

survey A way to collect data by asking questions of many persons.

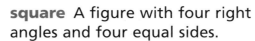

tessellate To fit plane figures together without overlapping or leaving gaps.

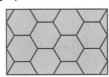

tessellation The pattern formed by tessellating figures.

theoretical probability The probability of an event written as a ratio of the number of favorable outcomes to the number of possible outcomes of the experiment.

trapezoid A quadrilateral with only one pair of parallel sides.

tree diagram An organized list that shows all possible outcomes of an event.

triangle A polygon with three sides and three vertices.

turn A motion in which a figure moves around a center.

turn center The point around which a figure is turned.

turn image The position of a figure after a turn.

half-turn image

unit price The cost of one item.

variable A letter such as *p, x,* or *n* that represents one or more values in an algebraic expression.

Venn diagram A drawing that shows relationships among sets of objects.

Numbers Divisible by 5 / Odd Numbers

vertex (vertices) The corner point of an angle, polygon, or solid.

vertical axis A vertical reference line on a grid.

Vertical Axis

volume The number of cubic units of space taken up by a solid.

whole number Any of the numbers 0, 1, 2, 3, 4, 5, and so on.

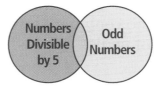

zero property of addition The sum of zero and any number is that number.
Examples: $4.9 + 0 = 4.9$
$0 + 6.7 = 6.7$

Test Prep Handbook

Contents

Test Prep Strategies

Cumulative Tests

Chapter 1 Test Prep Strategies

Monitor

When you first read a word problem, make sure that the problem makes sense to you. Then read the problem again to look for details and important information.

Sample Test Item

1 Mike started reading a book 5 weeks ago. To finish the book, Mike read 21 pages the first week, 24 the second week, 29 the third week, 32 the fourth week, and 25 the fifth week. Which is the best estimate for the total number of pages that Mike read?

- **A** 100
- **B** 110
- **C** 130
- **D** 150

1 Understand **Using Monitor Strategy**

You need to estimate the total number of pages that Mike read. Look at the answer choices and think about the method you would use.
- Is there any information in the problem that you don't need?

2 Plan **Choosing an Estimation Method**

Rounding and then adding is a reasonable method for estimating the total. Think about how to round each number.
- To what place should you round each number?

3 Try It **Using Make a Table**

List the numbers. Then round each to the nearest 10. Add.
- What other operation could you use to find the answer quickly?

21	→	20
24	→	20
29	→	30
32	→	30
25	→	30

$20 + 20 + 30 + 30 + 30 = 130$

4 Look Back **Checking for Reasonableness**

Look at the answer you chose. Then look at the other choices.
- How can you use number sense to tell why the other choices are incorrect?

Try These!

2 Keisha bikes each week. Last month she biked 18 miles the first week, 14 the second week, 19 the third week, and 13 the fourth week. What is the best estimate for the total number of miles?

- **A** 40 miles
- **B** 60 miles
- **C** 70 miles
- **D** 80 miles

3 Fernando is saving money to buy a new CD. Fernando has $11.67. He still needs to save $5.32. What is the best estimate for the cost of the CD?

- **A** $13.00
- **B** $15.00
- **C** $17.00
- **D** $18.00

Chapter 2 Test Prep Strategies

Reading Strategy
Summarize

When you summarize the information in a problem, try to interpret what the question is asking.

Sample Test Item

1 Scott bought four birthday presents. Each present cost $19.00. What is a reasonable estimate for the cost of all four presents?

A between $40 and $50

B between $50 and $60

C between $60 and $70

D between $70 and $80

1 **Understand** **Using the Summarize Strategy**

The problem tells you that Scott bought four presents at $19.00 each. The question asks for a reasonable estimate.
* How will you use the estimate to select an answer choice?

2 **Plan** **Choosing an Estimation Method**

Round the cost of each present, and then multiply to estimate.
* How can you use mental math to round and estimation to solve this problem?

3 **Try It** **Using Rounding**

Round $19.00 to $20.00 then multiply by 4 to find the total cost for four gifts.
4 × $20.00 = $80.00
* Is the actual cost greater than or less than $80.00?

4 **Look Back** **Check for Reasonableness**

Reread the problem. Look at your answer.
* Does it make sense?
* Is there another way to solve the problem?

Test Prep Handbook

....

Try These!

2 Carmen walks for 25 minutes 7 days a week. What is a reasonable estimate for the number of minutes Carmen walks in a week?

A between 100 and 140 minutes

B between 150 and 200 minutes

C between 220 and 275 minutes

D more than 300 minutes

3 Each student in a fifth-grade class will write 8 book reports during the school year. There are 24 students in the class. What is a reasonable estimate for the total number of book reports that the students will write this year?

A between 160 and 170

B between 190 and 200

C between 220 and 230

D between 240 and 250

Chapter 3 Test Prep Strategies

Reading Strategy

Predict/Infer

When you read a problem, try to picture the situation and predict what information you need to solve the problem.

1 **Understand**

Using Predict/Infer Strategy

Organize the ideas so you can interpret what is being asked.
- How many books did each fifth-grader borrow on Tuesday?

2 **Plan**

Choosing a Method for Solving

- What information will you use from the graph?
- What operations will you use?

3 **Try It**

Using the Graph

The problem is about division.
- About how many books did the fifth grade borrow?

Use compatible numbers.

108 ÷ 4 = 27 students
- What other compatible numbers could you have used to estimate?

4 **Look Back**

Checking for Reasonableness

Reread the problem. Check that you used the correct numbers.
- Does your answer make sense?

Sample Test Item

1 Use the graph to answer.

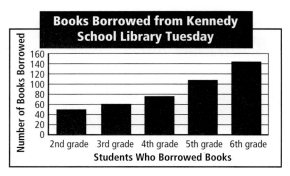

Books Borrowed from Kennedy School Library Tuesday

If each fifth-grade student borrowed 4 books, about how many fifth-graders borrowed books on Tuesday?

- **A** between 25 and 30 students
- **B** between 35 and 40 students
- **C** between 45 and 50 students
- **D** between 100 and 120 students

Try These!

Use the graph above.

2 About 24 sixth-grade students borrowed books on Tuesday. If each borrowed the same number of books, which is the best estimate for how many books each sixth-grader borrowed?

- **A** about 2 books
- **B** about 6 books
- **C** about 24 books
- **D** about 150 books

3 The same number of second-graders and fourth-graders borrowed books on Tuesday. The fourth-graders borrowed 3 books each. How many books did each second-grader borrow?

- **A** 6 books
- **B** 3 books
- **C** 2 books
- **D** 1 book

Chapter 4 Test Prep Strategies

Reading Strategy
Evaluate

Sometimes there is hidden information in a problem. As you read, make sure you have all the information you need.

1 Understand **Using Evaluate Strategy**

Rosa practices every day after school. You know that there are 5 school days in a week. There are 5 days that Rosa practices, but only 3 numbers in the problem.
- What is the hidden information in the problem?

Sample Test Item

1 Rosa has soccer practice every day after school. On Mondays she practices for 2 hours, on both Tuesdays and Fridays she practices for 3.5 hours, and on Wednesdays and Thursdays she practices for 2.5 hours. What is the best estimate for the number of hours Rosa practices each week?

A 7 hours

B 8 hours

C 11 hours

D 16 hours

2 Plan **Choosing a Problem Solving Strategy**

You can organize the information in a table. Making a table may also help you to identify hidden information. Then estimate the total number of hours.
- How can you use rounding to estimate a decimal sum?

3 Try It **Using Make a Table**

Make a table. Find the number of hours for *each* day. Add to estimate the total.

M	2 h	→	2 h
Tu	3.5 h	→	4 h
W	2.5 h	→	3 h
Th	2.5 h	→	3 h
F	3.5 h	→	4 h
Total			16 h

4 Look Back **Checking Your Estimate**

Reread your table. Make sure that you rounded and added correctly.
- How can you eliminate the incorrect answer choices?

Try These!

2 Eileen started collecting shells four years ago. Four years ago she collected 25 shells, and three years ago she collected 62 new shells. Last year she added 74 shells to her collection, and this year she collected the same number. Which is the best estimate for the total number of shells in Eileen's collection?

A about 160 shells

B about 200 shells

C about 230 shells

D about 250 shells

3 Javier volunteers at the community center every week. He is at the center for 3 hours each week. About how many hours does Javier spend at the community center during a two-month period? (Hint: 1 month = about 4 weeks)

A about 6 hours

B about 12 hours

C about 24 hours

D about 36 hours

Chapter 5 Test Prep Strategies

When you read a problem, pay attention to the vocabulary words. Before you can solve the problem, you will need to understand what the vocabulary means.

1 Understand **Using Think About Words Strategy**

The problem asks you to find a figure *congruent* to *rectangle MNOP*.
- What do you know about these words that can help you eliminate answer choices?

2 Plan **Choosing a Method for Solving**

Use logical reasoning and your understanding of *congruent* and *rectangle* to compare rectangle *MNOP* to the answer choices. You know that congruent figures have the same size and shape.
- What are the properties of rectangles?

3 Try It **Using Logical Reasoning**

Choice A is a rectangle, but all the sides are the same length. It is not the same shape as rectangle *MNOP*. Choice B is not a rectangle. Choice C seems to be congruent to rectangle *MNOP*. The measures of the sides seem to be the same as those of rectangle *MNOP*.
- How can you eliminate choice D?

4 Look Back **Checking Your Answer**

Reread the problem. Compare your answer choice with rectangle *MNOP*.
- Does your choice fit what you know about congruent figures?

Sample Test Item

1 Which figure appears to be congruent to rectangle *MNOP*?

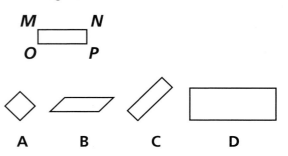

Try These!

2 Which figure appears to be congruent to triangle *JKL*?

   A

   B

   C

   D

3 Which figure appears to be congruent to polygon *RSTUV*?

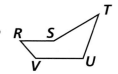

   A

   B

   C

   D

Chapter 6 Test Prep Strategies

Reading Strategy
Self-Question

Read the problem carefully. Ask yourself questions about the numbers in the problem and how they relate to one another.

1 **Understand** **Using Self-Question Strategy**

Reread the problem. Ask yourself what question is being asked and how the facts fit this question.
- Is there any information you don't need?

2 **Plan** **Choosing a Method for Solving**

You can start with a word equation.
Then, use the word equation to help you write a number sentence.
- What facts and operations will the number sentence contain?

3 **Try It** **Writing a Number Sentence**

money from ticket sales	**equals**	number of tickets sold	**times**	cost of each ticket
T	=	(75 + 129)	×	$2.25

- Does your equation fit the problem?

4 **Look Back** **Checking the Answer Choices**

Find the answer choice that matches. You may need to use the order property to find an equivalent equation in the answer choices.
- How do you know that the answer choice you chose is equivalent to your equation?

Sample Test Item

1 The basketball team has its first game at 8:00 P.M. tonight. The players have sold 75 tickets for the game. The ticket office has sold 129 tickets. One ticket costs $2.25. Which number sentence could you use to find T, the amount of ticket sales for tonight's game?

A $T = \$2.25 \times (75 + 129)$

B $T = (129 + 75) \div \$2.25$

C $T = \$2.25 + (129 \times 75)$

D $T = (129 - 75) \times \$2.25$

E None of these

Try These!

2 Maura works 16 hours each week delivering newspapers in her neighborhood. She delivers 32 newspapers each day. In one hour she earns $5.15. Which number sentence could Maura use to find how much she will earn in one week, W?

A $W = 16 \times \$5.15$

B $W = 16 \times (7 \times 32)$

C $W = (16 \times 32) \div \$5.15$

D $W = (16 \times 7) \times \$5.15$

3 Jeff needs 5 pounds of apples for each apple pie he will make. Jeff bought apples for $19.35. Each pound of apples cost $1.29. Which number sentence could you use to find P, the number of pies Jeff is planning to make?

A $P = (\$19.35 \div 5) \times \$1.29$

B $P = \$19.35 - (\$1.29 \times 5)$

C $P = (\$1.29 \times \$19.35) \div 5$

D $P = \$19.35 \div (\$1.29 \times 5)$

Chapter 7 Test Prep Strategies

Reading Strategy
Summarize

Sometimes when you read a test item, it helps to quickly summarize the given information.

1 Understand **Using Summarize Strategy**

When you summarize, include only the facts that will help you solve the problem.
- What is the distance you must travel?
- How many days will it take to travel that distance?

2 Plan **Choosing a Problem Solving Strategy**

You know that you will travel the same mileage on each of 3 days and that the total mileage is 811.5.
- What operation does this idea suggest?

3 Try It **Using Compatible Numbers**

Use compatible numbers to divide.
900 miles in 3 days ➡ 900 ÷ 3 = 300; 300 mi a day
- How does this help you choose the correct number sentence?

4 Look Back **Checking for Reasonableness**

Reread the problem to verify that you have summarized the facts well.
- How can you decide whether you have chosen the correct number sentence?

Sample Test Item

1 You decide to visit New York City, which is 811.5 mi from your town. Your plan is to drive the same number of miles each day for 3 days. Which number sentence could be used to find the number of miles you will drive each day?

A $811.5 - 3 = \square$

B $811.5 + 3 = \square$

C $811.5 \times 3 = \square$

D $811.5 \div 3 = \square$

Try These!

2 You are to take part in a cycling race that totals 203.2 km. If the course has 4 checkpoints equally spaced, which number sentence shows how many km are between the second and third check points?

A $203.2 + 203.2 = \square$

B $203.2 \times 4 = \square$

C $203.2 \div 4 = \square$

D $203.2 \div 5 = \square$

3 In the Grand Prix circuit race held in Monaco, a motor racing driver must complete 78 laps for a total of 259.74 km. Which number sentence shows how to find the halfway distance consisting of 39 laps?

A $259.74 \div 2 = \square$

B $259.74 - 2 = \square$

C $259.74 \times 39 = \square$

D $259.74 \div 78 = \square$

Chapter 8 Test Prep Strategies

As you read a problem, keep track of the mathematical ideas that are expressed. If you do not know the meaning of some vocabulary, use other information in the problem to guess the meaning.

Sample Test Item

1 Look at the grid. Which vertex of triangle *ABC* is represented by the ordered pair (2,3)? Explain how you made your choice.

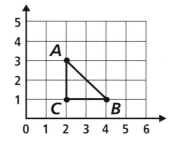

1 **Understand** **Using Monitor Strategy**

There are many math ideas in this problem to think about.
- What is a vertex?
- Where will you find the ordered pair?

2 **Plan** **Choosing a Method for Solving**

The problem states that one vertex is represented by the ordered pair (2,3). You need to locate that point on the grid.
- How do you locate the point for the ordered pair on a grid?

3 **Try It** **Finding Points on a Grid**

- What letter is at (2,3)?

Explain how you located the point for the ordered pair (2,3) on the grid.
  The "2" tells me to count 2 spaces across from 0 to 2.
  The "3" tells me to count 3 spaces up from 0 to 3.
  At the vertex I found the letter *A*.

4 **Look Back** **Checking for Reasonableness**

Make sure you located the point correctly on the grid.
- Why can you eliminate points *B* and *C*?

Try These!

2 Look at the grid. Which vertex of trapezoid *ABCD* is represented by the ordered pair (4,1)? Explain how you made your choice.

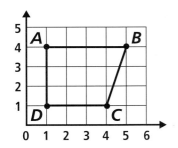

3 Look at the grid. Which vertex of pentagon *EFGHI* is represented by the ordered pair (1,3)? Explain how you made your choice.

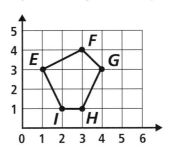

Test Prep Handbook

519

Chapter 9 Test Prep Strategies

Reading Strategy
Self-Question

After you read a problem, it helps to ask yourself questions to check your understanding. Think about how the problem connects with math skills that you already know.

1 Understand **Using Self-Question Strategy**

Reread the problem and look at the graph. Ask yourself: Which lunch item is the most popular? How many students took part in the survey? How many students voted for the most popular item?
- How can you organize the answers to your questons?

2 Plan **Choosing a Method for Solving**

Make a list of the information you got from the bar graph.
- What information do you need to find and write in the form of a fraction?

3 Try It **Using a List**

List the necessary information.
- most popular item — Chicken
- number of students who voted for it — 25
- total number of students surveyed — 60
- How do you write this information as a fraction?

4 Look Back **Checking for Reasonableness**

- Is your answer reasonable?
- Have you written the fraction in simplest form?

Sample Test Item

1 Sixty students were surveyed about school lunches. The graph shows how the students responded. What fraction of the students chose the most popular item? Write the fraction in simplest form.

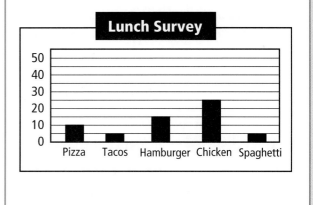

Try These!

2 Look at the bar graph. What fraction of the students voted for Pizza? Write the answer in simplest form.

3 Look at the bar graph. What fraction of the students voted for the Hamburger and Spaghetti lunch items? Write the answer in simplest form.

Chapter 10 Test Prep Strategies

Monitor

One way to monitor your reading of a problem is to try to identify the important details and information needed to solve the problem.

1 Understand   Using Monitor Strategy

Think about important details. The problem asks for an estimate of the total amount of ribbon needed. The fractions have unlike denominators.

• What do you need to do to answer the question?

2 Plan   Choosing a Method for Solving

You can simplify the problem by rounding.
• Round the fractions to the nearest whole numbers.
• Use the rounded numbers to estimate the sum.

3 Try It   Using Rounding

Round $\frac{1}{3}$ down to 0. Round $\frac{5}{6}$ up to 1. Round $1\frac{1}{2}$ up to 2.

$0 + 1 + 2 = 3$ A reasonable amount of ribbon is about 3 ft.
• How can you decide whether the total is more than or less than 3 ft?

4 Look Back   Checking for Reasonableness

Check your estimate.
• Have you rounded correctly?

Sample Test Item

1 Three different lengths of blue ribbon are needed for an art project. The three lengths are $\frac{1}{3}$ ft, $\frac{5}{6}$ ft, and $1\frac{1}{2}$ ft. What is a reasonable amount of blue ribbon to buy?

A   less than 1 ft

B   between 1 and 2 ft

C   between 2 and 3 ft

D   between 3 and 4 ft

Test Prep Handbook

Try These!

2 Jonathan has stored three bags of dog food in the cupboard. There are two small bags weighing $\frac{7}{8}$ lb each and one larger bag weighing $2\frac{1}{2}$ lb. What is a reasonable estimate of how much dog food Jonathan has stored?

A   less than 3 lb

B   between 3 and 4 lb

C   between 4 and 5 lb

D   more than 5

3 Three boxes are stacked on a shelf. Their heights are $1\frac{1}{4}$ in., $4\frac{3}{6}$ in., and $8\frac{1}{2}$ in. What is a reasonable total height for the three boxes?

A   less than 6 in.

B   between 6 and 12 in.

C   between 12 and 18 in.

D   more than 18 in.

Chapter 11 Test Prep Strategies

Predict/Infer

Identify the important information given in the problem. Think about what you already know about it. Look for important words or phrases. Then think about what you need to find out.

① Understand

Using Predict/Infer Strategy

Reread the problem slowly. See if you can predict what operations are not appropriate and can be eliminated.
- What choices can you eliminate?

② Plan

Choosing a Method for Solving

You need to decide whether to multiply or divide.
- How can estimation help you to solve the problem?

③ Try It

Using Estimation

Maria has $\frac{5}{6}$ lb of apples — $\frac{5}{6}$ is close to 1.

Maria peeled $\frac{2}{3}$ lb — $\frac{2}{3}$ is a little more than $\frac{1}{2}$.

- Which answer choice shows that she peeled a little more than $\frac{1}{2}$ a pound and less than 1 pound?
- Why isn't D the correct answer choice?

④ Look Back

Checking for Reasonableness

- Why do you think your answer is reasonable?

Sample Test Item

Choose the best solution sentence.

1 Maria has $\frac{5}{6}$ lb of apples. She peels $\frac{2}{3}$ of the apples. What part of a pound does Maria peel?

A $\frac{2}{3} + \frac{5}{6} = \square$

B $\frac{5}{6} - \frac{2}{3} = \square$

C $\frac{2}{3} \times \frac{5}{6} = \square$

D $\frac{5}{6} \div \frac{2}{3} = \square$

Try These!

Choose the best solution sentence.

2 Bill has $\frac{7}{8}$ of a pizza. He and a friend share it equally. How much will each person get?

A $\frac{7}{8} + \frac{7}{8} = \square$

B $\frac{7}{8} - \frac{7}{8} = \square$

C $\frac{7}{8} \times 2 = \square$

D $\frac{7}{8} \div 2 = \square$

3 Everyday by noon the parking garage is $\frac{9}{10}$ full. If $\frac{2}{3}$ of the cars park there by 9:00 A.M., what part of the garage is filled at that time?

A $\frac{2}{3} \times \frac{9}{10} = \square$

B $\frac{2}{3} \div \frac{9}{10} = \square$

C $\frac{9}{10} \div \frac{2}{3} = \square$

D $\frac{9}{10} - \frac{2}{3} = \square$

Chapter 12 Test Prep Strategies

After you read the problem, think about what the problem asks and what information it provides. By evaluating these facts, you should then be ready to solve it.

1 Understand **Using Evaluate Strategy**

Focus on words in the question: *probability*.

- What does it mean to find the probability?

2 Plan **Choosing a Method for Solving**

You need to think about the total number of students who were surveyed and about how many of them chose apples.

3 Try It **Using Probability**

You know that 7 students selected Apples.
You know that 15 students were surveyed.
You can say the *probability* is 7 out of 15.

4 Look Back **Checking for Reasonableness**

Reread the problem and review the chart information.
- Why could you eliminate choices B and C?

Sample Test Item

1 Fifteen students answered a survey about their favorite fruits. The chart shows the results.

Favorite Fruit

Fruit	Tallies	Number of Students
Pears	I I	2
Grapes	I	1
Peaches	I I	2
Apples	⊮ II	7
Bananas	III	3
Total	⊮ ⊮ ⊮	15

If a student is selected at random, what is the probability that the student's favorite fruit is apples?

A 2 out of 5
B 1 out of 15
C 3 out of 15
D 7 out of 15

Try These!

2 Use the chart above. If randomly asked, what is the probability that a student will select Peaches?

A 1 out of 15
B 2 out of 15
C 3 out of 15
D 3 out of 30

3 Use the chart above. If randomly asked, what is the probability that a student will select Bananas?

A 1 out of 3
B 2 out of 15
C 3 out of 15
D 3 out of 30

Chapter 13 Test Prep Strategies

Reading Strategy
Think About Words

Sometimes a problem contains an unfamiliar word. Reread the problem. Then figure out the meaning of the word from its context and/or parts.

1 Understand **Using Think About Words Strategy**

Check your understanding of the math vocabulary used.
- What does *area* mean?
- What is a *polygon*?

2 Plan **Choosing a Problem Solving Strategy**

Solve by working a simpler problem.
- How will visualizing the figure in smaller, separate parts help?

3 Try It **Using Work a Simpler Problem**

Look at the polygon as three parts each with its own area. You can use an expression to show the area of each part.
- How would you combine the three expressions to show the entire area?

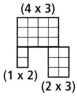

(4 x 3)
(1 x 2)
(2 x 3)

4 Look Back **Checking for Reasonableness**

Reread the problem. Then review the other answer choices.
- Why could you eliminate the other answer choices?

Sample Test Item

1 Which is one way to find the **area** of the polygon?

A $(3 \times 4) + (3 \times 3)$
B $(4 \times 6) \times 2$
C $(6 \times 4) - 3$
D $(4 \times 3) + (1 \times 2) + (2 \times 3)$

Try These!

2 Which is one way to find the area of the polygon?

A $(2 + 5) + (2 \times 6)$
B $(6 \times 5) \times 2$
C $(6 \times 5) - 8$
D $(8 \times 5) - 6$

3 Which is one way to find the area of the polygon?

A $(4 \times 6) - (4 \times 2)$
B $(6 \times 4) + (3 \times 4)$
C $(2 + 4) + 6$
D $(3 + 6) + 4$

Cumulative Tests

Chapter 1 Cumulative Test

Mark your answer on the answer sheet.

1. Which is the greatest number?

   A   999,888,204
   B   1,294,302,000
   C   2,194,302,000
   D   2,419,846,307

2. Which is the standard form for:
   3,000,000,000 + 90,000 + 800 + 20 + 4

   F   3,000,090,824
   G   3,000,098,024
   H   3,000,908,204
   J   3,000,980,024

3. Which model shows 0.31?

   A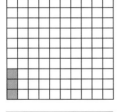

   B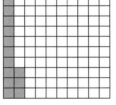

   C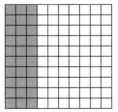

   D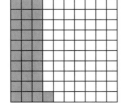

4. The average rainfall during the summer months in Arbor County was 5.42 cm. When rounded to the nearest tenth, what is the average rainfall?

   F   5.4 cm
   G   5.5 cm
   H   6.0 cm
   J   6.5 cm

5. During the first year, a department store was visited by 47,294 people. In its tenth year, the number of yearly visitors was 23,596 people more. How many people visited the store during its tenth year?

   A   23,698
   B   70,890
   C   70,970
   D   80,890

6. Suppose you plan to take a trip that is 894 miles long. After three days, you have traveled 536 miles. How many more miles do you need to travel to complete the trip?

   F   1,430 miles
   G   538 miles
   H   358 miles
   J   268 miles

GO ON

7. Which pair of numbers when rounded will give a sum of about 10 and a difference of about 1.4?

A 4.57 and 4.26

B 5.63 and 4.19

C 6.53 and 3.28

D 7.54 and 2.96

8. Jean skied 0.23 second faster than Paul. If her time was 45.98 seconds, what was Paul's time?

F 45.75 seconds

G 46.01 seconds

H 46.11 seconds

J 46.21 seconds

9. The graph shows how many cars stop at a stop sign. During the first hour, 30 cars stop. How many cars stopped in total during the 4 hours?

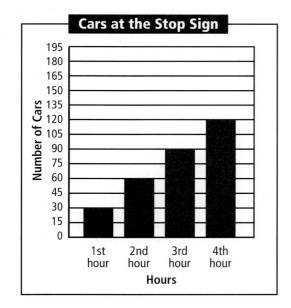

A 60 cars

B 90 cars

C 150 cars

D 300 cars

10. After the first week of practice your best race time was 24.78 seconds. After 4 more weeks of practice, you improved your time by 0.9 second. What number sentence gives you a reasonable estimate for your race time now?

F $25 + 1 = \blacksquare$

G $25 - 1 = \blacksquare$

H $4 \times 25 = \blacksquare$

J $25 - 4 = \blacksquare$

Please note that items 11–12 have *five* answer choices.

11. Which decimal below, when rounded to the nearest tenth, does not round to 10.0?

A 9.95

B 9.99

C 10.03

D 10.08

E Not here

12. Which point best represents a number greater than 0.5, but less than 0.8?

F point A

G point B

H point C

J point D

K point E

Chapter 2 Cumulative Test

Mark your answer on the answer sheet.

1. A pair of socks costs $4. If Jack buys 2 pairs of socks, which number sentence shows the total cost of both pairs?

   A $c = 4 \times 2$

   B $c = 4 - 2$

   C $c = 4 \div 2$

   D $c = 4 + 2$

2. During October, a restaurant serves chicken every 6th day. It serves mashed potatoes every 8th day. On what day will it serve chicken and mashed potatoes?

   F 6th day

   G 14th day

   H 16th day

   J 24th day

3. There are 48 cartons on a shelf. Each carton contains 64 boxes of crayons. What is a good estimate of how many boxes are on the shelf?

   A 300

   B 3,000

   C 4,000

   D 30,000

4. Bill can write his name 8 times in one minute. How many times can he write his name in an hour?

   F 16 times

   G 60 times

   H 160 times

   J 480 times

5. A chair weighs 25 pounds. How much will 12 chairs weigh?

   A 30 pounds

   B 300 pounds

   C 500 pounds

   D 3,000 pounds

6. A notebook costs $1.89. What is a good estimate of how much 5 notebooks cost?

   F more than $10

   G less than $10

   H less than $5

   J less than $2

GO ON →

7. You and 3 friends meet each other at school. Each of you shakes hands with each other one time. How many handshakes are there in total?

A   4 handshakes

B   6 handshakes

C   10 handshakes

D   12 handshakes

8. A recipe calls for 5 pounds of potatoes to make 12 servings of potato salad. How many pounds of potatoes are needed to make 48 servings?

F   10 pounds

G   17 pounds

H   20 pounds

J   32 pounds

9. Which number completes this pattern:

4.1, 3.95, 3.8, 3.65, ▓

A   3.6

B   3.55

C   3.5

D   3.45

10. What is the value of the underlined digit?

56,234,<u>1</u>02,098

F   10,000

G   100,000

H   1,000,000

J   10,000,000

Please note that items 11–12 have *five* answer choices.

11. Which statement is true about the estimated sum of 223,198 and 116,539?

A   The sum will be less than 300,000.

B   The sum will be more than 300,000 and less than 400,000.

C   The sum will be about 400,000.

D   The sum will be more than 400,000 and less than 500,000.

E   The sum will be more than 500,000.

12. After removing some potatoes from a bag, you weigh the bag and find that it is 6.8 kg. If the bag had 15 kg of potatoes to begin with, how many kg of potatoes did you empty out?

F   9.2 kg

G   9.8 kg

H   11.2 kg

J   21.8 kg

K   Not here

STOP

Chapter 3 Cumulative Test

Mark your answer on the answer sheet.

1. Suppose you have 48 cupcakes to share equally among 4 friends. Which number sentence represents how many cupcakes each friend will get?

   A $48 + n = 4$

   B $48 - n = 4$

   C $48 \times n = 4$

   D $48 \div n = 4$

2. James is reading a book that is 438 pages long. About how many pages should be read each day if he wants to finish reading the book in 6 days?

   F   30

   G   70

   H   80

   J   100

3. Which expression does *not* have the value of 6?

   A $600 \div (5 + 5)$

   B $(6 \div 3) \times 3$

   C $60 \div (5 \times 2)$

   D $(6 - 3) + (30 \div 10)$

4. The last number of a combination to a safe is a 3-digit number that is divisible by 4, 6, and 9. Which number below is the last number of the combination?

   F   150

   G   216

   H   233

   J   457

5. An adult heart pumps about 300 L every hour. About how much blood is pumped in a minute?

   A   30 L

   B   20 L

   C   10 L

   D   5 L

6. Which is the greatest common factor of 15 and 27?

   F   2

   G   3

   H   5

   J   9

GO ON

7. Which number is *not* a prime number?

A   11
B   17
C   33
D   47

8. You write down two 2-digit numbers on a piece of paper. The sum of the two numbers is 95. The product is 2,200. Which are the two numbers?

F   11 and 200
G   22 and 100
H   40 and 55
J   50 and 45

9. Kosei buys 3 items in a store. The lowest-priced item is $8 and the highest is $12. Before tax, what is a reasonable total cost for the items?

F   less than $12
G   between $12 and $22
H   between $22 and $32
J   more than $42

Please note that items 10–12 have *five* answer choices.

10. What is the total cost for buying 3 dozen donuts and 1 pie?

1 Dozen Donuts	$1.42
1 Dozen Muffins	$2.15
1 Pie	$3.29

A $7.55
B $6.13
C $5.71
D $4.26
E   Not here

11. Which value best represents point *V* on the number line?

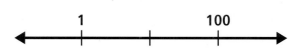

A   0. 413
B   0.632
C   0.721
D   0.9
E   Not here

12. Which is the value of the missing number?
4 + (2 + 9) = (4 + ▨) + 3

F   98
G   99
H   4
J   0
K   Not here

STOP

Chapter 4 Cumulative Test

Mark your answer on the answer sheet.

1. What is the median of these 5 test scores: 90, 85, 95, 75, 80?

A 80

B 85

C 90

D 95

Use the table to answer questions 2 and 3.

Ice Cream	
Vanilla	Chocolate
⊥⊥⊥⊥ ⊥⊥⊥⊥ ⊥⊥	⎮⎮⎮⎮

2. What fraction of all the votes for favorite ice cream were votes for chocolate?

F $\frac{1}{2}$

G $\frac{1}{3}$

H $\frac{1}{4}$

J $\frac{1}{8}$

3. What if you choose to show the data in the table as a pictograph. If you choose to use 🍦 to represent 4 votes for a flavor, how many 🍦 would you draw for vanilla?

A 12 🍦🍦🍦🍦🍦🍦🍦🍦🍦🍦🍦🍦

B 4 🍦🍦🍦🍦

C 3 🍦🍦🍦

D 1 🍦

4. Suppose you are paid 5¢ the first day, 10¢ the second day, 20¢ the third day, and so on. If this pattern continues, on which day will you be paid over $1.00?

F 3rd day

G 4th day

H 5th day

J 6th day

5. Use the line graph to answer questions 5 and 6.

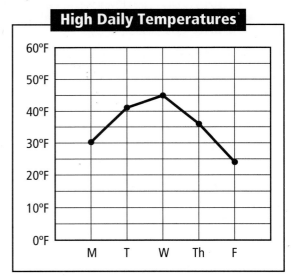

About what was the difference between the highest and the lowest temperatures shown?

A 40°

B 20°

C 30°

D 10°

GO ON ▶

6. Using the graph in #5, find which answer shows the days ordered from the lowest to the highest high temperature.

F Monday, Tuesday, Wednesday, Thursday, Friday

G Friday, Monday, Thursday, Tuesday, Wednesday

H Friday, Monday, Tuesday, Thursday, Wednesday

J Wednesday, Tuesday, Thursday, Monday, Friday

7.

Which of the following is a reasonable conclusion from the graph?

A About $\frac{1}{4}$ of the people chose either Quiz Shows or Talk Shows

B Quiz Shows and Adventures were equally popular

C About $\frac{2}{3}$ of the people chose Comedy

D Adventures were the most popular

8. The average height of four plants is 26 in. One plant is 28 in. tall. Another plant is 28 in. tall. A third plant is 30 in. tall. How tall is the fourth plant?

F 18 in.

G 22 in.

H 26 in.

J 28 in.

9. Which statement is true about the numbers 3 and 27?

A Both are prime numbers.

B Both are composite numbers.

C 3 is a prime factor of 27.

D Both are even numbers.

Please note that items 10-12 have *five* answer choices.

10. You have $8.48 to share equally among yourself and three friends. How much will you each receive?

F $4.24

G $3.16

H $2.12

J $2.02

K Not here

11. Which is the missing value for *n*?

$n - 4.24 = 13.76$

A 18

B 17.76

C 9.9

D 9.52

E Not here

12. Your sister is 6 years younger than your older brother. If your brother is 14 years old, which expression represents your sister's age?

F $6 - 14 = \blacksquare$

G $14 - 6 = \blacksquare$

H $6 + 14 = \blacksquare$

J $14 \div 6 = \blacksquare$

K $6 \times 14 = \blacksquare$

STOP

Chapter 5 Cumulative Test

Mark your answer on the answer sheet.

1. What is the length to the nearest $\frac{1}{8}$ in. of the pin?

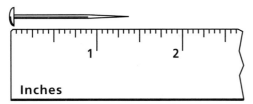

A $1\frac{1}{8}$ in.

B $1\frac{1}{4}$ in.

C $1\frac{3}{8}$ in.

D $1\frac{5}{8}$ in.

2. Which statement is not true about all regular polygons?

  F   They have sides that are congruent (same length).

  G   They have angles that are congruent (same measure).

  H   They are closed figures.

  J   They have an even number of sides.

Use the table to answer question 3.

	Triangle	Quadrilayeral	Pentagon	Hexagon	Heptagon
Number of Sides	3	4	5	6	7
Number of Diagonals	0	2	5	9	n

3. If the pattern continues, how many diagonals will a heptagon have?

  A   14

  B   11

  C   9

  D   7

4. The perimeter of the rectangle is 38 cm. What is the length of $\overline{BD}$?

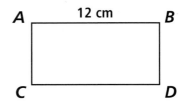

  F   26 cm

  G   14 cm

  H   7 cm

  J   4 cm

5. James awoke at 7:45 a.m. He left his house 1 hour and 30 minutes later. When did he leave his house?

  A   9:00 a.m.

  B   9:15 a.m.

  C   10:00 a.m.

  D   10:15 a.m.

6. Brian has a desk that is 2 ft 11 in wide. How wide is this in inches?

  F   62 in.

  G   48 in.

  H   35 in.

  J   13 in.

GO ON ➡

7. Brina practiced ballet 1.75 hours the first week, 2.3 hours the second week, and 3.25 hours the third week. What is the best estimate of her practice time for all 3 weeks?

A   6 hours

B   7 hours

C   8 hours

D   9 hours

8.

4 cm

The diameter of the circle is 4 cm. What is the circle's approximate circumference? [Use $\pi \approx 3.14$]

F   12 cm

G   4 cm

H   8 cm

J   3 cm

9. After you remove 7 cookies from a bag, you share the remainder equally among 3 friends. They each receive 4 cookies. How many were in the bag originally?

A   11 cookies

B   15 cookies

C   19 cookies

D   25 cookies

Please note that items 10-12 have *five* answer choices.

10. Danna bought an 18.5 lb Thanksgiving turkey. What is the weight in ounces?

A   20

B   34.5

C   148

D   296

E   3496

11. Which statement about the graph is true?

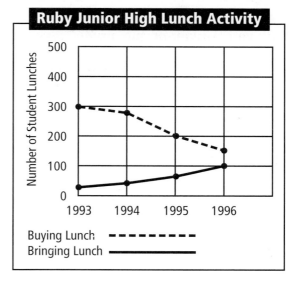

Ruby Junior High Lunch Activity

Buying Lunch - - - - - - -
Bringing Lunch —————

F   Students buying lunch decreased. Students bringing lunch increased.

G   Students buying lunch and bringing lunch both increased.

H   Students buying lunch and bringing lunch both decreased.

J   Students buying lunch increased. Students bringing lunch decreased.

K   Students buying lunch remained unchanged.

12. Which statement is not true?

F   No odd number is divisible by 2.

G   All even numbers are divisible by 2.

H   A number divisible by 4 is also divisible by 2.

J   The product of two whole numbers greater than 1 is greater than either factor.

K   The quotient of two whole numbers is greater than the divisor.

STOP

Chapter 6 Cumulative Test

Mark your answer on the answer sheet.

1. Which is the best estimate for the product of 6 × 234?

- A   2,000
- B   1,400
- C   1,300
- D   1,200

2. A snail crawled 1.43 meters in one day. If it maintains this pace, how far will it travel in 100 days?

- F   14.3 meters
- G   14.43 meters
- H   101.43 meters
- J   143 meters

3. Which number makes this number sentence true?

5.4 × ■ < 6.3

- A   1
- B   2
- C   2.2
- D   3

4. A meter of fabric costs $3.64. How much will 2.8 meters of this fabric cost to the nearest cent?

- F $6.44
- G $10.19
- H $11.19
- J $101.92

5. A towel that cost $8.49 was on sale for $6.89. Jeff decided to buy 3 towels. How much did he spend?

- A $25.47
- B $22.47
- C $20.67
- D $17.98

6. You have 4 different color pairs of pants, and 3 different color shirts. How many different outfits can you make?

- F   6
- G   7
- H   12
- J   15

GO ON ▶

7. A bowl weighs 2.6 kg. What is the weight of the bowl in grams?

   A   2,600 g
   B   260 g
   C   126 g
   D   26 g

8. Here are the heights of 4 people:

Phil	4 ft. 2 in.
Karen	47 in.
Lyle	53 in.
Joan	4 ft. 7 in.

Which of the following is a reasonable conclusion?

   F   Phil is shorter than Karen.
   G   Karen is the tallest.
   H   Lyle is the same height as Phil.
   J   Joan is taller than Lyle.

Please note that items 9-12 have *five* answer choices.

9. For which set of data is the range 20 and the mode 8?

   A   5, 15, 8, 8, 7
   B   5, 25, 5, 15, 8
   C   5, 8, 7, 8, 25
   D   5, 15, 25, 8, 15
   E   Not Here

10. For which pair of numbers is the greatest common factor 6?

   F   6, 9
   G   9, 12
   H   12, 18
   J   12, 24
   K   15, 24

11. Moyra bought presents for each of 5 friends. The lowest-priced gift cost $3.50, including tax, and the highest-priced gift cost $8.50, including tax. Which is a reasonable total for the 5 gifts?

   A   Between $3.50 and $20
   B   Between $8.50 and $20
   C   More than $40
   D   Less than $18
   E   Between $17 and $43

12. What is the perimeter of the triangle?

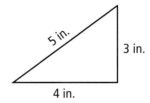

   F   7 in.
   G   9 in.
   H   10 in.
   J   11 in.
   K   Not Here

STOP

Chapter 7 Cumulative Test

Mark your answer on the answer sheet.

1. Which quotient is less than 10?

   A   946 ÷ 100

   B   2,580 ÷ 100

   C   183.4 ÷ 10

   D   7,500.4 ÷ 100

2. A record snowfall of 24.5 in. fell on December 15 in 5 hours. About how many inches of snow fell each hour?

   F   24.5 in.

   G   9.5 in.

   H   4.9 in.

   J   4.5 in.

3.

What is the cost of buying 1 pound of apples?

   A $.75

   B $1.25

   C $2.00

   D $2.25

4. Which is the most reasonable estimate for the quotient of $234.39 ÷ 7?

   F $300

   G $30

   H $3

   J $.30

5. Janice ran a total distance of 2540 meters. How many kilometers did she run?

   A   254 km

   B   25.4 km

   C   2.54 km

   D   0.254 km

6. Which yard needs the least fencing to go around its perimeter?

   F   5.21

   G   6.23 m   1.96 m

   H   7.4 m

   J   8.5 m   5.1 m   6.8 m

GO ON ▶

7. Which number below will make this number sentence true?

14.3 ÷ ▓ = 0.0143

A 1

B 10

C 100

D 1,000

Please note that items 8-12 have *five* answer choices.

Use the double bar graph to answer questions 8 and 9.

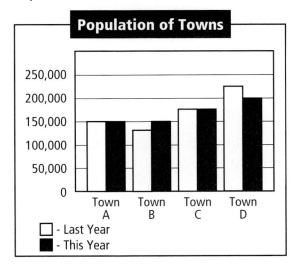

Population of Towns

- □ - Last Year
- ■ - This Year

8. Which of the following is a reasonable conclusion from the graph?

A Town A shows an increase in population.

B Town A shows a decrease in population.

C Town D shows an increase in population.

D Town D shows a decrease in population.

E Town B shows a decrease in population.

9. What was the approximate population of Town B last year?

F 100,000

G 130,000

H 150,000

J 170,000

K Not here

10. Which number sentence is true?

A 848 mm > 9.2 m

B 14.9 m > 203 cm

C 0.31 km < 250 m

D 1.49 m < 202 cm

E 100 m > 100 km

11. Jason earns an average of $38 a week babysitting. Which is the best estimate of how much he would earn over a 4-week period?

A $40

B $80

C $120

D $160

E $200

12. What is the missing number in the pattern?

62, 56, 50, ▓, 38, 32

F 40

G 42

H 44

J 48

K 52

STOP

Chapter 8 Cumulative Test

Mark your answer on the answer sheet.

1. Triangle *DCE* is congruent to triangle *FHG*.

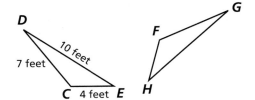

What is the length of segment GH?

A   4

B   5

C   7

D   10

2. Which number sentence could be used to find a reasonable estimate for the increase between 1994 and 1995?

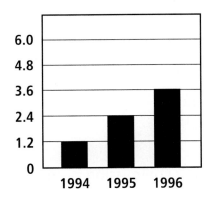

G   2 − 1 = ■

H   4 − 2 = ■

J   4 + 2 = ■

K   3 − 2 = ■

3. What statement below gives the measure of angle X and what type of angle it is?

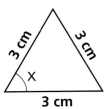

A   45°, obtuse

B   60°, acute

C   60°, obtuse

D   90°, right

4. The figure has a line of symmetry as shown below.

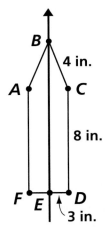

What is the length of line segment AF?

F   3 in.

G   4 in.

H   8 in.

J   15 in.

GO ON

Use the grid to answer questions 5–7.

```
7
6   B
5
4
3
2   A         D
1
0   1  2  3  4  5  6  7
```

5. If you connect points *A*, *B* and *D*, what figure do you make?

   A   an equilateral triangle

   B   an obtuse triangle

   C   a right triangle

   D   a scalene triangle

6. Which ordered pair does point *C* have in order to form square *ABCD*?

   F   (2, 6)

   G   (5, 5)

   H   (5, 6)

   J   (6, 6)

7. How many faces does this rectangular prism have?

   A   4

   B   6

   C   8

   D   12

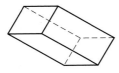

8. You get on an elevator on the 10th floor. It goes down 3 floors, then up 2 floors. Then it goes down another 5 floors and you get off. On what floor did you get off?

   F   4th floor

   G   5th floor

   H   8th floor

   J   9th floor

Please note that items 9–11 have *five* answer choices.

9. If you organize this data into a table using tally marks, which tally shown below would you see for 1994?

1990, 1991, 1991, 1991, 1991, 1992, 1993, 1993, 1994, 1994, 1994, 1994, 1994, 1994, 1995, 1995, 1996, 1996

   F   ///

   G   ////

   H   ⊬ /

   J   ⊬ ⊬

   K   Not here

10. Which statement is not true?

   A   5.1 m = 510 cm

   B   0.8 km = 80 m

   C   2.41 m = 241 cm

   D   350 m = 0.35 km

   E   48 cm = 0.48 m

11. A train leaves at 4:20 p.m. It is now 2:15 p.m. How much time is there until the train leaves?

   F   2 hours 5 minutes

   G   2 hours 15 minutes

   H   1 hour 45 minutes

   J   1 hour 20 minutes

   K   Not here

STOP

Chapter 9 Cumulative Test

Mark your answer on the answer sheet.

1. During math class, John's teacher placed 4 green marbles and 3 red marbles in a bag. What fraction of the marbles placed in the bag were red?

A $\frac{3}{4}$

B $\frac{4}{3}$

C $\frac{3}{7}$

D $\frac{4}{7}$

2. Which set of fractions are equivalent fractions?

F $\frac{1}{2}, \frac{2}{4}, \frac{4}{8}, \frac{8}{16}$

G $\frac{1}{3}, \frac{1}{6}, \frac{1}{9}, \frac{1}{12}$

H $\frac{2}{3}, \frac{3}{4}, \frac{4}{5}, \frac{5}{6}$

J $\frac{1}{3}, \frac{2}{4}, \frac{3}{5}, \frac{4}{6}$

3. Which fraction is closest to $\frac{1}{2}$?

A $\frac{1}{8}$

B $\frac{3}{8}$

C $\frac{3}{4}$

D $\frac{7}{8}$

4. After a party, the pizza shown below was left over. What fraction is this?

F 2 pizzas

G $2\frac{1}{8}$ pizzas

H $1\frac{7}{8}$ pizzas

J $\frac{10}{8}$ pizzas

5. The chart shows the weight of 4 kittens.

Kitten	Weight
Frisky	$2\frac{1}{8}$ lb
Pretzel	$1\frac{3}{4}$ lb
Fanny	$1\frac{1}{2}$ lb
Tiger	$1\frac{7}{8}$ lb

Which is a reasonable conclusion about these kittens?

A Tiger is heavier than Frisky

B Frisky is the lightest

C Tiger is the heaviest

D Frisky is heavier than Fanny

GO ON

6. The scale showed that a chicken weighed $2\frac{1}{2}$ lb. A heavier chicken weighed P pounds. Which value for P is a heavier chicken?

    F $P = \frac{5}{2}$ lb

    G $P = 2\frac{1}{8}$ lb

    H   P = 2.5 lb

    J   P = 2.7 lb

7. There are 24 pieces of fruit in a fruit basket. One-half are apples, one-third are oranges, and the rest are pears. How many pears are in the basket?

    A   3 pears

    B   4 pears

    C   6 pears

    D   8 pears

8. Which numbers would you multiply to estimate 48 × 195?

    F   40 × 100

    G   40 × 200

    H   50 × 100

    J   50 × 200

Please note that items 9–12 have *five* answer choices.

9. *STUV* is a parallelogram.

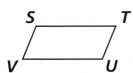

    Which statement is true?

    A   ∠S is congruent to ∠T

    B   ∠S is congruent to ∠U

    C   ∠S is congruent to ∠V

    D   ∠T is congruent to ∠U

    E   ∠V is congruent to ∠U

10. Which figure completes this sequence?

    F

    G

    H

    J

    K   Not here

11. Which pair of numbers when multiplied will give a product between 50 and 100?

    A   0.4 × 100

    B   7.2 × 8.13

    C   2.3 × 100

    D   4.16 × 7.85

    E   6.8 × 4.9

12. Which point on the number line represents $\frac{3}{4}$?

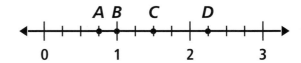

    F   point *A*

    G   point *B*

    H   point *C*

    J   point *D*

    K   Not here

STOP

Chapter 10 Cumulative Test

Mark your answer on the answer sheet.

1. Which model shows $\frac{3}{8} + \frac{2}{8}$?

A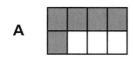

B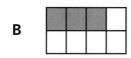

C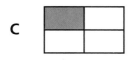

D

2. A cake is divided into 12 equal pieces. After 4 pieces are eaten, what fraction of the cake is left? Which number sentence could be used to find the solution?

F $\quad \frac{8}{12} - \frac{4}{12} = $ ■

G $\quad \frac{4}{12} - \frac{1}{12} = $ ■

H $\quad \frac{12}{12} - \frac{1}{12} = $ ■

J $\quad \frac{12}{12} - \frac{4}{12} = $ ■

3. Which is the best estimate for 1.25 + 4.61?

A   less than 3

B   between 3 and 4

C   between 4 and 5

D   more than 5

4. Which model shows $\frac{3}{4} - \frac{1}{8}$ shaded?

F

G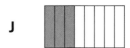

H

J

5. Which shaded region does *not* represent $\frac{1}{2}$ of the figure?

A

B

C

D

6. Mrs. Lynch had 20 papers to grade. She graded 6 this morning. What fraction of the papers did she grade?

F $\quad \frac{2}{5}$

G $\quad \frac{6}{7}$

H $\quad \frac{3}{10}$

J $\quad \frac{3}{4}$

GO ON ➡

7. Which is *not* another name for $1\frac{1}{2}$?

A $1\frac{4}{8}$

B $1\frac{3}{6}$

C $\frac{9}{6}$

D $\frac{6}{3}$

8. A contest begins with 2,000 people. After each week, there are one-half as many people left in the contest as the week before. At the end of which week will there be fewer than 50 people left in the contest?

F after week 5

G after week 6

H after week 8

J after week 10

Please note that items 9–12 have *five* answer choices.

9. Which set of ordered pairs when graphed and then connected will make a triangle?

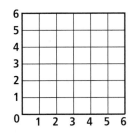

A (1, 1), (2, 2), (3, 3)

B (1, 1), (1, 2), (1, 3)

C (1, 1), (2, 3), (3, 1)

D (1, 1), (2, 1), (3, 1)

E Not here

10. How many vertices does a parallelogram have?

F 4 vertices

G 8 vertices

H 9 vertices

J 10 vertices

K 12 vertices

11. Which point on the number line is closest to the value of these models?

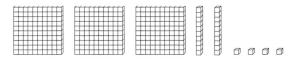

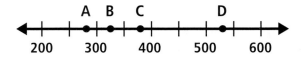

A point *A*

B point *B*

C point *C*

D point *D*

E Not here

12.

Which statement is true?

F $\frac{1}{2} = \frac{2}{3}$

G $\frac{2}{3} < \frac{1}{2}$

H $\frac{3}{4} > \frac{1}{2}$

J $\frac{5}{8} < \frac{1}{2}$

K $\frac{5}{8} > \frac{3}{4}$

STOP

Chapter 11 Cumulative Test

Mark your answer on the answer sheet.

1. There are 32 ounces in a quart. If a quart container of orange juice is $\frac{3}{4}$-full, how many ounces of orange juice are in the container?

   A   24 ounces

   B   16 ounces

   C   8 ounces

   D $\frac{3}{4}$ ounce

2. A dress sells regularly for $48.99. In a sale, the price has been reduced by $\frac{1}{5}$. About how much do you save if you buy the dress on sale?

   F   about $8

   G   about $10

   H   about $15

   J   about $20

3. My house is $\frac{3}{4}$ mile from the supermarket. I walked halfway from my house to the supermarket. Which number sentence shows how to find the distance that I walked?

   A $\frac{1}{2} + \frac{3}{4} = \square$

   B $\frac{1}{2} - \frac{3}{4} = \square$

   C $\frac{3}{4} - \frac{1}{2} = \square$

   D $\frac{1}{2} \times \frac{3}{4} = \square$

4. What is $5 \div \frac{1}{2}$?

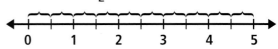

   F $2\frac{1}{2}$

   G   5

   H $5\frac{1}{2}$

   J   10

5. Which phrase below completes this sentence?

   Dividing a whole number n by $\frac{1}{3}$ is the same as _?

   A   multiplying the number by $\frac{1}{3}$.

   B   multiplying the number by 3.

   C   multiplying the number by n.

   D   dividing the number by 3.

6. Which set of fractions is in order from least to greatest?

   F $3\frac{1}{8}, 4\frac{1}{3}, 4\frac{1}{3}, 3\frac{1}{2}$

   G $3\frac{1}{2}, 3\frac{1}{8}, 4\frac{1}{3}, 4\frac{1}{4}$

   H $3\frac{1}{8}, 3\frac{1}{2}, 4\frac{1}{4}, 4\frac{1}{3}$

   J $4\frac{1}{3}, 4\frac{1}{4}, 3\frac{1}{2}, 3\frac{1}{8}$

7. Which number completes this pattern:

   4,200, 420, 42, ▮ ?

   A   4.2

   B   41

   C   402

   D   420

GO ON

Please note that items 9–12 have *five* answer choices.

8. Which set of data when graphed would produce a line graph that looks like the one below?

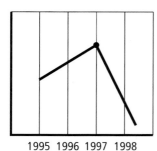

1995 1996 1997 1998

F

1995	1996	1997	1998
600	650	700	450

G

1995	1996	1997	1998
600	650	700	700

H

1995	1996	1997	1998
600	600	600	600

J

1995	1996	1997	1998
600	550	500	700

K   Not here

9. Which is a reasonable conclusion from the graph above?

A   There is a decrease between 1997 and 1998

B   There is a decrease between 1996 and 1997

C   There is an increase between 1997 and 1998

D   There is a decrease between 1995 and 1996

E   Not here

Use the diagram to answer questions 11–12.

C C
C C = pt pt   =   qt qt
C C   pt pt
C C

10. What fraction of a quart is 1 cup?

F $\frac{1}{2}$ or $\frac{2}{4}$

G $\frac{4}{8}$ or $\frac{1}{2}$

H $\frac{2}{8}$ or $\frac{1}{4}$

J $\frac{1}{3}$ or $\frac{2}{6}$

K   Not here

11. A cafeteria serves 480 children. It will serve each child a cup of milk. How many quarts of milk will it need to buy?

A   120 quarts

B   60 quarts

C   30 quarts

D   15 quarts

E   10 quarts

12. The length of a rectangle is 14 cm. Its width is half of that. What is its perimeter?

F   14

G   21

H   22

J   32

K   42

STOP

Chapter 12 Cumulative Test

Mark your answer on the answer sheet.

1.

Which does not show the ratio of circles to all of the shapes?

A   4 to 8

B $\frac{4}{8}$ or $\frac{1}{2}$

C   4 to 3

D   4 out of 8

2. Which ratios are equivalent to $\frac{2}{3}$?

F $\frac{4}{6}, \frac{6}{9}, \frac{8}{12}$

G $\frac{3}{4}, \frac{4}{5}, \frac{5}{6}$

H $\frac{4}{6}, \frac{6}{12}, \frac{12}{24}$

J $\frac{3}{2}, \frac{9}{6}, \frac{12}{8}$

3. There are 48 egg cartons on the shelf. Each contains 12 eggs. What is a good estimate of how many eggs are on the shelf?

A   500

B   1,000

C   1,200

D   5,000

4. Which fraction and decimal are another name for 12%?

F   1.2, $1\frac{1}{5}$

G   0.12, $\frac{3}{25}$

H   0.12, $\frac{12}{50}$

J   0.012, $\frac{12}{1000}$

5. About what percent of the circle is shaded?

A   About 80%

B   About 75%

C   About 50%

D   About 30%

6. The total cost for purchasing 2 hot dogs and a shake is $5.40. The hot dogs cost $1.95 each. Which number sentence could you use to find n, the cost of one shake?

F $2n + \$1.95 = \$5.40$

G $\$5.40 - \$1.95 = 2n$

H $2n - \$1.95 = \$5.40$

J $2 \times \$1.95 + n = \$5.40$

GO ON ➡

Use the spinner to answer questions 7–8.

7. What is the probability of spinning blue?

A $\frac{1}{4}$

B $\frac{1}{3}$

C $\frac{1}{2}$

D 0

8. If you spin the spinner 40 times, about how many times would you expect to land on red?

F never

G always

H 10 times

J 20 times

Please note that items 9–12 have *five* answer choices.

9. Ilie bought 5 comic books. The lowest priced book cost $1 and the highest priced book cost $3. Which is a reasonable total for the cost of the 5 comic books?

A Less than $3

B Between $3 and $5

C Between $5 and $15

D Between $15 and $20

E More than $20

10. You have a number cube, numbered from 1–6, and a penny. You roll the number cube and flip the penny. How many different outcomes are possible?

F 6 outcomes

G 8 outcomes

H 10 outcomes

J 12 outcomes

K 16 outcomes

11. Which figure below has no line of symmetry?

A

B

C

D

E Not here

12. Which expression has a value of 20?

F $(3 \times 4) - 8$

G $3 \times (4 + 8)$

H $(3 \times 4) + 8$

J $3 \times (8 \div 2)$

K $3 \times (4 \times 8)$

STOP

Chapter 13 Cumulative Test

Mark your answer on the answer sheet.

1. Which rectangle below has the same area as a 6 cm-by-6 cm square?

   A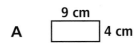
   9 cm
   4 cm

   B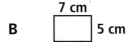
   7 cm
   5 cm

   C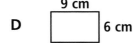
   10 cm
   3 cm

   D
   9 cm
   6 cm

2. What is the volume of this prism?

   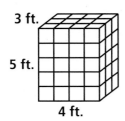
   3 ft.
   5 ft.
   4 ft.

   F 12 cubic feet
   G 20 cubic feet
   H 40 cubic feet
   J 60 cubic feet

3. What is the area of this triangle?

   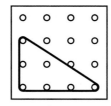

   A 12 square units
   B 8 square units
   C 6 square units
   D 4 square units

4. Marlys is making a small pizza for each of 3 friends. She wants to put 13 pepperoni slices on each pizza. Which number sentence could be used to find the number of pepperoni slices she will need?

   F $13 - 3 = $ ▨
   G $13 \times 3 = $ ▨
   H $13 + 3 = $ ▨
   J $13 \div 3 = $ ▨

5. What is the volume and surface area of this prism?

   A Volume = 3 cubic units; surface area = 12 square units
   B Volume = 3 cubic units; surface area = 14 square units
   C Volume = 6 cubic units; surface area = 14 square units
   D Volume = 6 cubic units; surface area = 18 square units

6. Which is one way to find the area of the polygon?

   A $(6 \times 8) - 5$
   B $6 \times 8 \times 5$
   C $(6 + 8) - 5$
   D $(6 \times 8) + 5$

GO ON ➡

7. Which figure below has a perimeter of 26 m and an area of 36 sq m?

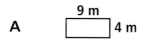

A 9 m, 4 m

B 6 m, 6 m

C 8 cm, 5 cm

D 18 m, 2 m

Please note that items 8–11 have *five* answer choices.

8.

Which point on the number line represents the decimal that is equivalent to the percent of the grid that is shaded?

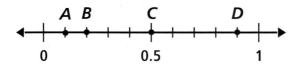

F Point A

G Point B

H Point C

J Point D

K Not here

9. What is the probability of rolling an odd number on a number cube numbered 1–6?

A $\frac{1}{6}$

B $\frac{1}{4}$

C $\frac{1}{3}$

D $\frac{1}{2}$

E 0

10. A hat costs $1.79. Which is a good estimate of how much 6 hats cost?

F more than $20

G more than $12

H less than $12

J less than $6

K less than $2

11.

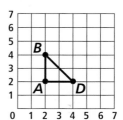

Suppose Triangle *DEF* slides one unit to the right. Which set of ordered pairs will show the new coordinates of points *D, E,* and *F*?

A (2, 2), (2, 4), (4, 2)

B (3, 2), (3, 4), (5, 2)

C (2, 3), (4, 3), (2, 5)

D (2, 3), (2, 5), (4, 3)

F (3, 2), (4, 3), (2, 5)

STOP

Index

Acknowledgments

For each of the selections listed below, grateful acknowledgment is made for permission to reprint copyrighted material as follows.

Cover of *Current Science* magazine, April 19, 1996 issue. Special permission granted, copyrighted ©1996, and published by Weekly Reader Corporation. *Current Science*® is a federally registered trademark of Weekly Reader Corporation. All rights reserved.

Cover of *Kids Discover: Garbage* magazine, April 1996 issue. Reprinted by permission of Kids Discover.

Cover of *Kids Discover: Gold* magazine, 1995 issue. Reprinted by permission of Kids Discover.

Cover of *Kids Discover: Oceans* magazine, 1996 issue. Reprinted by permission of Kids Discover.

Cover of *National Geographic World* magazine, April 1996 issue. Reprinted by permission of National Geographic Society.

Cover of *National Geographic World* magazine, December 1996 issue. Reprinted by permission of National Geographic Society.

Cover of *National Geographic World* magazine, November 1994 issue. Reprinted by permission of National Geographic Society.

Cover of *Ranger Rick* magazine. Reprinted from the August 1995 issue of *Ranger Rick* magazine, with permission of the publisher, National Wildlife Federation. Copyright 1995 by NWF.

Cover of *Scienceland* magazine, Vol. 18, No. 141 issue. Reprinted by permission of Scienceland Komat Inc.

Cover of *Zoobooks* magazine, August 1995 issue. Reprinted by permission of Wildlife Education, Ltd.

Cover of *Zoobooks* magazine, January 1995 issue. Reprinted by permission of Wildlife Education, Ltd.

Cover of *Zoonooz* magazine, March 1995 issue. Reprinted by permission of Zoological Society of San Diego.

Decimal Squares, Fraction Bars, and *Tower of Bars* were created by Professor Albert C. Bennett, Jr. and are registered trademarks of Scott Resources. They are used by permission of Scott Resources. All rights reserved.

Photo Credits

Cover: NASA/Corbis (background); Allan Landau Photography (front figure, screen inset); Image Copyright © 1996 PhotoDisc, Inc. (inset);
v Richard Hutchings/PhotoEdit; viii AP/Wide World; x-xi © Clara Von Aich Photography; xi NGW cover: Saturn; xii John Roberts/The Stock Market; 6(tl) Peter Menzel; 9(t) G. Brad/Lewis/Liaison; 9(b) Dave Bartruff/Stock Boston; 12(tl) © Royal Geographical Society; 12-13(bkgd) Alan Kearney/Tony Stone Images; 14(b) Mary Kate Denny/PhotoEdit; 16tl Ron Garrison (cover); 16 Wolfgang Kaehler/Liaison; 17(mb) Zoological Society of San Diego; 17(br) Ron Garrison/Zoological Society of San Diego; 17(t) Renee Lynn/Photo Researchers; 17(bl) Ron Garrison/Zoological Society of San Diego; 20(bl) Margot Conte/Animals, Animals; 26 R.B.-G.M.-J.O. Atlanta 96/Liaison International; 30 John Roberts/The Stock Market; 30-31(bkgd) Keith Kent/Peter Arnold Inc.; 32 Aaron Strong/Liaison; 34 Bob Daemmrich; 35 Zigy Kaluzny/Tony Stone Images; 36-37 Manoj Shah/Tony Stone Images; 38 Al Rendon; 39 Al Rendon; 55 Tim Phelps/The Stock Shop/Medichrome; 60(tl) C.M. Dixon; 60(br) Library of Congress; 60(mb) ©Archive Photos, 1996/PNI; 62 Kindra Clineff; 62-63(bkgd) NASA; 64(l) Kennan Ward/The Stock Market; 65 © Wolfgang Kaehler/Liaison; 68 Kelvin Aitken Peter Arnold; 68-69(bkgd) Norbert Wu/Peter Arnold; 70 NASA/JPL/California Institute of Technology (cover); 70(bkgd) NASA; 71(tl) NASA; 78(bkgd) Steve Winter/National Geographic Society; 78(t,m,b) John R. MacGregor/Peter Arnold; 79(tl) Hans Pfletschinger/Peter Arnold; 79(tr) Jeremy Thomas/Biofotos; 79(br) D. Cavagnaro/ Peter Arnold; 79(ml) Hans Pfletschinger/Peter Arnold; 79(mr) Jeremy Thomas/Biofotos; 79(bl) John R. MacGregor/Peter Arnold; 86-87(bkgd) Gene Peach/Liaison International; 87(tr) Chlaus Lotscher/Peter Arnold; 88-89(bkgd) Greg Adams/Tony Stone Images; 92(l) Erich Lessing/Art Resource; 96 Jack Vartoogian; 98-99(bkgd) Dallas & John Heaton/Stock Boston; 100(bkgd) Darryl Torckler/Tony Stone Images; 114 (bkgd) Remi Benali/Liaison International; 116 Bruce Esbin & Ruth Anderson/Photo Network/PNI; 124(l) Philippe Plailly/Photo Researchers; 124(m) Photo Researchers; 124(r) Scott Camazine/Photo Researchers; 126(tr) Courtesy of Central High School; 128(m) Chip Henderson/Tony Stone Images; 128(l) Image Copyright © 1996 PhotoDisc, Inc.; 128(ml) Image Copyright © 1996 PhotoDisc, Inc.; 128(mr) Image Copyright © 1996 PhotoDisc, Inc.; 128(r) Image Copyright © 1996 PhotoDisc, Inc.; 132 (bl) Robert Frerck/Odyssey; 132(bm) Science Museum / Science & Society Picture Library; 132(br) The Granger Collection; 132(l) Peabody Museum - Harvard University. Photograph by Hillel Burger; 133(bm) Culver Pictures, Inc.; 133(bl) Massachusetts Historical Society; 133(l) Massachusetts Historical Society; 134-135(bkgd) Library of Congress; 137 Richard Hutchings/PhotoEdit; 143 Gary Holscher/Tony Stone Images; 144(bkgd) © David Doubilet; 144 Walter looss (cover); 145 UPI/Corbis/Bettmann; 156(t) Image Copyright © 1996 PhotoDisc, Inc.; 156(b) Gail Shumway/FPG; 157(tr) Animals, Animals; 157(r) Heather Angel; 157(l) Hans Pfletschinger/Peter Arnold; 162(tl) © Yoav Levy 1994/Phototake/PNI; 164(b) R.T. Nowitz / Photo Researchers; 164(ml) Albright-Knox Art Gallery, Buffalo,

New York. Gift of Seymour H. Knox; 170(tr) Daemmrich/Stock Boston; 176(l) Telegraph Colour Library/FPG; 176-177(bkgd) John Sanford/Photo Researchers; 176-177(b) Jack Zehrt/FPG; 178(tr) Nancy J. Pierce/Photo Researchers;181 Jean Marc Giboux/Liaison; 182 Mitsuhiro Wada/Liaison; DLF Group; 184(bkgd) Ken Ross/FPG; 185(bkgd) Lee Foster/FPG; 186 Library of Congress (cover); 192(t) © Florida Museum of Natural History; 198-199(bkgd) Mula-Eshet/The Stock Market; 200(tr) Ilene Perlman; 201(tr) Ilene Perlman; 203(b) Charles D. Winters/Photo Researchers; 203(rm) Leonard Lessin/Peter Arnold, Inc.; 203(rt) Leonard Lessin/Peter Arnold, Inc.; 203(rt) Leonard Lessin/Peter Arnold, Inc.; 203(rb) Leonard Lessin/Peter Arnold, Inc.; 204(tr) Bob Daemmrich/Stock Boston; 208(t) Allan Morton & Dennis Milon/Photo Researchers; 210(m, ml) Smithsonian Institution; 211(l) Hugh Sitton/Tony Stone Images; 216(bkgd) Hans Pfletschinger/Peter Arnold, Inc.; 216(inset) Hans Pfletschinger/Peter Arnold, Inc.; 218 Lynn Hoffman/Photo Researchers; 224 © Clara Von Aich Photography; 224-225(bkgd) David Nunuk/Science Photo Library/Photo Researchers; 232 Ilene Perlman; 234 Courtesy Welch's Grape Juice Company; 236(tr) Lawrence Migdale/Stock Boston; 238(l) AP/Wide World; 238(b) From Suan Fa Thung Tsung, 1593.; 244(tl) Helen Williams/Photo Researchers; 245 Cosmo Condino/Tony Stone Images; 246(inset) Adam Smith/FPG; 246 Sarah Stone/Tony Stone Images; 246 G. Brad Lewis (cover); 248 Courtesy Naples High School Softball Team; 254(l) John Troha/Black Star/PNI; 254(r) ©Willinger/FPG; 260 M.C. Escher's "Symmetry Drawing E 67" ©1997 Cordon Art - Baarn - Holland. All rights reserved.; 266-267 © Glasgow School of Art; 270 (br) G. Brad Lewis/Liaison; 271 (bl) Daniel Beltra/Liaison; 272 (tr) Lee Foster/FPG; 276 Paul Merideth/Tony Stone Images; 281 ©Greg Vaughn 1994/AllStock/PNI; 284 Daniel R. Westergren/National Geographic Society; 284 Daniel R. Westergren (cover); 285 Daniel R. Westergren/National Geographic Society; 291 Detroit Institute of Arts; 296(tr) Gabe Palmer/The Stock Market; 301(m) NASA; 300-301(bkgd) NASA; 302 Horizon Design; 302(bl) Museum of Afro American History; 303 Massachusetts Historical Society; 304(bl) Nancy Sheehan/PhotoEdit; 306(m) Otis Imboden/National Geographic; 306(b) Eric A. Wessman / Stock Boston; 310(tl) Maslowski/Photo Researchers; 315(t) Peter Menzel; 314 DLF Group; 315(b) Peter Menzel; 316 Hank Iken; 320(r) John Cancalosi/Tom Stack; 320 Patti Murray/Animals, Animals (cover); 321(l) Animals Animals/Hans & Judy Deste; 321(r) Frans Lanting/Minden Pictures; 326(l) Nigel Cattlin/Holt Studios International/Photo Researchers; 326(r) Animals, Animals; 338(b) Steve Kaufman/Corbis; 339(tl) Alfred Pasieka/Peter Arnold, Inc.; 340-341(bkgd) Richard Clintsman / Tony Stone Images; 342 Jim Kern Expeditions; 346(tr) Rhoda Sidney; 346(b) Courtesy of Patricia Malarcher; 348(tl) R. Van Nostrand/Photo Researchers; 350(tr) Julie Marcotte/Stock Boston; 352(bkgd) Gary Alt; 353(tr) Steve Kaufman/DRK Photo; 353(bl) Donald M. Jones; 358 Mark Gibson; 358 Mark Gibson/The Stock Market; 364(b) Michael & Barbara Reed/Animals, Animals; 364(t) Jim Zipp/Photo Researchers; 364-365(bkgd) Lorentz Gullachsen/ Tony Stone Images; 366(bkgd) Aaron Haupt / Photo Researchers; 368(r) Tom Bean/Allstock/PNI; 368(l) Tom Bean/Allstock/PNI; 369 Richard Price/FPG; 372(tr) Mary Kate Denny/PhotoEdit; 376(l) Corbis-Bettmann; 376(b) Rafael Wollmann / Liaison; 382-383 Peter Menzel/Stock Boston/PNI; 384(bkgd) Norbert Wu/Tony Stone Images; 384 Joe McDonald/Bruce Coleman, Inc. (cover); 400(b) William Weems/Woodfin Camp/PNI; 400(t) Adam Woolfitt/Woodfin Camp/PNI; 413 Spencer Grant/Photo Researchers; 414 Stefan Merken/Tony Stone Images; 416 Hilprecht Collection of the University of Jena.; 421 Charles Thatcher/Tony Stone Images; 422(bkgd) Jess Stock/Tony Stone Images; 423(l) David Stoecklein/The Stock Market; 424-425(bkgd) Michael Grecco/Stock Boston; 436(inset) Virginia Weinland/Photo Researchers; 436 David Ulmer/Stock Boston; 437(t) Daniel J. Cox/Liaison; 437(b) Bruce M. Herman/Photo Researchers; 437(mt) Jess R. Lee/Photo Researchers; 437 (mb) Image Copyright © 1996 PhotoDisc, Inc.; 443 Frank Fournier/Contact Press Images/PNI; 444(br) Gianni Dagli Orti/Corbis; 446(t) Andy Washnik/The Stock Market; 454 John Running/Stock Boston/ PNI; 455(l) Liane Enkelis/Stock Boston; 455(r) Liane Enkelis/Stock Boston; 454 Richard T. Nowitz (cover)

Assignment Photo Credits

xiii(tr), 239(b), 307(b), 445(b) Karen Ahola; 150(b),151, 192-3(b), 200-1(bkgd), 290(t), 334-35(bkgd), 338(l), 339(b), 358-9(b), 417(ml), 430(b), 436(inset), 460 Petrisse Briel; 359(r) Dave Desroches; 255, 310-1(bkgd), 330-31(bkgd), 346(tl), 347, 348-49 (bkgd), 390(l), 430(t), 438(bkgd) Fayfoto; 15, 20(c), 21, 44, 45, 61, 78(b), 93, 120, 270(ml), 290-1(b) Allan Landau; 4(tr), 50(tr), 82,140(inset),141, 202, 205, 218(bl), 242, 260(insets), 261, 330(insets), 331(inset), 394, 407, 410, 420, 434(insets), 435(t), 447, 449 Parker/Boon Productions; 47(b), 81(b), 122(ml),123(bl), 129(tl), 150-1(b), 152(tl, ml, bl), 153(bl), 193(r), 194(tl), 195(b), 206(t), 207, 211(r), 226(tl), 227(bl), 257(b), 271(ml, inset), 275, 293(bl), 307(m), 327, 329(bl), 361(b), 377(m, b), 393(r), 433(r), 435(br) Tony Scarpetta; 133(r), 239(r), 390(b), 444(bl), 445(ml) Tracey Wheeler